Child Support Assurance

IRWIN GARFINKEL
SARA S. McLANAHAN
AND PHILIP K. ROBINS
Editors

CHILD SUPPORT ASSURANCE

Design Issues, Expected Impacts, and Political Barriers as Seen from Wisconsin

An Institute for Research on Poverty Study
University of Wisconsin
Madison, WI

THE URBAN INSTITUTE PRESS
Washington, D.C.

Copyright © 1992. The Urban Institute. All rights reserved. Except for short quotes, no part of this book may be reproduced or utilized in any form or by any means, electronic or mechanical, including photocopying, recording, or by information storage or retrieval system, without written permission from The Urban Institute Press.

Library of Congress Cataloging in Publication Data

Child Support Assurance: Design Issues, Expected Impacts, and Political Barriers as Seen from Wisconsin/Irwin Garfinkel, Sara S. McLanahan, and Philip K. Robins

1. Child support—Wisconsin. I. Garfinkel, Irwin. II. McLanahan, Sara S. III. Robins, Philip K.

| HV742.W6C47 | 1992 | 92-8638 |
| 362.7'1—dc20 | | CIP |

ISBN 0-87766-563-X (alk. paper)
ISBN 0-87766-562-1 (alk. paper; casebound)

Urban Institute books are printed on acid-free paper whenever possible.

Printed in the United States of America.

Distributed by:
    University Press of America

4720 Boston Way   3 Henrietta Street
Lanham, MD 20706   London   WC2E 8LU   ENGLAND

THE URBAN INSTITUTE is a nonprofit policy research and educational organization established in Washington, D.C., in 1968. Its staff investigates the social and economic problems confronting the nation and government policies and programs designed to alleviate such problems. The Institute disseminates significant findings of its research through the publications program of its Press. The Institute has two goals for work in each of its research areas: to help shape thinking about societal problems and efforts to solve them, and to improve government decisions and performance by providing better information and analytic tools.

Through work that ranges from broad conceptual studies to administrative and technical assistance, Institute researchers contribute to the stock of knowledge available to public officials and private individuals and groups concerned with formulating and implementing more efficient and effective government policy.

Conclusions or opinions expressed in Institute publications are those of the authors and do not necessarily reflect the views of other staff members, officers or trustees of the Institute, advisory groups, or any organizations that provide financial support to the Institute.

CONTENTS

Tables

Figures

ACKNOWLEDGMENTS

The research presented in this volume is the product of a series of contracts between the Institute for Research on Poverty at the University of Wisconsin and the Office of Child Support Enforcement in the Wisconsin Department of Health and Social Services. Most of the funding for the research was provided by the federal office of child support enforcement within the U.S. Department of Health and Human Services. The federal government pays for approximately two-thirds of state costs for administering child support enforcement. Because IRP research was integral to Wisconsin's administration of its child support enforcement program, two-thirds of the costs were paid for by the federal government.

Most of the state's share of the funding for the child support research came from a series of grants from the Ford Foundation program on urban poverty. The Russell Sage Foundation, the Foundation for Child Development, the University of Wisconsin graduate school, and the Wisconsin Department of Health and Social Services also provided funding.

We gratefully acknowledge the help of the state and federal government officials, foundation officers, and university faculty and administrators who made this research possible.

This book presents the highlights of the large body of research that resulted from a seminal project to design, implement, and evaluate a statewide child support assurance system (CSAS) in Wisconsin. A unique collaboration between the State of Wisconsin and the University of Wisconsin's Institute for Research on Poverty made this field test possible. It represents an outstanding example of the kind of policy research and program evaluation that the nation so badly needs to inform its policy design and implementation efforts, and The Urban Institute Press is proud to disseminate the research findings and implications that flow from it.

The objective of the CSAS is to hold noncustodial parents to their child support obligations while at the same time guaranteeing a minimum assured benefit to single-parent families. Three components combine to achieve this objective: child support guidelines, which establish the child support award; routine withholding, which deducts child support owed by the noncustodial parent from wages and other income; and an assured child support benefit, which is a government guarantee of child support to resident parents legally entitled to private support.

The research presented in this book has already had a profound effect on public policy in Wisconsin and in the nation. Wisconsin had adopted child support guidelines and routine wage withholding by 1987, and the Family Support Act of 1988 requires all states to do so by 1994. New York is experimenting with a limited version of the assured benefit, and bills are pending in the U.S. Senate that would establish federally sponsored CSAS experiments in several states.

Vulnerable single-parent families have been a central research and policy concern of the Institute ever since the 1975 pathbreaking study by Hether L. Ross and Isabel V. Sawhill, *Time of Transition: The Growth of Families Headed by Women*. Child support assurance is a promising approach to relieving the economic plight of such families. This book contributes to the debate on this policy alternative.

William Gorham
President

Part One

AN OVERVIEW OF THE CHILD SUPPORT ASSURANCE SYSTEM

FINDINGS OF THE WISCONSIN CHILD SUPPORT REFORM PROJECT: INTRODUCTION AND SUMMARY

Irwin Garfinkel, Sara S. McLanahan, and Philip K. Robins

Today in the United States, about one of every four children lives apart from one of his or her natural parents (U.S. Bureau of the Census 1990). Recent estimates also indicate that one of every two U.S. children born today will live apart from one of his or her parents some time before reaching adulthood (Martin and Bumpass 1989). Children who live apart from one of their parents are potentially eligible for child support, a transfer of income from the nonresident parent, or the government, to the child's caregiver.[1] Considering that one-half of the next generation will be potentially eligible for child support, the quality of our child support system is extremely important to the well-being of our citizens.

For well over a decade, the perceived inadequacies of the child support system that has operated historically in this country have been of great concern to policymakers and academics. Critics have claimed that the system condoned and therefore fostered parental irresponsibility, that it was rife with inequity, and that it contributed to poverty and welfare dependence (e.g., Cassetty 1978; Chambers 1979; Garfinkel and Melli 1982; Sawhill 1983). In 1979, the U.S. Bureau of the Census began gathering data on child support in alternate years. The first Census study indicated that less than half of the nonresident parents paid any child support (U.S. Bureau of the Census 1981). The study revealed weaknesses at every step in the child support process. Only 6 of 10 mothers potentially eligible for child support had child support awards, and only 1 of 10 never-married mothers had child support awards. Among mothers with awards, about half received the full amount to which they were entitled, and over a quarter received nothing. Few policymakers argued with the judgment that the system condoned parental irresponsibility. Other studies have documented inequities, such as widely varying child support awards for children and parents in similar circumstances (White and Stone 1976; Yee 1979). Notwithstanding the thousands of noncustodial fathers who were sent to jail for not paying child support, most such fathers paid no child support and suffered no consequences (Chambers 1979). And poor noncustodial fathers who were legally obligated to pay child support were required to pay a substantially higher proportion of their incomes than middle- and especially upper-income noncustodial fathers (Cassetty 1978). Finally, nearly half of all single mothers and their children were reported to be poor and dependent on welfare (Garfinkel and McLanahan 1986). The old system was clearly inadequate, necessitating renewed and stronger federal involvement.

CHILD SUPPORT RESEARCH AT THE INSTITUTE FOR RESEARCH ON POVERTY

As the caseload of the federal Aid to Families with Dependent Children (AFDC) program grew and shifted from orphans to children with living absent parents, federal interest in child support increased. The first federal child support legislation was enacted in 1950. Further bills were passed in 1965 and 1967, but it was not until 1974 that Congress added Title IV-D to the Social Security Act, thereby establishing the federal child support enforcement system. This legislation, signed into law in 1975, created a new federal Office of Child Support Enforcement in the then U.S. Department of Health, Education & Welfare (HEW, now the U.S. Department of Health and Human Services [DHHS]), it required all states to establish state offices of child support enforcement, and it provided for federal reimbursement for three-quarters of each state's enforcement costs.

In 1974, as the legislation neared passage, the Office of the Assistant Secretary for Planning and Evaluation (ASPE) in HEW requested that the Institute for Research on Poverty (IRP) at the University of Wisconsin–Madison undertake research on child support. This request led, in the near term, to a doctoral dissertation (that of Cassetty [1978]) and, ultimately, as described in chapter 2, to development of a proposal for a new child support assurance system (CSAS), a unique renewal of the tradition of collaboration between Wisconsin state government and the state university, implementation of key elements of a CSAS in Wisconsin and the nation as a whole, and a corpus of research on both the old and newly emerging child support systems.

The IRP conceived of child support assurance as an addition to our social security system. The underlying philosophy is that parents are responsible for supporting their children and that government is responsible for ensuring that children who live apart from a parent receive the amount to which they are entitled. The child support assurance system has three components: *child support guidelines,* which establish the child support award as a percentage of the nonresident parent's income; *routine income withholding,* which deducts child support owed from wages and other sources of income, just like income and payroll taxes; and an *assured child support benefit,* which provides a government guarantee of a minimum level of child support to the resident parent of a child legally entitled to private support.

Child support assurance is patterned after Survivors' Insurance. Like Survivors' Insurance, Child Support Assurance aids children of all income classes who suffer an income loss due to the absence of a parent. The cause of the absence differs, of course. Survivors' Insurance compensates for the loss of income arising from widowhood. Child support assurance compensates for the loss arising from divorce, separation, and nonmarriage. The percentage-of-income standard in conjunction with routine income withholding makes the bulk of the financing of Child Support Assurance similar to a proportional payroll tax, which is used to finance all of our social insurance programs. In the Child Support Assurance case, however, the "tax" applies only to those who are legally liable for child support. The assured-benefit component of Child Support Assurance makes the benefit structure of the system like all of our social insurance programs in that it provides greater benefits to low-income families than are justified on the basis of the family's contributions or taxes.

The Secretary of the Wisconsin Department of Health and Social Services (DHSS), Donald Percy, along with the attorney for the state's Office of Child Support Enforcement, Sherwood Zink, were sufficiently attracted by the proposal of a new child support assurance system to contract with the IRP to conduct research on the old child support system and to design, help implement, and evaluate the proposed new child support system. The contract, first signed in 1980, has been extended continuously since then to the present.

This volume is a representative collection of research on the old and new child support systems that have emanated from this lengthy state-university collaboration. The research has spawned numerous doctoral dissertations, journal articles, government reports, and at least two books (the Annex provides a comprehensive list). Whereas this wider body of work includes analyses that are qualitative as well as quantitative, normative as well as empirical, the dominant mode of research, as reflected in this volume, is a quantitative empirical analysis. The studies here were selected not only to illustrate the range of topics covered and research methods used (all but three relying exclusively on IRP data), but because together they tell a coherent story. Each of the following chapters stands on its own. Each addresses a different topic and the methods and data used vary. Each goes well beyond the original policy questions that motivated the research. The extensions reflect the unique academic questions of interest to the researchers and their disciplines. This diversity is an accurate reflection of the DHSS-IRP work on child support. Despite this diversity, all of the DHSS-IRP research had a common motivation—to evaluate the old and newly emerging child support system. Publishing these individual pieces of research together in a single volume makes clear the unity that underlies their diversity.

The next section of this chapter evaluates the old and new child support systems within the context of the overall research questions addressed in this book. The third section summarizes the content of each chapter, and the fourth and final section identifies the research tasks remaining.

RESEARCH QUESTIONS AND STUDY DESIGN

Normatively Motivated Factual Questions

To obtain federal reimbursement for expenditures incurred under its contract with the IRP, the Wisconsin DHSS had to make the case that the research would lead to improvements in its child support enforcement program. Thus all the research conducted by the IRP was ultimately focused on evaluating the old and newly emerging child support systems. Evaluation unavoidably includes normative components in addition to purely factual questions. (Most of the chapters in this book address only factual questions, although some, like chapter 3 and chapter 9, address both factual and normative issues.) This section places these factual issues within the normative framework that generated them. Broadly speaking, all of the research addresses the following two questions: Was the old system as bad as it seemed? and What are the costs and benefits of a CSAS?

WAS THE OLD SYSTEM AS BAD AS IT SEEMED?

State officials, first of all, encouraged the Institute for Research on Poverty to investigate the possibility that the apparent shortcomings of the old child support system were inherent or misleading. Specifically: Could fathers (or noncustodial mothers) really afford to pay more child support? Were low child support payments compensated for by generous property settlements? Were low child support payments a consequence of shared custody or frequent visitation? and Were there insuperable barriers to paternity establishment? Each of these questions is addressed briefly next.

Regarding the first of these questions, if nonresident fathers are too poor to pay more child support, reforms are unlikely to garner much more support, and any additional support elicited will be quite costly to the nonresident fathers. Furthermore, how much of their income *should* nonresident parents share with their children? Chapter 3 addresses the question of the ability of nonresident parents to pay more child support by combining estimates of income with the normative judgments embodied in the three most widely adopted child support guidelines.

Another possible explanation for low child support payments was that nonresident parents transferred property in lieu of support (see Mnookin and Kornhauser 1979). The extent to which low child support payments were compensated for by generous property settlements, however, was not known. This question motivated the empirical research reported in chapter 4.

Still a third possible explanation for low child support payments was that they were a consequence of frequent visitation or shared custody. That is, just as property can be a substitute for child support, time can be a substitute for money. On the other hand, it is possible that when it comes to child support, time spent with and money spent on a child reinforce one another—that is, they are complements rather than substitutes. Chapter 5 assesses the empirical relationship between visitation and child support.

Finally, the failure to establish paternity was so widespread that many believed there must be insuperable barriers to paternity establishment. However, neither the Wisconsin civil servants nor the academics at the IRP who were conducting this study subscribed to this view. In retrospect, we see that this was in part because Wisconsin was already performing much better than the overall dismal national record. Furthermore, by the time we actually undertook the relevant research, described in chapter 6, data confirmed that some states were doing much better at establishing paternity than others, and that nationally, paternity establishment rates had improved dramatically—a 50 percent increase from 1979 to 1986 (Nichols-Casebolt and Garfinkel 1991). Thus, the question addressed in chapter 6 is: Are there identifiable and correctable administrative barriers, rather than insuperable barriers, to paternity establishment?

WHAT ARE THE COSTS AND BENEFITS OF A CSAS?

The first question administrators and elected officials ask about a new proposal is, "How much will it cost?" From the start, estimating the costs of different variants of a child support assurance system (CSAS) in Wisconsin was a central endeavor. A parallel, though less central, task was to estimate the cost of a national system. These latter estimates are detailed in chapter 7.

Besides the costs to government, a child support assurance system entails costs to nonresident parents. Some observers have surmised that low child support payments have been due primarily to the low incomes of nonresident parents, and that, therefore, strengthening enforcement would at best merely shift poverty from women to men and at worst actually increase poverty.[2] Chapter 8 assesses the magnitude of the costs to nonresident parents and compares these to the benefits transferred to resident parent families.

The potential benefits of a CSAS that have been of greatest interest to policymakers have been its effects on poverty and welfare dependence. In the aftermath of the oversold initiatives from the War on Poverty, state and federal civil servants were not satisfied with purely qualitative claims; they pressed for hard numbers. How much of the poverty gap would a CSAS eliminate? What percentage of the AFDC caseload would exit welfare? As with costs, although we also developed estimates for Wisconsin, chapter 7 reports estimates for the nation as a whole.

To convert the CSAS from a vague proposal to a workable plan, the IRP had to investigate a number of vexing normative issues with regard to the child support guidelines. What percentage of income should nonresident parents be required to share with their children? Should the percentage vary with their income? and Should the child support obligation of the nonresident parent depend upon the income of the resident parent? As discussed further in chapter 2, these questions were addressed in a joint IRP-DHSS project working group. Chapter 9 outlines the guidelines adopted by Wisconsin and analyzes the benefits and costs of alternative child support guidelines.

Because the CSAS was first implemented in Wisconsin on a limited demonstration basis with a quasi-experimental design, it was possible to obtain some estimates of the actual effects of certain aspects of the system's design—specifically, of routine income withholding. The critical question here, of course, Does routine income withholding increase child support payments? Chapter 10 addresses this question, and chapter 11 investigates the actual effects of routine income with-holding on AFDC caseloads in Wisconsin.

Adverse side effects are also counted as costs of social programs. Among the more analyzed side effects of income transfer programs is their effect on the labor supply of program beneficiaries. In isolation transfer, programs are generally expected to reduce the labor supply of beneficiaries.[3] Thus, the CSAS may be expected to diminish the labor supply among those currently unaffected by other transfer programs. Among welfare recipients, however, the CSAS is likely to increase work because, unlike welfare, the CSAS is not income-tested and therefore does not reduce benefits as earnings increase. The net effects of the CSAS on labor supply are ambiguous and must be addressed empirically (chapter 7 also includes simulations of these effects). Chapter 12 estimates the actual effects on labor supply of routine income withholding.

A CSAS could also effect divorce, marriage, remarriage, and even birthrates. Of course, benefits as well as costs may be associated with induced changes in marital behavior. (The same applies to work behavior.) For example, by increasing the level and stability of income from child support, a CSAS may delay remarriage, but the delay may result in better matches. Despite the ambiguity associated with the normative meaning of changes in marital behavior, the CSAS research team believed it was important to ascertain whether child support affected marital behavior and if so, in what way. Chapter 13 therefore examines the relationship between child support and remarriage.

Finally, chapter 14 addresses a particular aspect of what might be thought of as the political benefits and costs of the CSAS: to wit, To what extent does public opinion support the major components of the CSAS? Specifically, the chapter addresses such questions as: Do most people think that child support awards should depend only upon the income of the nonresident parent as proposed under the CSAS, or do they think that the resident parent's circumstances should be taken into account as well? Is an assured child support benefit attractive to a broad range of the population? and To what extent does support for an assured benefit depend upon its cost?

Research Data and Methods

DATA COLLECTION

To evaluate the old and new child support systems, the Institute for Research on Poverty undertook several data collection efforts. Four distinct datasets were assembled and utilized—the Wisconsin Absent

Parent Income Study (WAPS), the children's income and program participation survey (CHIPPS), the Court Record Database (CRDB), and the paternity records data (PRD). Of these, the CRDB is by far the most commonly used; the analyses in chapters 4, 5, and 10–13 all rely upon this dataset, the sampling frame of which includes divorce and paternity cases commencing between 1980 and 1988 from 20 Wisconsin counties. In all, court records were abstracted from 10,915 cases. These records were matched with state income tax and welfare records, thus yielding an additional wealth of data on income and welfare receipt.

In addition, a random sample of about 2,000 cases entering the courts between 1984 and 1987 was selected for a telephone survey. Attempts were made to locate and interview both mothers and fathers. Interviews were obtained with 1,522 mothers, 1,281 fathers, and 979 matched pairs of mothers and fathers—corresponding to 65 percent, 55 percent, and 42 percent of the potential samples. For these subsamples, the survey provides data on income, demographics, location, remarriage, parent-child and parent-parent interaction, marital history, and so forth. The possibility of matching survey data to the court, welfare, and income tax records makes the CRDB a unique source of data for studying child support.

The other three datasets collected by the IRP—the WAPS, PRD, and CHIPPS—were essential for estimating the ability of nonresident fathers to pay more child support (chapter 3), the analysis of barriers to paternity establishment (chapter 6), and the estimates of the costs of and public support for the CSAS (chapters 7 and 14). But the analyses in chapters 3 and 7 rely more heavily upon the national data collected in the biannual Child Support Supplements to the Census Bureau's Current Population Survey (CPS—CSS) than upon the Wisconsin data. Chapter 8's analysis of the costs to nonresident parents of stronger child support enforcement relies exclusively upon the Panel Study of Income Dynamics (PSID—Institute for Social Research, University of Michigan, Ann Arbor). The AFYS, PRD, and CHIPPS, as well as the CPS—CSS and the PSID, are described in the relevant chapters.

METHODS OF ANALYSIS

Just as no single dataset enabled us to answer all the questions essential to evaluating the old and new child support systems, so too, no single method of analysis would have sufficed. The research in this volume employs a variety of methods, including historical and organizational analysis, regression analysis, microsimulation analysis, and policy analysis. Details of each method accompany the appropriate chapters.

WHAT ARE THE RESEARCH FINDINGS?

This section summarizes the major findings of the chapters in this volume as they relate to the policy evaluation issues that originally motivated the research: Was the old system really so bad? and What are the costs and benefits of the new system? Each chapter's research embodies a set of more detailed, mostly factual issues within these broad areas of inquiry. Readers are encouraged to consult the appropriate chapters for details on these and other specialized areas of interest.

Was the Old System As Bad As It Seemed?

CAN FATHERS AFFORD TO PAY MORE SUPPORT?

As reported in chapter 3, the average income of nonresident fathers in 1983 was $19,000, or about 14 percent below the average income of all working-age (25–64) males. Differences in income by race and marital status of the nonresident fathers are dramatic. The estimated incomes of nonwhite nonresident fathers are only half those of their white counterparts—$11,000 versus $22,000. Even more dramatic are the estimated differences in income levels between never-married ($7,700) and ever-married fathers ($24,000). In short, the average income of nonresident parents is somewhat below average, and some groups of nonresident parents have quite low incomes.

The income figures tell only part of the story, however, because the amount of child support a nonresident parent should pay depends not only on income but also on how much of this income should be expected to be devoted to child support. For example, if a nonresident parent's income is $19,000, his or her obligation will equal $1,900 if 10 percent is deemed the appropriate sharing rate. If 30 percent is deemed the appropriate rate, the nonresident parent's obligation increases to $5,700.

Is the question ultimately entirely subjective? Not quite, for as chapter 3 demonstrates, it is possible to combine estimated incomes with a variety of value judgments about what portion of the nonresident parent's income should be devoted to child support to derive a range of estimates of child support obligations. As mentioned, the chapter employs three child support guidelines used widely in the United

States. Each guideline indicates that nonresident parents should pay a great deal more child support than they now pay. Estimates suggest that nonresident fathers can pay from $24 to $30 billion, or at the least, about two and a half times their legal obligations under the old system ($9.7 billion), and more than three times the amount they were actually paying ($6.8 billion).

Unless one believes that nonresident parents should share dramatically less of their incomes with their children than suggested in these three guidelines, the huge gap between estimated ability to pay child support and the amount actually paid belies the argument that the low payments under the old system simply reflect an accommodation to the reality that "You can't get blood from a stone."

DOES PROPERTY COMPENSATE FOR LOW SUPPORT AWARDS?

The results reported in chapter 4 also provide little comfort to those who think that the low payments in the old system were compensated for by generous property settlements. The division of property is ordinarily not relevant to out-of-wedlock cases because the couple in these cases normally has no joint property.[4] Thus, chapter 4's analysis is limited to divorce cases.

About two-thirds of mothers divorced during 1980–84 received some property, typically a bit over half the total value of the couple's property. The median value of the mother's share was $7,800, an amount much too low to compensate for much of the difference between the postdivorce status of men and women. Even if the mother received 100 percent of the property, it would increase her postdivorce income by only $608. The average postdivorce income disparity equals $6,151.

On the other hand, there is sufficient property in many cases to make trade-offs between child support and property worthwhile. On average, the total value of property (assuming a 10 percent rate of return) equals 37 percent of the annual value of child support awards. For couples with combined annual incomes over $45,000, the property is worth 66 percent as much as the child support award. Except among the small group of couples where the incomes of the parents are roughly equal, however, below-average child support awards are associated not with generous property settlements but with below-average property settlements.

ARE LOW CHILD SUPPORT PAYMENTS A CONSEQUENCE OF SHARED CUSTODY OR FREQUENT VISITATION?

About 85 percent of American children potentially eligible for child support live with their mothers, and 15 percent live with their fathers.[5] Joint physical custody in which the child lives a substantial period of time with both parents is rare. In Wisconsin, only 2 percent of the couples share physical custody. Joint legal custody—under which both parents share legal responsibility for making decisions about the child—is much more common and is growing. In the Wisconsin sample, about 20 percent of the divorces involved joint legal custody.

As chapter 5 indicates, the amount of time that divorced fathers spend with their children varies widely. Nearly 10 percent failed to have any contact with their children during the previous year, but half had face-to-face contact with them during 36 or more days and one of five fathers saw their children twice a week or more.

Time and money turn out to be complements rather than substitutes. Other things being equal, nonresident parents who pay below-average child support payments also have below-average visits with their children. Conversely, those who pay more also spend more time with their children.

The positive association between child support and visitation lends credence to theoretical expectations that strengthening child support enforcement might indirectly lead to increases in visits. Increasing the parent's monetary investment in his or her children might increase the parent's stake in the child and the legitimacy of his or her involvement (Weiss and Willis 1985: 268–92).[6] But there are also good reasons to believe that the observed positive correlation between payments and visitation could result from a third unmeasured variable, such as degree of commitment to the child. At this point, we cannot distinguish between these two possibilities.

ARE THERE INSUPERABLE BARRIERS TO ESTABLISHING PATERNITY ?

For children born out-of-wedlock, paternity must be established for child support to be awarded. In most out-of-wedlock births, paternity is not established; however, the proportion of paternities established for such births increased between 1979 and 1985—from 19 percent to 28 percent (Nichols-Casebolt and Garfinkel 1991). Moreover, there is great variation across states in paternity establishment rates. Michigan and Wisconsin have two of the highest rates in the country—at about 66 percent and 50 percent, respectively. Both are in sharp contrast to the Texas record of about 1 in every 50 cases.

Both the high rate of paternity establishment in Wisconsin as a whole and the variation in rates across the state suggest that the barriers to establishing paternity are not insuperable. At least 20 percent and perhaps as much as 60 percent of the difference between paternity establishment rates in Milwaukee, Racine, and Dane counties—40 percent, 62 percent, and 70 percent, respectively—is attributable to how soon the counties start processing the cases. In Dane County, the intake interview with the mother of a child born out-of-wedlock takes place on average when the child is 55 days old; in Racine, the figure is 82 days; and in Milwaukee, the figure is 233 days (the latter apparently owing to a serious backlog of cases).

What Are the Costs and Benefits of the New System?

COSTS TO TAXPAYERS OF CSAS

Stronger paternity establishment laws, child support guidelines, and routine income withholding will increase child support payments, thereby reducing welfare costs and public child support costs. But the assured benefit will increase public child support costs.[7] How much CSAS costs as a whole will depend primarily upon the extent to which its collection-side components increase child support collections compared to the extra costs associated with an assured benefit.

At this point we have no way of knowing how much child support collections are likely to increase in the future. Thus, the best estimates that chapter 7 can provide are upper-bound and lower-bound (the estimates also ignore administrative costs and savings). The upper-bound estimates assume that collections do not increase at all. A CSAS with an assured benefit of $2,000 for the first child, an additional $1,000 each for the second and third child, and an additional $500 each for the fourth and fifth child would cost the nation $1.7 billion per year. The lower-bound estimates assume the ideal collection system—awards in 100 percent of the cases, award levels in accordance with the Wisconsin percentage-of-income standard, and full payment of all awards—in which case CSAS would actually save $2.1 billion. With a medium-range improvement in child support collections—award levels corresponding to the percentage-of-income standard, and award and collection rates improving to halfway between current and perfect rates—a CSAS with a $2,000 assured benefit would save $.5 billion. In short, it is quite possible that welfare savings from increased child support collections could more than offset the additional costs of an assured benefit.

The cost of a CSAS also depends, of course, upon the level of the assured benefit. For example, under the medium-range improvement in collections scenario, the costs (or savings) of an assured benefit of $1,000, $2,000, and $3,000 for the first child (and benefits for higher-order children as just described) are savings of $1 billion, savings of $0.5 billion, and costs of $0.9 billion, respectively. Taken together, these cost estimates suggest that a CSAS with a modest assured benefit—$2,000 for the first child—might have some initial cost, but could actually save money as collections improved over time.

Finally, the net costs of the assured benefit component of a CSAS—that is, if the savings in AFDC that result from increased collections are ignored—also depend upon how much child support collections improve. The greater the private child support payments to those eligible for it, the lower will be the net costs of the assured benefit. Thus, increases in award levels and payment rates will decrease the net costs of the assured benefit. However, increases in award rates—the proportion of cases with awards—will lead not only to increases in private support but also to an increase in the number of cases eligible for the assured benefit, because eligibility for this benefit is limited to those with legal entitlement to private child support. If an assured benefit of $2,000 for the first child were implemented nationwide in the absence of any improvement in any aspect of child support enforcement, the annual cost is estimated to be $1.7 billion. If the assured benefit were implemented in a world in which all child support awards were in accordance with the Wisconsin percentage-of-income guideline, even if award and payment rates were not improved, the cost would be only $0.6 billion. The latter suggests that a fiscally conservative method of implementing an assured benefit would make updating of the child support award a condition of initial eligibility for the assured benefit.

REDUCTIONS IN POVERTY AND DEPENDENCE

In addition to cost estimates, chapter 7 presents estimates of two benefits of CSAS: reductions in poverty and welfare dependence among those potentially eligible for child support. The benefits, like the costs, depend upon the extent and nature of improvement in the child support collections and the level of the assured benefit. Improvements in award rates are the most important determinant on the collection side of reductions in poverty and welfare dependence because they increase the number of families eligible for the assured benefit.

The long-run potential benefits of a CSAS are large. In terms of reductions in poverty and dependence, an upper-bound estimate (based on perfect enforcement) of the long-run effects of a CSAS with a $2,000 assured benefit for the first child indicates a reduction in the poverty gap of 30 percent, reduction in the proportion in poverty of 16 percent, reduction in AFDC caseloads of 33 percent, and reduction in average dependence—the average percentage of income that comes from either AFDC or the public portion of the assured child support benefit—of 19 percent. The benefits in the intermediate run (the medium enforcement improvement) are still substantial—reductions in the poverty gap and AFDC caseloads, for example, of 17 percent and 20 percent. Benefits in the short run (the no improvement scenario) are much smaller, yet still notable—for example, 5 percent and 8 percent reductions in the poverty gap and AFDC caseloads.

The sensitivity of reductions in poverty and dependence to improvements in award rates highlights the strong ties between paternity establishment and the assured child support benefit. Failure to establish paternity is the most common reason for the absence of a child support award among poor and welfare-dependent mothers.[8] The effectiveness of the assured benefit as an antipoverty weapon, therefore, hinges critically upon the nation's ability to increase paternity establishment rates. At the same time, the establishment of an assured benefit would increase the incentives for mothers (and civil servants and community activists with an interest in reducing poverty and welfare dependence) to establish paternity and secure a child support award.

COSTS TO FATHERS OF A CSAS

If the costs of CSAS to the public are small and the benefits to resident parents and their children are large, the costs to nonresident parents must be pretty large.

How can the gains to mothers be compared to the losses to fathers? Many economists respond that there is no scientific basis for comparison, because any comparison involves interpersonal utility comparisons, which have no scientific basis. Although value judgments have no scientific basis, science can trace the implications of value judgments. Which value judgments should be examined? As Myrdal has argued, the choice of value judgments should not and need not be subjective. Reducing poverty is now taken as a valid public objective. In our discussions with public officials, civil servants, academics, and the media, all wanted to know if the CSAS made as much new poverty among fathers as it eliminated among mothers.

Chapter 8 examines the relative income positions of resident mothers and nonresident fathers both under the existing child support system and under what we have called the perfect enforcement system. The analysis takes no account of the effects of an assured benefit and is limited to couples who have resided together. Poverty rates of nonresident fathers are much lower than those of resident mothers and their children—5 percent and 26 percent for white and nonwhite fathers, respectively, versus 29 percent and 44 percent for white and black mothers and children, respectively. A perfect child support enforcement regime would narrow, but hardly eliminate, the gap for whites—to 6 percent for fathers versus 22 percent for mothers and children. For nonwhites, the gap is almost eliminated—35 percent for fathers versus 36 percent for mothers. On the whole, the decrease in poverty rates for mothers and children is larger than the increase in the poverty rates for fathers.

Taking into account the assured benefit would substantially reduce the poverty rates for resident mother families.[9] On the other hand, if the sample included never-married mothers and fathers, the gap between the relative poverty rates of mothers and fathers would be somewhat narrower.[10] But the basic story remains the same. The CSAS destroys much more poverty than it creates.

BENEFITS AND COSTS OF ALTERNATIVE STANDARDS

Chapter 9 compares the two most widely adopted types of child support guidelines—the percentage-of-income model and the income-shares model. The former was designed by the IRP architects of CSAS and is the model for 17 states. The latter was designed by an advisory committee appointed by the federal Office of Child Support Enforcement and has been adopted in 33 states.[11]

Both guidelines begin with the philosophical premise of income sharing—that to parent a child is to incur a responsibility to share income with the child. Both also start with the judgment that the proportion of the nonresident parent's income to be shared with the child should be based upon the proportion that would have been shared with the child if the parent lived with the child.

The standards depart from one another in application, however, both because estimates of the extent and nature of income sharing in two-parent families range widely and because a host of other value judgments must be made to derive child support orders. Under the income-shares approach, the child support obligation declines as a percentage of the nonresident parent's income as total income increases, and consequently, the obligation decreases as the resident parent's income increases. Moreover, the obligation also depends upon expenses for child care and medical care. In contrast, under the percentage-of-income standard, the obligation is a flat percentage of the nonresident parent's income and depends neither upon the resident parent's income nor upon expenses for child care and medical care.

Economic research on two-parent families provides mixed evidence on whether the percentage of income spent on the children declines as incomes increase. Moreover, whereas the proportion of income that would have been spent on the child if the parents had remained together is a useful starting point for determining the proportion of income that a nonresident parent should share with his or her child, whether or not that should be the end point is a value judgment.

Similarly, whether the resident parent's income should affect the nonresident parent's child support obligation is principally a value judgment. On the one hand, counting a resident parent's income seems intuitively fair. On the other hand, if both parents work in the two-parent family, the child's share of total family income does not decrease. Why should it be any different when the family is separated? Most Wisconsin residents report that they believe the economic circumstances of the resident parent are relevant for establishing child support award amounts.

One of the most attractive features of the Wisconsin percentage-of-income standard is its simplicity, that is, it is easy to comprehend, it is at least consistent with equity, and and it facilitates updating of awards. The last function may be the single most important consideration for states or the federal government in constructing future mathematical child support standards. Failure to update awards is a major source of inadequate child support awards.

ESTIMATED EFFECTS OF WITHHOLDING ON COLLECTIONS, DEPENDENCE, AND
LABOR SUPPLY

Chapters 10, 11, and 12 take advantage of the quasi-experimental nature of the way in which routine income withholding was implemented in Wisconsin to derive estimates of the effects of this CSAS component on child support collections, welfare dependence, and the labor supply of resident mothers, respectively. Chapter 10 concludes that the routine withholding of child support obligations from the outset of the obligation, as compared to a regime in which withholding was initiated only in response to a delinquency, led to a 10 percent–30 percent increase in child support collections. Chapters 11 and 12 report no discernible effects on caseloads and small-to-no effects on AFDC costs and labor supply.

These modest-to-no effects of routine income withholding are in contrast to the large simulated effects of the CSAS as a whole reported in chapter 7. Is there some contradiction? Is the difference due to the difference between theory and practice? The answer is no to both questions. The results are consistent with the simulations.

Routine income withholding directly affects only payment rates—the ratio of payments to obligations. Simulation analysis indicates that compared to the total gap of $17–$23 billion between the ability of nonresident parents to pay child support and what they actually pay, achieving 100 percent collection rates alone would eliminate only $2.9 billion. Increasing award rates and award levels are both much more important than increasing payment rates.[12] Furthermore, even under the best of circumstances, routine income withholding could not increase payment rates to 100 percent. Withholding changes nothing, for example, for the self-employed. Job changers can still avoid their obligation at least temporarily if they fail to report their obligation to their new employer.[13]

For two additional reasons, increases in child support payments resulting from routine income withholding in Wisconsin are likely to be smaller than the nationwide increases. First, withholding within only one state affects only those who live within the state, so consequently, nearly a third of obligors are unaffected. Second, Wisconsin already had one of the most effective collection systems in the country and was one of only seven states that required all child support payments to be made through a public agency. In 1984 when the pilot counties in Wisconsin began implementing routine income withholding, all counties in the state had already been required to institute withholding in response to a delinquency for the previous five years. On the other hand, Wisconsin's experience suggests that increases will occur slowly over time because implementation proceeds slowly and affects mainly new cases.

Routine income withholding affects welfare costs and caseloads and the resident parent's labor supply only indirectly through its effects on child support payments. Increases in child support collections do not automatically translate into decreases in welfare costs and caseloads. Increases in payments to those not on welfare obviously have no effect. Even for those on welfare, there will be no effect on costs or caseloads so long as the increase does not push total payments above the $50 per month child support set-aside. Thus, the effects of routine income withholding on welfare costs and caseloads should be even smaller than its effects on payments. Similarly the effects of withholding on labor supply should be smaller than the effects on payments. Indeed, as discussed in chapter 12, economic theory predicts opposite effects for those who are and are not welfare recipients.

Finally, in comparing the small effects of routine income withholding on AFDC caseloads and the labor supply of resident mothers as reported in chapters 11 and 12 with the much larger simulated effects of CSAS as a whole in chapter 7, it is useful to bear in mind that the largest effects in the latter result from the assured child support benefit in combination with increases in award rates.

CHILD SUPPORT AND REMARRIAGE

Economic theory suggests that child support payments could either hasten or retard remarriage (Becker 1981). Child support facilitates marital search and increases the economic attractiveness of the recipient as a potential partner. On the other hand, it makes life in the single state more pleasant and thereby increases choosiness of the recipient. Chapter 13 provides evidence that child support both hastens and retards remarriage. As compared to no support, low levels of child support and irregular payments actually hasten remarriage. Regularly paid high levels of child support delay remarriage. Furthermore, there is some evidence that the delays in remarriage lead to husbands with higher incomes.

PUBLIC OPINION ABOUT CSAS COMPONENTS

Chapter 14, the final chapter in this volume, uses a series of vignettes to explore public opinion in Wisconsin about the percentage-of-income child support standard, routine income withholding, and the assured child support benefit. As such, it provides evidence of the potential for political support for or opposition to each of these components.

With one major exception, there is strong public support for establishing awards in conformance with the Wisconsin standard. On average, respondents support child support awards slightly higher than the percentages called for in the Wisconsin standard. A strong majority supports automatically changing awards in response to changes in the nonresident parent's income, but only a minority supports reducing obligations in response to the remarriage of the nonresident parent. In contrast to the Wisconsin standard, however, which bases awards solely on the income of the nonresident parent, there is strong support for reducing awards if the resident mother either has substantial earnings or remarries.

Support for routine income withholding is modest and increases with both the extent to which obligors become delinquent in its absence and the extent to which withholding reduces welfare costs. Surprisingly, support for withholding was not very sensitive to its effectiveness in increasing collections.

Support for an assured benefit was surprisingly high even under the most adverse of postulated circumstances—an increase in total transfer costs (welfare plus assured benefit) of 20 percent and a decrease in welfare caseloads of only 10 percent. Support increases if total costs do not increase or actually decrease. Larger reductions in AFDC caseloads also increase support, but support is more sensitive to total costs than to AFDC caseloads.

SOME QUESTIONS REMAINING

The previous section summarized the findings reported in the chapters which follow. While these research findings shed a great deal of light on various benefits and costs of a child support assurance system and suggest that CSAS is promising, they do not amount to a full cost-benefit analysis. Because routine income withholding was implemented earlier in Wisconsin than either the child support guidelines or the assured benefit, we have been able to learn more about it from the Wisconsin experience. Yet, as noted above, withholding is arguably the least important of the three major provisions and it is certainly the least controversial. For example, we are only beginning to study the effects of expressing child support orders in percentage terms rather than as a fixed dollar amount. Similarly, because an assured benefit has not been implemented, we have no way of estimating what effect it will have on paternity establishment. Finally, no attempt has been made to estimate administrative cost savings or cost increases resulting from a full fledged CSAS.

In recent years, the United States Congress has enacted two major pieces of legislation that entice and/or require the states to incorporate collections-side features of a CSAS into their enforcement of private child support. The Child Support Enforcement Amendments of 1984 required states to adopt numeric child support guidelines that courts could use at their discretion to determine child support obligations, and also bound them to withhold child support obligations from wages and other income of nonresident parents who become one month delinquent in their child support payments. The bill furthermore encouraged states to develop expedited processes—that is, administrative or bureaucratic rather than judicial processes—for establishing paternity.

The 1988 Family Support Act immensely strengthened the 1984 child support guidelines, withholding, and paternity establishment provisions. Whereas the 1984 Child Support Enforcement Amendments allowed the courts to ignore the guidelines, the 1988 legislation makes the guidelines the presumptive child support award. Judges may depart from the guidelines only if they construct a written justification that can be reviewed by a higher court. Furthermore, the Family Support Act requires that by 1993 states must review child support awards of Title IV-D cases (those handled by the federal Office of Child Support Enforcement) at least every three years and directs the DHHS to study the impact of requiring periodic review of all child support cases. The 1988 legislation also requires withholding of the child support obligation from the outset for all IV-D cases as of 1990 and for all child support cases as of 1994.

Three major paternity provisions are included in the Family Support Act: (1) states must either establish paternity in at least half of the out-of-wedlock cases on AFDC or increase the proportion of such cases in which they establish paternity by 3 percentage points each year; (2) states must obtain the social security numbers of both parents in conjunction with the issuance of birth certificates; and (3) all parties in a contested paternity case must take a genetic test upon the request of any party, with the federal government paying 90 percent of the cost of the test.

The 1984 and 1988 legislation also took two extremely cautious steps in the direction of an assured child support benefit by directing the secretary of the Department of Health and Human Services to grant the state of Wisconsin (in 1984) and the state of New York (in 1988) waivers that would allow them to use federal AFDC funds to pilot an assured child support benefit.[14]

These dramatic changes in our child support system raise a number of additional important research and policy questions. At the most general level, the standard evaluation questions apply: To what extent are the reforms being implemented? What are the effects of the reforms on child support payments, on incomes and welfare dependence of resident parent families, and ultimately on the well-being of the child? We are now in the process of designing such an evaluation.[15]

There are also a number of specific questions. For example, What accounts for the vast differences across states in paternity establishment rates? Would we be better advised to routinely establish paternity at birth in hospitals, as the Swedes have done for decades and the state of Washington has just begun doing?

In addition, What are the benefits and costs of taking the trend from judicial discretion to bureaucratic regularity to its logical conclusion by completely shifting child support enforcement from the judiciary to the executive branch of government? Would total administrative costs increase or decrease and by how much? Can the judicial system cope with the mandate to update all child support awards every three years? To what extent will state-local administration of child support enforcement in our mobile society limit improvements in the system? More generally, what are the benefits and costs of federalizing our child support system?

Finally, what is the best way to learn more about the actual effects of an assured child support benefit? Would a small microexperiment, or a large-scale demonstration in several states, or nationwide implementation of a real program provide the best information?[16]

Questions like these led to the establishment of a close working relationship between the Institute for Research on Poverty and the Wisconsin Department of Health and Social Services. This book demonstrates the fruitfulness of that collaboration in terms of both research and policy. It is hoped that these new areas of inquiry will stimulate comparable collaborations in the future.

Notes

1. Private child support is paid for by the nonresident parent. Public child support, such as Aid to Families with Dependent Children (AFDC), is paid for by the U.S. Government.

2. The latter possibility could occur if strengthening enforcement impoverished nonresident fathers but did little to reduce poverty among poor mothers because the mothers were already receiving welfare and the increased child support resulted primarily in reduced welfare expenditures.

3. If time spent in activities other than market work is a normal good, an increase in income will lead to a reduction in work. Income-tested transfers also reduce the reward for work via their benefit reduction rates. Non-income-tested transfers, like the CSAS, may also indirectly reduce the reward for work among beneficiaries via the increase in taxes that is required to finance them. A wage subsidy is an exception in that it increases the rewards for work even as it increases income. The net effect of a wage subsidy is therefore an empirical question.

4. Indeed, in most cases neither individual has much property. On the other hand, a lump sum payment in lieu of child support used to be common. This is no longer legal under the laws of Wisconsin.

5. Data are from the Survey of Income and Program Participation (SIPP) and ignore children who live with neither parent. See Meyer and Garasky (1991).

6. Nonpayment of support is frequently given as a reason for denying visitation (Weiss and Willis 1985).

7. By increasing the incentive to leave welfare, an assured benefit will indirectly lead to some offsetting reductions in costs. But these reductions are much smaller than the direct increases in outlays.

8. More generally, the link exists between award rates and the assured benefit.

9. According to the results in chapter 5, a perfect enforcement regime accompanied by a $2,000 and a $3,000 assured benefit would reduce poverty rates by an additional 6 and 15 percentage points, respectively.

10. Oellerich (1990) reported that poverty rates for mothers and fathers were 40.3 percent and 7.6 percent, respectively. With a perfect enforcement regime, the rates for mothers decrease to 33.3 percent, and those for fathers increase to 12.8 percent.

11. Three jurisdictions—Washington, D.C., Puerto Rico, and the Virgin Islands—use the Melson formula devised by Judge Melson from Delaware.

12. In addition, total payments are a product of award rates, award levels, and payment rates. Thus, the improvement in any single component of the system is smaller than the simultaneous improvement of all three components.

13. Once the employer reports wages paid to the Social Security Administration, it is possible to find out that the obligor has a new employer. But there is a three- or six-month lag before this information first becomes available on a computer, and the search for an obligor's social security number might not be initiated that quickly.

14. In effect, Wisconsin was to be given a block grant to run both a child support assurance system and the AFDC system at the same cost to the federal government as the old AFDC system alone. Extra costs or savings were solely to be borne by or benefit the state.

15. For our preliminary thoughts, see Garfinkel and McLanahan (1990: 205–34).

16. For a discussion of the limits of a microexperimental approach, see Garfinkel, Manski, and Michalopoulos (forthcoming in 1992).

References

Becker, Gary. 1981. *A Treatise on the Family.* Cambridge, Mass.: Harvard University Press.

Cassetty, Judith. 1978. *Child Support and Public Policy: Securing Support from Absent Fathers.* Lexington, Mass.: D.C. Heath and Co.

Chambers, David. 1979. *Making Fathers Pay: The Enforcement of Child Support.* Chicago: University of Chicago Press.

Garfinkel, Irwin, and Sara S. McLanahan. 1986. *Single Mothers and Their Children: A New American Dilemma.* Washington, D.C.: Urban Institute Press.

Garfinkel, Irwin, and Sara S. McLanahan. 1990. "The Effects of the Child Support Act of 1988 on Child Well-Being." *Population Research and Policy Review* 9(3, Sept.):205–234.

Garfinkel, Irwin, Charles Manski, and Charles Michalopoulos. Forthcoming. "Are Micro-Experiments Always Best? Randomization of Individuals or Sites." In *Evaluating Welfare and Training Programs,* edited by Charles Manski and Irwin Garfinkel. Cambridge, Mass.: Harvard University Press.

Martin, Teresa Castro, and Larry Bumpass. 1989. "Recent Trends in Marital Disruption." *Demography* 26:37–51.

Meyer, D. R., and S. Garasky. 1991. "Custodial Fathers: Myths, Realities, and Child Support Policy." Technical Analysis Paper 42. Washington, D.C.: U.S. Department of Health and Human Services, Office of Human Service Policy.

Mnookin, Robert H., and Lewis Kornhauser. 1979. "Bargaining in the Shadow of the Law: The Case of Divorce." *Yale Law Journal* 88(5, Apr.):950–97.

Nichols-Casebolt, Ann, and Irwin Garfinkel. 1991. "Trends in Paternity and Adjudications and Child Support Awards." *Social Science Quarterly* 27(1):89.

Oellerich, 1990. "The Income Distributional Impacts of Private Child Support Transfers in the United States." In Johann Kurt Brunner, Hans-Georg Peterson (eds.) *Simulation Models in Tax and Transfer Policy*. Campus Verlag Frankfurt/New York, pp. 399–421.

Sawhill, Isabel V. 1983. "Developing Normative Standards for Child Support Payments." In *The Paternal Child Support Obligation*, edited by Judith Cassetty. Lexington, Mass.: Lexington Books.

U.S. Bureau of the Census. 1981. *Child Support and Alimony: 1978. Current Population Reports*, Special Studies ser. P-23, no. 112. Washington, D.C.: U.S. Bureau of the Census. September.

_____. 1990. *Marital Status and Living Arrangements. Current Population Reports*, ser. P-20, no. 450. Washington, D.C.: U.S. Government Printing Office. March.

Weiss, Yoram, and Robert J. Willis. 1985. "Children as Collective Goods and Divorce Settlements." *Journal of Labor Economics* 3:268–92.

White, Kenneth R., and R. Thomas Stone. 1976. "A Study of Alimony and Child Support Rulings with Some Recommendations." *Family Law Quarterly* 10(1):75–91.

Yee, Lucy M. 1979. "What Really Happens in Child Support Cases: An Empircal Study of the Establishment and Enforcement of Child Support Awards in the Denver District Court." *Denver Law Journal* 57(1):21–70.

Chapter Two

THE WISCONSIN CHILD SUPPORT ASSURANCE SYSTEM: FROM PLAUSIBLE PROPOSALS TO IMPROBABLE PROSPECTS

Thomas Corbett

In 1991, the National Commission on Children—commonly known as the Rockefeller Commission—recommended several important steps toward assuring economic security for children. It called for the introduction of refundable tax credits, the expansion of the Earned Income Tax Credit (EITC), expanded training and job opportunities, and the reorientation of welfare into a short-term form of relief in periods of unanticipated unemployment, disability, or other economic hardship. Critical among the steps suggested by the commission was a call to develop a child support assurance system (CSAS):

> We recommend that a demonstration of suitable scale be designed and implemented to test an insured child support plan that would combine enhanced child support enforcement with a government-insured benefit when absent parents do not meet their support obligations. Contingent on positive findings from this demonstration, the Commission recommends establishment of the insured child support benefit in every state. (p. xxi)

Almost a dozen years earlier, in 1979, the Wisconsin Welfare Reform Study Advisory Committee had also recommended several steps toward assuring the economic security of children. Like the Rockefeller Commission, it called for the use of refundable tax credits, introduction of a state EITC, and expanded training and job opportunities. The advisory committee also made child support a central component of its reform package:

> The Department of Health and Social Services should initiate a study to design and implement on an experimental basis a universal child support tax program to replace much of the existing AFDC program. This program would be financed through a specific tax on natural or adoptive parents which varies with the number of dependent children and income, plus state general revenues and federal funds normally expended in this programmatic area. (p. 45)

The "insured child support plan" and the "universal child support tax program" are different labels for a set of proposals designed to enhance the economic well-being of children, generally known as the child support assurance system. The dozen years between the initial proposal to enact such a program in Wisconsin and its partial reintroduction through the Rockefeller Commission represent a conventional example of the challenges associated with "doing" public policy (Bardach 1977; Beyer and Trice 1978). Proposing a plausible concept is neither equivalent to enacting a new policy or institutionalizing a new program. Although approval by the governing authorities and legitimization through the political process are important preconditions for realizing reform, the ultimate litmus test for success is the capacity to translate proposals into a working reality. The story of the CSAS in Wisconsin is instructive in terms of the prospects and perils of undertaking fundamental social change.

CSAS—DEFINITIONS AND CHALLENGES

Three provisions of the Wisconsin version of the child support assurance system have been considered central to its success from the beginning. The first of these is that of establishing adequate child support obligations in an equitable manner. Under the CSAS, the obligation of the noncustodial parent is set as a simple percentage of gross income and varies only with the number of children the noncustodial parent is required to support: 17 percent for one child, 25 percent for two children, 29 percent for three children, 31 percent for four children, and 34 percent for five or more children. The basic rationale behind this Percentage of Income and Asset Standard (PIAS) is that liable, noncustodial parents ought to share a legislatively prescribed portion of their income with those children not living with them. This is typically referred to as the income-sharing concept.

The second principal provision is that support obligations are to be withheld from earnings, and other sources of income if feasible, and forwarded by the employer to the clerk of courts office. This contrasts with a prior practice in which withholding was used only if child support is not paid. This provision assumes that child support is a preeminent debt, to be paid before other obligations, and is often referred to as the "taxation at the source of income" concept.

The final provision is that all children participating in the program will receive a socially assured minimal level of economic support

each month. If the private child support transfer from the noncustodial parent falls below the assured benefit, a publicly financed subsidy,
known as the Child Support Supplement, makes up the difference.
The concept underlying this provision is consistent with "advanced
payment" programs found in several European countries: children
eligible for child support should be able to count on an assured level
of support that is not dependent upon the ability or willingness of
the noncustodial parent to provide that support.

The first two provisions—those dealing with how awards are set
and collected—are considered collections-side initiatives or interventions designed to enhance private child support transfers and thereby
reduce public responsibility. The course of these reform initiatives
over the 1980s was generally positive, though some difficulties remain. The Wisconsin experience in this area served as a model for
the child support provisions of the Family Support Act of 1988.[1]

The fate of the "socially assured" benefit concept, which came to
be known as the assured benefit (AB), was less fortuitous. Despite
almost universal support from the academic/policy community,[2] the
AB initiative was never tried in Wisconsin. In fact, progress toward
actually implementing the assured benefit program in Wisconsin
stalled in the late 1980s.

A CONFLUENCE OF IDEAS

The history of the private child support system in the United States
is fraught with failure. Although the needs of children in single-parent
households had been recognized as acute early in this century, when
the National Conference of Commissioners on Uniform State Laws
directed its committee on marriage and divorce to study the problem,
enforcement of private child support was viewed as strictly a state
and local problem.[3] The attitude of benign neglect changed in the
1940s when congressional interest in absent fathers emerged in response to an upward trend in divorce, separation, desertion, and out-
of-wedlock births. Because of this trend, children with living but
absent parents replaced orphans as the most numerous dependents in
the Aid to Families with Dependent Children (AFDC) Program. The
U.S. Congress enacted the first federal legislation regarding private
child support in 1950, requiring state welfare agencies to notify law
enforcement officials when a child receiving AFDC benefits had been

deserted or abandoned. Further legislation, enacted in 1965 and 1967, allowed states to request addresses of absent parents from the U.S. Department of Health, Education & Welfare (HEW, now the U.S. Department of Health and Human Services [DHHS]) and from the Internal Revenue Service (IRS). States were also required to establish a single organizational unit to enforce child support and establish paternity.

The most significant federal legislation was enacted when Congress added part D to Title IV of the Social Security Act, establishing the Child Support Enforcement (IV-D) program. Former Senator Russell Long, of Louisiana, had been the principal sponsor of the legislation, which President Gerald Ford signed into law in early 1975. The legislation established an Office of Child Support Enforcement in HEW and required each state to establish a corresponding agency to help enforce child support in all AFDC cases and, on request, in non-AFDC cases. It also required states to maintain a parent locator service, which tied in with a federal service. In short, the 1975 act created the public bureaucracy to enforce child support obligations.

However, social and economic trends outpaced the modest policy initiatives that had taken place. Aggregate poverty rates reached their lowest levels in the 1970s, but other patterns—some not generally appreciated until the decade following—generated pressure for additional change. First, children, particularly those living in single-parent households, replaced the elderly in 1974 as society's most economically disadvantaged group (Danziger and Weinberg 1986). Second, the growth of single-parent households with children was becoming an observable and troubling trend (Pearce 1978; Sawhill 1975); where 1 in 12 children would live in such households in 1960, more than 1 in 5 would be so situated in the early 1980s (Garfinkel and McLanahan 1986). Third, public economic support systems for children were entering a period of decline. The real value of AFDC benefit guarantees decreased by over 40 percent between 1970 and 1990; the proportion of poor children receiving help through AFDC declined from 80 percent in 1973 to less than 60 percent a decade later (Green Book 1991). Fourth, a period of long-term economic restructuring would occur after 1973; wage inequality would increase and inflation-adjusted wage opportunities would deteriorate for many—particularly young family heads (Danziger and Gottschalk 1986). Finally, the historic problems with the private child support system were beginning to be acknowledged and supportive data were being collected. By the end of the decade, it was common knowledge that only 60 percent of eligible children were covered by a support award and that only half of those received the full amount.[4] In addition to these trends, the era of reliance on "solutions from the center" was over. President Jimmy Carter's Program for Better Jobs and Income (PBJI) initiative was the last gasp of megareform. Thereafter, state-sponsored initiatives would increasingly dominate the poverty policy and welfare reform dialogue.

The Institute for Research on Poverty (IRP) had been established at the University of Wisconsin–Madison in 1966 by the federal Office of Economic Opportunity (OEO) to serve as a think tank for the War On Poverty. Wisconsin was chosen as the site for the IRP because its economics department had both expertise in poverty research and a long tradition of university-government cooperation in the social welfare area. In the early part of this century, at the dawn of the Progressive era, Professor John R. Commons had worked with Wisconsin Governor Robert M. La Follette to establish the first workmen's compensation system, the first child and labor legislation, and the first progressive income tax in the nation. A generation later, Professor Edwin Witte, Commons's student, helped Wisconsin establish the first state unemployment insurance system in 1932 and, in 1934, served as the executive director of President Roosevelt's Committee on Economic Security, which drafted the landmark 1935 Social Security Act. Still one generation later, Professor Robert Lampman, Witte's student, had become one of the nation's foremost academic analysts of poverty and coauthored, with Burton Weisbrod, the famous chapter in the 1963 Economic Report of the President that put poverty back on the public agenda. This long tradition of university-government collaboration gave rise to the oft-cited notion of the "Wisconsin Idea," where the boundaries of the university are the boundaries of the state.

By the mid-1970s, the poverty research functions of OEO had been transferred to the Office of the Assistant Secretary for Planning and Evaluation (ASPE) within HEW. The ASPE asked Professor Irwin Garfinkel, the director-designate of IRP, to initiate a line of research on child support. Garfinkel was not enthusiastic about the idea, assuming, like many others at the time, that noncustodial parents of poor children in particular probably had little to share with their offspring. He did motivate Judith Cassetty, who was then a doctoral candidate in social work, to write her dissertation on the topic. The dissertation, subsequently revised and published as a book entitled *Child Support and Public Policy,* was the first child support research done at the IRP and provoked considerable attention.

The CSAS proposal, first expressed publicly to the Wisconsin Welfare Reform Committee and the Wisconsin legislature in 1978, was the product of several sources. The idea for the standard came from Judith Cassetty and contemporaneous work by Isabel Sawhill, an economist doing highly respected research on the poverty of women and children. The idea to use immediate income withholding to collect support obligations emerged circuitously. The original concept involved collecting obligations through the tax system, much like FICA taxes. That general notion can be traced to Harold Watts, a former director of the IRP, who proposed a complex method for using tax returns to help collect support obligations in *All Our Children: The American Family under Pressure* (in Keniston 1977). Lack of interest by the Department of Revenue in assuming this responsibility led to the withholding concept (a relatively minor extension of the "conditional withholding" statute enacted in Wisconsin in 1978). The idea of an assured benefit probably came from Sweden's advanced child support payment program, or perhaps as an extension of the social security menu in the Commons/Witte/Lampman tradition.

Good public policy is, in part, a matter of getting the question right. The emergence of the CSAS concept in the late 1970s reflected important shifts in how key policy issues were posed. First, the philosophical premise underlying CSAS is that parents are responsible for sharing income with their children and that government is responsible for ensuring that children who live apart from their parents receive the share to which they are entitled. Thus, the prevailing viewpoint shifted somewhat away from government responsibility for the economic well-being of children and toward a form of shared responsibility. Second, the CSAS may be thought of as an addition to the social security system, analogous to Survivors' Insurance. Like Survivors' Insurance, CSAS is designed to include children from *all* income classes who suffer an income loss due to the absence of a parent. The collections-side provisions resemble a proportional payroll tax—similar to that used to finance social insurance programs—and the benefit structure of the assured-benefit component of CSAS is like that found in all U.S. social insurance programs, because it provides greater benefits to low-income families than are justified on the basis of the family's contributions or taxes. Most critically, the CSAS concept, like other social insurance programs, is designed to prevent poverty and welfare dependence. Welfare programs relieve poverty; social insurance prevents it. Welfare replaces earnings and thus is inconsistent with self-sufficiency; the CSAS proposal would supplement the earnings of custodial parents and thereby encourage self-sufficiency.

When first proposed, the CSAS appeared consistent with the emerging societal standard that valued personal responsibility as well as with a respected U.S. tradition of social responsibility. The plausibility and attractiveness of the concept notwithstanding, the road to reality was paved with unexpected obstacles. We examine that road in the two sections following.

GETTING STARTED

As noted, the CSAS was conceived as part of a broad reform package to aid the economically disadvantaged in Wisconsin. It was adopted in 1979 by the Wisconsin Welfare Reform Advisory Committee appointed by Governor Martin Schreiber. The chairman of the committee, Robert Haveman, was on the faculty of the Department of Economics at the University of Wisconsin–Madison and was a former director of the university's Institute for Research on Poverty (IRP). Thus, from the outset, a close working relationship was established between the university and the state.

At the time, the environment within the state Department of Health and Social Services (DHSS) and in Wisconsin state government in general was one of innovation, risk-taking, and disregard for protocol. As the prospect for national reform diminished, Wisconsin reformers felt that the task of designing fundamental reform devolved upon them, as it had in the past. Donald Percy, the secretary of the DHSS, was a gifted administrator who called for "lateral thinking" in approaching reform and generated considerable enthusiasm for being innovative.

The recommendations of the Welfare Reform Advisory Committee contained an antipoverty agenda that was designed to promote work and reduce poverty and welfare dependence primarily through creation of new nonwelfare programs. The agenda included a credit income tax, an earned income tax credit, a cash out of the Food Stamp Program (i.e., substitute cash for the value of Food Stamp coupons), and a child support reform concept originally known as the universal child support tax initiative. The agenda was received favorably by the media, government officials, and members of the state legislature. The new governor of Wisconsin, Lee Sherman Dreyfus—representing a different party—affirmed that the state was prepared to undertake fundamental reform and appointed an interdepartmental task force to help design and implement the various proposals. But the difficulty of translating abstract concepts into practical programs proved overwhelming, and progress at the governmental level diminished and eventually stopped in most areas where recommendations had been made.

Work on the child support reform was carried on at the Institute for Research on Poverty under the direction of Irwin Garfinkel. The pieces for an interorganizational effort also began to fall into place. Judith Cassetty, while working on her dissertation, became acquainted with Sherwood Zink—legal counsel for the Wisconsin Office of Child Support—and helped forge a relationship between that agency and the IRP. Moreover, a key member of the 1978 Welfare Reform Committee—State Representative Thomas Loftus—quickly assumed a position of legislative leadership and maintained an interest in the child support concept. A collaborative relationship among academic, bureaucratic, and legislative institutions began to emerge.

A two-pronged attack was then launched: to secure outside financial support and to formalize a relationship between the IRP and the DHSS. The IRP proposal for outside support described the reform being designed and suggested a program of public education, including a national conference; the overall proposed budget was over a million dollars. However, the proposal was greeted with nearly universal skepticism; a mere $10,000 was obtained from the Ford Foundation in 1982.

At this point the politics of the reform required a delicate balancing act. Continued interest from the state bureaucracy and legislative supporters depended in part on the attention the plan received from outside sources, such as the Ford Foundation, the academic community, advocacy groups, and federal officials. At the same time, the legislature needed assurance that the ideas being thrust upon it were reasonable. The Institute and DHSS could take the project no further unless they had sufficient funds to hire additional staff.

Refusing to give up, IRP researchers and their colleagues at the DHSS worked out a contractual arrangement that enabled developmental work to continue, although with a lengthened timetable. The state, having received the Ford money and university contributions (and initially adding state dollars), was entitled to a federal matching grant on a four-to-one basis. The federal support obtained through this symbiotic university-state relationship permitted a small number of dedicated persons at the institute and in the DHSS to continue to work on the project.

From 1980 through 1982, specifications for the universal child support tax program were worked out. A model law for implementing both the collections and benefit sides of the proposal was drafted by

Margo Melli, professor of law at the University of Wisconsin–Madison. A process for developing databases was initiated, to simulate costs and benefits under various program parameters.

During this period a national conference was held to learn what work had been done on child support nationally, to seek feedback on the direction taken in Wisconsin, and to garner publicity for the undertaking. In 1982 the IRP published a three-volume report (Garfinkel and Melli 1982) that not only described the new system but discussed related issues such as eligibility, collections, benefits, and administration, and included a method for implementing the reform program at the state level.

The plan for moving from concept to program was to be accomplished in two stages. First, the so-called collections-side proposals (the percentage-of-income standard and immediate income withholding) would be designed and implemented. At a later date the assured benefit would be introduced. This strategy was both fiscally conservative and reflected the complexities of the benefit side of the package. Thus, by early 1983, the plan was ready for implementation on a demonstration basis. Yet, many continued to view it as an academic exercise, and in March 1983, the Ford Foundation again rejected a request to provide significant financial support.

THE COLLECTIONS SIDE OF CSAS

The first practical steps toward implementing the reform took place when the Wisconsin State Legislature passed a bill in 1983 that included directives for the state DHSS to test the automatic wage withholding provision in 10 counties and publish a percentage-of-income standard as an alternative guideline for establishing support obligations in its 1983–85 budget package. The bill also contained a provision requiring all Wisconsin counties to begin to use immediate income withholding in all support cases after July 1987, depending upon the outcome of the pilots. This partial success in the legislature was due, in large part, to the work of Representative Loftus, who had risen to the position of speaker of the state Assembly. The new Wisconsin secretary of the DHSS, Linda Reivitz, supported the project; however, the new Democratic governor of Wisconsin, Anthony Earl, was only lukewarm to the idea. Like many others, he underestimated both the importance of child support to the economic well-being of children and the ability of absent parents to pay significant amounts of support. Only a small piece of the reform package was being tested, but it generated considerable controversy.

The Percentage-of-Income-and-Asset Standard (PIAS) was criticized for not taking into account: (1) unusual debts encumbering the obligor, (2) remarriage and start of a new family by the noncustodial parent, and (3) the income or remarriage of the custodial parent. The PIAS was also attacked for being inflexible, eroding judicial discretion, and diminishing the ability of parents to negotiate a child support arrangement uniquely tailored to their circumstances. Further, this provision called for administrative rather than legal procedures to be used to modify support obligations. If the obligation is expressed as a percentage of income, it changes automatically as the obligor's income changes. Some argued that all changes in support orders should be based on a judicial review of relevant factors.

The immediate income withholding provision evoked positive and negative reactions. Many believed that it was the most efficient mechanism for collecting support obligations: it avoided the necessity of making sensitive decisions regarding when to impose such an order— an action traditionally representing a penalty for noncompliance— and it minimized the accumulation of unpaid support, with all the resulting legal and economic complexities. Others, however, construed withholding as an unnecessary intrusion of government into a private transaction—a variant of the "big government" argument. Opponents also argued that the withholding provision penalized obligors who intended to meet their obligation, and that it eliminated the personal touch associated with paying child support. Finally, it was argued that employment-related problems would ensue, either because employers would object to the costs associated with administering the wage assignment or because employees would experience embarrassment vis-à-vis their employer.

At that time, the publicly guaranteed child support benefit had had little public exposure, so little was known about possible reaction to this provision. Several potential objections appeared likely. First, the guarantee could be seen as an unwarranted extension of government responsibility by those who view child support—unless welfare is involved—as essentially a private transaction. Second, there would likely be concerns about potential costs, particularly with respect to how large an increase (if any) the public would accept. And third, some viewed the guarantee as an extension of welfare under a different name.

Yet the modest 1983 legislation and administrative effort proved to be a watershed. Its cautious character effectively muted some of the prevailing concerns—for example, that the withholding provision would be a burden for employers and infringe on the constitutional rights of noncustodial parents. Furthermore, the permissive language of the standard did not threaten the judiciary by statutorily depriving them of flexibility in setting support amounts. Until this time three of the major actors—the state government, the federal government, and the Ford Foundation—appeared to be waiting for one of the others to make a substantive move. The proposed reforms were sufficiently different from the staus quo that doubt remained about their feasiblity as public policy. The Ford foundation was waiting for government to accord the ideas some legitimacy while government was waiting for some recognized outside entity, like a major national foundation, to indicate interest. The legislation also demonstrated to federal and foundation officials that the plan was more than an academic exercise: it gave the DHSS something tangible to implement, and it gave the IRP something real to evaluate. In subsequent years, significant fiscal support was forthcoming from the Ford Foundation.

The initial stages of implementing the withholding provision were not easy—given that Wisconsin employs a state-supervised and county-administered approach to managing many of its social welfare programs. Convincing 10 counties to participate meant persuading a combination of locally elected individudals and program-management officials and obtaining a contract with each county board. All did not go smoothly. Indeed, the first county ready to sign a contract was persuaded not to do so by a large turnout of noncustodial parents at a public hearing to consider the proposed contract between the DHSS and the county. Other counties, too, presented their own sets of difficulties.

Persuading the judicial community that the percentage-of-income standard was the appropriate means for setting obligations also was not easy. Although it was generally agreed that the standard simplified the process, saved time, and lessened antagonism between the parties, there was considerable concern that the automatic determination of support amounts would fail to treat equitably those individuals whose circumstances set them outside the guidelines. Self-interest also generated resistance, with some judges and commissioners fearing that the procedure would erode their discretion and reduce their roles to those of administrative functionaries. Some attorneys feared they would lose part of their livelihoods. Noncustodial parents objected to the size of the awards calculated under the standard, which, they claimed, did not take into account their current needs. They also

resented immediate income withholding because it implied a reluc-
tance on their part to provide support voluntarily to their children.

Clearly, the relevant organizational environment was confused during the pilot period; it was not always apparent how the key institutions would line up. The Wisconsin Child Support Enforcement Association (WCSEA) indicated concern about the policy direction being
taken—perhaps fearing change, or simply resisting apparent new state
mandates, or concluding that these reforms would threaten their traditional role or undermine job security. Although feminists were generally supportive, this was not a guarantee. Some argued, for example,
that the percentage standard would shift the divorce negotiations away
from advantageous property settlements (which were considered a
"bird in the hand") toward promises of future income sharing—something viewed as far less certain.

The troika of academic, bureaucratic, and legislative supporters
patiently dealt with the objections raised. For example, Sherwood
Zink, the attorney for the Wisconsin Office of Child Support, worked
to allay the fears of those in the legal community. In part, the approach
of not mandating the standard worked in its favor. Some judges and
commissioners tried it, found it helpful, and convinced others to use
it. Other state bureaucrats worked within the bureaucracy and with
community groups to develop acceptance of the proposals. In the
legislature, Representative Loftus used his position as Assembly
speaker to sell the idea politically. Finally, the steady stream of academic papers that began emanating from the IRP moved the debate,
at least in part, from a theoretical to an empirical basis.

By 1985, some of the more egregious fears about, and opposition to,
the collections provisions of what was now becoming the child support assurance system had been muted. This encouraged Governor
Earl to successfully enact several changes in the Wisconsin child
support law that moved the state well along toward a full-fledged
program. The budget bill for the 1985–87 biennium contained new
child support legislation to permit additional counties to begin immediate income withholding prior to July 1, 1987, when the withholding provision became state law. The bill also made the percentage-of-
income standard presumptive as of July 1987, which meant that
awards could depart from the standard only if the judge submitted a
written finding to the case record justifying such a departure.

By 1986, despite some half-dozen years since the inception of a
formal planning process, proponents of child support reform were
satisfied with the progress being made. Immediate income withholding proved so popular that the DHSS could not keep up with the

counties requesting to become "withholding pilots." Milwaukee County, by far the state's largest jurisdiction, became a pilot in January 1986—a year and a half before the state mandate would take effect. It was also clear that use of the percentage-of-income standard was increasing, though the numbers supporting this concept would not be available for some time. And the Ford Foundation, despite its earlier reservations, began to contribute substantial amounts in support of the "Wisconsin Demonstration."

As called for in the 1985 legislation, the use of immediate income withholding was mandated statewide in July 1987, and the percentage-of-income standard was made presumptive a month later. The ultimate testimony to the success of this portion of the CSAS is found in how closely the child support provisions of the 1988 federal Family Support Act parallel the Wisconsin experience. As of 1991, both provisions remain in effect in the state, though a number of issues and questions remain. For example, it was originally hoped that, under the standard, awards would be set in percentage terms and allowed to automatically rise or fall as income changed. For a variety of reasons, some related to the ease of calculating arrearages, the standard generally has been used to set the initial award, which is then set forth in absolute dollar, not percentage, terms. Erosion of the "real" value of awards, on average, resulted in state efforts to routinely update awards periodically. And other pockets of discontent continue to arise. As late as August 1991, the percentage standard was challenged on constitutional and other validity grounds in a legal brief filed by a member of the Fathers for Equal Justice. Finally, some issues that were not originally part of the CSAS concept, such as finding efficient ways to establish paternity, have been recognized as important to a fully effective child support system.

Flushed with some success, the proponents of CSAS anticipated similar outcomes on the benefit side of the reform proposal.

THE BENEFIT SIDE OF CSAS

The assured benefit (AB) had always been considered an essential part of the CSAS package. A commonly used analogy for that package is that it was like a three-legged stool—establishing adequate support orders, collecting those orders efficiently, and publicly guaranteeing a minimal amount of child support when the collection provisions (or legs) failed for whatever reason. If one of those legs were missing, then the integrity of the CSAS as a strategy for helping children economically would be undermined.

The assured benefit was conceptualized as a universal program that would provide benefits both to the middle class and the poor. Some proponents saw the AB as a fundamental step toward dismantling the welfare approach to aiding children. If implemented, the AB would ensure children from middle- and upper-middle-income families against the risk that their nonresident parent would fail to pay child support. When the percentage-of-income standard is fully implemented and child support orders are expressed in percentage terms, a sudden decline in the nonresident parent's income will result in a precipitous decline in the private child support transfer, unless the AB is present to cushion the fall.

The AB would also enable those with low earnings ability and low child support entitlements to escape poverty. In the absence of an assured benefit, a large proportion of welfare mothers would still be poor even if they worked full time and received all the private child support to which they were entitled. Moreover, the AB would encourage work and reduce welfare dependence. Unlike welfare, the AB would not be reduced by one dollar for each dollar of earnings. Rather, the assured benefit would function as an income floor on which earnings of the custodial parent could be added. This policy would supplement earnings and not, like welfare, substitute for earnings.

Finally, the AB would offer an effective means of reinvesting the savings of increased child support collections. Currently, much of the increased child support for poor children goes to offset AFDC costs. This, in effect, results in a system where child support tranfers collected from poorer absent parents are not spent on their children but are used for the benefit of middle- and upper-income taxpayers. Sharing the gains of increased collections with poor custodial-parent families who have child support awards not only bolsters their incomes in times of hardship, but gives them an incentive to cooperate in establishing paternity and locating the other legally liable parent of their child.

From the first, it was recognized that the decision to separate the *collections* (or income-enhancement) provisions from the *benefit* (or expenditure) provisions had merit as a short-term strategy but represented a considerable gamble over the longer term. Withholding and the percentage-of-income standard, despite the numerous objections and concerns raised, had the advantage of helping children without increasing the public fiscal burden. In fact, expenditures on welfare would decrease if the program were successful. The publicly guaranteed child support minimum—the assured benefit—was thought to be controversial from several perspectives: first, when viewed as an unwarranted extension of public responsibility; second, when viewed as a possible source of increased public expenditures; and third, when considering the difficulty of explaining how broadening access to a public transfer would be consistent with reducing welfare dependency. Although the decision to proceed on the collections side accorded the project recognition and support, it isolated the assured benefit and rendered it more vulnerable to attack. The proponents of the CSAS always saw the collection and benefit provisions as interrelated—particularly in calculating benefit-cost ratios. Whether or not that linkage could be sustained remained to be seen.

Developmental work on the assured benefit had never really ceased. The early work took place in the form of joint university-state planning sessions where a formal planning process dominated. By 1983, enough progress had been made to seek the necessary federal waivers and support. It was determined that the best way to secure federal support would be to appeal to Congress, rather than seek a normal federal waiver of social security regulations (this was prior to the creation of the Low Income Opportunity Board by President Ronald Reagan in 1987). State executive agency officials (particularly Bernard Stumbras and Sherwood Zink) and legislative Representative Loftus made the case while the U.S. Department of Health and Human Services (DHHS) opposed Wisconsin's apparent end run around their prerogative to grant waivers. Then-DHHS Secretary Margaret Heckler personally testified against granting Wisconsin any special legislative consideration in this matter.

Despite DHHS opposition, Congress, in 1984, passed legislation allowing Wisconsin to use the money normally paid to the state as part of the AFDC matching formula to finance the assured benefit and to waive relevant parts of titles IV-A and IV-D of the Social Security Act. To effectuate these provisions, the state would have to submit a formal waiver request to the secretary of DHHS, who could only turn it down *if* the proposed plan was demonstrably harmful to children. As specified in the enabling legislation, the state's window of opportunity extended from 1986 to 1994.

The pace of the planning process then picked up and shifted from the university to the state bureaucracy. The Committee to Review Innovations in Child Support (CRICS) was created by Wisconsin DHSS Secretary Linda Reivitz to assist the department in making program design and policy decisions on the path toward implementation. In 1985, the Wisconsin State Legislature approved a proposal to pilot the assured benefit in principle—pending further review of a detailed proposal by the powerful Joint Finance Committee (JFC) in 1986. The DHSS, with input from CRICS and the IRP, was moving ahead on several fronts; preparing the federal waiver proposal, as well as a detailed plan for consideration by the JFC, and organizing the work with the pilot counties. When the JFC approved the departmental plan (albeit by a close 9–7 vote) and the waiver application was readied for submission, the transition from planning to implementation appeared imminent.

Then the momentum stalled. Already, modifications to the concept's original intent and design had compromised its integrity. For example, the original program would not have been means-tested at all. The proposal that emerged would have imposed a benefit reduction rate (or tax) on the publicly guaranteed portion of the AB—though far less than the one in AFDC. Other compromises would also be proposed: establishing an income ceiling and restricting eligibility to working custodial parents. The year 1986 was an election year, and the incumbent Governor Earl feared being labeled a "big spender" and a social tinkerer. A debate broke out within the bureaucracy about whether welfare reform should focus on expanding child care resources (which everyone understood) or moving ahead with the assured benefit pilots (which was much harder to explain). With AFDC caseloads expanding to their peak in early 1986, the opponent—a conservative Republican—campaigned on a platform that stressed retrenchment in the area of social welfare. (The assured benefit appeared to be an expansion of government.) Governor Earl lost the election and, despite intense lobbying, never sent the waiver request to Washington, D.C. He reportedly felt that the new administration should decide on its own if this concept constituted good public policy.

The prospects of the reform were not promising in the spring of 1987. The new governor, Republican Tommy Thompson, had a different view of welfare reform. To him, alleviating poverty was less important than reducing welfare costs and caseloads. Reform proposals that were hard in character (designed to push recipients out of dependency) were more credible to the new administration than soft reforms designed to induce recipients into self-sufficiency. One of the governor's appointees, the new administrator of a major division in the DHSS, the Division of Community Services (DCS), strongly opposed the assured benefit concept. In short order, staff within the division were forbidden to work on the AB program, though several continued to do so unofficially.

Again, the complexity of the interorganizational network played a key role. The state Assembly was controlled by the Democrats, with Representative Loftus continuing as speaker. This meant that controversial issues such as welfare reform would require some form of bipartisan negotiation. From the beginning, the fate of the assured benefit depended upon how forcefully Speaker Loftus brokered the issue—particularly during preparation of the 1987–88 biennial budget.

In the bargaining that ensued, the Democrats agreed to part of the governor's plan for welfare reform, that of Learnfare (a program that linked welfare benefits to school attendance) and to a dramatic expansion of welfare-to-work programs that had been initiated under the previous administration. The governor, in turn, accepted part of the speaker's agenda—the assured benefit pilots and pilots to test ways to increase health insurance coverage among the working uninsured. The assured benefit pilots were reduced from four to two, but the concept remained alive.

Some events proved favorable. The governor appointed Timothy Cullen, a Democratic state legislator and close associate of Speaker Loftus, as secretary of the DHSS. Undoubtedly prompted by political motivations, this unusual appointment subdued some of the opposition to the CSAS within the department. Secretary Cullen was thus able to appoint *some* of the division administrators—in particular, the head of the powerful Division of Policy and Budget, therefore permitting some work to continue in that division and bypassing the opposition in the Division of Community Services.

In rapid succession, the waiver application was submitted; a pilot implementation manager position was created and ably filled by a tenacious public servant named Ingrid Rothe;[5] and the hostile administrator of the DCS was transferred to a less influential position. Though the waiver application was initially rejected by the DHHS in Washington, D.C., on grounds of insufficient information, reform advocates were not overly dismayed. Federal attitudes toward the reform were becoming more positive, perhaps in response to the increasing national attention being paid to the concept by social policy experts.

By mid-1988, prospects were upbeat. Two pilot counties had been selected, and detailed operational plans were under way. The federal waiver request was resubmitted in July 1988 and was finally favorably received. A start-up date of January 1989 was set. But the complexity of the implementation process could not be avoided. Advocates for the reform in Washington County, the first pilot county, had to seek political permission from the county board to proceed. At the crucial board meeting, opponents implied that the governor actually opposed the program. One opponent noted that "what this program really is, is the first step of a vast program of social engineering and redistribution of wealth under the guise of welfare reform." Confusion ensued and, despite intervention by departmental officials, the motion to officially become an AB pilot county was defeated on a 16–14 vote. Shortly afterward, the second pilot county withdrew from the project, citing insufficient management resources for such an undertaking.

In a real sense, the fate of the assured benefit had already been sealed, though, like a classic tragedy, the actors continued to play out their roles. The planning process for implementing the assured benefit continued; new pilot counties were found; and revised implementation schedules were arranged. And the outside world continued to discuss the "Wisconsin Demonstration" as though it were a reality. A July 29, 1988, editorial in the *Wall Street Journal* noted that "Wisconsin's widely hailed welfare overhaul provides a casebook example of how states function as a kind of laboratory of government, experimenting with innovative solutions that the federal government is either too bureaucratic, or too politically riven, to try" (p. 32).

Unfortunately, Wisconsin state government had become just as bureaucratic and politically riven. From 1986 to 1991, there would be four different secretaries of the DHSS and a correspondingly heavy turnover in major departmental policy positions. Even with good intentions, it was highly unlikely that the assured benefit pilot could have been implemented successfully. In the end, the assured benefit died with a whimper rather than a bang. By mid-1989, the plan had become a partisan issue. Assembly Speaker Loftus had made it clear that he intended to run for governor, and welfare and child support reform were two of his key issues. Governor Thompson sequestered the funds for the administration of the AB pilots. In fall 1989 the legislature passed a bill directing the governor to spend these funds, but the governor vetoed the bill. Through the middle of 1990 four counties had been AB pilots at one time or another (Washington, Rock, Dane, and Oneida)—with Washington County having pilot status on two occasions. As late as mid-1990, Washington and Oneida counties were still engaged in serious planning efforts in preparation for implementing the pilots in January 1991, though planning activity diminished after this point.

On the campaign trail, however, welfare was not emerging as a seminal topic, and the CSAS clearly did not lend itself to the kind of sound bites that grab an audience. The DHSS quietly withdrew any semblance of support and the local planning processes ceased—pending an expression of interest from the department or the governor. Such support was not forthcoming. Rather, the final gasps of CSAS in Wisconsin took on a humorous tone. The department decided that the IRP would not be allowed to do the formal evaluation of the CSAS pilots. The IRP had prepared the evaluation methodology, which had been approved by the U.S. Department of Health and Human Services and reviewed by a national panel of experts on program evaluation. Further, the institute had arranged a way to finance the evaluation without any expenditure of state tax dollars (General Purpose Revenue, or GPR) by using Ford Foundation grants to the institute to leverage federal matching funds. Based on the rationale that a conflict of interest would exist if the IRP conducted the evaluation, the department rewrote the evaluation and obligated GPR funds to select an outside evaluator. The revised evaluation plan was rejected by federal officials, who also indicated in writing that they did not concur with the department's concerns about the alleged "conflict of interest." Rejection of the evaluation plan effectively rescinded the waiver to proceed with the pilots. The AB concept was dead in Wisconsin.

As a concept, however, CSAS had become public property. In early 1986, Governor Mario Cuomo of New York had appointed a panel of national experts to advise him on how to reduce poverty and welfare dependency. In December of that year, the panel issued a written report recommending adoption of a new child support assurance system. Governor Cuomo proposed that the state adopt a percentage-of-income standard and routine income withholding immediately, and pilot the assured child support benefit in eight counties. In 1987, the New York State Legislature adopted neither a new child support standard nor routine income withholding, but did approve piloting a version of an assured child support benefit that was steeply income tested and limited to welfare recipients. In 1989, the legislature adopted a modified version of the Wisconsin percentage-of-income standard and, owing to federal requirements included in the Family Support Act, immediate income withholding will be adopted by 1994. In 1989, seven New York counties began piloting a version of an assured child support benefit known as the Child Assistance Program. The bipartisan National Commission on Children (1991) has also called for a national program of research on the AB concept, and Congressman Robert Downey of New York, among others, is preparing legislation that would move the country closer to a national AB program.

The bottom line, however, is that the child support assurance concept—as originally conceived—did not succeed despite its broad appeal within the policy community and numerous attractive characteristics.

ANALYSIS AND LESSONS

The CSAS experience in Wisconsin contained both successes and failures. The income-sharing and taxation at the source of income principles were realized, in part at least, in the form of the PIAS and immediate income withholding provisions. Though radical when first proposed, these principles are now part of the national public policy fabric. The assured benefit principle, the most visionary and dramatic component of the package, was not realized.

It is somewhat premature to do a complete postmortem on the AB experience in Wisconsin. Some initial speculation is appropriate, however, and perhaps useful to those engaged in making public policy a political reality.

Among the plausible explanations for why the complete CSAS program was not implemented in Wisconsin, are the following. First, the benefit side of the package—the AB provision—generated conceptual confusion. That is, it was difficult for some key actors in politics, the bureaucracy, and the media to understand that the AB provision was not an expansion of welfare and would not result in extending counterproductive public dependency. Second, the AB provision encountered contextual difficulties. At key points in the analysis, design, and legitimization stages of the planning process, proponents encountered countervailing normative trends and adverse fiscal realities. For example, whereas the AB argued for an expansion of public responsibility the 1980s were a decade where advocates for a minimalist government prevailed. Moreover, states became increasingly wary of entertaining new responsibilities as the federal government continued its retreat from an activist social policy role. Third, there is the serendipity factor. If the incumbent governor had been reelected in 1986, the subsequent course of the CSAS *might* have been quite different.

Even with conceptual clarity, contextual affinity, and dumb luck, the prospects of the AB principle succeeding might still have been uncertain. It represented, after all, an example of fundamental reform outside the comfortable way of doing business. As such, it required a long developmental time frame, during which initial enthusiasm might wane and the sheer complexity associated with introducing new programs and procedures would prove too daunting. Within this context, much was expected from the state-university relationship, particularly in getting the idea past the "embryonic" stage where many plausible proposals simply disappear. Unfortunately, those expectations were not realized.

When both breadth of vision and constancy of vision were required, the assured benefit confronted an environment better understood in terms of limited attention spans and narrow scopes of substantive interest. Typically, academics propose new ideas but are reluctant to engage in policy legitimization and implementation. Politicians address policy questions along time lines punctuated by reelection bids and assume, oddly enough, that a social problem is solved with the passage of legislation. Program officials transform policy/political intent into detailed operational plans and administrative rules within institutional environments dominated by conservative forces that redirect innovation into conventional and comfortable programmatic forms. And new programs must ultimately be introduced through a complex array of existing subsystems whereby changing prevailing attitudes and practices demands extraordinary commitment and sustained energy. And at each step—from inception of an idea to its institutionalization—those perceiving themselves as likely losers emerge to exert countervailing pressures against change (Pressman and Wildavsky 1979).

In a rational world where academia and government collaboratively address social issues, social policy could be expected to be governed by a set of logical steps. Theory and program experience would motivate research and social experimentation. The results of that research and experimentation would inform subsequent policy development and the process of political legitimization. With policy formally articulated, program design and implementation would proceed in a logical fashion—guided by continuing policy analysis and implementation evaluation. Such a process would be iterative—replicating itself in an ever-changing world—but it would remain orderly. That was the vision of the new public policy in the early 1960s when faith in national government remained high (Haveman 1986), and it was the vision in Wisconsin in the early 1980s when states inherited large segments of the domestic policy agenda (Corbett 1982).

However, sustained relationships between the academic and operational worlds necessitate that both sides work to bridge the confines of their own experiences. Generally, academics involved in social policy issues interact with the world indirectly. The data upon which they formulate views is truncated and largely restricted to "the literature." Despite increasing methodological sophistication, the academic orientation is toward theoretical simplicity and elegance. Not surprisingly, academic thought can appear abstract and irrelevant to program managers, encompassing only a portion of the extraordinary complexity of the real world.

The inherent difficulties of state-university relationships do not account entirely for the disintegration of the "Wisconsin Idea" during the 1980s. In retrospect, a change in the relationship between the governor and most executive agencies also damaged this interorganizational relationship. During the mid-1970s, Wisconsin moved toward a cabinet form of government,[7] under which top policymakers are appointed by—and serve at the pleasure of—the state's chief executive. For at least two reasons, Wisconsin's preeminence as a progressive arena for testing public policy deteriorated substantially under this governance structure. First, political allegiance, not competence, emerged as the basis for agency appointments. Not surprisingly, the institutional level of agency management became more attentive to the political sector of the organization's environment. Second, the anticipated tenure of top administrators substantially decreased, so that by the time a new management team—typically selected from outside the agency and sometimes the program area—became technically competent, they were likely to be replaced (Heclo 1977; Pfeffer 1981). Within such a governance framework, it becomes difficult to maintain the administrative continuity essential to competent management and fundamental reform. Organizational memory is absent; relevant timeframes are shortened; political expediency replaces programmatic merit; and the kind of organizational inputs provided by academic-based organizations like the IRP become increasingly irrelevant and, in the extreme, threatening. Certainly, complex reforms requiring multiyear timetables such as the CSAS become more problematic to implement.

The history of the CSAS suggests that fundamental change is a complex process better thought of as a marathon than a sprint. Over the decade of the 1980s policy analyses and program planning strategies evolved from "empirical-rationalist" and "rational decision-making" approaches, premised on the belief that planned change was possible and that salient elements of the situation were controllable, to, once in the political arena, a "disjointed-incrementalist" model that assumed that the planning process was governed by "satisficing" decisions (i.e., those designed to just get by) responding to largely uncontrollable circumstances. The "rational" planning process thus evaporated.

When the CSAS concept was still largely an academic proposal, the "empirical-rationalist" mode of planning prevailed. Issues were identified, analyses conducted, alternative solutions proposed, and a decision made. As the CSAS concept moved out into the political-bureaucratic arena, the degree of rationality and precision governing the planning process evaporated. Though work plans were made and milestones set, unanticipated events intruded continually. A rational decision-making process continued but the outcomes of that process increasingly were subject to subsequent review and political compromise. Progress apparently would be made only to be undone summarily when changes in personnel and/or in the sociopolitical environment intervened. The "rational" planning process evaporated.

A continuing and intense working relationship between academic and operations-oriented individuals can offset the constraints and distortions that tend to short-circuit the rational planning process. The capacity of the academic community to concentrate on the broad dimensions of social policy issues, to assess such dimensions from a more encompassing historical vantage point, and to examine interrelationships among presumably distinct phenomena provides policymakers with a unique perspective regarding their programmatic responsibilities. At the same time, the sensitivities to the operational nuances of both policy formation and policy execution displayed by those operating in "real world" and "real time" environments represent a valuable input to those involved in describing and understanding social policy. Such a cross-fertilization of perspectives cannot occur, however, if contact between the two cultures is episodic or asymmetric in character. A re-creation of the "Wisconsin Idea"—whether in Wisconsin or elsewhere—could be a necessary and fundamental step toward moving beyond the paralysis currently dominating social policy.

Notes

1. Senator Daniel Patrick Moynihan, of New York, is credited as the primary congressional sponsor of the landmark Family Support Act. Erica Baum, who was on Moynihan's staff at the time and was instrumental to the drafting and passage of this legislation, had briefly been a faculty member of the School of Social Work at the University of Wisconsin–Madison and was familiar with the child support work being done in the state.

2. A wide spectrum of academics and policy analysts endorsed the CSAS either in writing or in public comments, particularly the assured benefit provision. Support was particularly forthcoming from mainstream academics such as Sheldon Danziger, David Ellwood, Robert Haveman, Robert Lerman, Isabell Sawhill, William Julius Wilson, and conservatives such as Lawrence Mead and Charles Murray. Conventional liberals were rather silent on the topic. A typical discussion of the "Wisconsin Demonstration" can be found in Cottingham and Ellwood (1989).

3. Some of the material in this and the following two sections of the chapter is drawn from earlier works by Irwin Garfinkel and the author (see references).

4. The U.S. Bureau of the Census did not begin to collect systematic data on child support until 1979.

5. Within the bureaucracy, there was some risk involved in being overly identified with this project. Historically, executive agencies in Wisconsin had been immune from partisan politics. This began to change during the 1980s, and by late in the decade, Wisconsin looked much like other states in terms of the politicization of executive agencies. An association with the CSAS was particularly hazardous after it became apparent that Representative Thomas Loftus was mounting a political challenge to the incumbent governor.

6. The Learnfare program—a high priority of the governor's that had received national attention—was so poorly implemented that a federal judge enjoined the program in Milwaukee County (which accounted for half of all those covered by the program), and federal officials imposed extensive terms as a condition for extending the waiver for the program. Moreover, reform in Wisconsin had become little more than a battle over public relations sound bites. Symbolic initiatives that would attract media attention took precedence over substantive progress against child poverty.

7. Up to this point, the heads of most executive agencies reported to citizen boards. Members of these boards were appointed for fixed terms on a staggered basis. Moreover, governors were elected for two-year terms until the mid-1970s and seldom were in office long enough to fully control the boards. Power was shifted to the chief executive's office throughout the 1970s. By the early 1980s, there were clear signs that the bureaucracy was being politicized and that notions of merit and objectivity that had given Wisconsin a comparative advantage were being compromised.

References

Bardach, Eugene. 1977. *The Implementation Game.* Cambridge, Mass.: Massachusetts Institute of Technology Press.

Bergman, Barbara. 1987. "A Fresh Start on Welfare Reform." *Challenge* (Nov.-Dec.): 44–50.

Beyer, J., and H. Trice. 1978. *Implementing Change.* New York: Free Press.

Cassetty, Judith. 1978. *Child Support and Public Policy: Securing Support from Absent Fathers.* Lexington, Mass.: D.C. Heath and Co.

Corbett, Thomas. 1982. *State/University Relationships: Problems and Prospects.* Madison: University of Wisconsin–Madison, Center for the Study of Public Policy and Administration.

_____. 1988. "Social Policy: Essays on the Difference between Expectation and Actuality." Ph.D. diss. University of Wisconsin–Madison.

Corbett, Thomas, N. C. Schaeffer, and Irwin Garfinkel. 1988. "Public Opinion about a Child Support Assurance System." *Social Service Review*

Corbett, Thomas, et. al. 1986. "Assuring Child Support in Wisconsin." *Public Welfare:* 33–39.

Cottingham, P., and D. Ellwood, eds. 1989. *Welfare Reform for the 1990s.* Cambridge, Mass.: Harvard University Press.

Danziger, Sheldon, and P. Gottschalk. 1986. "How Have Families with Children Been Faring?" Institute for Research on Poverty Discussion Paper 808-86. Madison: University of Wisconsin–Madison, Institute for Research on Poverty.

Danziger, Sheldon, and Daniel Weinberg. 1986. *Fighting Poverty.* Cambridge, Mass.: Harvard University Press.

Ellwood, David. 1988. *Poor Support: Poverty in the American Family.* New York: Basic Books.

Garfinkel, Irwin. 1990. "A New Child Support Assurance System." Institute for Research on Poverty Discussion Paper 916-90. Madison: University of Wisconsin–Madison, Institute for Research on Poverty.

Garfinkel, Irwin, and Marygold Melli. 1982. *Child Support: Weaknesses of the Old and Features of a Proposed New System.* Madison: University of Wisconsin–Madison, Institute for Research on Poverty.

Garfinkel, Irwin, and S. McLanahan. 1986. *Single Mothers and Their Children: A New American Dilemma.* Washington D.C.: The Urban Institute.

Garfinkel, Irwin, and P. Wong. 1987. "Child Support and Public Policy." Institute for Research on Poverty Discussion Paper 854-87. Madison: University of Wisconsin–Madison, Institute for Research on Poverty.

Gilbert, N., and H. Specht. 1977. *Planning for Social Welfare.* Englewood Cliffs, N.J.: Prentice Hall.

Green Book. 1991. *Overview of Entitlement Programs.* U.S. Congress, Committee on Ways and Means. Washington, D.C.: U.S. Government Printing Office.

Haveman, Robert. 1986. *Poverty Research and Public Policy.* New York: Academic Press.

_____. 1988. *Starting Even: An Equal Opportunity Program to Combat the Nation's New Poverty.* New York: Academic Press.

Heclo, Hugh. 1977. *A Government of Strangers.* Washington, D.C.: The Brookings Institution.

Ikenberry, John, and Theda Skocpol. Fall 1987. "Expanding Social Benefits: The Role of Social Security." *Political Science Quarterly* 102: 389–416.

Keniston, Kenneth. 1977. *All Our Children.* New York: Harcourt Brace Jovanovich.

Lerman, Robert. 1988. "Non-Welfare Approaches to Helping the Poor." *Focus* 11 (1) (Spring): 29–34 (University of Wisconsin–Madison, Institute for Research on Poverty).

McQueen, Michael. 1988, July 29. "Wisconsin Welfare Innovations Blaze a Path for Other States and the Federal Government," *Wall Street Journal*, p. 32.

Mead, Lawrence. 1987. "Work and Dependency: Part II." Paper prepared for the Welfare Dependency Project of the Hudson Institute, New York. Photocopy.

National Commission on Children. 1991. *Beyond Rhetoric: A New American Agenda for Children and Families.* Washington D.C.: U.S. Government Printing Office.

New York. 1986. *A New Social Contract: Rethinking the Nature and Purpose of Public Assistance.* Albany, N.Y.: State of New York.

Pearce, Diana. 1978. "The Feminization of Poverty: Work, Women, and Poverty." *Urban and Social Change Review* pp: 28–36.

Pfeffer, Jeffrey, 1981. *Power in Organizations.* Marshfield, Mass.: Pittman Co.

Pressman, Jeffrey and Aaron Wildavsky. 1979. *Implementation.* Berkeley: University of California Press.

Sawhill, I. 1975. *Time of Transition: The Growth of Families Headed by Women.* Washington, D.C.: The Urban Institute.

Wilson, W.J. 1987. *The Truly Disadvantaged.* Chicago: Univeristy of Chicago Press.

Wisconsin Department of Health and Social Services. 1979. *Report and Recommendations of the Welfare Reform Study Advisory Committee.* Madison: Wisconsin Department of Health and Social Services.

Part Two

WAS THE OLD SYSTEM AS BAD AS IT SEEMED?

Chapter Three

NONCUSTODIAL FATHERS' ABILITY TO PAY CHILD SUPPORT

Irwin Garfinkel and Donald T. Oellerich

We define child support as the transfer of income from a child's living noncustodial parent to the child's custodial parent. The ability to pay child support on the part of noncustodial fathers—who represent nearly 90 percent of all noncustodial parents[1]—is an important national issue for two reasons. First, given current divorce and out-of-wedlock birthrates, at least one-half of the next generation will be potentially eligible for private child support before they reach adulthood (Bumpass 1984; Hofferth 1985). Second, the current child support system is generally considered to be inadequate. Only 60 percent of noncustodial fathers have a legal obligation to pay child support; of those with a legal obligation, only half pay the full amount and 24 percent pay nothing; and more than half of the mothers with children potentially eligible for support receive nothing (U.S. Bureau of the Census 1987).

In response to this state of affairs (as described in chapter 1), the U.S. Congress has enacted a series of increasingly stronger federal laws to strengthen child support enforcement. Can strengthening public enforcement of private child support transfers substantially reduce economic insecurity or welfare dependence? In large part, the answers to these questions depend on the noncustodial parent's ability to pay child support.

This chapter develops estimates of the noncustodial father's ability to pay child support. The first section describes the major data sources and the methods for estimating the noncustodial parent's income. The second section presents estimates of the incomes of noncustodial parents and evaluations of the reliability of these predictions. The third section combines the income estimates with simulations of three prototypical state child support standards for how much absent parents should be expected to contribute to the costs of rearing their children. The resulting estimates of the noncustodial father's ability to pay child support are then compared with the amounts currently ordered and paid.

DATA AND METHODS FOR INCOME ESTIMATION

To estimate the aggregate ability of noncustodial fathers to pay child support, one must have data on both the income of the noncustodial father and the number of children for whom he owes support. Unfortunately, no national dataset contains a representative sample of noncustodial fathers. Although divorced and separated males are identified in the Current Population Survey (CPS) and many other datasets, these two demographic groups are not equivalent to noncustodial fathers. More than half of noncustodial fathers are married (see table 3.5). Furthermore, many divorced and separated men are not noncustodial fathers. What is ideally required is a male fertility and income study, which is uncommon.

Though the 1976 Survey of Income and Education (SIE) (U.S. Bureau of the Census 1976) and the June 1980 CPS each contained a male fertility study, Cherlin, Griffith, and McCarthy (1983) documented the severe undercount of noncustodial divorced and separated fathers in the June 1980 CPS.[2] Further, because the fertility questions in these surveys were addressed only to the ever-married, they also omitted all never-married noncustodial fathers. A crude estimate is that they undercounted noncustodial fathers by about 50 percent.[3] Finally, though the SIE contained income data on noncustodial fathers, this was not very helpful for obtaining an estimate of the income distribution of noncustodial fathers, because we knew neither the income nor the demographic characteristics of the unidentified noncustodial fathers.

In view of the unavailability of a representative sample of noncustodial fathers, the necessity of having information on the number of children owed support, and the abundance of data on the custodial family (e.g., the 1976 SIE and the 1979, 1982, and 1984 CPS April Child Support Supplements [CPS—CSS]), we have developed an indirect method for imputing the income and other characteristics of the noncustodial father based on the characteristics of the custodial mother. The method uses regression analysis to estimate the relationship between a wife's characteristics and her husband's income for married couples with children. This relationship is then modified based on several assumptions about how it may differ for formerly married and never-married parents.[4]

The basic model estimates the relationship between wives' characteristics and husbands' income for a sample of married couples with children under 18 years old. The equation takes the following form:

$$y = xb + e, \tag{3.1}$$

where y is the natural log of the men's income from all sources except welfare, x is a set of demographic characteristics normally found in human capital income regressions, and e is a random disturbance assumed uncorrelated with x.

If the coefficients estimated in this regression were used to impute income for noncustodial fathers, the resulting incomes would be too high if formerly married and never-married noncustodial fathers are poorer earners than their married counterparts. In addition, we required estimates of the incomes of noncustodial fathers of children receiving welfare, and these fathers are likely to be poorer earners ceteris paribus than noncustodial fathers whose children are not on welfare. To account for these differences, we estimated two additional equations employing other samples:

$$y = x_f C_1 + dm + u \tag{3.2}$$

$$y = x_m C_2 + gw + v, \tag{3.3}$$

where y remains the same, x_f in equation (3.2) is the father's demographic characteristics, x_m in equation (3.3) is the mother's characteristics, m in equation (3.2) is a set of dummy variables for different marital statuses with the married state as the excluded category, and w in equation (3.3) is a dummy variable for welfare status of the custodial family (Aid to Families with Dependent Children [AFDC]).

To impute income for the noncustodial father for each custodial family, the coefficients estimated in equation (3.1) together with the dummy variable coefficients estimated in equations (3.2) and (3.3) were combined with the known demographic and welfare status characteristics of the custodial mother and the predicted marital status of the noncustodial father.[5]

$$Y = bx + dm + gw \tag{3.4}$$

The first regression was estimated by using a sample of married couples with children under 18 years old extracted from the 1979 CPS. The dependent variable is the natural log of the man's income. Because the natural log of zero or a negative number is indeterminate, we assigned a small positive income ($50) to those men with zero or negative income. The explanatory variables (x) include the wife's age, education, number of children, residence outside a standard metropolitan statistical area (SMSA), size of SMSA, residence outside a central city, region of the country, ethnicity, and an income dummy. The income dummy variable was included to capture the effect of assigning $50 to those men with zero or negative incomes. This permitted these observations to affect the estimated slopes (b coefficients). Rather than including a dummy variable for race, we estimated separate equations for whites and nonwhites. This avoided the misspecification of any interactions between race and the other explanatory variables in the equation. The sample for the white regression contained 10,590 couples, and the nonwhite regression used a sample of 1,214 couples.

The results of estimating equation (3.1) by ordinary least squares regressions appear in table 3.1. Wives' characteristics provide an adequate explanation of the variation in married men's income. All of the coefficients are in the expected direction, and all but a few are statistically significant. The R^2 is artificially high because of the inclusion of the income dummy variable. In a comparison regression estimated by excluding those with zero and negative income and without the income dummy variable, the R^2 was closer to 0.15, which is still respectable for human capital/income regressions.

The regression estimating equation (3.2) utilizes a sample from the 1976 SIE. The sample consisted of self-identified noncustodial divorced, separated, and remarried fathers, married men with children, and never-married men. The dependent variable is the natural log of the man's income. The explanatory variables (x_f) are specified in the same manner as in equation (3.1), but the characteristics are those of the men. The dummy variables (m) have the married state as a reference group and include variables for divorce, separation, and never-married statuses. (Earlier regressions included a dummy variable for remarried men, but the coefficient for this variable was approximately zero and was never statistically significant. Therefore this group was combined with the reference married group.)

The results of the regression appear in table 3.2. The coefficients of the marital status dummy variables are of the expected sign, are large, and are statistically significant. It is also interesting to note that the other coefficients in this regression are similar in direction and magnitude to the regression coefficients found in the estimation of equation (3.1). This provides further evidence supporting our use of the women's characteristics as substitutes for the men's.

Table 3.1 HUSBAND'S EARNINGS AS FUNCTION OF WIFE'S CHARACTERISTICS

Explanatory Variables	Dependent Variable: Log of Annual Income of Husband	
	Whites	Nonwhites
Age	0.0621	0.08476
	(0.0006)	(0.01829)
Age Squared	−0.0008707	−0.00111
	(0.0000808)	(0.00022)
Age times education	0.00116	0.00563
	(0.00015)	(0.00038)
Education		
<9 years	−0.1799	−0.09772
	(0.0438)	(0.1147)
9–11 years	−0.08367	−0.12788
	(0.0236)	(0.0647)
>12 years	0.10191	0.16861
	(0.02285)	(0.0669)
Noncentral city	0.09671	0.05817
	(0.01961)	(0.05162)
Non-SMSA	−0.22725	−0.16827
	(0.0159)	(0.0592)
Children		
2	0.05064	0.03103
	(0.01693)	(0.05175)
3 or more	0.06684	−0.04254
	(0.01943)	(0.05567)
Region	−0.01481	−0.17811
Northeast	(0.0201)	(0.0705)
South	−0.03063	−0.20191
	(0.01846)	(0.06094)
West	−0.00087	−0.00297
	(0.0212)	(0.07271)
Income dummy	−5.5793	−5.533261
	(0.06811)	(0.1444)
Intercept	8.04844	7.71464
R_2	0.4362	0.5759
F test	605.83	116.41
Number of observations	10,590	1,214
Mean squared error	0.54216	0.54369
Mean of dependent variables	9.543	9.212

Note: Standard errors are in parentheses.

Table 3.2 MARITAL STATUS AND AFDC STATUS REGRESSIONS

| | Dependent Variable: Log of Annual Income of Man | | | |
| | Marital Status (1976 SIE) | | AFDC Status (1979 CPS—CSS) | |
Explanatory Variables	White	Nonwhite	White	Nonwhite
Age	0.07972	0.04872	-0.02619	-0.0632
	(0.00308)	(0.01041)	(0.0208)	(0.07441)
Age Squared	-0.0009982	-0.0006179	-0.00034476	0.000459
	(0.0000312)	(0.000115)	(0.000222)	(0.000659)
Age times education	0.00148	0.00112	0.00101	0.00259
	(0.00009)	(0.000314)	(0.000595)	(0.00265)
Education				
<9 years	-0.10232	0.02918	-0.32782	1.06146
	(0.02951)	(0.1000)	(0.18151)	(1.0534)
9–11 years	-0.15142	-0.10701	-0.11419	0.32022
	(0.01917)	(0.06295)	(0.08927)	(0.34252)
>12 years	-0.05271	0.11863	0.08559	0.09431
	(0.01645)	(0.06583)	(0.08485)	(0.39639)
Noncentral city	-0.16936	-0.23008	0.06346	-0.14493
	(0.01665)	(0.0800)	(0.07574)	(0.27316)
Non-SMSA	-0.03644	0.10943	-0.06212	-0.33731
	(0.01722)	(0.06341)	(0.06212)	(0.32569)
Children				
2	—	—	0.01231	-0.11549
			(0.06294)	(0.25498)
3 or more	—	—	0.06232	0.18084
			(0.07393)	(0.2925)

Region				
Northeast	—	—	-0.02421	0.35425
			(0.08485)	(0.37441)
South	—	—	0.03443	-0.3532
			(0.07147)	(0.2839)
West	—	—	0.01854	0.5486
			(0.07681)	(0.30954)
Income dummy	-4.70438	-3.92412	—	—
	(0.03961)	(0.09033)		
Marital status				
Divorced	-0.26646	-0.37883	—	—
	(0.03146)	(0.0997)		
Separated	-0.23966	-0.51656	—	—
	(0.06915)	(0.1182)		
Never married	-0.68797	-0.91063	—	—
	(0.01606)	(0.06175)		
AFDC recipient	—	—	-0.43357	-0.44746
			(0.08537)	(0.28329)
Intercept	7.3776	7.78489	8.69303	10.00843
R^2	0.5720	0.7486	0.1779	0.2973
F test	2,216.38	350.38	9.169	1.299
Number of observations	21,570	1,544	608	58
Mean of dependent variable	9.516	9.2219	9.581	9.385

Note: Standard errors are in parenthese. Dashes (—) denote variables not included in the model.

The regression estimating equation (3.3) employs a sample from the 1979 CPS—CSS. This dataset provides a sample of 608 white and 58 nonwhite custodial families who reported the income of the noncustodial father. The dependent variable is the same as for prior regressions, and the explanatory variables (x) are also the same as in equation (3.1). The dummy variable (w) is coded one if the custodial family received AFDC and zero otherwise. The resulting coefficient provides the regression-controlled mean difference between noncustodial fathers' income of AFDC families and non-AFDC families. The results of this regression for whites and nonwhites also appear in table 3.2. The coefficients for the dummy variable are in the same direction and of the same magnitude for both groups, although the coefficient for the nonwhites is not statistically significant. The small sample size may explain the weaker relationship for the latter group. Overall these results strongly suggest that the welfare status of ever-married custodial families is related to the income of the noncustodian. Consequently, we use these coefficients to adjust the estimated incomes for divorced and separated families of both groups.

Finally, an estimated noncustodial father's income was imputed for each custodial family, using equation (3.4). Here the relevant coefficients from equations (3.1)–(3.3) were combined with the known characteristics of the custodial family. As noted earlier, however, the application of the marital status coefficients requires us to estimate the marital status of the male noncustodian.

For separated women, it is reasonable to assume that the marital status of the male is separated. Such an assumption will lead to an underestimate of income resulting from bigamy or underreporting, but this error should be small. For never-married women, we assumed that the male was also never married. Because some fathers of children of never-married mothers are ever-married men, this will clearly lead to an underestimate of the noncustodians' income for this subgroup. For divorced and married women, the noncustodian can either be divorced or remarried; remarried men have the same income on average as married men. To avoid underestimating the remarried noncustodians' income, we first obtained an independent estimate of the probability that the ever-divorced noncustodian is remarried. The probability was obtained by using logit regression; this procedure is explained in some detail in the upcoming section on "Simulation Methodology" and is fully detailed in Oellerich (1984: 97–104). The probability was used to produce a weighted average income for each ever-divorced custodial family.

ESTIMATED INCOMES AND REPLICATIONS
FOR SELECT SUBSAMPLES

This section applies the income estimation procedure to supplement available data on the custodial families contained in the 1979 CPS—CSS, the first national survey of families eligible to receive child support. The 1979 CPS—CSS is a match file that combines the annual March demographic file with the April supplement. The file contains the records for 3,547 women potentially eligible for child support in 1978. The women in the file had children under 18 years old whose fathers were absent from the household. The child support supplement contains numerous questions on child support, including the amounts of child support legally owed and actually paid. As such, the CPS—CSS is the best dataset for obtaining national estimates of (1) the population of children living in families potentially eligible for child support, (2) the amount of support these families are entitled to, (3) the amount of support they actually receive, and (4) for a small subsample of the divorced and separated mothers, their estimates of the noncustodial father's income.

Table 3.3 presents the estimates of the mean income of noncustodial fathers by the race and marital status of the custodial mother. The overall estimated mean income in 1983 dollars equaled $19,346. The average income of all prime-aged males (25–64 years old) was $22,482 (U.S. Bureau of the Census 1983b: 146). In short, noncustodial fathers have about 14 percent less income than prime-aged working males.

Differences in income by racial and marital status of the mother are dramatic. Not surprisingly, the incomes of nonwhite noncustodial fathers are only half those of their white counterparts. Even more dramatic are the differences within each group between the never

Table 3.3 MEAN INCOME OF NONCUSTODIAL PARENTS IN DOLLARS BY MARITAL STATUS OF CUSTODIAL PARENT AND RACE (in 1983 dollars)

Marital Status of Custodial Parent	White ($)	Nonwhite ($)	All ($)
Never married	9,952	6,285	7,775
Separated	17,747	10,551	14,712
Divorced	24,760	17,824	23,600
Widowed	21,533	20,188	21,261
Remarried	25,379	21,257	25,006
All	22,533	11,285	19,346

married and the remarried. Among whites the ratio of the income of married men to the income of never-married men is nearly 3:1, whereas among nonwhites the ratio is greater than 3:1.

To assess the reliability of the income estimation methodology that uses the mothers' characteristics as substitutes for the fathers', we used the methodology to predict the incomes for three datasets for which we had both the custodial mothers' characteristics and the noncustodial fathers' income. The imputed incomes were then compared with the reported incomes within each dataset. Each of these datasets suffered from severe nonresponse or missing data on the noncustodians' incomes, precluding their use for estimating the mothers' characteristics/fathers' income regressions.

The first sample consisted of the 20 percent of the respondents who reported the noncustodial father's income in the 1979 CPS—CSS (U.S. Bureau of the Census 1979). Regarding the question on the noncustodian's income, never-married women were not asked this question, and a large portion of the ever-married women either did not respond to it or did not know the noncustodian's income. Consequently, the sample of respondents constituted only 20 percent of all custodial mothers and is not representative.

The second dataset was the Michigan Panel Study of Income Dynamics (PSID) (Institute for Social Research 1980), a longitudinal study that began in 1968 with a representative sample of American families. We used the 1980 data. Our sample consisted of the 700 married fathers who experienced a divorce or separation during the 13 years of the study and who had children at the time of the marital split. Of the 700 cases selected, in 343 cases the father became a nonrespondent after the marital split. In these cases, predivorce income inflated by the average increase in earnings was used to measure income in 1983.

The third dataset was the Wisconsin Absent Parent Income Study (WAPS) (Institute for Research on Poverty 1980). WAPS is a random sample of 2,021 AFDC cases with mothers potentially eligible for child support in Wisconsin as of September 1980. In some cases there was more than one noncustodial father. In all, 2,259 noncustodial fathers were identified.[6] Social security numbers were taken from child support enforcement records and were then used to obtain the noncustodial fathers' income as reported in state and federal income tax returns. Social security numbers were obtained for only 1,468 of the 2,259 noncustodial fathers, and tax returns were obtained for only 821 of these noncustodial fathers.

Table 3.4 presents the actual and predicted incomes and the percentage differences between them for the three subsamples of noncustodial fathers in the CPS—CSS, the PSID, and the WAPS. The results are disaggregated by race. In five of the six comparisons, predicted income was less than reported income. In the one case in which predicted income exceeds reported income—CPS—CSS whites—the difference is only 2 percent. These results strongly suggest that we are not overestimating the noncustodial fathers' income as measured in these three subsamples.

The only sizable differences between the predicted and reported incomes are for nonwhites in the CPS—CSS and WAPS samples (see table 3.4). An explanation for the discrepancy is that reported incomes in the CPS—CSS and WAPS are likely to be too high because of income-related selectivity bias. In the CPS—CSS, women are more likely to know the noncustodial father's income, the more regular and stable the noncustodial father and his income. In the WAPS, the more stable the noncustodial father, the more likely that his whereabouts and social security number would be known and that he filed an income tax return. It seems plausible that the selection bias is stronger for nonwhites than for whites, in that a greater percentage of the former are likely to be both unattached to the conventional labor force and uncaptured by conventional surveys. An alternative explanation is that our estimates overcorrect for the AFDC selection bias in the nonwhite sample.

Table 3.4 REPLICATION OF NONCUSTODIAL FATHER INCOME ESTIMATES
(in 1983 dollars)

Sample	Reported Income ($)	Predicted Income ($)	Percentage Difference, (Col. 2 − Col. 1)/Col. 1
CPS—CSS[a]			
Whites	24,822	25,352	+2.1
Nonwhites	21,375	17,060	−20.2
PSID[b]			
Whites	20,653	20,427	−1.1
Nonwhites	13,318	12,217	−8.3
WAPS[c]			
Whites	13,895	12,345	−11.2
Nonwhites	11,736	8,828	−24.8

[a]Custodial reports of noncustodian's income.
[b]Divorced and separated noncustodians.
[c]Income tax returns for noncustodians of AFDC children.

SIMULATION OF ABILITY TO PAY CHILD SUPPORT

Our estimates of noncustodial fathers' incomes indicate that their average income in 1983 equaled about $19,000. We suspect that to most people this would suggest a substantial ability to pay child support. Ability to pay depends, however, on both income and a normative standard that specifies the proportion of a given income that should be devoted to child support. For example, should the child support obligation of the noncustodial parent depend on the income of the custodial parent or whether the noncustodial parent has started a new family? Should a portion of the noncustodial parent's income be set aside for his or her own needs before any obligation is assessed?

The first part of this section describes three radically different child support standards that are prototypical and have received a great deal of national attention. Each standard is akin to a tax schedule. The second part of this section simulates the amount of revenue raised by applying these standards. We thereby derive three different estimates of ability to pay child support that correspond to different sets of normative judgments about how much of noncustodial parents' income should be shared with their children. These estimates are then compared with the amounts ordered and paid under our current child support system.

The Standards

Although states have traditionally given local courts nearly complete discretion in determining child support obligations, the 1984 Social Security Amendments require states to develop and adopt normative standards or guidelines to be used in setting the levels of child support. We have chosen three standards, from Wisconsin, Colorado, and Delaware, that have received considerable national attention[7]. The standards vary in their complexity. We begin with the simplest, the Wisconsin standard.

1. *Wisconsin Standard.* Under the Wisconsin standard, the child support obligation of the noncustodial parent is based on gross income and the number of eligible dependent children. The obligation for one child is set at 17 percent of the noncustodian's gross income. The respective obligations for two, three, four, and five or more children equal 25 percent, 29 percent, 31 percent, and 34 percent.

2. *Colorado Standard.* Under the Colorado standard, the costs or needs of the child(ren) are based on a declining proportion of the

combined incomes of the parents. The costs of the child(ren) are then shared proportionately by the parents based on the proportion of gross income each receives. Therefore, unlike the Wisconsin standard, the implied marginal tax rate on the noncustodial parent declines as the income of either parent increases.

3. *Delaware Standard.* In contrast to the Wisconsin standard, the Delaware standard considers both parents' incomes, contains personal exemptions for both parents, provides for exemptions for the noncustodian's new dependents (spouse and/or children), uses net income rather than gross, and employs very high marginal tax rates on the noncustodian's nonexempt income: Under the Delaware standard, federal, state, and local income taxes, Social Security taxes, and some work-related expenses are deducted from the gross income of each parent.[8] From the resulting net incomes, an exemption of $4,800 is subtracted to arrive at the amount of income available for the initial support obligation. If the noncustodian's net income is below the exemption, there is no support obligation. The marginal tax rate on the noncustodian's available income is 100 percent, up to an income level sufficient to pay his or her share of a minimum level of the children's needs. The children's needs are based on a percentage of the parents' basic needs of $4,800: 40 percent, or $1,920, for the first child, and 30 percent, or $1,440, for each additional child (if the custodian is remarried, then the first child's needs are 30 percent rather than 40 percent). The noncustodian's share equals the ratio of the noncustodian's income to the parents' combined income. Further, the tax rate on the noncustodian's income in excess of that required to pay the level of minimum needs equals 15 percent of excess income for one child and 10 percent for each additional child. If the noncustodian has any new dependents, the rate is applied to income that exceeds an exemption for these additional dependents.

Simulation Methodology

The simulation of the Wisconsin standard was straightforward. For each observation, the estimate of the noncustodial father's gross income was multiplied by the percentage appropriate for the number of eligible dependent children reported in the survey. The result was multiplied by the Census Bureau's March/April family weight, and the result was summed over all observations to obtain the aggregate amount of child support due.

The simulation of the Colorado standard was a little more complex. For each observation, the estimate of the noncustodial father's gross income was combined with the reported nonwelfare gross income of the custodial mother. This combined income was used to determine the needs of the children from a schedule provided in the standard. The child support obligation level was determined by multiplying the need times the ratio of the noncustodian's income to the combined incomes. The result for each observation was multiplied by the Census Bureau's March/April family weight and was summed over all observations.

The simulation of the Delaware standard was the most complex and required three additional pieces of information: the number of new dependents of the noncustodian, the net incomes of each parent, and the distribution of the noncustodian's income for each observation. The number of new dependents was estimated by using a method similar to our income estimation procedure. A subsample of ever-married noncustodial fathers from the 1976 SIE provided the sample (U.S. Bureau of the Census 1976). Using logit regression, we estimated the probability that each ever-married father has zero to four (or more) new dependents. The dependent variable is a set of four dichotomous variables representing four levels of new dependents: one (new spouse or child), two (new spouse and child or two children), three (new spouse and two children or three children), and four (new spouse and three or more children). The independent variables are the demographic characteristics of the men (Oellerich 1984). The coefficients (presented in table 3.5) from these logit regressions were combined with the characteristics of the custodial mother to impute the probability of each discrete number of new dependents for each observation. These probabilities were then incorporated into the simulation of the Delaware standard. Net income estimates, the second piece of information, were made for each observation by simulating federal and FICA taxes for both parents. These simulations used several simplifying assumptions, including the standard deductions. The number of possible new dependents was incorporated into the calculation of personal exemptions by producing five net incomes for each ever-divorced father, one for each possible level of new dependents.

Finally, because the Delaware standard tax structure is nonlinear (due to the personal and new-dependent exemptions), we needed estimates of the distribution of income for each sample observation, rather than the expected value or point estimate produced from the imputation. This point estimate for each observation represents the noncustodian's mean income for all of the noncustodians represented by the sample observation. Not all of these noncustodial fathers have the same income. Rather, their incomes comprise a distribution of income that we are summarizing by the point estimate. Using the

Table 3.5 NEW DEPENDENT LOGIT REGRESSIONS USED FOR MARITAL STATUS INCOME ADJUSTMENT AND SIMULATIONS OF NORMATIVE STANDARDS INVOLVING NEW DEPENDENTS

Dependent Variable	Dependents			
	1 or More Versus None	2 or More Versus 1 or None	3 or More Versus 2 or Less	4 or More Versus 3 or Less
		White Subsample		
Explanatory Variables:				
Age				
25–34 years	1.038 (0.1616)	0.9892 (0.2214)	1.964 (0.4915)	4.330 (1.936)
35–44 years	1.624 (0.1645)	1.280 (0.2215)	2.619 (0.4899)	5.455 (1.933)
>44 years	1.258 (0.1649)	0.3975 (0.2263)	1.800 (0.4941)	4.327 (1.937)
Education				
9–11 years	0.1005 (0.1179)	-0.1145 (0.1213)	0.0742 (0.1475)	0.0892 (0.2044)
12 years	0.1101 (0.1043)	-0.3153 (0.1078)	-0.2927 (0.1341)	-0.5521 (0.1926)
>12 years	-0.2184 (0.1058)	-0.6452 (0.1137)	0.6736 (0.1452)	-1.082 (0.2225)
Region				
Northeast	-0.0109 (0.0939)	-0.0288 (0.1033)	-0.0044 (0.1291)	-0.0568 (0.2037)
South	0.1770 (0.0784)	0.0848 (0.0841)	-0.0496 (0.1082)	0.1128 (0.1644)
West	0.0897 (0.0838)	0.0012 (0.0971)	-0.1877 (0.1208)	-0.1922 (0.1930)
Non-SMSA	0.3420 (0.0828)	0.1256 (0.0872)	0.1265 (0.1142)	0.1168 (0.1806)
Noncentral City	-0.2158 (0.8914)	0.01256 (0.0919)	0.0511 (0.1186)	0.1502 (0.1821)
Intercept	-0.8001	-1.678	-3.741	-7.346
Number of observations	5352	5352	5352	5352
Mean of dependent variables	0.676	0.28	0.14	0.05

continued

Table 3.5 NEW DEPENDENT LOGIT REGRESSIONS USED FOR MARITAL STATUS INCOME ADJUSTMENT AND SIMULATIONS OF NORMATIVE STANDARDS INVOLVING NEW DEPENDENTS (continued)

Dependent Variable	Dependents			
	1 or More Versus None	2 or More Versus 1 or None	3 or More Versus 2 or Less	4 or More Versus 3 or Less
		Nonwhite Subsample		
Explanatory Variables:				
Age				
25–34 years	0.6745 (0.5770)	0.9509 (0.8275)	2.887 (2.554)	4.816 (6.631)
35–44 years	1.130 (0.5799)	1.181 (0.8296)	2.806 (2.556)	4.740 (6.632)
>44 years	0.9406 (0.5834)	0.7311 (0.8365)	2.523 (2.560)	4.378 (6.635)
Education				
9–11 years	−0.5722 (0.2952)	−0.8901 (0.3365)	−0.7237 (0.4464)	−1.033 (0.5577)
12 years	−0.1656 (0.2712)	−0.2317 (0.2808)	−0.1602 (0.3583)	−0.8733 (0.4407)
>12 years	−0.3693 (0.2991)	−0.4383 (0.3202)	−0.2981 (0.4128)	−0.2014 (0.4746)
Region				
Northeast	−0.0686 (0.2748)	−0.3511 (0.3679)	−0.2114 (0.5329)	−1.067 (0.8947)
South	0.3519 (0.2146)	0.5714 (0.2480)	0.5529 (0.3478)	0.5393 (0.4187)
West	−0.0281 (0.2435)	0.3969 (0.2841)	0.7689 (0.3765)	0.2680 (0.5432)
Non-SMSA	0.5209 (0.2492)	0.3930 (0.2559)	0.3158 (0.3368)	0.3835 (0.4298)
Noncentral City	−0.2024 (0.3073)	0.0698 (0.3069)	0.2537 (0.3862)	0.3409 (0.4757)
Intercept	−0.6626	−2.023	−4.950	−7.002
Number of observations	543	543	543	543
Mean of dependent variables	0.582	0.28	0.155	0.085

Note: Sample includes ever-divorced men with children from 1976 Survey of Income and Education (U.S. Bureau of the Census 1976). Numbers in parentheses are standard errors.

point estimate will underestimate noncustodial fathers' ability to pay child support for standards like Delaware's that incorporate exemptions.[9] To further define these distributions, we used the mean squared error from the ordinary least squares income regressions as an estimate of the variance of income. This enabled us to define the income distributions by two parameters: the mean estimated by the point estimate and the variance. In addition, we assumed that income was distributed log normally for each observation. The distributions for each sample observation allowed us to simulate nonlinear normative standards, such as Delaware's, that incorporate an income exemption or set-aside.

Although the actual simulation of the Delaware standard was similar for all families, there were some important differences between ever-divorced families and separated or never-married families, because some of those who are divorced are assumed to remarry and start new families. The simulation was performed five times for ever-divorced families—once for each possible number of new dependents that incorporates the concomitant net income. Since each sample observation represented many in the population, a proportion of the Census Bureau's family weight was allocated to each possible outcome (i.e., 0–4 new dependents). This was done by multiplying the family weight by the five probabilities of new dependents. (This new weight is referred to as the Census Bureau's family weight throughout this discussion.) The sample observation was then passed through the simulation procedure five times, each time with a new weight, net income, and number of new dependents.

The first step for all families was to determine the basic needs of the dependent eligible children for each observation. This was done by adding $1,920 for the first child (unless the mother is remarried, in which case the amount was $1,440) plus $1,440 times the number of children other than the first. The next step was to determine the amount of income available to support the children. For the custodial parent, this amount equaled net income, determined from the income tax simulation, minus the $4,800 exemption. For the noncustodial parents the procedure was more complicated. First, we determined the number of noncustodians with net income above the initial exemption of $4,800. This was done for each observation by finding the probability that net income was greater than $4,800 and multiplying the result by the Census Bureau's family weight; this produced an adjusted weight. For those with income above the exemption, the expected value of the truncated distribution was calculated. The

$4,800 exemption was then subtracted from this amount to produce an estimate of available income for the noncustodian.

The next step was to determine the noncustodial father's share of the child(ren)'s basic needs. This was computed from the ratio of the noncustodian's available income to the combined available income of the two parents. The resulting ratio was multiplied by the child(ren)'s needs.

Next, we determined three groups of noncustodians for each observation: (1) the number whose income was insufficient to pay all of their share of the child(ren)'s needs, (2) the number who could pay their total share of basic needs but no more, and (3) the number who could pay their share of basic needs and have income sufficient to pay a supplement. For the first group we determined the expected value of the truncated distribution (income above the exemption but below the need share), and subtracted the exemption from this. The result was the average child support obligation for this group. Note that the marginal tax rate is 100 percent until the noncustodian meets this basic obligation. This amount was then multiplied by the adjusted family weight and summed over all observations. For the second group, the noncustodian's child support obligation equaled his or her share of the basic needs; this amount was multiplied by the adjusted family weight and summed over all observations.

Finally, for the last group we first subtracted from the available income the basic obligation and an exemption for any new dependents. Next, we determined the probability that the income was greater than the new-dependent exemption for each possible number of new dependents (zero to four). For those whose income was less than the new-dependent exemption, there was no supplemental award, and the child support obligation equaled the noncustodian's share of the eligible child(ren)'s basic needs. This amount was multiplied by the adjusted family weight and summed over all observations. For those with income greater than the new-dependent exemption, we determined the mean of the truncated distribution (i.e., the income distribution truncated from below by the new exemptions). From this mean we subtracted the personal exemption, the basic obligation, and the new-dependent exemption. The result was the income available for a supplemental award. This income was taxed at a proportional rate of 15 percent for the first child plus 10 percent for each additional child. The supplemental award was then added to the basic obligation to determine the total obligation for each observation. The result is multiplied by the Census Bureau's family weight and summed over all observations.

Noncustodial Fathers' Ability to Pay Child Support

The first column of table 3.6 presents estimates of the aggregate ability to pay child support based on the Wisconsin, Colorado, and Delaware standards (first three rows, respectively), as well as the aggregate amounts of child support owed and paid (fourth and fifth rows, respectively). The second column contains estimates of the percentage of noncustodial fathers with no child support obligations under each of the standards, as well as the percentages who owe nothing and pay nothing under current practices.

What is most striking is that the difference between what is currently owed and paid is dwarfed by the difference between either of these numbers and the three estimates of ability to pay that correspond to the application of the Delaware, Colorado, and Wisconsin standards. Unless these standards are highly unrepresentative of the range of current American norms with regard to how much of noncustodial parents' income should be shared with their children, table 3.6 clearly indicates that noncustodial fathers can afford to pay substantially more child support. Even the lowest estimate, that for the Delaware standard, suggests that noncustodial fathers can afford to pay about two and one-half times their current legal obligations and more than three times what they are actually paying.

According to the Delaware standard, about one-quarter of the noncustodial fathers are unable to pay child support. This is less than half of the proportion who actually pay no support. In contrast, according to the Wisconsin and Colorado standards, all noncustodial parents can afford to pay at least some child support. Despite these differences in normative judgments, the differences in aggregate estimates of ability to pay child support are quite small. This is because, compared with the standards without exemptions, the Delaware stan-

Table 3.6 ESTIMATES OF AGGREGATE ABILITY TO PAY CHILD SUPPORT BASED ON THREE DIFFERENT STANDARDS AND CURRENT PRACTICE (in 1983 dollars)

Standards and Practice	U.S. Ability to Pay ($ billion)	Percentage with Zero Obligation
Wisconsin	28.5	0.0
Colorado	30.1	0.0
Delaware	23.8	25.8
Current orders	9.7	51.4
Current payments	6.8	62.8[a]

[a]Includes 40.4 percent without orders and 14.1 percent who received none of the ordered amount.

dard—in common with other standards that exempt parents with very low income—imposes higher support obligations on parents whose income exceeds the exemption. Although the aggregate ability to pay child support is relatively insensitive to the standard chosen, the distribution by income class of ability to pay is quite sensitive to the choice of a normative standard.

SUMMARY AND CONCLUSION

This chapter addresses a question of current great national interest: Can noncustodial fathers afford to pay substantially more child support? Assuming our methodology is anywhere near correct, the answer is clearly yes. Even our lowest estimate suggests that noncustodial fathers can pay about two and one-half times their current legal obligations and more than three times what they are actually paying.

Unless it can be shown that either (1) our income estimates are substantially too high or (2) on average Americans believe noncustodial fathers should share much less of their income with their children than is implied in the Colorado, Delaware, and Wisconsin standards, our central conclusion is unlikely to be reversed. Even though three replications provide some evidence that our estimates of noncustodial income are reliable, further research on the incomes and marital statuses of noncustodial parents is clearly warranted. In this regard it is regrettable that the federal government has recently chosen not to fund a study of noncustodial fathers after the pretest revealed that such a study was feasible. Similarly, it would be useful in future work to incorporate standard errors from the income estimation equations into the simulation to obtain a range or confidence interval, rather than just a point estimate of ability to pay child support. Clearly, the lower end of such a confidence interval would be much closer to actual child support payments than our point estimate of ability to pay.[10] Finally, research is warranted on the representativeness of the norms embodied in the three standards we chose to simulate.[11]

Notes

Reprinted with permission. This research was supported by funds provided to the Institute for Research on Poverty by the Ford Foundation, the Wisconsin Department of Health and Social Services, and the U.S. Department of Health and Human Services.

1. This estimate is derived from Wisconsin data (Nichols-Casebolt, Garfinkel, and Wong 1988).

2. The structure of the questions in the SIE was similar to that in the 1980 June CPS; and in a Wisconsin survey of custodial and noncustodial parents known as CHIPPS (Institute for Research on Poverty 1985), we also obtained a much smaller proportion of noncustodial fathers than custodial mothers.

3. Cherlin et al. (1983) found that ever-married noncustodial fathers are undercounted by about 40 percent. Never-married mothers constitute 20 percent of those potentially eligible for child support (U.S. Bureau of the Census 1983a: table B). Multiplying 40 percent by 80 percent yields 32 percent, and adding 20 percent for the never-married mothers (assuming that each one is matched by a never-married father) yields 52 percent.

4. An alternative specification would be to treat the estimation of the noncustodian's income as a sample selection problem and apply the two-stage procedure (Heckman 1979). Keep in mind that our intention was to develop a methodology to supplement the abundance of available custodial family data with noncustodial fathers' income. Therefore, the explanatory variables are the women's characteristics.

Let Y' be married men's income and Y'' be unmarried men's income; let X_{f1} be the married women's characteristics and X_{f2} be the custodial mothers' characteristics; and let I be a dummy variable equal to one if the man is present in the home and zero otherwise. Then the model could be specified as follows:

$$Y' = a + bX_{f1} + e_1 \; if \, I = 1 \qquad (3.A)$$

$$Y'' = a + bX_{f2} + e_2 \; if \, I = 0 \qquad (3.B)$$

$$I^* = a + cX_f + u \qquad (3.C)$$

$$I = 1 \; if \, I^* \geq 0$$

$$I = 0 \; if \, I^* < 0.$$

Equation (3.A) is a human capital equation for a man's income using his wife's characteristics as proxies for his own. Equation (3.B) is similar, but for fathers who are not married; the characteristics are those of his former mate. Equation (3.C) determines the probability that the man is present in the home. We have information on all variables except Y''' (income for noncustodial fathers); thus we cannot directly estimate equation (3.B).

It is likely that the es are correlated with u, so we could estimate equation (3.C) by using probit regression and construct a lambda term and insert it in equation (3.A) to obtain unbiased estimates of bs by using ordinary least squares regression. The bs from equation (3.A) combined with the x_{f2}, and the lambda term for those not in equation (3.A) can then be used to impute income for equation (3.B).

The application of this model to the CPS—CSS data failed to produce the expected results. That is, the sign of the coefficient of the lambda term in the stage-two ordinary least squares regression (estimating equation [3.A]) was perverse (negative) and not statistically significant. Given our a priori assumptions concerning the incomes of noncustodial fathers relative to married men, we opted to develop the method presented in the text as an alternative to the Heckman procedure.

5. The welfare coefficient, g, is used both to adjust downward the estimated income of absent fathers of children on welfare and to adjust upward the estimated income of absent fathers of children not on welfare. The adjustments are constrained such that the mean estimated income of all noncustodial fathers after the adjustment equals the preadjustment mean. For those on welfare the adjustment is equal to $\log\{1/[P + (1 - p)\exp(-g)]\} + Y_1$. For those not on welfare, the adjustment is equal to $-\log[p + (1 - p)\exp(-g)] - g + Y_1$, where p = proportion of custodial families on welfare and Y_1 = mean income of all noncustodial fathers.

6. For more details on the sample, see McDonald, Moran, and Garfinkel (1983).

7. The Delaware standard, discussed in the text following, is one of the oldest, and served as a model for standards in many other states. The Colorado standard is based on the income-shares model recommended by a report on standards commissioned by the federal Office of Child Support, DHHS. Michigan used to have a standard that, like Wisconsin's, depended almost exclusively on the income of the noncustodial parent and the number of children owed support. Texas has adopted a similar standard; in 1989 New York adopted a modified version of the Wisconsin percentage-of-income standard.

8. Owing to the unavailability of data, our simulations ignore state and local income taxes as well as work-related expenses. This will result in some overestimation of net income and the resulting ability to pay.

9. To demonstrate this, suppose that fathers are obligated to pay child support only if they earn at least $5,000 per year. Suppose also that fathers with some set of characteristics have average earnings of $5,000 but that incomes for the group are distributed uniformly over the interval $0–$10,000. If the mean is assigned to each noncustodial father with these characteristics, all fathers will be assigned zero obligation. If the distribution were used, however, half the fathers would be expected to pay child support.

10. We are grateful to one of our referees for this suggestion.

11. The results from a Wisconsin survey suggest that the public would impose sharing rates similar to those in the standards simulated (see the last chapter in this volume).

References

Bumpass, L. 1984. "Children and Marital Disruption: A Replication and an Update." *Demography* 21:71–82.
Cherlin, A., J. Griffith, and J. McCarthy. 1983. "A Note on Maritally Disrupted Men's Reports of Child Support in the June 1980 Current Population Survey." *Demography* 20:385–89.
Corbett, T., N. C. Schaeffer, and I. Garfinkel. 1987. "Public Opinion about a Child Support Assurance System." Institute for Research on Poverty Discussion Paper 834-87. Madison: University of Wisconsin–Madison, Institute for Research on Poverty.
Heckman, Joseph. 1979. "Sample Selection Bias as a Specification Error." *Econometrica* 47(1):153–161.

Hofferth, S. 1985. "Updating Children's Life Course." *Journal of Marriage and the Family* 47:93–115.

Institute for Research on Poverty. 1980. *Wisconsin Absent Parent Income Study (WAPS.)* Machine-readable data files. Madison: University of Wisconsin–Madison, Institute for Research on Poverty.

————. 1985. *Wisconsin Children, Incomes, and Program Participation Survey (CHIPPS).* Machine-readable data files. Madison: University of Wisconsin–Madison, Institute for Research on Poverty.

Institute for Social Research. 1980. *Michigan Panel Study of Income Dynamics (PSID).* Machine-readable data files. Ann Arbor: University of Michigan, Institute for Social Research.

McDonald, T., J. Moran, and I. Garfinkel. 1983. *Wisconsin Study of Absent Fathers' Ability to Pay More Child Support.* Institute for Research on Poverty Special Report 34. Madison: University of Wisconsin–Madison, Institute for Research on Poverty.

Nichols-Casebolt, A., I. Garfinkel, and P. Wong. 1988. "Reforming Wisconsin's Child Support System." In *State Policy Choices: The Wisconsin Experience,* edited by S. Danziger and J. White (172–86). Madison: University of Wisconsin Press.

Oellerich, D. 1984. *The Effects of Potential Child Support Transfers on Wisconsin AFDC Costs, Caseloads, and Recipient Well-being.* Institute for Research on Poverty Special Report 35. Madison: University of Wisconsin–Madison, Institute for Research on Poverty.

U.S. Bureau of the Census. 1976. *Survey of Income and Education (SIE).* Machine-readable data files. Washington, D.C.: U.S. Bureau of the Census.

————. 1979, Mar.-Apr. *Current Population Survey—Child Support Supplement (CPS—CSS).* Machine-readable data files. Washington, D.C.: U.S. Bureau of the Census.

————. 1983a. *Child Support and Alimony: 1981. Current Population Reports,* ser. P-23, no. 124. Washington, D.C.: U.S. Government Printing Office.

————. 1983b. *Money Income of Households, Families, and Persons in the United States. Current Population Reports,* Consumer Income, ser. P-60, no. 146. Washington, D.C.: U.S. Government Printing Office.

————. 1987. *Child Support and Alimony: 1985. Current Population Reports,* ser. P-23, no. 52. Washington, D.C.: U.S. Government Printing Office.

Chapter Four

INEQUALITY IN DIVORCE SETTLEMENTS: AN INVESTIGATION OF PROPERTY SETTLEMENTS AND CHILD SUPPORT AWARDS

Judith A. Seltzer and Irwin Garfinkel

Social scientists study the process of marital dissolution to gain insights into spouses' and parent-child relationships. Financial settlements at divorce are particularly revealing for the insights they provide into family relationships. This chapter investigates inequality between husbands and wives in the United States using data from a representative sample of recent divorce cases. We address three questions. First, how do property settlements affect differences between fathers' and mothers' postdivorce economic well-being? Second, are property settlements potentially large enough to induce parents to consider a trade-off between property and a child support award? Third, which is more important in determining divorce outcomes: power inequalities or bargaining? In the sections following we describe why these questions are significant for social research, we review the previous literature on divorce settlements, and we discuss its limitations. We then describe the data, followed by a discussion of our methods of analysis and a presentation of our results. We conclude by considering the implications of our findings.

DIVORCE SETTLEMENTS AS A PROBLEM FOR SOCIAL RESEARCH

The proportion of U.S. children in households headed by single mothers continues to grow. In 1985, nearly 21 percent of children lived in households with their single mothers, more than double the percentage who lived with single mothers in 1960 (U.S. Bureau of the Census 1986b: table A8). High separation and divorce rates combined with increasing rates of unmarried childbearing mean that half of the children in recent cohorts may spend time in a single-mother household (Castro Martin and Bumpass 1989). Children separated from a parent suffer economic and social disadvantages (Garfinkel and McLanahan 1986; McLanahan and Bumpass 1988). Households maintained by single mothers—the majority of single parents—suffer from poverty and economic insecurity (Garfinkel and McLanahan 1986).

Because most children who reside with a single mother have a living father, they have a potential claim to child support. Yet, only 61 percent of mothers with children eligible for support have a child support award; of these, less than half receive the full amount due (U.S. Bureau of the Census 1987). Inadequate child support payments contribute to the hardships of a childhood spent with a single mother by lowering the household's income, a key factor affecting children's school behavior and educational attainment (Hetherington, Camara, and Featherman 1983; McLanahan 1985). In addition to their effects on income, child support payments have also been found to reduce children's behavioral problems at school (Furstenberg, Morgan, and Allison 1987). The division of property at divorce may also affect children's welfare, but previous research on economic aspects of divorce has focused primarily on child support awards rather than on the division of property (Beller and Graham 1988; Cassetty 1978). Except for studies of the effects of legal reforms on property settlements (Peters 1986; Weitzman 1985), the role of the division of property in divorce settlements has been neglected.

Mnookin and Kornhauser (1979), in their classic article "Bargaining in the Shadow of the Law," characterized divorce settlements as the outcome of parents' private negotiations about child support awards and the division of property. In the authors' view, parents trade off child support and property to maximize their own preferences, and courts ratify parents' informal agreements. This suggests that low or nonexistent child support awards may be offset by generous property settlements. Some evidence supports this view of the divorce process as an economically rational exchange of property and support. Divorcing parents have described their maintenance, child support, and property settlements in the same breath (Weitzman 1985). In addition, Landes (1978) found a negative effect on alimony of the amount of property that women receive. A few mothers have even stated explicitly that they got more property because they gave up a support award (U.S. Bureau of the Census 1986a).

Yet, there are reasons to doubt the Mnookin-Kornhauser picture of the divorce process. Weitzman's (1985) California data suggest that the division of property is unimportant compared to wives' potential loss of husbands' income. The value of tangible assets in divorce settlements is less than the amount that an average couple earns in the year before divorce. National data and findings from studies in other states also show that few custodial mothers receive valuable property at divorce (McLindon 1987; U.S. Bureau of the Census 1981; Wishik 1986). Thus, property settlements may neither offset the dramatic difference between women's and men's economic welfare after divorce nor provide much opportunity for parents to trade off property and support awards.

Even if property values are high relative to income, Mnookin and Kornhauser's (1979) view of informal divorce negotiations may be flawed by its emphasis on consensus. Their portrayal of divorce as an informal process downplays the acrimony that characterizes the resolution of uncontested divorces (Erlanger, Chambliss, and Melli 1987; Kressel 1985). Furthermore, they assume that a settlement accepted by both spouses reflects each person's preferences equally. This is inconsistent with research on marital conflict and decision making, which shows that one spouse, usually the husband, has more control in resolving disagreements (Blood and Wolfe 1960; Gillespie 1971; Scanzoni 1982). Mnookin and Kornhauser ignore the implications of husbands' greater authority, access to economic resources, and information about the value of assets (e.g., pensions, credit) that they can use to their advantage in a divorce settlement.

Contemporary marriage patterns suggest wide variation in the degree to which husbands have power over wives. Some spouses may be relatively equal because of women's increasing economic independence (Moore and Sawhill 1976) and the adoption of egalitarian sex-role attitudes (Bianchi and Spain 1986). Among couples who adopt a traditional division of labor in which husbands provide market work and wives provide housework, however, greater male dominance is found. Couple differences in spouses' relative power may affect the distribution of property and child support in divorce settlements. The greater the inequality between spouses, the more likely it is that the more powerful parent will receive a disproportionate share of property *and* an advantageous support award (e.g., when noncustodial fathers are relatively more powerful, the child support award will be lower).

Divorce settlements also reflect parents' concern for their children's economic welfare. Although Mnookin and Kornhauser (1979) contended that parents seek settlements to achieve both self-interested and altruistic goals, their view does not evaluate the relative importance of these goals to individual spouses. Parents share deep-rooted concerns about the effects of divorce on their children (e.g., Arendell 1986; Goode 1956), but differ in their willingness to place children's interests ahead of their own. The custodial parent, usually the mother, may be more committed to the children's goals than the father, both because her economic interests coincide with the children's economic interests and because she identifies emotionally and psychologically with the children.[1] Noncustodial parents' economic interests compete with those of their children. However, when noncustodial parents are strongly committed to maintaining their children's economic welfare, they may act against their own economic interests and agree to larger property settlements and support awards for the custodial parent and children. Thus, commitment to children as well as relative power inequality may describe divorce settlements more accurately than bargaining to a mutually acceptable property settlement and support award.

PROPERTY SETTLEMENTS AND MEN'S AND WOMEN'S POSTDIVORCE ECONOMIC WELFARE

Divorce is costly for both men and women, but the economic consequences for women are undoubtedly more severe. Approximately 40 percent of women who remain single in the first year after divorce lose more than half their family income. Fewer than 17 percent of men experience such a sizable drop in income (Duncan and Hoffman 1985a). Children share women's economic fate; 59 percent of children living with single mothers live in poverty, compared to about 10 percent of children in two-parent households (U.S. Bureau of the Census 1988: table 24). Men, on the other hand, experience a rapid economic recovery from divorce, in part because they no longer share as much of their incomes with their children (Duncan and Hoffman 1985a).

As indicated earlier, previous research suggests that property settlements are unlikely to reduce the gap between women's and men's postdivorce economic well-being. Couples who divorce have lower incomes prior to separation than stably married couples (Duncan and Hoffman 1985a), an income differential that is reflected in the limited value of property holdings at divorce. Property settlements are more likely to include cars or household furnishings than more valuable assets such as houses, businesses, or pensions (Weitzman 1985), so that the net value of assets owned at divorce is quite low (McLindon 1987; Weitzman 1985). Even if women received all of the property, the low total value of assets might not be enough to offset their post-divorce economic disadvantage. Of course women rarely receive all of the property at divorce, even when they have custody of children (McLindon 1987; Weitzman 1985; Wishik 1986).

Property settlements, however, may play an important role in divorce negotiations if the value of property is high *relative to the amount of support awarded.* Although Weitzman's (1985) evidence suggested that the total value of the property divided is low compared to couples' predivorce income, the value of maintenance and child support awarded to custodial mothers is also low. Support awards may be a more appropriate standard than income for evaluating the significance of property in divorce negotiations because support awards are the other component of financial settlements. Despite the direct relevance of the comparison between the amount of property each person receives and the amount of support awards for theories of divorce bargaining, no studies investigate systematically the association between property and support.

THE DIVORCE PROCESS: COMPETING PERSPECTIVES AND THEIR LIMITATIONS

Most divorce settlements are determined by informal negotiations outside of court (Erlanger et al. 1987; Melli 1983; Mnookin and Kornhauser 1979). Couples typically treat litigation as a last resort because of its high emotional and financial costs (Albrecht 1980; Arendell 1986; Spanier and Casto 1979; Spanier and Thompson 1984). Some types of informal negotiation, such as mediation, may decrease postdivorce conflict and improve compliance with divorce settlements (e.g., Pearson and Thoennes 1984). Yet emphasis on private agreements, emotional adjustment, and improved compliance are inconsistent with inequality in bargaining resources, intense conflict between parents, and competition between self-interest and concern for children.

Consensus: Trade-Offs between Property and Support

Consensus-oriented views of divorce settlements, best exemplified by Mnookin and Kornhauser (1979), treat settlements as the outcome of each parent's preferences for property (lump-sum payments) and support awards (periodic payments). As in economic theories of family life (e.g., that of Becker 1981), consensus models assume that once parents decide to divorce, they negotiate to maximize the joint utility of their settlement. Parents consider property and support to be substitutable goods, subject to discounts for inflation, availability of liquid assets, and expected compliance with support awards. For example, in a sociolegal environment in which support awards are rarely or haphazardly enforced, it is in the custodial parent's economic interest to request a larger share of property as part of the divorce settlement, rather than a larger amount of child support. Divorce lawyers frequently advise their clients that a large property settlement is worth more than a hard-to-enforce maintenance or child support award (Weitzman 1981, 1985). Because the settlement is a compromise division of property and child support responsibilities, the net association between the amount of property and support awarded to custodial mothers will be negative. Although Mnookin and Kornhauser acknowledged that husbands and wives may differ in their bargaining chips (resources), they do not consider the problems of conflicting preferences and spouses' differential ability to achieve preferences.

Conflict and Inequality

Divorce occurs as a result of conflict between spouses. The way that conflicts are resolved within marriage depends on differences between husbands' and wives' power (Scanzoni 1982; Straus, Gelles, and Steinmetz 1980); thus power differences may play an integral role in resolving divorce disputes. In fact, competing preferences and relative inequality between husbands and wives may be more important than trade-offs in determining the relationship between property settlements and child support awards.

Inevitably, spouses differ in power when one is more eager to leave the marriage than the other. The spouse more anxious to leave has a bargaining disadvantage and may have to give up more joint assrts as the "price" of a divorce (e.g., Erlanger et al. 1987). However, disparity between the postdivorce living standards of women and children, on the one hand, and those of men, on the other hand, suggests that, on average, men have a systematic bargaining advantage because they control more economic resources. Husbands usually know more about the value of their pensions and insurance policies. This gives them an advantage because they can understate the value of the joint assets they control (Wishik 1986). Husbands' financial status at divorce is generally more secure than that of wives, enabling husbands to freeze joint assets (e.g., bank accounts) or withhold mortgage payments to coerce wives to accept a less advantageous settlement (Erlanger et al. 1987; Foster and Freed 1984; Weitzman 1985). Differences between men's and women's knowledge and earning capacity suggest that, in general, private negotiations do not optimize divorce settlements for *both* spouses, just for husbands.

Couples vary, however, in the degree of husband-wife inequality. Married women's economic dependence on husbands has declined dramatically during this century (Sørensen and McLanahan 1987). As women earn more of their families' incomes, their monetary contributions to the purchase of joint property increase. Monetary contributions are more likely to be recognized in property settlements than unpaid contributions to family property, such as housework or child care. For instance, studies show that, controlling for other factors, wives who are employed and/or who have separate bank accounts have more control in decisions about how to spend money than wives who do not have their "own" money (Blumstein and Schwartz 1983; England and Farkas 1986). In cases where the balance of power is relatively more favorable for wives, wives may use their stronger bargaining position to acquire larger property settlements and support awards. Conversely, when the balance of power is relatively more favorable for husbands, wives will receive less of both property and support.

Although courts rarely alter parents' property and support agreements (Melli 1983), expectations about judges' preferences may enhance or diminish parents' relative bargaining positions (Erlanger et al. 1987; Mnookin and Kornhauser 1979; Weitzman 1985). Other things being equal, couples who anticipate that their case will be heard by a judge who favors custodial mothers and children are likely to arrange a settlement that gives more property and support to the mother than couples who anticipate a judge who favors noncustodial fathers. Thus, judges' potential ability to alter divorce settlements influences parents' relative inequality, further suggesting a positive association between the amount of property and child support that custodial parents receive (e.g., if the judge is sympathetic to mothers and their children, both property settlements and support awards will be larger).

Property and Commitment to Children

Parents' concern for their children also affects the allocation of property and child support. Concerns include the negative effects of divorce on children's emotional welfare, the potential loss of contact between the noncustodial parent and child, social upheaval if children must move to a new residence, and decline in children's standard of living (Arendell 1986; Harrison and Tucker 1986; Wallerstein and Kelly 1980). Parents may attempt to protect children from conflict by negotiating a quick divorce settlement outside of court. They may also serve children's interests by ensuring that the custodial parent receives the house (when there is one) or sufficient child support to enable the children to remain in their current residence. Under the most common custody arrangements, where fathers are noncustodial and mothers are the custodial parents, these strategies affect husbands and wives differently. Private negotiations and a quick settlement may favor the father, whereas concern for children's economic welfare may favor the mother. When mothers are more committed to children's welfare than fathers are, fathers may acquire another advantage in financial negotiations. Mothers may comply with fathers' demands to give up property and claims to child support as a way to facilitate friendlier postdivorce relationships between the noncustodial father and children (Arendell 1986; Spanier and Thompson 1984; Wallerstein and Kelly 1980; Weitzman 1985). The divorce process, therefore, is influenced by parents' differing commitments to childrearing responsibilities and by conflict between achieving various childrearing goals (protection from conflict and fulfilling children's material needs).

Methodological Limitations

Despite the theoretical contributions of previous research, sample and measurement problems hamper the interpretation of findings about divorce. Legal studies are limited by the dearth of empirical work that tests assertions about divorce negotiations. Descriptions are impressionistic (Mnookin and Kornhauser 1979) or rely on small samples (McLindon 1987; Wishik 1986) and in-depth interviews (Erlanger et al. 1987; Spanier and Thompson 1984). Reliance on self-reports about the financial value of divorce settlements and retrospective reporting biases prevent studies from systematically evaluating the role of property settlements and child support awards in divorce settlements. Finally, research is limited by the absence of key variables. The most commonly used data source, the March-April Current Population Surveys (CPS), lacks information about the value of property awarded to each parent.[2] This prevents an assessment of property division. The CPS also lacks information about the amount of child support and maintenance awarded at divorce; rather, the survey includes the amount owed during the previous year (U.S. Bureau of the

Census 1987). These data limitations have prevented a consideration of the total value of divorce settlements, including both property and child support.

DATA SOURCES

We used data from a large, representative sample of recent divorces to examine the association between property settlements and child support awards. Unlike the CPS, our data include information about the total value of property in the settlement, the amount awarded each spouse, and the value of support awarded at the time of divorce. Because the information comes from official records, the data are not subject to retrospective reporting biases, as in the CPS and other smaller surveys of divorcing parents.

Sample and Measurement

We used court records of separation and divorce cases that were eligible for child support sampled from 22 Wisconsin counties with court dates between July 1980 and October 1984. Child support cases are those that include minor children and two living parents who live apart. The sample includes families with and without child support awards. Our analysis describes property settlements among approximately 1,800 divorcing families of all custody types and investigates the association between property settlements and support awards for the subsample of approximately 1,300 cases in which the family owned some property and sole legal custody was awarded to the mother. We treat the data as a cross-sectional sample of divorce cases sampled over the 4.5-year period. The population estimates reported here use sample weights that correct for variation in the probability of sample selection based on the year that the family entered the Wisconsin court system and the number of child-support-eligible divorce cases in each county (Garfinkel et al. 1988; Manning, Seltzer, and Schaeffer 1987).

Case records include information on parents' income, property ownership, division of assets, and support awards obtained from the financial statements filed by parents when they petitioned for divorce and from data on settlements in temporary orders (initial separation) and final orders (formal divorce decrees). The analysis uses data on property settlements and support awards specified in final orders whenever possible; for cases observed before parents had obtained final orders, we substituted information from temporary orders.[3]

The monetary value of parents' assets is defined as the net value of assets once mortgages, liens, and other debts have been taken into account. Couples or individuals who reported negative net worth, either because they owed money to each other or to outside parties, are treated in the analysis as though they have no assets (i.e., coded 0 on the value of property).[4] The data collection procedures do not enable us to determine the extent to which this assumption of zero net worth overestimates divorced parents' economic well-being. Overestimates of property values may be offset by underestimates attributable to missing data on property values when couples did not know the value because the property was still for sale at the time of divorce.

Wisconsin vs. National Sample Characteristics

Comparison of the Wisconsin court record data with national estimates from the CPS shows that divorce settlements in Wisconsin are very similar to settlements in the United States as a whole. Table 4.1 reports selected characteristics for the Wisconsin sample and recent divorce cases in the 1979 March-April CPS public use file. We used

Table 4.1 SELECTED CHARACTERISTICS FOR RECENT DIVORCE CASES IN WISCONSIN COURT RECORD SAMPLE AND 1979 MARCH-APRIL U.S. CURRENT POPULATION SURVEY, WEIGHTED PERCENTAGES

	Wisconsin (%)[a]	CPS (%)[b]
Mothers who received any property	66.4 (1,668)	60.3 (1,049)
Mothers who had a support award at divorce	85.3 (2,237)	83.8 (1,049)
Value of property awarded to mother:[c]		
<$5,000	49.7	51.1
$5,000–$9,999	11.3	13.3
$10,000–$19,999	13.8	17.7
$20,000–$29,999	11.0	6.1
$30,000–$39,999	3.5	4.2
$40,000–$49,999	2.4	2.9
$50,000–$74,999	4.5	2.4
$75,000+	3.8	2.3
Total	100.0 (1,151)	100.0 (566)

Note: Unweighted sample sizes are in parentheses.
[a]Restricted to cases in which mothers have legal custody.
[b]Restricted to cases in which mothers have physical custody.
[c]For mothers who received any property; excludes mothers who did not receive a settlement.

the 1979 Child Support Supplement because it was the last year that the survey included questions about the dollar value of property awarded to mothers (U.S. Bureau of the Census 1983). The CPS estimates in table 4.1 describe the subset of divorces that occurred in the five years before the survey to mothers who live with support-eligible children. The first row shows that the percentage of custodial mothers who receive at least some property in the divorce settlement is similar for Wisconsin and the nation (66 percent compared to 60 percent, respectively). In addition, the Wisconsin and CPS data estimate approximately the same percentage of cases with alimony and/or support awards at the time of separation (85 percent and 84 percent, respectively). Finally, the data sources show similar distributions for the value of property that mothers received as part of their divorce settlement, with an index of dissimilarity of 8.5. The comparison suggests that it is appropriate to use the Wisconsin court record data to explore the relationship between property settlements and support awards and that inferences from our analyses may apply to divorce settlements nationally.

METHODS AND RESULTS

This analysis is in three parts. The first considers the importance of property for postdivorce economic welfare. We describe the composition and value of property settlements and evaluate the effects of property settlements on mothers' and fathers' postdivorce incomes. The second part compares the value of property settlements to child support awards to assess the potential for trade-offs between property and support. The third part investigates whether trade-offs or inequalities of power and commitment to children explain the relationship between property settlements and support awards. We develop a multivariate model and evaluate the relative merits of the trade-off and inequality hypotheses by comparing divorce settlements in which husbands and wives have relatively equal access to economic resources with those in which husbands have more resources.

Effects of Property on Men's and Women's Postdivorce Economic Welfare

Table 4.2 shows that most families own some property at the time of divorce. The top panel reveals that 84 percent of all divorce cases have at least some property.[5] Despite the high percentage of divorce

Table 4.2 PROPERTY OWNERSHIP, MEDIAN VALUES OF PROPERTY, AND SHARE
OF PROPERTY AWARDED TO MOTHERS: DIVORCE CASES, WISCONSIN,
1980–84

Type of Property	Percentage of Cases Including the Item	Median Value ($)[a]	Mean Percentage of Total Property Value Awarded to Mothers
All custody types:			
Any property	84	7,800	54
House	52	22,000	
First car	80	1,000	
Other assets[b]	18	15,500	
Mother custody:			
Any property	82	6,000	57
House	48	21,000	
First car	79	1,000	
Other assets[b]	16	15,500	

Notes: Estimates are calculated using weighted data. Unweighted sample size for
calculating total property value for all custody types equals 1,807. For mother-custody
cases, the unweighted sample size for total property value equals 1,326. Sample sizes
vary due to missing data.
[a]Restricted to subset of cases that included the property item in their settlement.
Values are rounded to the nearest hundred.
[b]Restricted to property valued at more than $5,000.

cases involving property settlements, the value of most people's assets
is relatively low—the median dollar value of all property being $7,800.
Most people own only a car. The family house is clearly the couple's
most valuable asset, with a median net value of approximately
$22,000 for those who own one. Less than one-fifth of divorce cases
involving children include more than $5,000 worth of property other
than a house or cars. On average, families divide their property relatively equally between the two parents. Mothers receive 54 percent of
total assets, regardless of custody arrangements. Finally, a comparison
of the top and bottom panels of table 4.2 shows that compared to
families with other custody arrangements, those in which mothers
have legal custody of the couples' children have two slight economic
disadvantages: they are somewhat less likely to own property, and the
property that they own is worth somewhat less than for all families.

Distributional data on property values also show the low value of
assets in most divorce settlements. Figure 4.1 presents the distribution
of the value of property available for division when mothers have
custody and the settlements involve at least some property. Nearly 60
percent of all mother-custody families own property valued at less

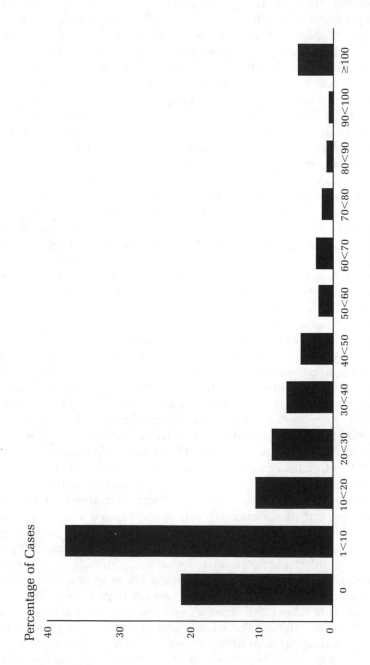

Figure 4.1 DISTRIBUTION OF TOTAL VALUE OF PROPERTY INVOLVED IN NEGOTIATIONS FOR MOTHER-CUSTODY CASES IN WISCONSIN, 1980–84.

than $10,000 at the time of divorce. In about 80 percent of the cases, the property is worth less than $30,000. Only 5 percent of mother-custody cases own property worth $100,000 or more. The unequal distribution of property suggests that few parents have an opportunity to acquire much wealth as part of their divorce settlement.

Despite the low value of property divided at divorce, small property settlements may be important for parents' economic welfare if the settlement is large relative to their other economic resources. To consider the effects of property settlements on postdivorce economic welfare, we compared property (a stock) to income (a flow) by estimating the income that spouses would receive if they invested their share of joint property; we then compared this investment income or flow of money to other postdivorce income. The income return to the invested assets, relative to couples' postdivorce annual income, indicates the degree to which property settlements affect the economic welfare of men and women. We assumed that assets acquired in property settlements yield an investment income of a simple 10 percent per year. Table 4.2 shows that the median value of property awarded in mother-custody cases is $6,000. Of this, 57 percent ($3,420) is awarded to mothers, while fathers receive the remaining 43 percent ($2,580). Investment income for our hypothetical example is $342 for custodial mothers and $258 for noncustodial fathers.

To evaluate the relative importance of this investment income for mothers and fathers, we compared it to estimates of women's and men's mean income for the first year after separation or divorce. Although our data do not include information about incomes the year after divorce, we estimated postdivorce incomes by combining our data on family income at the final divorce hearing (i.e., approximate predivorce family income) with Duncan and Hoffman's (1985b: table 14A.3) estimates of percentage declines in income after divorce. We used Duncan and Hoffman's estimates for whites with above-median predivorce family incomes, so that their estimates would be appropriate for our predominantly white, court-based sample of property owners. We treated parents' combined income at the final (or temporary) divorce order as predivorce family income (mean = $29,291). Duncan and Hoffman estimated that for women with higher socioeconomic status who do not remarry in the year after divorce, family incomes decline to 61 percent of their predivorce level. For men, the decline is to 82 percent of predivorce income. Using this information, we estimated that custodial mothers in our sample who do not remarry in the year after divorce have an average income of $17,868 for the first year after divorce, whereas fathers have an average income of $24,019.[6]

The comparison of parents' investment income from property settlements to average postdivorce incomes shows that mothers' share of property interest provides an additional 1.9 percent of income ($342 divided by $17,868), whereas fathers' share provides 1.1 percent of additional income ($258 divided by $24,019). Although the proportionate increase in women's economic well-being is nearly twice as high as the improvement in men's well-being, neither women nor men benefit appreciably from property settlements. Even if mothers received all $6,000 worth of joint property, its investment value would only increase their postdivorce income by 3.4 percent ($600 divided by $17,868). The small effects of property settlements on parents' postdivorce incomes indicate that taking property settlements into account does not diminish divorced mothers' economic disadvantage.

Potential for Trade-Offs between Property and Support

We compared the investment value of property settlements to the size of annual child support awards to determine whether a trade-off between property and support is feasible for those who own property. If the investment value of property is trivial relative to the size of child support awards, parents are unlikely to negotiate an exchange between property and support. Table 4.3 reports the ratio of the hypothetical investment income from the property that custodial mothers receive to the amount of noncustodial fathers' child support obligations.[7]

Table 4.3 COMPARISON OF AVERAGE PROPERTY SETTLEMENT VALUES TO AVERAGE CHILD SUPPORT AWARDS: DIVORCE CASES WITH MOTHER AS SOLE LEGAL CUSTODIAN, WISCONSIN, 1980–84

Mother's and Father's Combined Annual Income at Divorce ($) (1)	10% of Value of Property Received by Mother ($) (2)	Annual Child Support Award ($) (3)	Ratio of Property Investment Value to Support[a] (4)	Unweighted Number of Cases (5)
Less than 15,000	558	1,530	.29	126
15,000–24,999	486	2,906	.30	285
25,000–34,999	1,095	4,059	.31	298
35,000–44,999	1,595	4,307	.40	145
45,000 or more	3,840	7,068	.66	104
All	1,299	3,869	.37	958

Note: Estimates are calculated using weighted data.
[a]Excludes cases without support awards.

The data in table 4.3 show that property settlements do offer the potential for a trade-off between property and support. The mean investment value of mothers' property settlements equals nearly 40 percent of the value of fathers' support obligations among families with both a property settlement and a support award.[8] This ratio, moreover, underestimates the relative importance of property compared to support, because it assumes that the amount that noncustodial fathers are obligated to pay in child support is the same as the amount that they, in fact, pay. The ratio of property to actual child support payments is likely to be much higher, given the low compliance with child support awards (U.S. Bureau of the Census 1987: table A).

The relative size of invested property values and support awards varies among families of different income levels at divorce (see table 4.3). Among those with incomes less than $15,000, invested property values equaled approximately one-third of support obligations, while among those in the highest income category, property settlements totaled two-thirds of the annual support obligation. Other things being equal, families with higher incomes at divorce may have more property to divide, thus increasing the ratio of property to support. Families who have higher predivorce incomes are also more likely to include two earners. When mothers have their own earnings, they may use this resource to demand a divorce settlement with a larger property component. All else being equal, mothers may prefer a lump-sum property settlement because it is awarded immediately and is given directly to them, whereas child support awards may not be forthcoming and, in a sense, are more for the children's use than the mother's. At the same time, mothers who earn more are also better able to support their children without child support (i.e., have less "need" for fathers' support contributions) than mothers with lower earnings (Beller and Graham 1986; Cassetty 1978). Our results suggest that mothers from lower-income families are disadvantaged because they are forced to rely more on child support—a precarious arrangement—than on property for their share of the divorce settlement.

Relative Importance of Trade-Offs and Power Inequalities

Two dimensions govern the outcome of property and child support negotiations: parents' relative power to achieve their goals and whether parents seek their own self-interest or are altruistically motivated by concern for their children. Predictions about divorce outcomes can be made based on the interaction of these dimensions.

Predictions about the effects of relative inequality on settlements assume that parents negotiate in their own self-interest. To the extent that divorce settlements are compromises between relatively equal, self-interested parents who strike a bargain on property and child support, the net relationship between these two outcomes should be negative—that is, a gain in one would be balanced by a loss in the other. If, on the other hand, variation in mothers' and fathers' relative power dominates the outcome of divorce negotiations, the net relationship between mothers' property and support would be positive. On average, custodial mothers with more power relative to their husbands will obtain both larger property settlements and larger child support awards. Conversely, for couples in which custodial mothers have less relative power, mothers will receive smaller property settlements and smaller child support awards.[9] Predictions based on altruistic motives also suggest a positive association between property and child support. Noncustodial fathers may pursue altruistic goals as a way to express their commitment to children. All else being equal, the more committed noncustodial fathers are, the larger the awards of both property and child support to custodial mothers. Fathers who are less committed (or more self-interested) express this by giving custodial mothers smaller property and smaller support awards.[10]

Thus, by examining the association between property settlements and child support awards, we can ascertain the relative importance of trade-offs, which seek to accommodate parents' self-interested preferences for property and child support, compared to inequalities of power and commitment to children. If, for given levels of earnings and assets, the association is negative, we would conclude that trade-offs are the critical phenomenon. By contrast, if the association is positive, we would conclude that either inequalities in power or commitment to children are more important.

The bivariate relationship between property settlements and support awards provides initial support for the power inequality and commitment hypotheses. The correlation[11] between the dollar values of property and child support awarded to custodial mothers is .478, suggesting, according to the power interpretation, that within couples the more powerful parent gets more favorable property and support awards. However, the high positive association between the dollar values of property and support awarded to custodial mothers may also reflect parents' predivorce wealth. Wealthier parents can afford larger property settlements and larger child support awards. Thus, we investigated the association between property and child support awards, controlling for each parent's predivorce income, the total value of assets in the divorce settlement, and other family characteristics that affect divorce settlements. We evaluated the relationship between property settlements and support awards for the entire sample and for subsamples that differ in the degree of husband-wife power inequality. We expected trade-offs, if they occurred at all, to characterize divorce settlements in cases where spouses are relatively equal. The analysis distinguishes two couple types: "egalitarian" couples in which the wife's income is at least 70 percent of the husband's income and "husband-dominated" couples in which the wife's income at divorce is less than 70 percent of the husband's income.

MULTIVARIATE MODEL OF PROPERTY AND CHILD SUPPORT AWARDS

We estimated two-equation models in which one equation predicts the dollar value of property awarded to custodial mothers and one predicts the amount of support awarded per month.[12] The equations were estimated simultaneously with correlated disturbances. Both property and support have a large number of cases with zero values; therefore, we used a bivariate tobit model to estimate the joint association between property and support and to take account of the censoring of their distributions (Maddala 1983).[13] We interpret the residual association as evidence of either a trade-off between property and support (indicated by a negative correlation) or inequalities of power or commitment to children (indicated by a positive correlation). We estimated a pooled model for the entire sample to describe divorce settlements for all parents. We then estimated separate models for couples with high and low levels of inequality to determine whether or not trade-offs between property and support more accurately characterize settlements between relative equals than settlements between unequals.

INDEPENDENT VARIABLES

Table 4.4 summarizes the variables included in our models. Marital duration (DURATION) and the number of children eligible for child support (KIDS) are indirect indicators of the couple's investment in their marriage. The longer the parents have been married, the more property they have accumulated, and ceteris paribus, the greater each spouse's contribution (through paid or unpaid work) to accumulated assets. Number of children indicates the need for support. We included the quadratic term (KIDSQ) to take into account economies of scale associated with larger family sizes (Espenshade 1984).

We measured individual spouses' economic resources as their gross

Table 4.4 DEFINITIONS OF VARIABLES AND DESCRIPTIVE STATISTICS, WISCONSIN, 1980–84

Abbreviation for Variable	Description	Notes on Operationalization	Unweighted Mean	Standard Deviation
—	Value of property awarded to mother	In thousands of dollars	13.472	27.349
—	Support obligation per month	In dollars; equals 0 if no award	292.6	301.8
DURATION	Length of marriage in years	Calculated as of initial divorce petition date	10.350	6.463
KIDS	Number of minor children in the couple's family	Restricted to children eligible for support in the divorce action	1.820	.932
KIDSQ	Number of children squared		4.181	5.436
TOTVALUE	Total value of property distributed in the divorce case	In thousands of dollars	23.578	43.854
TOTVALSQ	Total value of property squared		2477.6	1310.7
FINCOME	Father's gross monthly income	In thousands of dollars	1.591	1.458
MINCOME	Mother's gross monthly income	In thousands of dollars	.838	.543
FDUMINC	Father's income is missing	1 = missing; 0 otherwise	.191	.393
MDUMINC	Mother's income is missing	1 = missing; 0 otherwise	.134	.341
MOTHREP	Mother is represented by an attorney, but father is not	1 = mother has an attorney and father does not; 0 otherwise[a]	.315	.465
FATHREP	Father is represented by an attorney, but mother is not	1 = father has an attorney and mother does not; 0 otherwise[a]	.042	.201
NEITHER	Neither parent is represented by an attorney	1 = neither parent has an attorney; 0 otherwise[a]	.040	.196
MILWAUKEE	County in which divorce was awarded	1 = case heard in Milwaukee; 0 otherwise	.113	.317

[a]Omitted category for the legal representation variables is "both parents have an attorney."

monthly income at the time of their final or temporary order (table 4.4, FINCOME for fathers; MINCOME for mothers). Parents' incomes indicate their control of bargaining resources. All else being equal, the higher the mother's income, the greater her power to achieve property and support settlements in her favor. The father's income is also a bargaining resource that determines his share of divorce settlements. However, the traditional division of labor in families suggests that the father's income is also a family resource. Men have more control over their income than other family members do, but wives and children also have a claim on men's income (England and Farkas 1986; Sørensen and McLanahan 1987). The father's income, therefore, indicates both his own resources and his ability to contribute to property settlements and child support awards. We cannot predict the net effect of the father's income on settlements. Income as the father's own resource suggests a negative effect on property and support awarded to the mother; as a family resource, the effect is likely to be positive.

Both income variables are missing for a large number of cases. To avoid reducing the sample, we recoded missing values to the sample mean and included dummy variables for cases with missing data on parent's income (FDUMINC, MDUMINC, in table 4.4). We also took into account parents' wealth by including linear and quadratic terms for the total value of property in the divorce settlement (TOTVALUE, TOTVALSQ).

In addition to family characteristics, we included variables that indicate the effects of the legal environment on property settlements and child support awards. Access to legal advice is a resource that may increase each parent's ability to acquire a favorable settlement. We contrasted cases in which only one parent has an attorney (MOTHREP, FATHREP, in table 4.4) and cases in which neither parent has an attorney (NEITHER) with the omitted category—both parents have attorneys. Administrative procedures may also affect the outcome of property and support negotiations. In Wisconsin, child support is administered by counties. Milwaukee, the state's largest county, is somewhat less efficient in enforcing and distributing child support payments ("County Spends $101,000 Studying Child Support Backlog" 1985), in part, due to the difficulties of pursuing delinquent payers in a large urban environment (see Chambers 1979). If child support collection is inefficient, custodial mothers have a greater incentive to bargain for a larger property settlement in exchange for a smaller or no support award. We included a dummy variable indicating whether or not the divorce occurred in Milwaukee.

FINDINGS: POOLED MODEL

Table 4.5 reports the parameters for the pooled, bivariate tobit model of the amount of property and support awarded to custodial mothers. The bottom of the table shows the correlation (ρ) between the residuals for the two equations. Controlling for common predictors, the correlation between the amount of property and child support awarded to custodial mothers is .156. Although this is lower than the .478 bivariate correlation reported earlier, the positive association between property and support is still statistically significant. Controlling for the total value of property explains more of the association between

Table 4.5 PARAMETERS FROM BIVARIATE TOBIT ANALYSIS OF VALUE OF PROPERTY AND AMOUNT OF SUPPORT AWARDED TO MOTHERS: DIVORCE CASES WITH MOTHER AS LEGAL CUSTODIAN, WISCONSIN, 1980–84

Variable	Value of Property Awarded to Mother		Child Support Awarded per Month	
	Parameter	t-statistic	Parameter	t-statistic
DURATION	.268*	5.38	3.980*	3.37
KIDS	.274	.35	121.176*	6.30
KIDSQ	−.045	−.34	−13.766*	−4.10
TOTVALUE	.454*	36.01	.565	1.86
TOTVALSQ	$.477 \times 10^{-3}$*	12.18	$.707 \times 10^{-2}$*	7.37
FINCOME	.387	1.92	69.117*	13.94
MINCOME	1.913*	3.70	−63.332*	−5.07
FDUMINC	1.284	1.73	−115.055*	−6.43
MDUMINC	.077	.09	−15.458	−.79
MOTHREP	−.495	−.78	−29.219	−1.93
FATHREP	−1.883	−1.31	−65.891*	−2.08
NEITHER	−1.072	−.71	−75.961*	−2.20
MILWAUKEE	−.109	−.12	11.152	.52
Constant	−4.718*	−3.97	24.563	.87
σ	9.866*	47.27	247.148*	48.40
Number of cases	1,301			
−2(log likelihood)	25,110			
ρ (correlation between residuals)	.156*			
	(9.23)[a]			
ρ (zero-order)	.478*			
	(38.06)[a]			
ρ (controlling for TOTVALUE and TOTVALSQ)	.160*			
	(9.50)[a]			

Notes: Property and income are measured in thousands of dollars.
Asterisk (*) denotes parameter is at least twice its standard error.
[a]*t*-statistic.

property and support than other variables, including parents' incomes, number of children, and legal representation ($\rho = .160$, controlling only for wealth).[14] These findings suggest that, in the aggregate, the outcomes of divorce settlements are determined more by variations in power inequalities and altruistic concern for children's material well-being than by trade-offs to maximize differences in parents' preferences for property or child support.

The upper part of table 4.5 provides additional evidence for the role of power differences and concern for children in explaining divorce settlements. The first two columns of the table show the net effects of individual and family characteristics on the value of property that custodial mothers receive.[15] Both property and income are measured in thousands of dollars.

The most striking finding is the large positive effect of mother's income on her share of the property. Just as wives' earnings increase their control over economic decisions within marriage (Blumstein and Schwartz 1983; Scanzoni 1982), women use their earnings to improve their share of property at divorce. Parents and courts may view a wife's earnings as entitling her to more joint property. Her financial contributions to joint assets go beyond the requirements of the traditional marriage contract and so are more likely to be recognized in property settlements. Father's income also increases custodial mother's property settlements, but the effect is smaller than for mother's income. The positive net effect of fathers' income on property settlements to custodial mothers is consistent with the view that men's earnings are, in part, a family resource. Fathers who have more resources are able to give more to their children in divorce settlements.

Couples who were married longer allocate more property to the custodial mother. Each year of marriage is worth an increment of $268 in mothers' property awards (table 4.5). The positive effect of marital duration on property awards may occur because wives in long-term marriages may have more relationship-specific power over their husbands (e.g., ability to anticipate and circumvent husbands' bargaining tactics) (England and Farkas 1986). Alternatively, marital duration may reflect a cohort effect. That is, couples who married in earlier periods are more likely to view the marriage contract as an agreement about the economic division of labor. Husbands, according to this contract, must fulfill breadwinning responsibilities while wives care for the home and children. Under the traditional marriage contract, even if husbands want to leave the marriage, their economic responsibilities to their former wife and children continue (Weitzman and Dixon 1980). Other family characteristics have little or no effect on the amount of property that custodial mothers receive.

The second two columns of table 4.5 show the effects of the same independent variables on the amount of child support awarded to custodial mothers. Again, socioeconomic characteristics are more important than other factors in determining support awards. As anticipated, mother's income decreases the amount of support awarded, whereas father's income increases the amount awarded. The custodial mother's income is inversely related to her need for support; mothers with more income have the potential to support children by themselves. The father's income, on the other hand, indicates his ability to pay support (Beller and Graham 1986; Cassetty 1978). Other indicators of need, such as marital duration and number of children, also affect the amount of awards. The positive effect of marital duration on awards may reflect parents' commitment to children. Parents who have been married longer generally have older children, and the child's age indicates parental time invested in childrearing. The relationship between legal representation and child support awards is also generally consistent with inequality and children's needs interpretations. When both parents have attorneys, support awards are higher. This may occur because both spouses are likely to retain attorneys when mothers seek large support awards. By contrast, when neither parent or just the father has an attorney, men's bargaining advantage is enhanced and women receive less support. When mothers have attorneys but fathers do not, less support is awarded than when both parents have attorneys, but the effect is not quite statistically significant. Although legal resources should increase the amount of child support that mothers receive, divorces in which only the mother is represented by an attorney may be more likely to occur because of desertion. The father's absence from divorce proceedings limits the likelihood of a support award.

FINDINGS: WITHIN HUSBAND-WIFE INCOME GROUPS

Although the results in table 4.5 suggest that inequality in spouses' power or commitment to children dominates trade-offs in negotiations between property settlements and child support, it is possible to identify subgroups in which trade-offs may be more common or less common. Specifically, we expected that when spouses have relatively equal control over economic resources, they would be more likely to compromise about how much property and support each receives than when one spouse is considerably more powerful. We also expected that, net of other factors, divorce settlements for couples in which husbands and wives have approximately equal incomes would award a larger proportion of the total settlement to wives than settlements for couples in which husbands have much higher incomes than wives. Table 4.6 reports parameter estimates for our model of property settlements and support awards for two types of couples: those in which the wife's income is at least 70 percent of the husband's income and those in which the wife's income is less than 70 percent of her husband's.[16] Of those with complete income information, approximately 40 percent of the cases are in the former group, and 60 percent are in the latter group.

A comparison of the residual association between the amount of property and child support awarded to custodial mothers within each husband-wife income category shows general support for our hypothesis that trade-offs are more common among relative equals. The residual correlation (ρ) for couples with relatively equal incomes is $-.086$, whereas for couples in which husbands have much higher incomes, the correlation is .123 (see table 4.6). The difference between the correlations is statistically significant ($z = -5.05$, $p < .001$). Controlling for the difference between spouses' incomes also diminishes the effects of other independent variables on property settlements and support awards. The negative effect of mother's income on the child support award becomes insignificant when parents' incomes are approximately equal. Among couples in which husbands have higher incomes, the positive effect of mother's income on her property settlement also becomes insignificant.[17]

That divorce settlements between relative equals reflect trade-offs whereas those between unequals benefit one party suggests support for the hypothesis that inequality plays an important role in determining the outcome of divorce negotiations. Stronger support for the inequality hypothesis could come from comparing the total settlements received by wives in each husband-wife income group. When wives have relatively more power (i.e., those whose incomes are approximately equal to their husbands), we would expect them to receive a larger portion of the total divorce settlement. Wives' share of the settlement is the sum of the yearly child support award and the investment value of the property they receive in the settlement.[18] We defined the total assets available for distribution at divorce as the sum of the noncustodial father's annual income and the investment value of all property available for distribution at the time of divorce. Contrary to our expectations, differences between husbands' and wives' incomes did not affect the portion of total settlements awarded to wives. Regardless of the degree of husband-wife income inequality, wives in both groups received 23 percent of the total settlement. This finding suggests that at least some husbands may use their greater economic power to achieve the altruistic goal of providing for children's material welfare rather than to achieve their own self-interest.

Table 4.6 BIVARIATE TOBIT ANALYSIS OF PROPERTY AND CHILD SUPPORT AWARDED TO MOTHERS BY HUSBAND–WIFE INCOME INEQUALITY: DIVORCE CASES WITH MOTHER AS LEGAL CUSTODIAN, WISCONSIN, 1980–84

| | Husband and Wife Have Similar Incomes | | | | Husband's Income is Greater Than Wife's | | | |
| | Value of Property Awarded to Mother | | Child Support Awarded per Month | | Value of Property Awarded to Mother | | Child Support Awarded per Month | |
Variable	Parameter	t-statistic	Parameter	t-statistic	Parameter	t-statistic	Parameter	t-statistic
DURATION	.109	1.45	-1.48	-1.32	.222*	2.83	-1.71	.936
KIDS	.119	.125	75.7*	5.32	1.22	.665	114.4*	2.73
KIDSQ	-.011	-.082	-8.49*	-3.94	-.266	-.691	-6.92	-.798
TOTVALUE	.651*	16.1	.077	.130	.474*	19.0	1.97*	3.32
TOTVALSQ/1000	-.708*	-2.03	5.23	.993	.368*	3.30	-3.25	-1.21
FINCOME	-.452	-.619	135.2*	12.2	.625	1.38	154.5*	14.1
MINCOME	1.82*	3.19	-4.93	-.566	.603	.500	-149.1*	-5.18
MOTHREP	.226	.267	2.69	.218	-.808	-.776	22.2	.912
FATHREP	5.12*	2.31	-44.2	-1.30	-4.83*	-2.27	-43.02	-.889
NEITHER	.647	.350	-30.7	-1.17	-.662	-.289	-27.7	-.510
MILWAUKEE	-1.29	-.964	-25.8	-1.29	.080	.061	43.5	1.41
Constant	-4.27*	-2.66	-36.3	-1.54	-4.56*	-2.08	-70.7	-1.40
σ	7.24*	25.0	111.6*	26.1	10.1*	31.2	246.0*	32.8
Number of cases	378				562			
-2(log likelihood)	6,417				11,291			
ρ (correlation between residuals)	-.086* (-2.62)[a]				.123* (4.87)[a]			
ρ (zero-order)	.157* (4.92)[a]				.461* (24.2)[a]			
ρ (controlling for TOTVALUE and TOTVALSQ)	-.060 (-1.83)[a]				.156* (6.22)[a]			

Notes: Both property and income are measured in thousands of dollars. Husbands and wives are assumed to have similar incomes if the wife's income is at least 70 percent of the husband's. Asterisk (*) denotes parameter is at least twice its standard error.

[a]t-statistic

An alternative definition of total settlements, however, provides evidence that economic power is used for self-interest. Our assumption that the noncustodial father's entire income can be drawn on for child support conflicts with some guidelines for uniform child support awards (e.g., Williams 1986). Parents (and courts) may treat part of the noncustodial father's income as exempt from child support because the income is needed for the father's own living expenses. According to this perspective, we recomputed the total value of assets available for distribution at divorce as the sum of the noncustodial father's net annual income and the investment value of all property. The father's net income is his gross income minus his living expenses. We conservatively defined living expenses as the poverty level income for a single adult under age 65. For 1982, a year included in our study, the poverty level was $5,019 (U.S. Bureau of the Census 1984: table A2). By this revised definition, wives in couples with relatively equal incomes receive 41 percent of the total settlement, whereas wives in couples in which husbands have much higher incomes receive 30 percent.[19] The difference in percentages is statistically significant. This is consistent with the view that wives use their income resources to acquire a larger share of the total divorce settlement. Our assumption about the father's minimum living expenses results in a difference between the two husband-wife income categories, because husbands in the "egalitarian" income group have lower mean incomes than those in the "husband-dominated" income group ($12,878 vs. $24,482, respectively). The choice of which comparison—the one using all of the noncustodial father's income or the one using his net income—better represents the mother's share of the total settlement depends on philosophical beliefs about the appropriate standard for child support (Williams 1986).

CONCLUSIONS

Our findings show that property settlements do not alter the disparity between men's and women's postdivorce economic welfare. Divorcing couples own little valuable property. Even if women received all joint assets at divorce, they would still be severely disadvantaged compared to men. Despite the low absolute value of joint assets, property is a significant element in financial settlements *compared to* child and family support awards. The investment value of property is worth between one-third and two-thirds of yearly support awards. Property settlements have the additional advantage that they provide material transfers at the time of divorce. Support awards promise future income, but these promises are not always kept. Thus, compared to the other economic component of divorce settlements, property is important and provides the potential for parents to trade one for the other to achieve their preferences.

The picture of relatively equal parents bargaining and trading until they reach agreement is inaccurate. Inequality characterizes most divorce negotiations. In most cases the parent who receives a favorable property settlement also receives a favorable support award. As in the resolution of marital conflict, spouses' relative power determines the outcome of divorce conflict about property and support. Among the subset of couples in which husbands and wives are relatively equal, property settlements and child support awards reflect trade-offs. For these couples, outcomes of divorce negotiations depend, largely, on bargaining and compromise. Thus, Mnookin and Kornhauser's (1979) theory of divorce bargaining may be accurate for subsets of the population in which husbands and wives have approximately equal earnings *and* couples own enough property to make trade-offs between property and support feasible. For the remainder of the population, where inequality between husbands and wives is greater, the outcome of divorce negotiations reflects either the relatively more powerful spouse's attempt to achieve self-interest or the noncustodial father's altruistic concern for children.

Better understanding of divorce settlements requires research on variation in parents' inequality. Specifically, why are some mothers more successful in achieving favorable financial settlements than others? Other research should examine more systematically the resources to which men and women have differential access (e.g., various sources of income, aggressive legal advice, information about asset value), variation in the effectiveness with which they use the same resources, and which resources are the best bargaining tools. Future research should also investigate the degree to which parents seek self-interested and altruistic goals in divorce negotiations.

In general, our analyses do not support the consensus view underpinning policies that leave negotiations up to spouses. According to this view, although spouses (and attorneys) anticipate judges' decisions, the law can and should remain removed from the divorce process (Mnookin and Kornhauser 1979).[20] But laws have strong, direct effects on the process and outcome of divorce negotiations. No-fault divorce laws, for example, alter the balance of power in property negotiations (McLindon 1987), in part by reducing the legitimacy of women's claims on men's breadwinning capacity. This leaves women and children with a smaller share of joint property than under previous laws (Weitzman 1985). Child support reforms, on the other hand, may improve the bargaining position of custodial mothers. Recent federal legislation requires that child support awards be determined by uniform standards and encourages more rigorous enforcement. Both strategies place a lower bound on noncustodial fathers' contributions to children's postdivorce support, thereby further limiting the potential for informal negotiations involving property settlements and child support awards. Our findings suggest that limits to informal negotiations may be particularly important for the well-being of children in the majority of cases when the mother's predivorce income is lower than the father's.

Notes

Reprinted by permission from Academic Press, Orlando, Fl.

This is a slightly shortened and edited version of "Inequality in Divorce Settlements: An Investigation of Property Settlements and Child Support Awards," which originally appeared in *Social Science Research* 19: 82–111 (1990). The research was supported by contract 144W857 between the Wisconsin Department of Health and Social Services and the Institute for Research on Poverty as well as the Center for Demography and Ecology, which receives core support from the Center for Population Research of the National Institute for Child Health and Human Development (HD-5876). Seltzer also received support from the University of Wisconsin Graduate School. Opinions expressed here are the authors' alone. We are grateful to L. Bumpass, R. Mare, S. McLanahan, I. Rothe, N.C. Schaeffer, and J. Sweet for comments on earlier versions of this chapter. We also thank P. Brown, A. Lewis, T. Orbuch, Q. Sullivan, and the computing staff of the Center for Demography and Ecology for technical assistance, as well as E. Uhr for editorial suggestions.

1. Allocation of custody rights also plays an important role in divorce negotiations. Parents may trade rights to money (property and child support) for custody. This chapter explores financial issues, focusing primarily on cases in which mothers get custody. In other research, we are examining the association between decisions about custody and financial settlements.

2. Since 1979, the CPS has not included questions about even the dollar value of property awarded to mothers (U.S. Bureau of the Census 1983).

3. Temporary and final order data were coded from a file of case records in which court actions for each case were recorded chronologically. By searching each of the first four court actions, we identified final or temporary orders for slightly over 95 percent of the divorce cases. Fifteen percent of the cases had information only from temporary orders. Preliminary analyses show no differences between cases with information from temporary and final orders. This is consistent with the Melli, Erlanger, and Chambliss (1985) finding that awards in final orders are usually the same as those in temporary orders.

4. We constructed the variable indicating the total value of all assets from a series of items reporting the value of individual assets. To include as many cases as possible in the analysis, we used the following procedure. Consider a couple with two cars. If they owed money on one car, but had no outstanding loans on the other, the value of the first car was coded as zero whereas the value of the second car was treated as a positive number.

5. Bivariate tables not included here show relatively little variation in whether or not couples own at least some property across various social, demographic, and economic characteristics.

6. Our estimates of postdivorce income are quite similar to those reported by Duncan and Hoffman (1985b: table 14.A.3) for their comparable subsample: $17,719 for women and $26,533 for men.

7. We define child support awards as the sum of alimony (maintenance), child, and family support awards. For cases with child-support-eligible children, these awards are substantively equivalent.

8. Note that the ratio reported in column 4 of table 4.3 is not the ratio of the means in columns 2 and 3. Column 3 includes cases without support awards (i.e., zero values). These cases are not included in the computations reported in column 4 because division by zero is not defined.

9. To the extent that judges' preferences enhance inequality between spouses, this also suggests a positive association between the amount of property and child support awarded to custodial mothers. Our analysis does not distinguish between power exercised by parents and power exercised by courts.

10. As noted earlier, custodial mothers' self-interest and altruistic concerns for children's material welfare coincide in negotiations about property settlements and child support awards.

11. The correlation takes into account censoring of both variables at zero. We estimated the correlation between dollars of property and dollars of support in a bivariate tobit model without independent variables. These models are explained in the text upcoming.

12. We treated both property and support as the dollar amounts awarded to custodial mothers to enable a more straightforward comparison between property and support awards than alternate, ratio specifications, such as the proportion of total property awarded to custodial mothers and the ratio of the child support award to the noncustodial father's income. Ratio variables make it difficult to assess the net effects of total wealth and parents' incomes on divorce settlements.

13. We estimated this model by maximum likelihood using HOTZTRAN (Avery and Hotz 1983).

14. In analyses not shown here, we investigated the association between property and support for two subsamples of cases: those with the most valuable property (total values of $27,000 or more) and those with both property and support awards (i.e., excluding those with zero awards). The former analysis focuses on parents who have the greatest flexibility to engage in trades between property and support because they have more assets and income. The latter focuses on the potential for exchanges between property and support, given that settlements include both types of awards. In both subsamples, the positive statistically significant association between property and support persists. In a third analysis, we specified the support award as a dichotomy (i.e., whether or not the settlement included a support award) instead of as a continuous variable; property awards remained as a continuous variable. We were unable to achieve convergence in our models using the combination of the continuous property variable and a dichotomous support variable.

15. Coefficients in tobit regressions can be interpreted like those in ordinary least squares regressions (i.e., they represent the change in the dependent variable produced

by a unit change in the independent variable). In tobit regressions, however, the coefficients refer to the latent distribution of the dependent variable or the distribution that the variable would have if it were not censored (McDonald and Moffitt 1980). In this analysis, the two outcomes, property and support, are censored at zero.

16. This analysis excludes cases with missing data on either spouse's income (361 cases, or 28 percent of the cases in the pooled model).

17. The only other important difference between tables 4.5 and 4.6 in the effects of the independent variables on property settlements and child support is that the sign changes on the dummy variable indicating whether or not the father is the only one represented by a lawyer. Among cases with relative income equality, when only the father has a lawyer, mothers receive a larger property settlement than when both parents have a lawyer. By contrast, among cases with greater income inequality, when only the father has a lawyer, mothers receive a smaller property settlement than when both parents have a lawyer. The negative effect of the father's legal representation suggests that a lawyer is a resource that parents can use to improve their chances of a favorable settlement. We are reluctant to interpret the difference in signs because of the small number of cases in which only fathers have lawyers, but suspect that among "egalitarian" couples, mothers may not use lawyers if they think that they are in a particularly strong bargaining position.

18. As in our previous examples, we treat the investment value of the property as 10 percent of its total value.

19. Here, as previously, calculations exclude cases in which the denominator is less than zero.

20. Mnookin (1984) proposed exceptions to judicial nonintervention only in extreme cases.

References

Albrecht, S. L. 1980. "Reactions and Adjustments to Divorce: Differences in the Experiences of Males and Females." *Family Relations* 29: 59–68.

Arendell, T. 1986. *Mothers and Divorce: Legal, Economic, and Social Dilemmas.* Berkeley: University of California Press.

Avery, R. B. , and V. J. Hotz. 1983. "HOTZTRAN User's Manual." Economics Research Center/NORC, Chicago. Photocopy.

Becker, G. S. 1981. *A Treatise on the Family.* Cambridge, Mass.: Harvard University Press.

Beller, A. H., and J. W. Graham. 1986. "The Determinants of Child Support Income." *Social Science Quarterly* 67: 353–64.

Beller, A. H., and J. W. Graham. 1988. "Child Support Payments: Evidence from Repeated Cross Sections." *American Economic Review* 78: 81–85.

Bianchi, S. M., and D. Spain. 1986. *American Women in Transition.* New York: Russell Sage Foundation.

Blood, R. O., Jr., and D. M. Wolfe. [1960] 1965. *Husbands and Wives: The Dynamics of Married Living*, 2nd ed. New York: Free Press.

Blumstein, P., and P. Schwartz. 1983. *American Couples: Money, Work, Sex.* New York: William Morrow.

Cassetty, J. 1978. *Child Support and Public Policy.* Lexington, Mass.: Lexington Books.

Castro Martin, T., and L. Bumpass. 1989. "Recent Trends in Marital Disruption." *Demography* 26: 37–51.

Chambers, D. L. 1979. *Making Fathers Pay: The Enforcement of Child Support.* Chicago: University of Chicago Press.

"County Spends $101,000 Studying Child Support Backlog." 1985. *Milwaukee Journal*, June 27.

Duncan, G. J., and S. D. Hoffman. 1985a. "A Reconsideration of the Economic Consequences of Marital Disruption." *Demography* 22: 485–97.

————. 1985b. "Economic Consequences of Marital Instability." In *Horizontal Equity, Uncertainty, and Economic Well-Being*, edited by Martin David and Timothy Smeeding (427–67). Chicago: University of Chicago Press.

England, P., and G. Farkas. 1986. *Households, Employment, and Gender: A Social, Economic and Demographic View.* New York: Aldine.

Erlanger, H. S., E. Chambliss, and M. S. Melli. 1987. "Participation and Flexibility in Informal Processes: Cautions from the Divorce Context." *Law and Society Review* 21: 585–604.

Espenshade, T. J. 1984. *Investing in Children: New Estimates of Parental Expenditures.* Washington, D.C.: Urban Institute Press.

Foster, H. H., Jr., and D. J. Freed. 1984. "Law and the Family: Politics of Divorce Process—Bargaining Leverage, Unfair Edge." *New York Law Journal* 192(7, July 11): 1, 6.

Furstenberg, F. F., Jr., S. P. Morgan, and P. D. Allison. 1987. "Parental Participation and Children's Well-being after Marital Disruption." *American Sociological Review* 52: 695–701.

Garfinkel, I., and S. S. McLanahan. 1986. *Single Mothers and Their Children: A New American Dilemma.* Washington, D.C.: Urban Institute Press.

Garfinkel, I., T. J. Corbett, M. MacDonald, S. McLanahan, P. K. Robins, N. C. Schaeffer, and J. A. Seltzer. 1988. "Evaluation Design for the Wisconsin Child Support Assurance Demonstration." Report produced for Wisconsin Department of Health and Social Services and Institute for Research on Poverty, University of Wisconsin–Madison. Photocopy.

Gillespie, D. L. 1971. "Who Has the Power? The Marital Struggle." *Journal of Marriage and the Family* 33: 445–58.

Goode, W. J. [1956]. 1970. *Women in Divorce*, 2nd ed. Westport, Conn.: Greenwood Press.

Harrison, M., and T. Tucker. 1986. "Maintenance, Custody and Access." In *Settling Up: Property and Income Distribution on Divorce in Aus-*

tralia, edited by Peter McDonald (259–78). Sydney: Prentice-Hall of Australia.

Hetherington, E. M., K. A. Camara, and D. L. Featherman. 1983. "Achievement and Intellectual Functioning of Children in One-Parent Households." In *Achievement and Achievement Motives: Psychological and Sociological Approaches*, edited by Janet T. Spence (208–84). San Francisco: Freeman.

Kressel, K. 1985. *The Process of Divorce: How Professionals and Couples Negotiate Settlements*. New York: Basic Books.

Landes, E. M. 1978. "Economics of Alimony." *Journal of Legal Studies* 7: 35–63.

Maddala, G. S. 1983. *Limited-Dependent and Qualitative Variables in Econometrics*. Cambridge, England: Cambridge University Press.

Manning W., J. A. Seltzer, and N. C. Schaeffer. 1987. "Wisconsin Child Support Project Data Sets." Paper prepared for the Institute for Research on Poverty, University of Wisconsin–Madison. October.

McDonald, J. F., and R. A. Moffitt. 1980. "The Uses of Tobit Analysis." *Review of Economics and Statistics* 62: 318–21.

McLanahan, S. 1985. "Family Structure and the Reproduction of Poverty." *American Journal of Sociology* 90: 873–901.

McLanahan, S., and L. Bumpass. 1988. "Intergenerational Consequences of Family Disruption." *American Journal of Sociology* 94: 130–52.

McLindon, J. B. 1987. "Separate but Unequal: The Economic Disaster of Divorce for Women and Children." *Family Law Quarterly* 21: 351–409.

Melli, M. S. 1983. "Child Support Awards: A Study of the Exercise of Judicial Discretion." Institute for Research on Poverty Discussion Paper 734-83. Madison: University of Wisconsin–Madison, Institute for Research on Poverty.

Melli, M. S., H. S. Erlanger, and E. Chambliss. 1985. "The Process of Negotiation: An Exploratory Investigation in the Divorce Context." Disputes Processing Research Program Working Paper ser. 7. Madison: University of Wisconsin–Madison, Institute for Legal Studies.

Mnookin, R. H. 1984. "Divorce Bargaining: The Limits on Private Ordering." In *The Resolution of Family Conflict: Comparative Legal Perspectives*, edited by John M. Eekelaar and Sanford N. Katz (364–83). Toronto: Butterworths.

Mnookin, R. H., and L. Kornhauser. 1979. "Bargaining in the Shadow of the Law." *Yale Law Journal* 88: 950–97.

Moore, K. A., and I. V. Sawhill. 1976. "Implications of Women's Employment for Home and Family Life." In *Women and the American Economy: A Look to the 1980s*, edited by Juanita M. Kreps (102–22). Englewood Cliffs, N.J.: Prentice-Hall.

Pearson, J., and N. Thoennes. 1984. "Mediating and Litigating Custody Disputes: A Longitudinal Evaluation." *Family Law Quarterly* 17: 497–524.

Peters, H. E. 1986. "Marriage and Divorce: Informational Constraints and Private Contracting." *American Economic Review* 76: 437–54.

Scanzoni, J. 1982. *Sexual Bargaining: Power Politics in the American Marriage*, 2nd ed. Chicago: University of Chicago Press.

Sørensen, A., and S. McLanahan. 1987. "Married Women's Economic Dependency, 1940–1980." *American Journal of Sociology* 93: 659–87.

Spanier, G. B., and R. F. Casto. 1979. "Adjustment to Separation and Divorce: A Qualitative Analysis." In *Divorce and Separation: Context, Causes, and Consequences*, edited by George Levinger and Oliver C. Moles (211–27). New York: Basic Books.

Spanier, G. B., and L. Thompson. 1984. *Parting: The Aftermath of Separation and Divorce*. Beverly Hills, Calif.: Sage Publications.

Straus, M. A., R. J. Gelles, and S. K. Steinmetz. 1980. *Behind Closed Doors: Violence in the American Family*. Garden City, N.J.: Anchor Press/Doubleday.

U.S. Bureau of the Census. 1981. *Child Support and Alimony: 1978*. Current Population Reports, ser. P-23, no. 112. Washington, D.C.: U.S. Government Printing Office.

———. 1983. *Child Support and Alimony: 1981*. Current Population Reports, ser. P-23, no. 124. Washington, D.C.: U.S. Government Printing Office.

———. 1984. *Characteristics of the Population Below the Poverty Level: 1982*. Current Population Reports, ser. P-60, no. 144. Washington, D.C.: U.S. Government Printing Office.

———. 1986a. *Child Support and Alimony: 1983*. Current Population Reports, ser. P-23, no. 148. Washington, D.C.: U.S. Government Printing Office.

———. 1986b. *Marital Status and Living Arrangements: March 1985*. Current Population Reports, ser. P-20, no. 410. Washington, D.C.: U.S. Government Printing Office.

———. 1987. *Child Support and Alimony: 1985*. Current Population Reports, ser. P-23, no. 152. Washington, D.C.: U.S. Government Printing Office.

———. 1988. *Poverty in the United States: 1986*. Current Population Reports, ser. P-60, no. 160. Washington, D.C.: U.S. Government Printing Office.

Wallerstein, J. S., and J. B. Kelly. 1980. *Surviving the Breakup: How Children and Parents Cope with Divorce*. New York: Basic Books.

Weitzman, L. J. 1981. "The Economics of Divorce: Social and Economic Consequences of Property, Alimony and Child Support Awards." *UCLA Law Review* 28: 1181–1268.

———. 1985. *The Divorce Revolution: The Unexpected Social and Economic Consequences for Women and Children in America*. New York: Free Press.

Weitzman, L. J., and R. B. Dixon. 1980. "The Transformation of Legal Marriage through No-Fault Divorce." In *Family in Transition*, 3rd ed., edited by Arlene Skolnick and Jerome H. Skolnick (354–67). Boston: Little, Brown.

Williams, R. G. 1986. "Guidelines for Setting Levels of Child Support Orders." *Family Law Quarterly* 21: 281–324.

Wishik, H. R. 1986. "Economics of Divorce: An Exploratory Study." *Family Law Quarterly* 22: 79–107.

Chapter Five

CUSTODY AND VISITING AFTER DIVORCE: THE OTHER SIDE OF CHILD SUPPORT

Judith A. Seltzer

Parents and the courts cannot divorce child support arrangements from two other aspects central to children's lives after divorce: custody and visitation. Family law is ambivalent about the separation of these issues, but families' behavior is not. Wisconsin family law, for example, requires that parents make arrangements for the care and maintenance of their minor children at the time of divorce. Thus, arrangements for where children live, who will care for them and make decisions about their lives, and who will provide financial support are all made within the context of a divorce settlement (e.g., *Wisconsin Statutes* 1987, chapter 767.25). At the same time, Wisconsin has decreed that access to children or visitation should not depend on whether a parent complies with child support obligations (*Wisconsin Assembly Bill 205* [1987], published 1988: section 34). Parents' behavior contrasts sharply with the judicial requirement that access be independent of paying child support. Several studies show that parents who pay support are more likely to spend time with their children, even when other factors, such as geographical proximity and parents' remarriage, that might constrain the ability to pay and visit are taken into account (Furstenberg et al. 1983; Seltzer 1990; Seltzer 1991b; Seltzer, Schaeffer, and Charng 1989).

Lack of clarity in family law results, in part, from the dearth of high-quality information about custody, child support, and visiting relationships after divorce. Thus, laws about custody and visitation have been subject to the influence of strong interest groups and commonsense notions of what life is like after divorce. Access to children has also been treated separately from compliance with child support awards because financial responsibilities are much more amenable to the manipulation of social policy and legislative and administrative reforms than is visitation (but see Bruch's 1987 suggestion that parents be penalized for not visiting their children). The dire economic straits of children in single-mother households is focusing public attention on ways to alleviate these disadvantages. The long-term costs of economic disadvantage are well-documented (Garfinkel and McLanahan 1986; McLanahan and Booth 1989). However, evidence about the effects of maintaining contact with both parents after divorce is mixed. National survey data show little, if any, improvement in children's emotional and social welfare if their nonresident parent, usually their father, stays involved with them after divorce (Furstenberg, Morgan, and Allison 1987; Seltzer 1990a). But evidence from clinical and other small studies suggests that paternal involvement benefits children (Hess and Camara 1979; Hetherington, Cox, and Cox 1982; Lund 1987; Wallerstein and Kelly 1980). Inconsistent evidence that nonresident parents' involvement with children affects their well-being fuels parents' contests for custodial and visitation rights.

This chapter discusses the social aspects of responsibility for children after divorce, especially questions of custody and visitation. Data are reported here from three Wisconsin studies: the Children, Incomes, and Program Participation Survey (CHIPPS), the Court Record Database (CRD), and the first Wisconsin Parent Survey (PS1). The chapter describes custody and visiting patterns for representative samples of recently divorced families and examines the relationships between custody and visiting on the one hand and child support awards and payments on the other hand.[1] Throughout, results of national surveys and other state-based studies are cited to demonstrate the generalizability of diverse aspects of the Wisconsin experience. State-based samples, including those from the Wisconsin project, provide valuable insight into the effects of child support reforms. Many national reforms are state-based, such as the principles used to define uniform support guidelines. Implementation is also almost completely at the state level. State-based analyses are therefore instrumental for policy evaluations because they include an implicit control for the legal environment in which family decisions are made and enacted. The CRD and PS1 are particularly useful for these studies because they sample families from throughout the state in large enough numbers to enable statistical controls for differences in county administrative practices, instead of relying on a small number of counties to describe child support and custody arrangements (e.g., Koel et al. 1988; Maccoby, Depner, and Mnookin 1988; McLindon 1987; Weitzman 1985). Finally, state-based datasets often provide more detailed information about specific aspects of family and court processes than is generally available in national surveys that must meet the goals of basic research as well as of policy evaluation.

DISTINGUISHING LEGAL CUSTODY FROM PHYSICAL CUSTODY

Policy debates often fail to distinguish between legal and physical custody of children. Wisconsin law distinguishes between formal decision-making rights about children and where children live or the parent(s) responsible for children's daily care (e.g., *Wisconsin Assembly Bill 205* [1987], published 1988).[2] Physical custody (or placement) indicates the parent with whom the children live.[3] Legal custody indicates the parent who has the formal authority to make decisions about the children's lives. Where and with whom children live clearly affect children's access to economic resources and provide opportunities for the intimate interaction necessary for children's socialization. The individual granted the right to make decisions about important things in the children's lives such as education and health care may also affect the children's welfare. This is particularly true in instances in which physical and legal custody do not coincide. For example, children may live with their mother after divorce, but their parents may hold joint legal custody and thereby share decision-making rights. When children live with their mother, but the parents share legal custody, nonresident fathers may try to use their formal authority to constrain the mother from moving the children to another state (Schepard 1985). The role of joint legal custodian may also hold symbolic importance that encourages nonresident fathers to be more involved with their children after divorce. Compared to fathers without joint legal custody, those with joint custody are more likely to comply with child support awards (Pearson and Thoennes 1988; but see Albiston, Maccoby, and Mnookin 1990 and Seltzer 1991a), and they spend more time with their children (Seltzer and Schaeffer 1989; Wolchik, Braver, and Sandler 1985).

Inattention to the distinction between legal and physical custody is mirrored in social research. Most studies examine either living arrangements and their consequences or legal custody, implicitly assuming that the two coincide. Yet instances in which legal and physical custody differ provide unique insights into the consequences of alternate divorce policies. Even studies that do distinguish between legal and physical custody offer little information about the effects of socioeconomic status and family composition on custody choices, because most such studies use small samples with limited variation on these characteristics (Clingempeel and Reppucci 1982). Knowledge of the extent to which families with differing custody arrangements vary

in their economic resources is critical for the development and implementation of child support reforms. Data from the Wisconsin Child
Support Reform Project provide much-needed information from a
large, representative sample of divorces about the degree of correspondence between legal and physical custody and the social and
demographic factors associated with various custody arrangements.

WHO GETS THE CHILDREN?

When couples divorce, they divide their joint assets and debts to try
to establish separate lives. When these couples are parents, rights to
children must also be reallocated. That children may be priceless in
emotional terms is irrespective of their clear economic costs, requiring the division of financial responsibilities as well. This section
describes the way children's time is divided, or with whom they live,
after divorce and the division of formal responsibilities for children
as indicated by legal custody arrangements.

That children in single-parent households are much more likely to
live with their mother than with their father is well-documented
(Sweet and Bumpass 1987). An incompatible shared belief is that a
large proportion of parents have joint physical custody of their children. Despite attention to joint custody in the popular press and in
clinical research, only a small proportion of U.S. children spend
equal amounts of time with both parents (Furstenberg 1988; Seltzer
1991b).[4] Much of the concern about the economic costs of divorce for
children hinges on the fact that children who live with their mothers
share her labor force disadvantages (Garfinkel and McLanahan 1986;
Holden and Smock 1991). Evidence of economic disadvantage comes
primarily from census data and from national surveys that do not
include information about legal arrangements after divorce. Therefore,
as stated, we know little about whether and how legal custody arrangements alter the costs of divorce for children. That most research
on joint custody uses samples of upper-middle-class families suggests
that joint legal custody may be more common among parents with
more economic resources. Certainly shared physical custody and establishing two households for children costs more than a single household (Patterson 1984), so upper-middle-class families may be better
able to maintain joint physical custody than working class or poor
parents.

Table 5.1 shows the distribution of legal and physical custody types for Wisconsin divorces between 1980 and 1985. Data from the court documents distinguish between legal custody (in the table, before the slash) and physical custody (after the slash). Information about physical custody is indicated on the data abstraction form as "Number of children living primarily with each parent." The coding instructions identify cases as joint physical custody if children spend equal time in each parent's household. This underestimates the extent to which children may spend significant portions of the year in each parent's household, but stay with one parent for just under half a year (e.g., a two-thirds versus one-third division of time).[5] However, the data provide more complete information about the correspondence between legal and physical custody arrangements than is generally available (but see Maccoby et al. 1988).

Table 5.1 reveals that in Wisconsin, children are much more likely to live with their mother than to live with their father or to divide their time between parents. Just over 73 percent of Wisconsin divorces awarded both legal and physical custody to the mother at divorce. Combined with cases in which the children live with their mother but parents have joint legal custody, over 88 percent of the divorced families arranged for children to spend most of their time in the mother's household. Only about 9 percent of children spend most of the year with their fathers. Of families in which children live with their fathers, almost half are ones in which parents share legal custody. Finally, the Wisconsin data are consistent with national survey data on children's living arrangements. Only 2 percent of families adopt joint physical custody, in which children spend equal time in each parent's household. Despite the attention devoted to joint phys-

Table 5.1 PERCENTAGE DISTRIBUTION OF CUSTODY TYPE (LEGAL/PHYSICAL) FOR WISCONSIN DIVORCE CASES ENTERING COURT, 1980–85

Custody Type	Distribution (%)
Mother/mother	73.3
Father/father	5.3
Joint/mother	15.2
Joint/father	3.9
Joint/joint	2.3
All cases	100
Unweighted N	4,038

Source: Wisconsin Court Record Database, as reported in Seltzer (1990b).
Note: Percentages are weighted.

ical custody, it applies to a very small percentage of all divorce cases *and* even a small percentage (less than 11 percent) of all cases in which parents share joint legal custody. For Wisconsin, the vast majority of parents award legal custody to the mother. Joint legal custody is a clear second, with just over 20 percent of the families choosing this arrangement. Table 5.1 also shows that legal and physical custody differ for about one-fifth of the divorces. Thus, studies that treat joint legal custody as though it is equally shared parenting greatly overestimate the percentage of families in which both parents contribute equally to child care after divorce.[6]

That legal and physical custody are distinct components of post-divorce family arrangements is reinforced by findings from a multivariate analysis of the family characteristics that predict custody type. In work reported in detail elsewhere, I show that economic characteristics, such as parents' incomes at divorce, determine legal custody arrangements, whereas children's ages affect physical custody in statistical models of combined legal and physical custody types (Seltzer 1990b).[7] In particular, when fathers have higher incomes, they are more likely to acquire joint legal custody than to allow mothers sole legal custody, regardless of where children live. Mothers' income also affects their acquisition of legal custody: compared to mother/mother custody, the likelihood of father/father custody decreases and joint/ joint custody increases when mothers have higher incomes. Parents' incomes may index their relative power to acquire custody, but the mother's income may also reflect her employment status. Mothers with higher incomes may have professional occupations and may be more likely to have had marriages that involved shared parenting before divorce compared to mothers with lower incomes, thus accounting for the effect of the mother's income on combined joint legal and physical custody. In contrast to the importance of economic factors for legal arrangements, when families have older children, fathers are more likely to have both legal and physical custody compared to mother/mother custody. The importance of children's ages for determining where they live is consistent with the Stanford Child Custody Study (Maccoby et al. 1988) and census data showing that children in single-father households are likely to be older than children in single-mother households (Sweet and Bumpass 1987).

That fathers' income increases the likelihood of both joint legal custody and sole-father custody is consistent with the notion that joint legal custody is a compromise between parents. If joint legal custody is a compromise between parents, children may be exposed to more conflict after divorce as the parents adjust to an arrangement that neither wanted. These findings also suggest that legal and physical custody choices may perpetuate couples' predivorce division of labor. Mothers are more likely to be responsible for the care of younger children. Fathers are more likely to get custody when children are older. That both parents' incomes increase the likelihood of joint legal and physical custody is also consistent with the idea that parents who share breadwinning and child-care tasks before divorce continue this arrangement in the early period after divorce.

DOES IT MATTER WHO GETS CUSTODY?

Reasons that Joint Legal Custody Matters

Many child support studies begin by limiting investigations to families in which the children live with their mother and their father has potential child support obligations. For Wisconsin in the early and mid-1980s, this was a sensible analytic strategy. Even in California, a state known for its innovations in divorce and custody laws, most children spend more time in their mothers' household than in their fathers' household, even when both parents have legal custody (e.g., Maccoby et al. 1988). In both settings, joint legal custody has become more common compared to sole-mother custody (Seltzer 1990b; Mnookin et al. 1990).

Focusing on children who live with their mothers leaves open the question of whether legal decision-making rights, alone, affect child support and other aspects of family relationships after divorce. Child support laws and uniform guidelines for establishing child support awards focus on where children live, not on who has legal control over them (e.g., Wisconsin Department of Health and Social Services 1987). However, opponents of joint legal custody argue that fathers use their designation as legal custodian to acquire lower child support awards and to pay less support; the fathers claim that they contribute to children's support by having (legal) custody and so should owe less support than fathers who do not have custody (California Senate 1987; Fineman 1988). On the other hand, child support awards might be higher when fathers have joint legal custody if, as Arendell (1986) and Weitzman (1985) suggest, mothers trade rights to child support for sole legal custody of their children.

Custody Effects on Average Child Support Awards and Payments

The formal codification of responsibilities for child support specifies the amounts of support awards regardless of who has legal custody of the children. This implies that any association between joint legal custody and child support arrangements is attributable to informal processes, either in the courts or in families. There are three interpretations of an association between joint legal custody and child support arrangements. First, the socioeconomic characteristics of families who choose joint legal custody may explain their higher awards and payments. Second, families in which parents share joint legal custody may differ in the quality of family relationships, either between parents or between fathers and children, from families in which only the mother is the legal custodian. For example, parents with joint legal custody may be more cooperative and may agree more about how to care for their children than families in which one parent has sole custody. Fathers who agree with their children's mother on basic values and who trust her judgment about how to spend child support money are more likely to agree with high child support awards and to comply with them. A variant on this interpretation is that fathers with joint legal custody may seek these legal rights as an indication of their concern for children. This same concern explains higher child support awards and payments with joint legal custody. Finally, adopting the role of legal custodian may, itself, alter nonresident fathers' commitment to children and participation in children's care after divorce. Expectations of a "good" father include providing for children's material support. Fathers who adopt this role pay more support to fulfill role expectations. All of these interpretations suggest differences in the average amounts of child support paid by fathers with and without joint legal custody.

Custody Alters the Determinants of Child Support Payments

The premise of joint custody is that it makes children's lives as similar as possible before and after divorce (Felner and Terre 1987; Goldstein 1984; Wallerstein and Blakeslee 1989). A neglected implication in child support research of joint custody legislation is that it may increase the *effects* of fathers' characteristics on children. That joint custody may strengthen the effects of fathers on children is a long-standing concern of opponents of joint legal custody and liberal visitation because these policies expose children to fathers who are physically or emotionally abusive (California Senate 1987; Schulman and

Pitt 1982). In terms of child support, the status of legal custodian may be associated with greater opportunities for nonresident fathers to exercise discretion about how to look after their children. Compared to nonresident fathers without custody, fathers with joint legal custody may choose to spend more money on child support, either because joint custody formally recognizes paternal responsibilities and good fathers provide for their children or because joint custody increases the informal benefits of paternity (Weiss and Willis 1985). When fathers have lower incomes, joint custody may allow them to pay less child support than under other custody arrangements because they can more easily explain their financial constraints to their children or former wives. Thus, joint legal custody may increase variation in payments, at the same time that states are adopting uniform standards for child support awards to limit variation in payments.

Wisconsin Evidence on Legal Custody, Awards, and Payments

Data from the Wisconsin court records show that among families in which children live with their mothers, fathers with joint legal custody have higher average awards and pay more child support than do fathers without custody in the first year after divorce. Fathers with joint custody owe an average of about $3,650, whereas those without custody owe just under $2,630.[8] Fathers with joint legal custody also pay more support, but the difference by custody type is reduced to about $550 (roughly $2,640 joint legal custody vs. $2,090 mother legal custody). The amounts paid are roughly similar to child support receipts among recently divorced resident mothers in the National Survey of Families and Households (Seltzer 1991b: table 4). Gross custody differences do not take into account the high incomes of fathers in families with joint legal custody. Once such factors as parents' incomes, number and age of children, marital duration, and the use of attorneys are controlled statistically, the positive association between awards and joint legal custody disappears (Seltzer 1991a). A detailed investigation of these associations suggests that socioeconomic status is a major source of differences in child support awards. Together with the results described earlier, these findings suggest that both high child support awards and joint legal custody are the results of parents', and especially fathers', high incomes.[9]

Controlling for parents' incomes and other characteristics also reduces the mean difference in child support payments by custody type. The first row of table 5.2 shows how much child support fathers with each type of legal custody would pay if families in the two custody

Table 5.2 SIMULATED ANNUAL CHILD SUPPORT PAYMENTS IN WISCONSIN BY
          LEGAL CUSTODY TYPE

	Child Support Payment by Legal Custody Type ($)		Payment Difference, Joint Custody Minus Mother Custody ($)
	Joint	Mother	
All characteristics at the pooled sample means	2,263	2,219	44
Father's income high, mother's income high	2,514	2,328	186
Father's income high, mother's income low	2,972	2,621	351
Father's income low, mother's income high	1,905	1,998	− 93
Father's income low, mother's income low	2,341	2,277	64

Source: Wisconsin Court Record Database, cases entering court 1980–85, as reported in Seltzer (1991a).
Notes: Data are for children living with their mothers; payments are for the first year after divorce. The simulation assumes that both custody types have the same distribution on family characteristics. It controls for number of minor children, number of children squared, whether payments were routinely withheld from the father's earnings, number of months of payment information observed in the court record, amount of child support awarded, and whether either parent's income information was missing from the court record. Parents' income categories are defined by the sample distribution. For fathers, high equals $31,915, average equals $16,501, and low equals $11,363. For mothers, high equals $12,790, average equals $8,096, and low equals $3,402.

types had the same incomes, family composition, and child support awards. There is virtually no custody difference in average payments. However, the Wisconsin data also show that the effects of parents' incomes differ for the two legal custody types. Income effects on payments are larger for families with joint legal custody than for those with sole-mother custody. In other words, payments are more responsive to variation in parents' economic circumstances when fathers share joint legal custody. Subsequent rows of table 5.2 show how much child support nonresident fathers would pay for different combinations of parents' incomes and custody types. Within categories of mothers' income, among those with joint legal custody, fathers who have high incomes pay from about $610 to $630 more in child support per year than fathers with low incomes (column 1, $2,514 − $1,905;

$2,972 − $2,341). The difference in payments between fathers with high and low incomes for those in mother-custody families is about $330 to $340 (column 2, $2,328 − $1,998; $2,621 − $2,277). The custody difference in the effects of father's income on child support payments is approximately $280, more than the average monthly payment for either custody type (about $220 for fathers with joint legal custody [$2,640/12]; just under $175 for those in families with mother custody).[10]

These findings support the notion that joint legal custody is consequential for children's economic well-being, but the effects do not operate in the manner usually investigated in studies of custody and child support. Joint legal custody is not associated with higher *levels* of child support payments. Instead, it is associated with different *patterns* of income-sharing than for fathers without custody. The results reported in table 5.2 and my related finding (not shown here) that fathers with joint legal custody are less likely to comply fully with their child support awards than fathers in families in which mothers have sole legal custody suggest that fathers with joint legal custody may have greater discretion to respond to fluctuations in their own and the children's mothers' financial circumstances (Seltzer 1991a). When fathers have more resources, children benefit economically from joint legal custody, but when fathers are disadvantaged, children suffer. In the absence of longitudinal data on variation in fathers' incomes, my cross-sectional findings suggest that by increasing fathers' opportunity to use discretion, joint legal custody may decrease resident mothers' ability to rely on regular child support payments. Regular and steady income is important for mothers' emotional welfare, stable childrearing patterns, and through these, children's adjustment (Braver et al. 1989; Hetherington, Cox, and Cox 1982; Wallerstein and Huntington 1983).

SPENDING TIME WITH CHILDREN AND CHILD SUPPORT

Nonresident fathers contribute to their children's welfare by investing time and money. Like fathers who live with their children, they juggle competing demands and resource constraints to determine what mix of time and money to provide their children.[11] Reform of the child support system may alter the balance of time and money that fathers contribute to children. Research from the Wisconsin Child Support

Reform Project examines the association between spending time with children and child support to anticipate the effects of more rigorous enforcement on other aspects of children's lives after separation.

What is the Relationship between Visiting and Paying Child Support?

Growing evidence suggests that for most families, when fathers pay support they are more likely to visit their children as well (Fursten-berg et al. 1983; Seltzer 1990a; Seltzer 1991b). These studies focus primarily on children who live with their mothers because, as demonstrated earlier, these represent the vast majority of children in single-parent households. However, Grief (1985) reported a similar pattern for children who live with their fathers. The Wisconsin project contributes to this literature by investigating alternative explanations for an association between visiting and paying support.

Two interpretations of an association between visiting and paying support parallel those for an association between joint legal custody and payments: first, visits and payments are the result of common demographic causes (e.g., distance, parents' remarriage, parents' financial resources); and, second, they result from unobserved social-psychological causes such as commitment to children or feelings toward the former spouse. Visits and payments may also cause each other. For instance, nonresident fathers may pay more support when they visit children because visits provide information about children's material needs, children ask for money when they see their father, or fathers spend money on children during visits. Payments may increase visiting if nonresident fathers want to monitor the way the children's mother spends child-support money (Weiss and Willis 1985) or if mothers facilitate visits when they receive payments, but hinder visits when they do not receive support (Furstenberg 1988; Wright and Price 1986).

These explanations account for a positive association between visiting and paying support. However, the association between visiting and paying may be negative if parents trade off the scarce resources of time and money when they decide how to invest in their children. For example, parents may spend time with children instead of providing money to a babysitter to look after the children (e.g., Sawhill 1977). In the child-support case, nonresident fathers may prefer to spend fewer hours in the paid labor force and pay less child support; they would compensate for smaller payments by spending more time with the children (see Seltzer, Schaeffer, and Charng 1989, for a more complete discussion of the association between visiting and paying support).

Findings: Time and Money

Two sources of data from the Wisconsin project provide information about the relationship between visiting and paying support: CHIPPS, a random sample of maritally separated and divorced parents regardless of how long ago their separation occurred, and PS1, a representative sample of recent divorces (one to three years before the interview). Both datasets include information about periodic child support payments received as part of an award as well as informal financial contributions from nonresident fathers. The results reported here rely on resident mothers' reports about visiting and child support.[12]

Table 5.3 shows the frequency of contact between nonresident fathers and children in 1986, the year before the PS1 interview. The data come from a series of questions about how many days a randomly selected child spent "living" with the nonresident father, how frequently the child saw the father when they were not living together, and the length of the usual visit with the child. Note that children

Table 5.3 MEASURES OF FACE-TO-FACE CONTACT BETWEEN NONRESIDENT FATHERS AND CHILDREN BY LEGAL CUSTODY TYPE: DIVORCED RESIDENT MOTHERS, WISCONSIN, 1987

	Legal Custody Type (%)		
	Joint	Mother	Both Types
Frequency of face-to-face contact with father in 1986:			
No contact	2.9	10.9	8.6
Less than once a month	6.7	15.5	13.0
Once a month	11.9	17.3	15.7
Twice a month	13.3	15.0	14.5
Once a week	33.3	25.4	27.7
Twice a week or more	31.9	15.9	20.6
Total	100	100	100
Number of days:			
Median	48	24	36
Mean	71	43	51
Standard deviation	69	56	62
N	210	515	725

Source: Preliminary release of data file, Wisconsin Parent Survey 1, 1987.
Note: Percentages may not add up to 100 due to rounding error.

may spend most of the year in their mother's household, but their parents may think of them as "living" in both households. The analysis is restricted to families in which the parents were separated for the entire year of the reference period.

As table 5.3 indicates, most children saw their fathers at least once during the previous year. Nearly half saw their father once a week or more frequently (27.7 percent plus 20.6 percent). Frequency of spending time with the nonresident father is higher than for other national estimates of nonresident father–child contact because the latter describe the experience of all children, those separated for a short period, as well as those separated for many years (Furstenberg et al. 1983; Seltzer and Bianchi 1988). The PS1 estimates are roughly comparable to those from the 1987 National Survey of Families and Households, which showed that about 43 percent of children in families separated for two years or less saw their fathers once a week or more (Seltzer 1991b: table 4). Table 5.3 shows that legal custody differences in average amounts of time that nonresident parents spend with children mirror those for average child support payments. The median number of contact-days for children whose parents have joint legal custody is twice as high as for children whose mothers have sole legal custody (48 vs. 24 days, respectively). As with child support payments, custody differences in fathers' income account for part of this difference.

Multivariate analyses of the association between frequency of visits and the amount of child support paid using the CHIPPS data show a positive association between visiting and paying support.[13] Our findings do not support the interpretation that commitment to children explains both types of paternal involvement after divorce. Nor do we find direct evidence of reciprocal causation between visiting children and paying support. However, only part of the positive association is explained by family characteristics and geographic proximity. Although our cross-sectional data do not distinguish among the three alternate interpretations—common demographic causes, commitment, and reciprocal causation—the persistent positive association between visiting and paying support even with statistical controls for a wide range of family characteristics suggests that spending time with children and paying support are activities that go together (Seltzer, Schaeffer, and Charng 1989).

We pursued the problem of the association between time and money investments in children by asking whether the association differs for families with joint legal custody arrangements compared to those in which mothers have sole custody. As described earlier, nonresident fathers with joint legal custody appear to use more discretion about how much income to share with their children compared to mother-custody families. Legislative trends increasing the number of families with joint legal custody may result in greater similarity between divorced single-parent and two-parent households if it provides nonresident fathers greater opportunity to balance decisions about how much time and money to invest in children. In general, the more time they spend with their children, the fewer hours they are able to work, and the less child support they can pay. Thus, the greater flexibility associated with joint legal custody implies that time and money may be traded against each other in families with this custody arrangement.

PS1 data provide preliminary support for this expectation. The association between number of days children spend with nonresident fathers and the amount of child support paid is negative for families with joint legal custody, but remains positive for families with sole-mother custody, and the difference in the associations by custody type takes into account parents' incomes, number of children, geographic proximity, child support awards, and other family characteristics (Seltzer and Schaeffer 1989). That nonresident fathers trade off time and money does not mean that they contribute less to their children's support. For instance, when children spend more time in their nonresident father's household, he may spend more money directly on the children as well as incur housing and other living expenses associated with sharing a household with them. These direct payments to children and living expenses may limit the amount of child support that the father pays to the children's mother. Joint legal custody may enhance a nonresident parent's ability to invest in children in a way that is more responsive to the parent's own and, possibly the children's, needs.

LESSONS ABOUT POSTDIVORCE FAMILY LIFE FROM THE WISCONSIN PROJECT

The Wisconsin project addresses questions of national concern about how financial responsibilities relate to parents' legal and social responsibilities for children. Our findings to date suggest several conclusions. First, the emphasis on fathers as potential payers and mothers as potential recipients of child support is consistent with Wisconsin evidence that families are considerably more likely to arrange for children to live with their mothers after divorce than to adopt arrangements of equal sharing or awarding physical custody to the father. Recent child support and custody reforms may increase the proportion of families with other custody arrangements (Garfinkel and McLanahan 1990; Mnookin et al. 1990; Seltzer 1990b). Similarly, comparisons of nonresident mothers with nonresident fathers may illustrate instances in which ostensibly gender-neutral laws are not neutrally applied. Descriptions of most children's experiences after divorce, however, can reasonably focus on children who live with their mothers and may receive child support from their fathers.

Second, the legal status of joint custodian may alter fathers' relationships with children even when children live with their mothers. The Wisconsin studies cited here suggest that when fathers have joint legal custody their investments in children more closely resemble the investment strategies of fathers in two-parent households, compared to fathers in families where mothers have sole legal custody. Among families with joint legal custody, the effects of the father's income on payments are larger than among families with sole mother custody, suggesting that joint legal custody is associated with fathers' greater ability to contribute to child support, depending on fluctuations in parents' economic circumstances. Similarly, fathers with joint legal custody treat time and money as substitute resources for investing in children. In contrast, among fathers in families where mothers have sole custody, time and money investments go together, suggesting that in the absence of the symbolic status as legal custodian, fathers must spend time with children and pay more child support to establish their role as "good" fathers.

If fathers with joint legal custody have greater discretion about spending money on children, then an expansion of joint legal custody may undermine the goals of child support reforms that seek more universalistic enforcement of child support responsibilities (Garfinkel and Uhr 1984). The opportunity to make choices about how much child support to pay also threatens resident mothers' autonomy and ability to make financial plans based on their expectations of how much child support the children's father will pay. Some children, such as those with wealthier fathers, may benefit financially from fathers' increased discretion. That mothers may lose autonomy at the same time that children acquire economic advantages reinforces the view that parents' and children's interests do not always coincide (McLanahan 1991).

If joint legal custody is associated with mothers' losses and fathers' gains in ability to make decisions about their children, joint custody may both reflect and increase conflict between parents. Children suffer from parental discord, whether or not their parents are married

(Emery 1982; Hetherington et al. 1982; Peterson and Zill 1986; Rutter 1971). The Wisconsin findings suggest that social researchers should focus more attention on factors that may alleviate children's exposure to conflict or to certain types of conflict. For example, children have more negative reactions to parents' overt expressions of disagreement than when parents disagree privately but do not express this in front of the children and do not try to draw the children into the disagreement (Hetherington et al. 1982). Similarly, "parallel parenting" after divorce in which parents avoid contact with each other to limit conflict may facilitate children's beneficial involvement with both parents after divorce (Furstenberg and Cherlin 1991). The development and administration of more universal criteria for allocating and enforcing child support awards and payments may reduce parents' negotiations and disagreements about money, a major source of conflict between both married and formerly married parents. Thus, child support reforms may reduce conflict at the same time that custody and other changes in family law increase it.

Notes

This project was supported in part by a grant from the National Institute of Child Health and Human Development (HD-24751) to myself and Nora Cate Schaeffer and by a grant from the Office of the Assistant Secretary for Planning and Evaluation, U.S. Department of Health and Human Services, to the Institute for Research on Poverty (91ASPE236A). Computing was provided by the Center for Demography and Ecology, which receives core support from the Center for Population Research of the National Institute of Child Health and Human Development (HD-5876). The opinions expressed here are my own and are not those of the sponsoring institutions. A version of this paper was presented at the annual meeting of the Association for Public Policy Analysis and Management, Bethesda, Md., October 1991. I am grateful to Irwin Garfinkel, Robert Lerman, and Steven Sandell for helpful comments.

1. I focus on divorced families because the CRD and PS1 do not provide representative samples of children from all nonmarital relationships. The CRD does provide a reasonable sample of nonmarital families who are drawn into the family court system, but my emphasis throughout is on all children who might receive child support, both those in and outside the court system. See Seltzer (1991b) for a description of nonresident father–child relationships, based on a national sample of marital and nonmarital families.

2. California is another state that provides statutory definitions of legal and physical custody (e.g., Mnookin et al. 1990). Increased debate about joint custody may account for the legislative move to incorporate distinct definitions of legal and physical custody in state statutes. See Grove (1987) for a more general discussion of custody laws by state.

3. This discussion focuses exclusively on instances in which parents are responsible for children's care, even though physical and/or legal custody may be awarded to another adult guardian. Even taking into account formally arranged foster care, it is rare for nonparents to be awarded custody.

4. Attention to families with joint custody is well justified by the emphasis on this child care arrangement in family law and other public policy. Yet, this attention does not correspond to the proportion of children or families who adopt shared living arrangements.

5. Comparison of the court record specifications of where children lived for half of the year with parents' reports shows that the court records accurately reflect children's living arrangements during the first few years after divorce (Schaeffer, Seltzer, and Klawitter 1991).

6. These findings also suggest that questions such as the custody and visitation question in the 1990 Current Population Survey—Child Support Supplement (CPS—CSS) may confuse respondents by asking about "custody" without distinguishing between formal authority and where the children live. The CPS—CSS asks, "Does the child(ren)'s father have visitation privileges, joint custody, or neither?" and the number of days the father had custody of or visited the children (U.S. Bureau of the Census 1990, Form CPS-1) [emphasis added].

7. The analysis is a multinomial logit in which the dependent variable is a cross-classification of legal by physical custody type, as defined earlier in table 5.1. Independent variables include each parent's income, number of minor children, age of youngest child, marital duration, whether both parents had an attorney, date of the final divorce action, whether there were missing data on income, and whether the case was heard in Milwaukee County, the most urban area in the CRD.

8. These figures include cases without any child support awards. Nearly 90 percent of cases with joint legal custody and 83 percent of those with mother-custody had awards. The differential by custody type is diminished slightly for the subsample of cases with child support awards: about $3,950 vs. $3,110.

9. Evidence for the association between awards and custody comes from an analysis in which these components of divorce settlements are treated as jointly determined because decisions about custody are made in the context of other aspects of divorce settlements, such as child support. The analysis is a probit (joint legal custody vs. mother custody) and tobit (dollars of child support awarded) with correlated disturbances. For more details, see Seltzer (1991a).

10. The simulation shows custody differences in the effects of parents' incomes on child support based on an analysis in which the custody differences are statistically significant. The simulation in table 5.2 evaluates these differences at arbitrarily selected levels of income.

11. For a discussion of ambiguity in the father's role after separation, see Seltzer (1991b).

12. Comparisons of resident mothers' and nonresident fathers' reports about child support payments through the court system show that mothers' reports are more accurate, at least in aggregate comparisons with an external criterion. Nonresponse bias in child support estimates is also smaller for resident mothers than for nonresident fathers in divorced families (Schaeffer et al. 1991).

13. The analysis controls for parents' education, mother's household income from sources other than child support, receipt of Aid to Families with Dependent Children (AFDC), mother's remarriage, both parents' residence in Wisconsin, number of children, years separated, years separated squared, whether the parents had a child support

award, and age of child identified in the frequency of visits question. Visits and payments were modeled jointly in a bivariate tobit with correlated errors (see Seltzer, Schaeffer, and Charng [1989] for details of the analysis).

References

Albiston, Catherine R., Eleanor E. Maccoby, and Robert R. Mnookin. 1990. "Does Joint Legal Custody Matter?" *Stanford Law and Policy Review* 2(1): 167–79.

Arendell, Terry. 1986. *Mothers and Divorce: Legal, Economic and Social Dilemmas.* Berkeley: University of California Press.

Becker, Gary S. 1965. "A Theory of the Allocation of Time." *Economic Journal* 75: 493–517.

Braver, Sanford L., Nancy Gonzalez, Sharlene A. Wolchik, and Irwin N. Sandler. 1989. "Economic Hardship and Psychological Distress in Custodial Mothers." *Journal of Divorce* 12(4): 19–34.

Bruch, Carol S. 1987. "Problems Inherent in Designing Child Support Guidelines." In *Essentials of Child Support Guidelines Development: Economic Issues and Policy Considerations* (41). Washington, D.C.: U.S. Family Support Administration, Office of Child Support Enforcement.

California Senate. Task Force on Family Equity. 1987. *Final Report.* Sacramento, Calif. June.

Clingempeel, W. Glenn, and N. Dickon Reppucci. 1982. "Joint Custody after Divorce: Major Issues and Goals for Research." *Psychological Bulletin* 91: 102–27.

Emery, Robert E. 1982. "Interparental Conflict and the Children of Discord and Divorce." *Psychological Bulletin* 92(2): 310–30.

Felner, Robert D., and Lisa Terre. 1987. "Child Custody Dispositions and Children's Adaptation following Divorce." In *Psychology and Child Custody Determinations: Knowledge, Roles, and Expertise*, edited by Lois A. Weithorn (106–53). Lincoln: University of Nebraska Press.

Fineman, Martha. 1988. "Dominant Discourse, Professional Language, and Legal Change in Child Custody Decisionmaking." *Harvard Law Review* 101: 727–74.

Furstenberg, Frank F., Jr. 1988. "Good Dads—Bad Dads: Two Faces of Fatherhood." In *The Changing American Family and Public Policy*, edited by Andrew J. Cherlin (193–218). Washington, D.C.: Urban Institute Press.

Furstenberg, Frank F., Jr., and Andrew J. Cherlin. 1991. *Divided Families: What Happens to Children When Parents Part.* Cambridge, Mass.: Harvard University Press.

Furstenberg, Frank F., Jr., S. Philip Morgan, and Paul D. Allison. 1987. "Paternal Participation and Children's Well-Being." *American Sociological Review* 52: 695–701.

Furstenberg, Frank F., Jr., Christine Winquist Nord, James L. Peterson, and Nicholas Zill. 1983. "The Life Course of Children of Divorce." *American Sociological Review* 48: 656–68.

Garfinkel, Irwin, and Elizabeth Uhr. 1984. "A New Approach to Child Support." *Public Interest* 75: 111–22.

Garfinkel, Irwin, and Sara S. McLanahan. 1986. *Single Mothers and Their Children.* Washington, D.C.: Urban Institute Press.

————. 1990. "The Effects of the Child Support Provisions of the Family Support Act of 1988 on Child Well-Being." *Population Research and Policy Review* 9(3): 205–34.

Goldstein, Joseph. 1984. "In Whose Best Interest?" In *Joint Custody and Shared Parenting,* edited by Jay Folberg (47–55). Washington, D.C.: Association of Family and Conciliation Courts.

Grief, Geoffrey L. 1985. *Single Fathers.* Lexington, Mass.: Lexington Books.

Grove, Patricia L. 1987. "Joint Custody: A Concept that Has Come of Age but Needs Refinement." *American Journal of Family Law* 1: 23–55.

Hess, Robert D., and Kathleen A. Camara. 1979. "Post-Divorce Family Relationships as Mediating Factors in the Consequences of Divorce for Children." *Journal of Social Issues* 35: 79–96.

Hetherington, E. Mavis, Martha Cox, and Roger Cox. 1982. "Effects of Divorce on Parents and Children." In *Nontraditional Families,* edited by Michael E. Lamb (233–88). Hillsdale, N.J.: Lawrence Erlbaum.

Holden, Karen C., and Pamela J. Smock. 1991. "The Economic Costs of Marital Dissolution: Why Do Women Bear a Disproportionate Cost?" *Annual Review of Sociology* 17: 51–78.

Ilfeld, Frederic W., Holly Zingale Ilfeld, and John R. Alexander. 1984. "Does Joint Custody Work? A First Look at Outcome Data of Relitigation." In *Joint Custody and Shared Parenting,* edited by Jay Folberg (136–56). Washington, D.C.: Association of Family and Conciliation Courts.

Koel, Amy, Susan C. Clark, W.P.C. Phear, and Barbara B. Hauser. 1988. "A Comparison of Joint and Sole Legal Custody Arrangements." In *Impact of Divorce, Single Parenting, and Stepparenting on Children,* edited by E. Mavis Hetherington and Josephine D. Arasteh (73–90). Hillsdale, N.J.: Lawrence Erlbaum.

Lund, Mary. 1987. "The Non-custodial Father: Common Challenges in Parenting after Divorce." In *Reassessing Fatherhood: New Observations on Fathers and the Modern Family,* edited by Charlie Lewis and Margaret O'Brien (212–24). Beverly Hills, Calif.: Sage Publications.

Maccoby, Eleanor R., Charlene E. Depner, and Robert H. Mnookin. 1988. "Custody of Children following Divorce." In *Impact of Divorce, Single Parenting, and Stepparenting on Children*, edited by E. Mavis Hetherington and Josephine D. Arasteh (91–114). Hillsdale, N.J.: Lawrence Erlbaum.

McLanahan, Sara. 1991. "The Two Faces of Divorce: Women's and Children's Interests." In *Macro-Micro Linkages in Sociology*, edited by Joan Huber (193–207). Newbury Park, Calif.: Sage Publications.

McLanahan, Sara, and Karen Booth. 1989. "Mother-Only Families: Problems, Prospects, and Politics." *Journal of Marriage and the Family* 51(3): 557–80.

McLindon, James B. 1987. "Separate but Unequal: The Economic Disaster of Divorce for Women and Children." *Family Law Quarterly* 21: 351–409.

Mnookin, Robert H., and Lewis Kornhauser. 1979. "Bargaining in the Shadow of the Law." *Yale Law Journal* 88: 950–97.

Mnookin, Robert H., Eleanor E. Maccoby, Catherine R. Albiston, and Charlene E. Depner. 1990. "Private Ordering Revisited: What Custodial Arrangements Are Parents Negotiating?" In *Divorce Reform at the Crossroads*, edited by Stephen D. Sugarman and Herma Hill Kay (37–74). New Haven, Conn.: Yale University Press.

Patterson, Melissa. 1984. "The Added Cost of Shared Lives." In *Joint Custody and Shared Parenting*, edited by Jay Folberg (72–76). Washington, D.C.: Association of Family and Conciliation Courts.

Pearson, Jessica, and Nancy Thoennes. 1988. "Supporting Children after Divorce: The Influence of Custody on Support Levels and Payments." *Family Law Quarterly* 22: 319–39.

Peterson, James L., and Nicholas Zill. 1986. "Marital Disruption, Parent-Child Relationships, and Behavior Problems in Children." *Journal of Marriage and the Family* 48: 295–307.

Rutter, Michael L. 1971. "Parent-Child Separation: Psychological Effects on the Children." *Journal of Child Psychology and Psychiatry* 12: 233–60.

Sawhill, Isabel V. 1977. "Economic Perspectives on the Family." *Daedalus* 106: 115–25.

Schaeffer, Nora Cate, Judith A. Seltzer, and Marieka Klawitter. 1991. "Nonresponse and Response Bias: Resident and Nonresident Parents' Reports about Child Support." *Sociological Methods and Research* 20: 30–59.

Schepard, Andrew. 1985. "Taking Children Seriously: Promoting Cooperative Custody after Divorce." *Texas Law Review* 64: 687–788.

Schulman, Joanne, and Valerie Pitt. 1982. "Second Thoughts on Joint Child Custody: Analysis of Legislation and Its Implications for Women and Children." *Golden Gate University Law Review* 12: 539–77.

Seltzer, Judith A. 1990a. "Child Support Reform and the Welfare of U.S.

Children." National Survey of Families and Households Working Paper 34. Madison: University of Wisconsin–Madison.

————. 1990b. "Legal and Physical Custody Arrangements in Recent Divorces." *Social Science Quarterly* 71: 250–66.

————. 1991a. "Legal Custody Arrangements and Children's Economic Welfare." *American Journal of Sociology* 96(4): 895–929.

————. 1991b. "Relationships between Fathers and Children Who Live Apart: The Father's Role after Separation." *Journal of Marriage and the Family* 53(1): 79–101.

Seltzer, Judith A., and Suzanne M. Bianchi. 1988. "Children's Contact with Absent Parents." *Journal of Marriage and the Family* 50: 666–78.

Seltzer, Judith A., and Nora Cate Schaeffer. 1989. "Another Day, Another Dollar: Effects of Legal Custody on Paying Child Support and Visiting Children." Paper presented at the annual meeting of the American Sociological Association, San Francisco, August.

Seltzer, Judith A., Nora Cate Schaeffer, and Hong-wen Charng. 1989. "Family Ties after Divorce: The Relationship between Visiting and Paying Child Support." *Journal of Marriage and the Family* 51(4): 1013–31.

Sweet, James A., and Larry L. Bumpass. 1987. *American Families and Households.* New York: Sage Publications.

U.S. Bureau of the Census. 1990. *Questionnaire for Current Population Survey, Child Support Supplement.* Washington, D.C.: U.S. Bureau of the Census. April.

U.S. Family Support Administration. 1990. *Grant Guide for Child Access Demonstration Projects.* Washington, D.C.: U.S. Family Support Administration, Office of Child Support Enforcement.

Wallerstein, Judith S., and Joan Berlin Kelly. 1980. *Surviving the Breakup: How Children and Parents Cope with Divorce.* New York: Basic Books.

Wallerstein, Judith S., and Dorothy S. Huntington. 1983. "Bread and Roses: Nonfinancial Issues Related to Fathers' Economic Support of their Children following Divorce." In *The Parental Child-Support Obligation*, edited by Judith Cassetty (135–55). Lexington, Mass.: Lexington Books.

Wallerstein, Judith S., and Sandra Blakeslee. 1989. *Second Chances: Men, Women, and Children a Decade after Divorce.* New York: Ticknor and Fields.

Weiss, Yoram, and Robert J. Willis. 1985. "Children as Collective Goods and Divorce Settlements." *Journal of Labor Economics* 3: 268–92.

Weitzman, Lenore J. 1985. *The Divorce Revolution: The Unexpected Social and Economic Consequences for Women and Children in America.* New York: Free Press.

Wisconsin Assembly Bill 205 [1987], published 1988. Sec. 34.

Wisconsin Department of Health and Social Services. 1987. "Child Support

Percentage of Income Standard." *Register*, chap. HSS 80: 316-1–316-14.

Wisconsin Statutes. 1987. *Actions Affecting the Child*, chap. 767.25. Madison, Wis.

Wolchik, Sharlene A., Sanford L. Braver, and Irwin N. Sandler. 1985. "Maternal versus Joint Custody: Children's Postseparation Experiences and Adjustment." *Journal of Clinical Child Psychology* 14: 4–10.

Wright, David W., and Sharon J. Price. 1986. "Court-ordered Child Support Payment: The Effect of the Former Spouse Relationship on Compliance." *Journal of Marriage and the Family* 48: 869–74.

Chapter Six

PATERNITY ESTABLISHMENT IN AFDC CASES: THREE WISCONSIN COUNTIES

Sara S. McLanahan, Patricia R. Brown, and Renee A. Monson

A major weakness in the current U.S. child support system is its failure to establish paternity for children born to unmarried parents. Without paternity, these children have no legal claim on their fathers' income, and the decision to pay child support is left entirely to the fathers' discretion. In 1989, 77 percent of children living with a divorced mother had a child support award and 59 percent received child support payments. For children born to unmarried parents, the figures were 24 percent and 17 percent, respectively (U.S. Bureau of the Census 1991). In recognition of this disparity, the Family Support Act of 1988 contained several provisions explicitly aimed at increasing paternity establishment. The act required states to: (1) increase the proportion of Aid to Families with Dependent Children (AFDC) cases with child support awards; (2) obtain social security numbers from both parents in conjunction with the issuance of birth certificates; and (3) require parties in contested paternity cases to take a genetic test. The act also exhorted states to simplify paternity establishment by setting up civil procedures for voluntary acknowledgement of paternity and for resolving disputes in contested cases.

In December 1989 we began an evaluation of the paternity adjudication process in the state of Wisconsin. Our evaluation included interviews with key officials at the state and local levels, direct observations of several stages of the adjudication process in both the Office of Child Support Enforcement (OCSE) and the family court, and surveys of records from the OCSE caseload. This chapter reports on analyses based on the OCSE records in Dane, Racine, and Milwaukee counties. These counties differ substantially with respect to the size of the general population. Milwaukee is the largest county with a population of over 959,000 in 1990. Dane County has a population of over 367,000 and Racine County has about 175,000 people. The counties also differ in racial composition. Dane and Racine are 10 and 11 percent nonwhite respectively, and Milwaukee is 25 percent nonwhite. Paternity adjudication rates range from 42 percent in Milwaukee County to 69 percent in Dane County.

The remainder of this chapter is divided into five parts: first, an examination of the administrative structure of the paternity adjudication process in Wisconsin; second, a discussion of our sample and data collection techniques; third, a description of our findings regarding the paternity adjudication process in the three Wisconsin counties, including the demographic characteristics of each county's caseload and success rates at different stages of the process; and, fourth, a presentation of our results from a multivariate analysis. All of the analyses reported here are based on samples taken from the AFDC caseload and processed by the Office of Child Support Enforcement; the findings are therefore generalizable to this population only.

THE ADMINISTRATIVE PROCESS

The administrative process for identifying and locating the alleged father of a child whose mother is receiving AFDC is basically the same in each of the three Wisconsin counties we studied. The process comprises the following steps: (1) All AFDC cases with a child eligible for paternity adjudication are identified by the Social Services Office and a referral is made to the Office of Child Support Enforcement in that county. Basic demographic information concerning the mother and any child for whom AFDC benefits are claimed is collected and recorded by the Social Services Office. (2) After receiving a referral, the OCSE sends a letter to the mother, notifying her that she is required to cooperate with the paternity adjudication process as a condition of continued eligibility for AFDC benefits. The letter sets an appointment date for the mother and OCSE worker. (3) The mother comes in for an appointment, called an intake interview, and the interviewer collects information about the pregnancy, birth, and alleged father of the child. If the mother does not cooperate with OCSE, she may be sanctioned by having her AFDC grant reduced by an amount equal to her individual benefit for the period in which she refuses to cooperate. The OCSE has the authority to recommend sanctions, but the ultimate decision to sanction is made by the Social Services agency. (4) After information on the alleged father is obtained, the OCSE sends a letter asking him to appear in Family Court for a paternity hearing. At this stage, the alleged father can either admit or contest paternity. If he does not appear at the paternity hearing, the judge may enter a default judgment. (5) If he appears but contests paternity, blood tests are ordered for the alleged father and the child. In cases where the tests confirm the mother's allegation, the father is again asked to acknowledge paternity. If he continues to deny responsibility, the judge rules on the allegation.

DATA AND STUDY DESIGN

To obtain our sample, we scanned the AFDC caseload in each county in December 1988 and identified families with at least one child eligible for paternity adjudication (i.e., a child born to unmarried parents). From this universe, we randomly selected approximately 600 cases from each county (in Dane County the actual number of cases selected was 573; in Milwaukee County, 600; and in Racine County, 599). If a record contained more than one eligible child, the youngest child on each record was designated as the focal child. Thus, our sample is a sample of families with an eligible child rather than a sample of all children eligible for paternity adjudication.

Once the sample was selected, information on the parents and child in each case was obtained from the AFDC record and OCSE file. For the mother, we recorded information on current age (as of December 1988), age at child's birth, and number of children eligible for paternity adjudication listed on the AFDC record. In Milwaukee and Racine counties we also recorded information on the mother's race and current marital status. For the focal child, we recorded information on age (as of December 1988) and state of residence at birth. In cases where information on the state was not available on the OCSE record, we used the mother's AFDC record to determine whether the child was born before or after the mother moved to Wisconsin.

Information on the father was taken from the OCSE file and included age as of December 1988, age at child's birth, race, state of residence at the time of the intake interview, and social security number. In Racine and Milwaukee counties we also collected information on the father's employer. In many instances, complete information on the father was not available, because fathers' information was contingent on a successful intake interview with the mother.

In addition to gathering data on the characteristics of parents and children, we also recorded the dates of key administrative events, including the date a letter was sent to the mother asking her to come for an interview, the date the intake interview occurred, and the date paternity was established. This task turned out to be more difficult than we had anticipated. In Milwaukee and Racine counties there was often no record of an initial letter being sent to the mother, even though an intake interview had occurred. In some of these cases, the mother may well have been sent a letter but a copy was not placed in her file. In others, the mother may have contacted the OCSE herself or appeared for an intake interview without a letter. Similarly, in some cases a considerable amount of information on the father was found in a file, although no date for an intake interview was recorded. Again, this may reflect poor record-keeping or a different administrative procedure (e.g., information on the father was collected by phone or mail, from correspondence with other counties or states, or from Social Services).

In addition to collecting information on the date of the initial letter, the intake interview, and adjudication, we also recorded information on the use of sanctions (whether the OCSE recommended that sanctions be used against the mother) and on the type of adjudication (whether the father admitted paternity and whether blood tests were used). The decision to gather data on sanctions and contested adjudication was made after the Dane County data were collected, and therefore this information was available only for Milwaukee and Racine counties. Finally, in Milwaukee and Racine counties, we collected data on the reasons for nonadjudication. This information was used to examine unsuccessful cases in more detail.

Since the purpose of our study was to evaluate paternity establishment within the Office of Child Support Enforcement, four types of cases were eliminated from the sample prior to our analysis: (1) cases in which paternity was established outside the OCSE, including those adjudicated previously in another location, (2) cases in which the child was legitimated by the marriage of the parents, (3) cases where the father held custody of the child, and, (4) cases that were closed because the youngest child had reached age 18 or because the mother had left the county. These cases represented a trivial proportion of the caseload in all three counties.

THREE CASE STUDIES

This section describes the adjudication process in each of the three counties. The discussion is organized around the following questions: What did the paternity caseload look like in December 1988 in terms of the demographic characteristics of parents and children? How well were the counties doing with respect to (1) making referrals to the OSCE, (2) conducting intake interviews with the mother, (3) gathering information on the alleged fathers, and (4) establishing paternity? Where were the major roadblocks? Were they due to lack of administrative capacity or to noncompliance on the part of parents?

Dane County

The OCSE office in Dane County has a child support caseload of 7,100 cases and a staff of 24 people. Of the 573 cases yielded through our sampling procedure in Dane County, 21 were identified as having had paternity adjudicated outside of the OCSE, either through parents' marriage or prior adjudication, and 8 additional cases were marked closed. The remaining 544 cases were designated as the official OCSE caseload. We were unable to locate a file in the OCSE office for 10 of these cases, and they were treated as missing data.

DEMOGRAPHIC CHARACTERISTICS

Information on the demographic characteristics of mothers, focal children, and alleged fathers in the Dane County sample is reported in table 6.1. For mothers and children, the percentages are based on the entire OCSE caseload. Missing data for mothers and children were very low, ranging from 0 to 4.4 percent. For fathers, the percentages are based on a subsample of cases where a single alleged father was named by the mother. Missing data on fathers' characteristics ranged from 6.9 percent to 19.0 percent.

In 1988, the typical mother referred to the Dane County OCSE was in her late twenties (see table 6.1). Just over 30 percent of the mothers were in their teens when the focal child was born. Almost two-thirds had only one child listed on the AFDC record, and only 10 percent had more than two children listed. We did not collect information on mother's race or current marital status in Dane County. However, assuming that father's race is a good proxy for mother's race, it appears that over half the Dane County sample was white. Clearly, these women do not fit the stereotype of the nonwhite, welfare mother caring for several out-of-wedlock children born to different fathers.

The typical child in the Dane County OCSE caseload was between 2 and 3 years old (see table 6.1). About a third of the sample was under 18 months and another third was over 4 years old. A high proportion of the focal children were born in Wisconsin—about 71 percent.

The typical father was also in his late twenties at the time of the

Table 6.1 DEMOGRAPHIC CHARACTERISTICS OF MOTHERS, CHILDREN, AND
FATHERS IN THREE WISCONSIN COUNTIES SAMPLED

	Dane County	Racine County	Milwaukee County
Mothers' Characteristics:			
Age in 1988			
Under 20 years old	6.8	8.5	10.1
Over 30 years old	31.3	30.6	36.1
Missing data	(0.0)	(1.2)	(2.5)
Age at child's birth			
Under 20 years old	31.5	33.3	34.4
Race (nonwhite)	—	66.4	83.0
Missing data		(6.7)	(7.0)
Marital status (unmarried)	—	72.2	76.3
Missing data		(5.2)	(3.0)
Number of children on grant			
One only	64.2	56.8	48.0
More than 2	10.7	18.1	23.8
Missing data	(0.0)	(5.0)	(4.8)
Children's Characteristics:			
Age in 1988			
Under 18 months	31.2	26.0	27.3
Over 4 years	32.8	39.9	41.7
Missing data	(4.4)	(5.1)	(5.4)
Born in Wisconsin	71.0	68.8	57.5
Missing data	(13.8)	(24.2)	(38.5)
Data from AFDC record	—	82.8	82.3
Fathers' Characteristics:			
Age in 1988			
Under 20	4.6	10.2	5.5
Over 30	39.3	34.7	48.0
Missing data	(6.9)	(22.2)	(32.5)
Age at child's birth			
Under 20	15.3	23.9	21.8
Race (nonwhite)	45.9	72.3	84.9
Missing data	(12.1)	(11.7)	(28.4)
Lives in Wisconsin	71.5	83.3	83.4
Missing data	(19.0)	(17.9)	(28.4)

Note: Dashes (—) denote data not collected. See text for explanation of data.

intake interview (see table 6.1). Only 15 percent of these men were teenagers when the focal child was born. Again, this profile does not fit the stereotype of the teenage father too young to accept responsibility for supporting his offspring. Fifty-four percent of the fathers were white, and 71 percent lived in Wisconsin. It should be reemphasized that our estimates of fathers' characteristics were based on a subset of fathers for whom an intake interview with the mother was completed. Information for fathers is therefore less complete than that for mothers and children. In addition, some mothers were unable (or unwilling) to provide full information on the fathers, even though an interview was carried out. Missing information on fathers' characteristics for the subsample of cases with an intake interview ranged from a low of 6.9 percent, for age, to a high of 19 percent, for state of residence.

THE ADJUDICATION PROCESS

Table 6.2 provides an overall picture of the flow of cases through various stages of the paternity adjudication process. The first row reports the original OCSE caseload as determined from the AFDC records. The second and third rows report cases that were missing from the OCSE files. Row 4 reports the number of cases that were

Table 6.2 DATA ON CASE FLOW THROUGH DIFFERENT STAGES IN PATERNITY ADJUDICATION PROCESS IN THREE WISCONSIN COUNTIES

	Dane County	Racine County	Milwaukee County
Raw Numbers:			
1. Original OCSE caseload	552	577	590
2. Closed cases	8	5	7
3. Missing/out cases	10	79	79
4. Available cases	534	493	504
5. Cases with intake	484	447	358
6. Cases with full information	439	399	305
7. Cases adjudicated	381	352	247
Percentage of cases:			
8. With a file	96.7	85.4	85.4
9. With an interview	90.6	90.7	71.0
10. With full information	90.7	89.3	85.2
11. With paternity adjudicated	86.8	88.2	81.0
Total adjudication rate	69.0	61.0	41.9
Adjusted adjudication rate	71.3	71.4	49.0
Recent adjudication rate	74.0	71.6	37.5

located and therefore available for analysis, and rows 5 through 7 report the number of cases that progressed through each stage of the process.

The next panel of figures in table 6.2 report transition rates for each stage of the adjudication process. Row 8 reports the percentage of cases for which we were able to locate an OCSE record. Row 9 reports the percentage of cases with an OCSE record that had an intake interview. Row 10 reports the percentage of cases with an interview that provided full information on the father (name, date of birth, race, and address). And row 11 reports the percentage of cases with full information that had paternity adjudicated.[1]

The last three rows in table 6.2 report the total paternity adjudication rate (using the entire eligible OCSE caseload as the denominator), the adjusted adjudication rate (using the available cases as the denominator), and the recent adjudication rate (as of June 1990, using children born since January of 1988 in both the numerator and denominator), respectively.[2]

What is most striking about table 6.2 is the high success rate in Dane County at each of the stages. About 97 percent of the original sample had an OCSE file. Of this group, about 91 percent had been interviewed by an OCSE worker. Of those interviewed, about 91 percent provided full information on the father. And of those cases with full information, almost 87 percent had paternity adjudicated.

The overall paternity adjudication rate of the Dane County OSCE as of June 1990 was nearly 70 percent. Excluding cases for which there was no file, the rate was slightly higher, 71.3 percent. Given that the national average ranged between 25 percent and 33 percent at that time, and given that the average for the state of Michigan, which is generally acknowledged to have the best rate in the nation, was about 66 percent, we conclude that Dane County had an outstanding record in the area of paternity establishment.[3] Moreover, for the youngest children in our sample, the adjudication rate was 74 percent, which indicates that the Dane County system was moving swiftly as well as effectively. The high success rate was achieved by the time new entrants were 18 months old.

Table 6.3 provides more detailed information on the rate of the case flow. The top panel reports the age of the child when the case was first opened (defined here as the mailing date of the letter requesting the mother to come for an interview). The second panel reports the age of the child at the time of the intake interview, and the third panel reports the age of the child at the time of adjudication. These numbers are based on cases for which an OSCE file was found *and* for which

Table 6.3 ADMINISTRATIVE PRACTICES REGARDING PATERNITY ADJUDICATION
IN THREE WISCONSIN COUNTIES

	Dane County	Racine County	Milwaukee County
Age of child at start of case			
Median age (in days)	21	59	—
Case started before birth (%)	44.3	18.7	—
Missing data (%)	(16.8)	(27.6)	(83.1)
Age of child at intake interview			
Median age (in days)	55	82	288
Intake before birth (%)	37.4	17.7	5.2
Missing data (%)	(15.5)	(19.2)	(28.8)
Age of child at adjudication			
Median age (in months)	8.3	8.5	12.5
Adjudication by six months (%)	38.4	37.5	17.5
Missing data (%)	(3.7)	(0.0)	(7.3)
Sanctions			
Percentage of caseload	—	31.8	3.0
Prior to intake (%)	—	68.0	80.0
After intake (%)	—	32.0	20.0

Note: Information on the use of sanctions was not collected in Dane County.
Dashes (—) indicate not available.

information was available on the dates of the letter and interview. The
numbers in the third panel were based on successful cases only. The
amount of missing data for each variable is reported so that the reader
is aware of the extent to which the estimates are based on a subsample
that may be selective of the population as a whole.

The results in table 6.3 show that the paternity adjudication process
begins quite early in Dane County. The median age of the child when
the case was started was 21 days. Forty-four percent of the cases were
started *before* the child's birth. At the time of the intake interview, the
typical child was between 4 and 5 months old. Thirty-seven percent
of the interviews occurred before birth. Finally, for cases in which
paternity was established (over 70 percent), the median age of the
child at adjudication was 8 months. Information on the use of sanctions was not collected in Dane County.

Racine County

Data collection began in Racine County in August 1990 and continued
for three months. Since the number of months that elapsed between

the date of sample selection and the date of data collection was longer in Racine than in Dane County, one might have expected the paternity adjudication rate to be slightly higher in Racine County, all else being equal. (However, as will be discussed here, this was not the case.) The data collection instrument in Racine was an expanded version of the Dane County questionnaire. In addition to the information collected in Dane County, the survey recorded data on the mother's race and current marital status and whether sanctions and blood tests were used by OCSE workers.

The OCSE caseload in Racine County was 10,723 and the staff size was 21. Of the 599 cases in the sample taken from the AFDC caseload in Racine County, 22 of these were adjudicated prior to OCSE referral and another 5 were deemed ineligible because the case was closed. The remaining 572 cases were designated as the eligible OCSE caseload; of these, we were unable to locate 79. One explanation for the large number of missing cases is that our shortened data collection period (two and a half months instead of five months) did not allow enough time for files "in use" when we began our data collection effort to be returned to their original location. Racine County was in the midst of converting their manual filing system to a computerized system when our data collection began, and this overhaul could partly explain the higher incidence of missing files in that county.

DEMOGRAPHIC CHARACTERISTICS

As in Dane County, the typical mother in the Racine County caseload was in her late twenties when our sample was drawn (see table 6.1). About one-third were teenagers when the focal child was born. Over half of the mothers in Racine County had only one child listed on the AFDC grant, and only 18 percent had more than two children listed. This figure suggests a slightly large family size in Racine compared with Dane County. A majority of the mothers in Racine were non-white, and over two-thirds had never been married.

The typical child in the Racine County caseload was somewhat older than the typical child in Dane County (see table 6.1). About 40 percent were over 4 years old and about a quarter were under 18 months. At least 69 percent were born in the state of Wisconsin. Because of the large number of missing files in Racine County, we used information on the AFDC record to determine the child's state of birth. The latter showed that about 83 percent of the children in the Racine County sample were Wisconsin-born.

The average alleged father in Racine County was somewhat younger than his counterpart in Dane County (see table 6.1). About 35 percent of the fathers were over 30 years of age, and about 10 percent were under 20 years of age. Nearly a quarter were teenagers when their child was born. Eighty-three percent were reported as living in Wisconsin at the time of the intake interview. The latter figure is somewhat surprising, since Racine County is an urban area near the state border. This estimate may be biased because of the large amount of missing data on fathers' characteristics. Again, recall that our percentages are based on a subsample of cases in which a file was available and a single father was named during the intake interview. In addition, our estimates exclude cases in which the mother did not provide full information on the father. Missing data of the latter type ranged from a low of about 12 percent for fathers' race to a high of 22 percent for fathers' age. The biggest difference between fathers in Dane and Racine counties is race. Whereas a majority of Dane County fathers were white, less than 28 percent of Racine fathers fell into this category.

THE ADJUDICATION PROCESS

The flow of paternity cases in Racine County is reported in table 6.2. According to these numbers, 85.4 percent of eligible cases had a record on file at the Racine County OCSE. Of these, 90.7 percent had had an intake interview, and 89.3 percent of cases with an interview contained "full" information on the father.[4] Finally, 88.2 percent of the cases with full information on the father were successfully adjudicated by the time of our study. The principal difference between Racine and Dane Counties was the percentage of cases with a file. Dane County did a slightly better job of collecting full information from the mothers, and Racine was slightly ahead in establishing paternity for cases with full information. But these differences were minor.

The last panel in table 6.2 reports the overall paternity adjudication rate for Racine County as well as the rate for recent cases. Although Racine County's overall record (61 percent) is not quite as good as Dane County's (69 percent) or the state of Michigan's (about 66 percent), it is well above average for the nation as a whole. Moreover, if one excludes cases for which no file was found, the Racine record is nearly identical to that of Dane County. Similarly, when examining only recent cases, Racine County appears to be doing about as well as Dane County, even taking into account the cases with missing files.

Table 6.3 reports time-lapse information for Racine County. In Dane County, the start date for each case was designated as the date a letter was sent from the OCSE to the mother. The large number of missing letters makes this definition problematic for Racine County. Almost 28 percent of the cases with an OCSE file had no record of a letter being sent to the mother. For those cases with a record of a letter, the median age of the child at the time the letter was sent was about 2 months, with over 18 percent of letters being sent prior to the birth of the child. The median age of the child at the intake interview was 82 days, with about 19 percent of the interviews occurring prior to birth. These numbers suggest that Racine County begins the process of adjudication fairly early, although not as early as Dane County. Finally, for successful cases, the median age of the child at adjudication was 8.5 months, nearly identical to the median age in Dane County.

In Racine, we also collected information on the use of sanctions. The data identify cases where sanctions were *recommended* by the OCSE. The recommendations were in the form of a letter sent from the OCSE to Social Services, requesting that the mother's AFDC benefits (though not the AFDC benefit of her children) be eliminated, due to non-cooperation in paternity establishment. When and if these recommendations for sanctions were actually acted upon cannot be determined from the OCSE record. The data show that the letters were used primarily to "encourage" the mother to come in for an intake interview. In about one-third of the cases, sanctions were threatened in order to gain additional information from the mother after the intake interview.

Finally in Racine County, we recorded additional information on successful and unsuccessful cases. This information is reported in table 6.4. According to our data, in the overwhelming majority of successful cases, fathers admitted to paternity once they were contacted by the OCSE. In over 80 percent of the cases in which the father admitted his responsibility, he did so without a blood test. In only 33 cases was paternity established by default or over the father's objection.

Under "unsuccessful" cases we listed several different obstacles that appeared consistently in the files. These ranged from lack of a name for the father to cases dismissed because of administrative error. It is clear that the most common problems faced by OCSE workers were identifying the father and getting an address for the father. About 64 percent of the cases fell into these two categories. Another 15 percent of the problems were due to administrative delay (i.e., cases with addresses but no action and cases dismissed because of administrative delays).

Milwaukee County

The Milwaukee OCSE caseload was 77,776 in 1990 and the staff size was 104.[5] The Milwaukee sample contained 600 AFDC cases, 10 of

Table 6.4 ANALYSIS OF SUCCESSES AND FAILURES IN PATERNITY
ADJUDICATION IN TWO WISCONSIN COUNTIES

	Racine County	Milwaukee County
Successful Cases:	352	247
Father admits paternity	305	197
Without blood test	248	177
With blood test	57	20
Father does not admit paternity	48	50
Direct denial	6	6
Default judgment	27	30
Missing	15	14
Unsuccessful Cases:	141	257
No name/wrong name	25	36
No address	66	118
Out-of-state	11	28
Address, no action	14	29
Dismissed for error	7	21
Mother left AFDC	13	14
Other	5	11

which were adjudicated outside of OCSE and 7 of which were closed because the mother moved or the child turned 18 years old. Of the remaining 583 cases, 79 were missing from the OCSE system. As in Racine County, the large number of missing files in the Milwaukee OCSE makes our data less reliable than in Dane County.

DEMOGRAPHIC CHARACTERISTICS

The typical mother in the Milwaukee sample was in her late twenties when the sample was taken (table 6.1). Only 10 percent of the mothers were teenagers when we began our study, and only about 34 percent were teenagers when the focal child was born. The greatest difference across the three samples was in family size: less than half of the mothers in the Milwaukee sample had only one child on the AFDC record, and nearly 25 percent had more than two children. Eighty-three percent of the mothers in Milwaukee County were nonwhite, and about 76 percent had never been married.

The children in the Milwaukee sample were slightly older than the children in the other two samples: over 40 percent were over age four (table 6.1). A high percentage of children were born in Wisconsin, about 58 percent. When information from mothers' AFDC records was used instead of information from the OCSE file, the number was higher, about 82 percent, suggesting that about two-thirds of the cases with missing OCSE files were born inside Wisconsin.

Information on fathers' characteristics was even less reliable than information on mothers and children, insofar as additional cases were excluded owing to no intake interview or information missing from the intake interview. For cases with information, the numbers suggest that Milwaukee fathers were somewhat older than fathers in the other two counties (table 6.1). Nearly half were over 30 years old at the time the sample was taken. At the same time, over 20 percent were teen-agers when the child was born, just slightly less than in Racine County. A large proportion of the fathers in Milwaukee County were black—about 85 percent. Thus, the racial contrast between Milwaukee and Dane counties is quite pronounced. About eighty-three percent of the fathers were living in Wisconsin at the time of the intake interview. This number is 12 percentage points higher than the number for Dane County, although, again, it is probably distorted because of missing information.

THE ADJUDICATION PROCESS

Looking at the case flow in Milwaukee County (table 6.2), one sees that 85.4 percent of the original sample had a file at the OCSE that was readily available. Of those, 71 percent of the mothers had completed an intake interview, and 85.2 percent of the intakes had produced "full" information on the alleged father. Eighty-one percent of the cases with full information had paternity established. The last three rows of table 6.2 provide information on overall adjudication rates, adjusted rates, and recent rates, respectively. Milwaukee's adjudication rate is 41.9 percent when all cases are included, 49 percent when cases with missing files are excluded, and 37.5 percent when only recent cases are examined.

Comparing success rates at each stage in the paternity adjudication process, one sees that Milwaukee's performance is below that of Dane's and Racine's at all stages. The difference is especially pronounced at the interview stage. Had Milwaukee achieved the same intake level as Racine County, holding all else constant, its total adjudication rate would have been 53.4 percent instead of 41.9. In other words, over 60 percent of the difference between the two counties is due to differences in the rates of obtaining an intake interview. About 10 percent of the difference between Milwaukee and Racine is due to failure to collect full information, for cases that have an intake interview; and about 20 percent is due to differences in the rate of establishing paternity, for cases that provide full information.

The large number of missing files and the large amount of missing data on letter and interview dates make the time lapse analysis for

Milwaukee County highly unreliable (see table 6.3). In over 83 percent of the cases for which there was a file, no record of a letter being sent to the mother existed. Less than 21 percent of all adjudicated cases contained a record of letters to the mother. Records of intake interviews were more complete, with only 28.8 percent of the cases having missing data on this variable. Here we found that the average length of time between a child's birth and the intake interview was 233 days, between seven and eight months. This was over four times longer than the time lapse in Dane County and about three times longer than the lapse in Racine. For children who had paternity established, the average age at adjudication was just over one year.

Recommendations for sanctions were rare in Milwaukee County. It is possible that, owing to inconsistent record-keeping, sanctions were actually used more often than our figures show. To the extent that the threat of sanctions existed, the records suggest that they were used primarily to encourage the mother to come for an intake interview.

Table 6.4 provides more detailed information on successful and unsuccessful cases. According to our analysis, in successfully adjudicated cases, most fathers in Milwaukee County admitted paternity (197 out of 247 adjudicated cases). In another 30 cases the father did not appear in court and paternity was established in a default judgment by the court. In only six cases was paternity established in spite of the father's denial. With respect to unsuccessful cases, about 70 percent of the problems were due to the lack of a name (or incorrect name) for the father, lack of address for the father, or out-of-state location. Another 20 percent were due to administrative delays.

MULTIVARIATE ANALYSIS

This section presents a multivariate analysis of the determinants of paternity adjudication in Wisconsin. The analysis is designed to answer two questions: Which demographic and administrative characteristics are associated with successful adjudication in Wisconsin? and Which characteristics account for differences across counties? To answer these questions, we combined data from the three counties and estimated an equation that treated adjudication as the outcome variable and demographic and administrative characteristics as predictor variables. Since the outcome variable was dichotomous—adjudicated, not adjudicated—we used a logistic regression model to obtain our parameter estimates. The results are reported in table 6.5.

Table 6.5 EFFECTS OF DEMOGRAPHIC AND ADMINISTRATIVE
CHARACTERISTICS ON PATERNITY ADJUDICATION IN WISCONSIN

	(1)	(2)	(3)
Racine	−.002	−.149	−.048
Milwaukee	−.588*	−.677*	−.488*
Mother's age in 1988		−.026*	−.003
Mother's age at birth		.004	−.187
Mother's race			
Black		.377*	.376
Other		.549*	−.472*
Missing		−.634*	−.308†
Child's birth place			
Outside Wisconsin		−.965*	−.961
Missing		−1.540*	−1.017*
Intake			.903*
Age at intake (in months)			−.006*

Note: * = significant at .05 level, † = significant at .10 level.
See text for explanation of data.

The first column in table 6.5 presents results from a model that included only the county dummy variables. Dane County was the omitted variable. The purpose of the first model was to test whether the cross-county differences presented in table 6.2 were statistically significant. As expected, the coefficient for Racine County was not significant, whereas the coefficient for Milwaukee was.

The second column in table 6.5 reports results from a model that included demographic characteristics of mothers and children. The variables were mother's age in 1988, mother's age at the birth of the focal child, mother's race, and whether the child was born in Wisconsin. We hypothesized that the mother's age in 1988 would have a negative effect on adjudication. We also hypothesized that children born outside Wisconsin to teenage mothers would be less likely to have paternity adjudicated than other children. Finally, we expected nonwhites to have lower adjudication rates than whites. With the exception of race, the demographic composition of the caseloads in the three counties did not differ much, and therefore we did not expect the demographic variables to explain much of the cross-county difference. The coefficients reported in column 2 of table 6.5 behaved as we had expected, with one exception: mother's age at the child's birth was not significant. Similarly, the new variables did not "explain" any of the Milwaukee-Dane difference. In fact, the dummy for Milwaukee was larger in column 2 than in column 1.

The third column in table 6.5 reports results from a model that added two new administrative variables: whether an intake interview occurred and age of the child at the intake interview. We hypothesized that these two variables would be significantly related to adjudication and that they would account for a substantial part of the cross-county difference in adjudication. According to our estimates, both variables were significant and the point estimates were in the expected direction. Having an intake interview increased the likelihood of adjudication, and the age of the child at the time of the intake reduced adjudication. The two new variables accounted for less than 20 percent of the difference between Milwaukee and Dane counties. The fact that the intake variables did not account for more of the cross-county difference was probably because of the unreliability of the Milwaukee data. (Recall that many of the successful cases in Milwaukee had no record of an intake interview.) We suspect that had the data been more reliable, these two variables would have accounted for a much larger share of the difference across counties.

CONCLUSIONS

A number of conclusions can be drawn from the analysis of OCSE records in the three counties. First, and most important, all three of the Wisconsin counties are doing very well. Adjudication rates in Dane and Racine counties are well above the national average for OCSE cases and Milwaukee's rate is close to average. Second, a number of barriers remain which, for policy reasons, can usefully be distinguished as those due to client characteristics and those due to administrative capacity and practices.

We find that the demographic characteristics of the caseloads in all three counties are quite similar. Most of the parents in all three counties were *not* teenagers when their child was born. Most of the mothers did *not* have multiple nonmarital births on their AFDC records, most of the children were born in Wisconsin, and most of the fathers were still living in Wisconsin. Thus, while some of these client characteristics are related to adjudication, they cannot account for the difference in success rates across the three Wisconsin counties. The only major difference in caseload composition was racial composition: the Dane County caseload is over 50 percent white, whereas the Racine and Milwaukee caseloads are predominantly nonwhite. But again, the multivariate analyses shows that while race is related to adjudication, it does not account for the cross-county differences in adjudication rates.

Administrative factors appear to be more important in determining success. The biggest difference between the three counties is caseload size and staff/caseload ratios. In Dane and Racine counties, the ratio is about 300 to 400 cases per staff person whereas in Milwaukee County the ratio is 700 to one. Clearly, Milwaukee's administrative capacity is much weaker than that of Dane or Racine county. It is possible that all of the administrative practices that distinguish Milwaukee from the more successful counties are due to staff overload as opposed to inefficient management.

A second major difference across counties is in record keeping procedures. The Dane County records are more readily available and more complete than the records in Racine or Milwaukee County. We reiterate that Racine was moving offices at the time we were collecting our data, and therefore the absence of some records in that office may have been a temporary phenomenon. The fact that Racine has a very high success rate indicates that they are more efficient than their "missing files" would suggest.

Third, Racine and Dane counties do much better than Milwaukee County at getting an intake interview from the mother. This is very important because over 85 percent of cases with an intake provide full information, and over 80 percent of those with full information have paternity established. Differences in the intake interview account for over half of the difference in success rates across the three counties. Failing to conduct an interview appears to be related to two administrative practices (1) not getting an early start, and (2) not assigning responsibility for intake interviews to OCSE staff. In Dane County, the interview process starts well before the child is born. In both Dane and Racine counties, 38 percent of the cases are adjudicated by the time the child is 6 months old. In contrast, only 5 percent of the Milwaukee cases are interviewed before birth, and only 18 percent of the cases are adjudicated by age six months.

Fourth, about 10 percent of the difference between Racine and Milwaukee is associated with the failure to obtain full information from the mothers and another 20 percent is due to failure to establish paternity for cases with full information. If all of these failures are due to bad information, lack of client cooperation might account for as much as 30 percent of the difference between Racine and Milwaukee Counties. More realistically, at least some of the failure is probably due to administrative practices. The fact that Racine and Dane counties conduct their interviews closer to the time of birth means that mothers have more accurate information about the fathers and fathers are easier to locate.[7] Unfortunately we did not collect information on who conducted the intake interview (an OCSE worker or a social services worker) or where the intake was conducted (at the OCSE office, at the Department of Social Services, or by phone). The absence of information on the intake interview in the Milwaukee OCSE office suggests that this office relied more heavily on social service staff to conduct intake interview. This would make sense given the large client-staff ratio in the Milwaukee child support enforcement office. We recommend that future studies collect information on *who* conducts the intake interview and *where* it takes place.

A final point worth noting is that most fathers in Racine and Milwaukee counties eventually admitted paternity. Less than 20 percent of successful cases were adjudicated by default or in spite of fathers' denial and less than 20 percent required blood tests. This adds support to the argument that administrative practices rather than client cooperation are the key determinants of successful adjudication. It also argues for minimizing the proportion of the caseload that is subjected to judicial procedures.

Notes

1. For this part of the analysis we recoded the data so that each stage in the process was conditional on successful completion of the previous stage. For example, if paternity was established, we coded the case as having full information and as having an intake interview. Similarly, if full information was provided, we coded the case as having an intake interview.

2. Children born in 1989 appeared in our sample if the mother was receiving a maternity benefit in December 1988.

3. The percentage for the national average is based on all children born to unmarried parents whereas our percentages are for children in the AFDC caseload. The national average for AFDC cases is about 40 percent.

4. As in Dane County, we recorded our data so that cases with full information were all coded as having had an interview and cases with paternity established were all coded as having full information on the father.

5. In 1988 a backlog of 5,800 unprocessed paternity cases existed in Milwaukee County. Special funding from the Milwaukee IV-D Office was allocated to Milwaukee from June 1988 through January 1990 to hire additional personnel to work through the backlog. The numbers reported here are for the normal staff size rather than the augmented staff that existed during the catch-up phase. The Milwaukee sample used in our analysis is representative of paternity cases that were initiated during the backlog as well as the

catch-up phases. This should affect paternity adjudication rates in two ways. The large number of backlog cases should reduce adjudication rates, whereas the increased staff size during the catch-up phase should improve adjudication.

6. Of course, a mother may be less willing to provide information when the relationship with the father is ongoing and she is afraid of losing his affection (or his informal support).

References

Garfinkel, Irwin, and Sara S. McLanahan. 1986. *Single Mothers and Their Children: A New American Dilemma.* Washington, D.C.: Urban Institute Press.

Garfinkel, Irwin, Philip Robins, Pat Wong, and Daniel Meyer. 1990. "The Wisconsin Child Support Assurance System: Estimated Effects on Poverty, Labor Supply, Caseloads, and Costs." *Journal of Human Resources* 25 (1, Winter):1–31.

Monson, Renee A., and Sara S. McLanahan. 1990. "A Father for Every Child: Dilemmas of Creating Gender Equality in a Stratified Society." In *Proceedings of the Second Annual Women's Policy Research Conference.* Washington, D.C.: Institute for Women's Policy Research, June.

U.S. Bureau of the Census. 1988. *Statistical Abstracts of the United States.* Washington, D.C.: U.S. Bureau of the Census.

————. 1989. "Child Support and Alimony: 1985." *Current Population Reports,* ser. P-23, no. 154. Washington, D.C.: U.S. Bureau of the Census.

Part Three

WHAT ARE THE COSTS AND BENEFITS OF A CSAS?

Chapter Seven

WHO SHOULD BE ELIGIBLE FOR AN ASSURED CHILD SUPPORT BENEFIT?

Daniel R. Meyer, Irwin Garfinkel, Donald T. Oellerich,
and Philip K. Robins

Concern about the well-being of children in single-parent families, particularly female-headed families, has grown substantially in the last 20 years for a variety of reasons. First, the proportion of children living in female-headed families has dramatically increased (Garfinkel and McLanahan 1986). Second, female-headed families with children are the poorest of all major demographic groups (Garfinkel and McLanahan 1986). Third, there is growing evidence that the children in female-headed families are worse off on a number of dimensions than are children of two-parent families (Featherman and Hauser 1978; Hill, Augustiniak, and Ponza 1985; McLanahan 1988).

The growth, poverty, and adverse impacts on children of female-headed families have all contributed to a heightened interest by public policymakers in examining public policies affecting this group. Since the mid 1970s the child support system has received increased attention, and many have concluded that it needed drastic changes. As described in earlier chapters, the child support assurance system (CSAS) proposed by Garfinkel and Melli in 1982 included three reforms: (a) a uniform standard for establishing child support obligations; (b) immediate withholding of the child support obligation from the income of the noncustodial parent; and (c) an assured or minimum-guaranteed child support benefit for each family. The first two reforms were incorporated into the Family Support Act of 1988 and are currently being implemented nationwide. Although an assured benefit has not been implemented, it is receiving increased national attention (see, for example, the report of the National Commission on Children 1991).

In previous research, we have estimated some of the costs and effects of an assured benefit plan in the context of the child support assurance system. This chapter reviews those results and then focuses specifically on the costs and benefits of several assured benefit plans that vary in both generosity and eligibility rules. We begin with a brief discussion of the policy decisions involved; we then briefly review prior research; we discuss our data and research methodology; we summarize the costs and benefits of a basic assured benefit plan; and we conclude with a discussion of the effects of different levels of assured benefits and various eligibility rules.

DESIGN OF AN ASSURED BENEFIT PLAN

The philosophy behind Garfinkel and Melli's assured benefit proposal (1982) was that all parents should be required to share their income with their children. The assured benefit, then, was not proposed as a substitute for private support but as a backup for private support. All eligible families would be able to count on receiving at least a minimum level of child support each month. This would protect them against the insecurity that comes from irregular or late child support payments. In addition, some custodial-parent families (probably the poorest) would receive a supplement because the level of support obtained from the nonresident parent would be inadequate to meet the basic needs of the child(ren). Thus, an assured benefit would provide income support to the families of children with poor noncustodial parents as well as ensure the regularity of child support income for other families.

A number of design options are included within this basic idea of an assured child support benefit.[1] These options require decisions regarding two closely related areas: who would be eligible for the benefit and the level of the assured benefit. The debate regarding eligibility focuses on whether such a benefit should be available to all custodial families without regard to award, income, and/or marital statuses or whether the benefit should be restricted to some subgroup of custodial families. The following issues have received the most attention:

- Should the assured benefit be restricted to only those with awards?
- Should the assured benefit be available only to single parents?
- Should the assured benefit be restricted to only those with low incomes?
- Should the assured benefit be available only to recipients of Aid to Families with Dependent Children (AFDC)?

Other key decisions include the level of the assured benefit, whether the benefit is taxable, and whether any additional services will be provided to recipients. The interaction of the assured benefit with current programs will also require some decisions regarding the following issues:

- How is the assured benefit treated by the AFDC program—as unearned income (making it taxed at 100 percent, and thus there is no financial advantage to receiving both AFDC and the assured benefit), as a new category of income (perhaps taxed at 50 percent, as proposed by the National Commission on Children [1991]), or as the child support disregard (AFDC recipients could keep the first $50 per month only)? Also, would an assured benefit replace the child support disregard?
- How is the assured benefit treated in other means-tested programs? For example, does it count as income in the Food Stamp Program, in subsidized housing, or in the determination of eligibility for the Earned Income Tax Credit?

In addition, decisions would be needed with respect to the administration of the assured benefit, including such issues as the relative roles of different levels of government and the appropriate administrative agency. In terms of the latter, possibilities include the state child support agency, the state agency that distributes welfare benefits, a division of the family courts in each state, the state tax agency, the Social Security Administration, and the Internal Revenue Service, among others.

This chapter focuses on eligibility issues, while also touching on two others—first, that of taxation, since it is closely connected to whether the assured benefit should be available to only those with low income or to all income levels, and, second, that of the level of the assured benefit.

Should the Assured Benefit Be Restricted to Only Those with Awards?

The critical argument against limiting eligibility to those with child support awards is that it keeps some vulnerable children from receiving a potentially important benefit through no fault of their own. Even if their custodial parent has done all that is expected in cooperating with the child support system, but for some reason an award has not been established, should the family be penalized? One alternative would be to require cooperation with the child support agency rather than the existence of an award as one eligibility criteria for an assured benefit, similar to the AFDC program. Or an award could be required, but those who can demonstrate "good-cause" could be exempted.

Garfinkel (forthcoming) argues that limiting eligibility to those legally entitled to receive private child support is "essential to creating and preserving the system's integrity." He contends that restricting eligibility underscores the responsibility of parents to provide for their own children and limits the government's role to enforcing that responsibility and providing public support only when private efforts are inadequate. Providing the benefit only to those with awards differentiates it from current welfare programs and thus helps make the benefit less stigmatizing. Limiting eligibility to those with awards may also add new incentives for the custodial parent to pursue paternity establishment and to gain awards. A final argument is that a benefit with limited eligibility may cost less than a benefit available to all.

Given the controversial nature of this issue, this chapter presents estimates of the costs and benefits of an assured benefit plan that is restricted to those with current awards and a plan that is available to all custodial families, regardless of award status.

Should the Assured Benefit Be Available Only to Single Parents?

The argument for limiting the assured benefit only to single parents is that remarried custodial parents have access to the resources of the new spouse and less need of public support. Thus this limitation, like the others, reduces costs and targets more of the benefits to the poor.

One of the arguments against this limitation is that many remarried custodial families are near poverty, and thus may need assistance. Second, limiting benefits to single parents may discourage remarriage, when remarriage may eventually increase economic security. Third, private child support obligations do not terminate upon remarriage of the custodial parent, in part because stepparents have no legal obligation to support children that are not theirs. Since the assured benefit is closely tied to the private child support obligation, it can be argued that it should be treated similarly and not stop at remarriage.

The primary advantage of limiting eligibility for the assured benefit to single parents is cost. This chapter therefore presents estimates of the potential costs and effects of two types of assured benefit plans: those that are restricted to single parents and those that are unrestricted by current marital status.

Should the Assured Benefit Be Restricted to Only Those with Low Incomes?

The main reason for limiting eligibility for the assured benefit to those with low incomes is a pragmatic one, cost. When public resources are limited, targeting those resources to the most needy is appealing. Providing benefits to all custodial families would be more expensive than limiting them to the poor, but the magnitude of these additional costs is unclear. A second reason for limiting eligibility to low-income families is that an assured benefit that is available to all would lead to some wealthy custodial families receiving a public benefit.[2] It could be argued that the public should not be supporting a high-income custodial family, just because the noncustodial parent has not paid in a particular month.

On the other hand, other universal programs support high-income families without public outcry. Very few consider it an outrage that wealthy individuals receive social security or attend public schools. Similarly, unemployment insurance is available to all regardless of income and is primarily seen as an important buffer against insecurity for all individuals, not just for those with low incomes.

One key reason not to income test the benefit is that limiting eligibility may discourage work. Income-tested programs must reduce benefits as the recipient's income increases. This benefit reduction is equivalent to an extra tax placed on income. An advantage of a non-income-tested benefit is that it may supplement earnings, rather than replace them. However, the overall effect of a nonincome-tested benefit compared to an income-tested benefit is ambiguous because the income effect could discourage work.[3]

A second important reason for not limiting eligibility is that the assured benefit could then *prevent* poverty. A variety of recent empirical studies summarized by Lewin/IFC (1990) have all shown that children experience a substantial decline in their economic situation when their parents separate. An assured benefit available to all may help to cushion this fall for the near-poor and may prevent others from slipping into poverty.

A third argument against limiting the benefit is that it segregates the poor, which may stigmatize them. In contrast, a nonincome-tested program integrates the poor into the social mainstream, and receiving benefits may be less likely to be seen as an indication of moral failure.

Fourth, income-tested programs require larger administrative costs per recipient. A bureaucracy must be developed that checks income to determine eligibility, monitors income over time, and adjusts benefits based on income. In contrast, a nonincome-tested program would not have to check income at application or over time, and would not have to vary the amount of the benefit each month.

Finally, political support would be higher if benefits were available to all, not just to the poor. Again, because cost savings are the primary reason for limiting eligibility to the poor, we present the costs and effects of both an income-tested and a nonincome-tested assured benefit.

Should the Assured Benefit Be Available Only to Recipients of AFDC?

Again, the argument for this limitation is that it would cost less and would target benefits to the neediest. In addition, it would target the needy without requiring a new potentially large bureaucracy that determines eligibility.

However, this limitation makes the benefit available only to former welfare recipients. One hope for the assured benefit is that it might prevent welfare recipiency, yet this limitation on eligibility keeps this key benefit from occurring and might, in fact, actually encourage welfare recipiency, at least temporarily. This type of assured benefit would be inequitable in that it sets up two different income conditions: individuals must be very poor first (to be eligible for AFDC), but once on AFDC they can have substantial income and still be eligible for the assured benefit. In addition, this limitation changes the way the assured benefit would be viewed: it would be seen as an adjunct to the current welfare system rather than as an alternative, which means that recipients may be stigmatized and continue to be separated from the mainstream rather than integrated into it. The effects of restricting the assured benefit to AFDC-eligible families would be similar to the income-testing plan. We currently lack the model necessary to produce these estimates, but plan to incorporate this eligibility plan in our future work.

Should the Assured Benefit Be Subject to Income Taxes?

The issues involved in the taxation of an assured benefit are closely related to the income-testing arguments. Means-tested transfers have not been subject to income tax in this country; thus, if the assured benefit is limited to the poor, there is little justification for subjecting the public portion of the benefit to the income tax. Although originally no government transfers were taxed, there has recently been some support for taxing universal benefits (unemployment compensation, part of social security benefits, and so on). The rationale for taxing benefits is that the tax code already exempts poor individuals from paying taxes; presumably, if recipients are not poor, this income should be subject to income taxation. Making the public portion of the assured benefit taxable also reduces the cost of the program and targets more of the benefits to the poor, without limiting benefits only to the poor. In general, then, the most economical options for an assured benefit are either a benefit available only to the poor that is not taxed through the income tax system or a benefit available to all, in which the public portion of the benefit is subject to income tax. This chapter contains estimates of the effects of both types of assured benefit plans.

THEORY AND PREVIOUS RESEARCH

In recent years, various researchers have offered predictions about the effects of the various components of a child support assurance system. For instance, it has been asserted that the uniform standard will increase the dollar amounts of awards (Garfinkel, Oellerich, and Robins 1991); that immediate withholding will increase child support collections (Garfinkel and Klawitter 1990); and that poverty among custodial-parent families will decrease through increased private child support and the assured benefit (Meyer et al. 1991). A CSAS should also increase the number of families with child support awards, primarily because having an award will become more worthwhile economically.

A CSAS should, moreover, decrease AFDC recipiency. The traditional model of the welfare-recipiency decision is an extension of the static theory of labor supply, which holds that individuals consider the trade-offs between income and leisure in deciding the hours they will work. They then select the amount of work and whether they will receive welfare based on the option that maximizes their well-being (utility), given budget and time constraints. AFDC recipiency could be decreased by a CSAS for three reasons. First, for some women, the combination of private child support, the minimum benefit, and unearned income may provide more income than welfare, and thus they will choose to leave welfare. In fact, the minimum benefit alone may be greater than the AFDC maximum in some states, and women residing in those states may choose to leave AFDC. Second, the minimum benefit may provide enough support so that when it is combined with earnings, a woman is able to leave AFDC. The third possibility affects preferences rather than the budget constraint. A potential change in community values may have a feedback effect, in that dependence on child support rather than on AFDC may become the norm for single parents, further decreasing welfare recipiency (Garfinkel, Manski, and Michalopoulos 1992).

The static theory of labor supply also provides predictions about the effects of a CSAS on labor supply. In the absence of welfare, any increase in unearned income (whether an increase in private child support or an assured benefit) will decrease labor supply, partly because individuals could achieve the same total income as before while working fewer hours. So nonrecipients of AFDC would be expected to decrease their labor supply if they receive additional child support or an assured benefit. But AFDC recipients may increase their labor supply if the new combination of the assured benefit, private child support, and earnings is more attractive than staying on AFDC. The aggregate effect on labor supply, therefore, is ambiguous.

Although theory provides clear hypotheses about the direction of most of the effects of the CSAS (increased number of awards, increased award levels, increased collections, increased incomes for custodial families, decreased welfare recipiency, and decreased labor supply for nonwelfare custodial families), the magnitude of these effects is not clear, nor are there any a priori predictions about overall labor supply or program costs.

Some previous research has been completed on the possible effects of various configurations of a CSAS. For example, a simulation of the effects of a CSAS available only to low-income families in Wisconsin found that if there were a "medium" increase in awards and collections, an assured benefit of $3,000 may save money ($20 million) because increased collections from the noncustodial parents of AFDC recipients would offset part of the costs of AFDC (Garfinkel, Robins, Wong, and Meyer 1990). Welfare recipiency was predicted to decrease by 3 percent, the poverty gap for custodial families was predicted to decrease by 16 percent, and the labor supply of custodial families was predicted to decrease by 2 percent.[4]

Robert Lerman (1989) tested a simulation model that examines four different national child support systems: (1) the Wisconsin CSAS with an assured benefit (restricted to those with awards) of $3,000 a year for the first child and a surtax on custodial-parent income; (2) a lower assured benefit of $1,080 a year, restricted to those with awards; (3) a lower assured benefit ($1,080) available to all custodial mothers, not just those with awards; and (4) a lower assured-benefit plan ($1,080) available to all that also includes a tax credit of $1,080 a year for a family of three, replacing the $2,000 personal exemption for children. Lerman did not simulate increases in the percentage with awards or the percentage collected, nor did he allow a labor supply response. The four plans were estimated to cost from $1.1 billion (plan 2) to $3.6 billion (plan 3). They would reduce the poverty gap $0.4 billion (plan 2) to $11.3 billion (plan 4), and would reduce AFDC caseloads by about 4 percent (plan 2), 12 percent (plan 1), or 30 percent (plan 4).

Although Oellerich, Garfinkel, and Robins (1991) did not simulate an assured benefit, they provided simulation estimates of the effects of the collections-side reforms of a national CSAS. They found that implementing the Wisconsin child support guidelines without changing award or collection rates would decrease AFDC caseloads by 2.7 percent, decrease the poverty gap by 6.8 percent, and increase custodial income by 8.9 percent.

Robins (1986) also examined the effects of increased child support collections on AFDC participation and poverty. He concluded that the full enforcement of the child support obligations that existed in 1981 would have little effect on AFDC participation and would decrease the poverty rate of custodial families by only 3 percentage points over the child support system in effect in 1981.

Previous studies of the effects of a CSAS have several limitations, including the lack of predictions on the labor supply response (Lerman 1989; Oellerich et al. 1991; and Robins 1986), the failure to model increases in awards and collections resulting from the Family Support Act (Lerman 1989; Robins 1986), and the potential difficulty of generalizing the Wisconsin results to a national assured benefit (Garfinkel, Robins, Wong, and Meyer 1990). We have therefore recently developed estimates of a national assured benefit. These are summarized later in the chapter, along with information on the relative effects of several different eligibility options.

SIMULATING THE EFFECTS OF A NATIONAL CHILD SUPPORT ASSURANCE SYSTEM

Data

To perform the microsimulation, a data source was needed that provides information on all those eligible for the CSAS. The 1986 Current

Population Survey—Child Support Supplement (CPS—CSS), al-though not perfect,[5] is a national dataset of complete and relatively current information on most of those eligible for the CSAS. It includes demographic information on custodial parents (age, race, education, etc.); their children (number, age of the youngest, etc.); income and labor force information (annual earnings, amount of welfare reported, number of weeks worked in 1985, and number of hours per week usually worked); and information on the existence and amount of a child support award, as well as on the amount received. All women aged 18 and over who are eligible for child support (including remar-ried women) are included, for a total of 3,631 cases. Missing from the sample are the male custodial parents.

Model

The simulation analysis required estimating the amount of private child support each woman may receive, estimating the amount of AFDC received (because recipiency is underreported in the CPS), estimating a labor supply and welfare-recipiency response to the CSAS, and identifying the features of each CSAS and assured benefit plan tested.

ESTIMATING THE AMOUNT OF PRIVATE CHILD SUPPORT

Estimates of the amount of private child support each woman may receive depend on the existence of an award, the level of that award, and the percentage of the award collected. Because of legislation al-ready enacted that improves the establishment of paternity and makes having an award more worthwhile, it is likely that the percentage of cases with awards will increase in the future. Therefore, we included in our simulations an increase in the percentage of families with a child support award.[6]

To determine the level of an award, we needed to know the income of the noncustodial parent. Unfortunately, the CPS—CSS does not report the incomes of noncustodial parents, so to estimate noncusto-dial income we used procedures developed by Oellerich (1984) that based estimates of noncustodial parent income on the race, education, age, region, marital status, and AFDC use of the custodial parent. These procedures estimated the mean annual income of noncustodial parents as $20,379 in 1985 dollars.[7] The income of the noncustodial parent and the number of children were then used to determine the award amount using the Wisconsin percentage-of-income standard. The percentage of the award collected was then estimated based on a variety of custodial parents' demographic characteristics. Again, because of recent legislation requiring the use of wage withholding, we believe that compliance with awards is likely to increase and we included an increase in our simulations.

ESTIMATING AFDC RECIPIENCY

A second series of intermediate steps was required to estimate the amount of AFDC received, because AFDC is significantly underreported in the CPS—CSS (U.S. Bureau of the Census 1990), as in most self-reported surveys. Our approach basically ignored the amount of AFDC reported and used the maximum amount of AFDC available for each family (based on state of residence and family size) and an estimated tax rate on earnings (based on Fraker, Moffitt, and Wolf 1985) to determine if each family was income-eligible.[8] An AFDC benefit was then imputed to each recipient based on the maximum and the estimated tax rate. This approach yielded 2.7 million AFDC recipients and total AFDC payments of $10.0 billion, figures somewhat lower than those given in the administrative records, because all AFDC recipients are not in the CPS—CSS.[9]

ESTIMATING LABOR SUPPLY AND RECIPIENCY RESPONSES TO THE CSAS

The third part of the simulation model predicted welfare recipiency and labor force behavior after the CSAS is implemented. As stated, the static theory of labor supply suggests that women choose the number of hours they will work and choose to receive AFDC, the assured benefit, or neither, based on the alternative that provides the highest utility. The labor supply response model used in this chapter is based on the general theoretical approach developed by Burtless and Hausman (1978). It specifies a budget constraint, calculates utility on each segment of the budget constraint, and then assumes that custodial parents select the number of hours that provides the highest utility. The form of the utility function we used to derive the estimates of the effects of the CSAS is an augmented Stone-Geary direct utility function employed by Garfinkel, Robins, Wong, and Meyer (1990), as follows:

$$U(C, H) = (1-\beta) \ln(\frac{C}{m} - \delta) + \beta \ln(\alpha - \frac{H}{r}), \qquad (7.1)$$

where C = annual consumption of market goods;
H = annual hours of work;
β = marginal propensity to consume leisure $(1 - \beta$ = marginal propensity to consume market goods);

δ =   subsistence consumption;
α =   total time available for work; and
m, r =   indexes that normalize C and H in accordance
with the size and composition of the household.

To estimate directly the parameters of this utility function is beyond the scope of this discussion. Therefore, we drew on results from the existing labor supply literature. For our baseline estimates of the effects of our proposed CSAS, we used the results obtained by Johnson and Pencavel (1984) in their analysis of the labor supply response to the Seattle and Denver Income Maintenance Experiments (SIME-DIME). In particular, we assumed that β = .128, δ = -2,776, α = 2,151, m = 1-.401 ln(1 + K) (K being the number of children in the family under the age of 18), and r = 1-.071P (P being 1 if there are preschool-age children in the family, 0 otherwise). Hence, the total income elasticity estimated in the Johnson-Pencavel study was -.128 and the uncompensated wage elasticity was .303 (from .128 (n + 2,776m)/wH = .303), evaluated at the means of our analysis sample.[10]

The preceding utility function was used to estimate the effects of the CSAS. Using existing data, we defined a family's preprogram labor supply, welfare position, and an error term that could represent taste for work.[11] We then calculated a net wage and an amount of unearned income on each budget segment. Net wages were determined by adjusting gross wages for income taxes, payroll taxes, and implicit taxes on earnings for AFDC recipients.[12]

Given current net wages, current unearned income, changes in private child support, and the amount of the assured benefit, we could estimate optimal hours and utility on each budget segment. The segment with the highest utility level then determined the woman's postprogram labor supply and program participation status.

In summary, the model simulates the amount of child support women would receive and their AFDC program participation and labor supply responses to the implementation of the CSAS. By aggregating these individual responses, we could estimate the total costs, decreases in AFDC recipiency, effects on poverty and income, and effects on labor supply. The costs included in this model are the direct (nonadministrative) cost of the assured benefits paid to custodial parents and any decreased tax revenue that results from higher-income custodial parents who work less in response to increased child support. These costs are offset by taxing the public portion of the assured benefit, by savings in the AFDC program that result when women no longer receive AFDC, and by savings in the AFDC program that result from increased collections from noncustodial parents even when the custodial parent remains on AFDC. Administrative costs were not estimated.

Although the simulation provides some interesting information about the magnitude of some of the costs and benefits of our CSAS, a few words of caution are in order. To conduct the simulations, a number of simplifications had to be made. First, food stamps and Medicaid were ignored, which led to an overestimate of the number of women who will leave AFDC. (However, recent legislation that eventually makes Medicaid available to all poor children mitigates this error.) On the other hand, the Earned Income Tax Credit was also ignored, which could lead to an underestimate of the number of women who would leave AFDC. In addition, potential "macro" or "community" effects of changing norms were disregarded. We also did not include the effects of the CSAS on noncustodial parents: for example, an increase in child support obligations may (depending upon the precise guideline used) increase or decrease the labor supply of noncustodial parents, will increase noncompliance with child support awards, and may move some noncustodial parents and their families into poverty. An assured benefit will decrease the incentive for noncustodial parents to pay child support, since their children would receive benefits regardless of whether payments were made, although this may be mitigated by the universal use of wage withholding. Estimating the effects of a CSAS on noncustodial parents is beyond the scope of this research. Finally, we did not account for the absence of custodial fathers in the CPS—CSS, a group that may receive a substantial portion of assured benefit funds.[13]

IDENTIFYING THE FEATURES OF CSAS

The three major elements of the CSAS (guidelines for awards, immediate income withholding, and an assured benefit) could take a variety of forms. The particular CSAS that we tested has the following features:

1. Child support awards are initially set and updated using Wisconsin's percentage-of-income standard. Award levels are based only on the number of children and on the income of the noncustodial parent. For one child, the award is 17 percent of the first $75,000 of noncustodial income; for two children it is 25 percent; for three children, 29 percent, for four children, 31 percent, and for five or more children, 34 percent. Variants of percentage-of-income standards are currently used by 17 states (Lewin/ICF 1990).[14]

2. Three potential levels of assured benefits, with the first child entitling the custodial parent to either $1,000, $2,000, or $3,000 annually, are presented. In each plan the benefit increases by $1,000 for the second child, $1,000 for the third, $500 for the fourth, and $500 for the fifth child.[15]

The assured benefit plans reflect the following eligibility rules:

1. For our baseline simulations the availability of the assured benefit is restricted to only those custodial families with a current child support award. The public portion of the child support transfer (assured benefit) is subject to the federal income tax.
2. In the next two simulations we continue to restrict the assured benefit to those with awards and add the additional restrictions of (a) single-parent families only (again, the public portion of the child support transfer is subject to the federal income tax) and (b) low-income families, respectively.[16]
3. Our last group of simulations provides an assured benefit to all custodial families regardless of their award, income, and marital statuses. The public portion of the income transfer is subjected to the federal income tax.

In all simulations we assume that the AFDC program would tax the assured benefit at the rate of 100 percent. As a result, there would be no financial advantage to a custodial parent if he or she received both AFDC and the assured benefit.

RESULTS AND DISCUSSION

We examined the effects of an assured benefit under four different CSAS scenarios: (1) the child support situation in 1985; (2) a scenario in which there is no change in the percentage of cases with awards or the percentage of child support collected, but all awards are set according to the Wisconsin child support guidelines; (3) a "medium improvement" scenario, in which awards are set according to the Wisconsin standard, collection rates are increased by half the distance between the 1985 percentage and 100 percent, and 40 percent of those who do not have an award in 1985 are assumed to receive one; and (4) a scenario in which all cases are given awards, all awards are set according to the Wisconsin standard, and all award amounts are collected. We believe some increases in awards and collections will occur because the provisions of the 1984 Child Support Amendments and the 1988 Family Support Act are intended to generate increases in child support obligations and improvements in collections. The second scenario, in which all awards are based on the Wisconsin standard, could be implemented fairly easily by making updated child support awards a condition of eligibility for an assured benefit and by updating all the child support awards of AFDC recipients. The medium improvement can be interpreted as a level of improvement that could be expected from a CSAS in perhaps 15 to 20 years. The perfect system is the upper bound and could at best be approached, but never fully achieved, in the long run.

Within each CSAS scenario, we estimated the effects of the four assured benefit plans with the following eligibility options: (1) benefits restricted to all families with a current award; (2) benefits restricted to low-income families with current awards; (3) benefits restricted to single-parent families with current awards; and (4) benefits available to all custodial families, that is, regardless of current income, marital, and award statuses. The particular income-tested plan we simulated is modeled after a Wisconsin proposal that would restrict the benefit to custodial families with incomes below an income cutoff of $2,000 less than the median income. The tax on the custodial parents' earnings is set at a rate equal to the noncustodial parents' tax rate for the number of eligible children (i.e., 17 percent for one child and 25 percent, 29 percent, 31 percent, and 34 percent for two, three, four, and five or more children, respectively). In all nonincome-tested options the assured benefit is regarded as taxable income subject to federal income tax.

Our basic results, restricted to those with a current award, are summarized in table 7.1. Providing an assured benefit of $3,000 to those with awards regardless of current marital status or income level could cost $4.2 billion if the rest of the child support system remains as it was in 1985. However, if an assured benefit were combined with improvements on the collections side of the private child support system, costs would be reduced. For example, combining the $3,000 assured benefit with the universal use of the Wisconsin percentage-of-income standard to initially set and update award levels (scenario 2), and with no changes in compliance behavior, reduces the estimated cost to $2.2 billion.

The third scenario, medium improvements in awards and collections (see table 7.1) shows that these improvements by themselves could reduce public costs, primarily through AFDC savings, by $1 billion. These system improvements alone have beneficial effects on

Table 7.1 ESTIMATES OF DIRECT COSTS OF CSAS AND EFFECTS OF CSAS ON POVERTY, AFDC RECIPIENCY, AND LABOR SUPPLY OF CUSTODIAL FAMILES UNDER FOUR SCENARIOS

Scenario	Percentage Decrease in Poverty Gap	Percentage of Caseload Leaving AFDC	Nonadministrative Cost (1985)	Percentage Change in Labor Supply		
				AFDC Recipients	Non-AFDC Recipients	All
1. Child support system in 1985:						
Assured benefit $0	0	0	0	0	0	0
Assured benefit $1,000	2	3	448	5	0	0
Assured benefit $2,000	5	8	1,759	15	-1	1
Assured benefit $3,000	9	13	4,239	26	-1	1
2. Percentage standard implemented:						
Assured benefit $0	2	2	- 144	3	-1	-1
Assured benefit $1,000	3	4	- 47	6	-1	0
Assured benefit $2,000	5	9	552	14	-1	0
Assured benefit $3,000	9	14	2,166	23	-2	1
3. Medium improvements in awards and collections:						
Assured benefit $0	10	8	-1,026	9	-3	-2
Assured benefit $1,000	12	11	- 943	13	-3	-1
Assured benefit $2,000	15	18	- 461	24	-3	0
Assured benefit $3,000	21	28	850	45	-3	1
4. Perfect awards and collections:						
Assured benefit $0	24	19	-2,775	25	-5	-3
Assured benefit $1,000	25	22	-2,667	29	-5	-3
Assured benefit $2,000	30	33	-2,157	46	-6	-1
Assured benefit $3,000	39	50	- 749	79	-6	2

Source: Microsimulation results based on 1986 Current Population Survey—Child Support Supplement (CPS—CSS).
Notes: Assured benefit is restricted to those with an award, and the public portion of the transfer is subject to federal income tax. Cost figures are in millions of 1985 dollars.

the economic well-being of custodial families, decreasing their poverty gap by 10 percent and decreasing the AFDC caseload by 8 percent. The addition of an assured benefit of $2,000 does more for custodial families under this scenario, decreasing the poverty gap by an additional 5 percent and AFDC recipiency by an additional 10 percent, at an estimated cost of about $500 million. A perfect system (scenario 4) would of course do even more and shows the maximum potential benefits.

Aggregate changes in labor supply for custodial families are quite small under every scenario tested. However, these low aggregate changes are the result of two offsetting effects. Women originally receiving AFDC increase their labor supply substantially, showing a 45 percent increase in average hours worked under the medium improvement scenario with a $3,000 benefit. In contrast, those not receiving AFDC decrease their hours of work, by 3 percent in the medium improvement scenario. Thus, it appears that an assured benefit as low as $1,000 targeted to those families with a current child support award could make substantial inroads in reducing poverty and AFDC participation while having only a marginal impact on labor supply.

Table 7.2 compares the effects of the eligibility options we explored. The table contains four panels, one for each of the four scenarios. Within each scenario we report the results of four eligibility plans. The costs and effects of the plans reported in the table indicate the additional change in outcomes due to the minimum benefit level and are calculated relative to the costs and effects of a base plan that has no minimum. For example, if medium improvements (scenario 3) were achieved, we would estimate a 10 percent reduction in the poverty gap. If this improvement were combined with an assured benefit plan based at $1,000, we would estimate an additional 2 percent reduction in the poverty gap for a total of 12 percent.

Within each panel in table 7.2, the first set of results (1a, 2a, 3a, 4a) are restatements of the results in table 7.1, our base estimates for an assured benefit available to all families with awards. The second set of results in each panel in the table (1b, 2b, 3b, 4b) is for the income-tested benefit that is available to families with awards. The income-tested assured benefit is designed to decrease the benefit by 17 percent to 34 percent (depending on the number of children) for each dollar of custodial income and to ensure that those families with annual incomes above an income cutoff of $2,000 less than the median income are not eligible. This plan costs substantially less than the assured benefit restricted simply to all those with awards, decreasing

Table 7.2 INCREMENTAL EFFECTS OF FOUR TYPES OF ASSURED BENEFITS ON POVERTY, AFDC RECIPIENCY, AND LABOR SUPPLY OF CUSTODIAL FAMILIES UNDER FOUR SCENARIOS

Scenario	Percentage Decrease in Poverty Gap	Percentage of Caseload Leaving AFDC	Net Nonadministrative Cost Compared to 1985	Percentage Change in Labor Supply, Custodial Mothers
1. Child Support System in 1985	0	0	0	0
Additional Changes from Assured Benefit:				
1a. Families with awards:				
$1,000	2	3	448	0
$2,000	5	8	1,759	1
$3,000	9	13	4,239	1
1b. Low-income families with awards:				
$1,000	0	1	72	0
$2,000	2	4	253	0
$3,000	5	10	837	0
1c. Single-parent families with awards:				
$1,000	2	3	288	0
$2,000	4	7	1,065	1
$3,000	8	13	2,532	2
1d. Families with and without awards:				
$1,000	10	16	2,728	2
$2,000	22	35	5,936	5
$3,000	35	52	10,673	6
2. Percentage Standard Implemented	2	2	−144	−1
Additional Changes from Assured Benefit:				
2a. Families with awards:				
$1,000	1	2	97	1
$2,000	3	7	696	1
$3,000	7	12	2,310	2

	$				
2b. Low-income families with awards:	$1,000	0	1	31	0
	$2,000	1	3	136	0
	$3,000	4	9	503	0
2c. Single-parent families with awards:	$1,000	1	2	94	1
	$2,000	3	6	467	1
	$3,000	6	11	1,456	2
2d. Families with and without awards:	$1,000	10	15	2,404	2
	$2,000	21	34	4,856	5
	$3,000	34	51	8,771	4
3. Medium Improvements in Awards and Collections *Additional Changes from Assured Benefit:*		10	8	−1,026	−2
3a. Families with awards:	$1,000	2	3	83	1
	$2,000	5	10	565	2
	$3,000	11	20	1,876	3
3b. Low-income families with awards:	$1,000	1	1	53	0
	$2,000	2	6	207	0
	$3,000	7	15	685	1
3c. Single-parent families with awards:	$1,000	1	2	83	1
	$2,000	4	10	507	2
	$3,000	10	19	1,528	3
3d. Families with and without awards:	$1,000	7	11	1,452	2
	$2,000	15	26	3,055	4
	$3,000	26	43	5,750	6

continued

Table 7.2 INCREMENTAL EFFECTS OF FOUR TYPES OF ASSURED BENEFITS ON POVERTY, AFDC RECIPIENCY, AND LABOR SUPPLY OF CUSTODIAL FAMILIES UNDER FOUR SCENARIOS (continued)

Scenario	Percentage Decrease in Poverty Gap	Percentage of Caseload Leaving AFDC	Net Nonadministrative Cost Compared to 1985	Percentage Change in Labor Supply, Custodial Mothers
4. Perfect Awards and Collections	24	19	−2,775	−3
Additional Changes from Assured Benefit:				
4a. Families with awards:				
$1,000	1	3	108	0
$2,000	6	14	618	2
$3,000	15	31	2,026	5
4b. Low-income families with awards:				
$1,000	0	2	62	0
$2,000	2	8	317	0
$3,000	8	13	946	1
4c. Single-parent families with awards:				
$1,000	1	3	101	1
$2,000	6	14	608	2
$3,000	15	30	1,925	5

Source: Microsimulation results based on 1986 CPS—CSS.
Notes: Cost figures are in millions of 1985 dollars. A perfect scenario for assured benefit plan "Families with and without awards" is not shown, since if all cases have awards it is redundant with the first plan, "Families with awards."

costs by about $1.2 billion for the $3,000 assured benefit in the medium scenario. It also provides fewer benefits, reducing the poverty gap by only an additional 7 percent, rather than 11 percent, and enabling only an additional 15 percent of the caseload, rather than 20 percent, to leave AFDC. The difference in costs between the award-only plan and the income-tested benefit is largest ($3.4 billion) if the old system does not improve. An income-tested assured benefit is estimated to have no effect on the labor supply of recipients. The effect of income testing on labor supply is less than the award-only plan for two reasons: first, moderate-income custodial families would not be eligible, and thus would not decrease their labor supply; and second, and perhaps more important, moving into the labor force would be less attractive if the assured benefit were subjected to a surtax, so fewer women would leave AFDC to begin working.

The third set of results in table 7.2 (1c, 2c, 3c, 4c) shows an assured benefit that is limited to single-parent families with awards (i.e., those who remarry would not be eligible for the assured benefit). This also saves money, but produces less savings than limiting the benefit to those with low incomes. In contrast to directly income-testing the benefit, categorically limiting the benefit to single-parent families costs less, while still helping poor custodial families. Because a relatively small percentage of remarried custodial parents are poor or on AFDC, confining benefits to single mothers with awards reduces poverty and AFDC recipiency almost as much as a benefit available to all custodial mothers with awards regardless of current marital status.

Finally, not restricting eligibility (1d, 2d, 3d in table 7.2) for the assured benefit results in much larger economic impacts in terms of increases in both benefits and costs. For example, under the medium improvement scenario, an assured benefit plan available to all families (with and without an award) of $3,000 would reduce the poverty gap by an additional 26 percent, at a projected nonadministrative cost of $5.8 billion. This same benefit restricted to those with an award would result in a lower reduction in the poverty gap (11 percent) and would cost $3.9 billion less than the plan available to families with and without awards.

The impacts on AFDC participation are most dramatic when the assured benefit is provided without regard to award status. This is due to the relatively low award rate for AFDC recipient families; in 1985 less than one-third of these families had a current award.

We could try to attain the long-run benefits of the program by not requiring an award, but the cost could be quite high. Without concomitant improvements in collections and award levels, extending

benefits to all—without regard to award, income, and marital statuses—would result in costs of over $10 billion. In addition, such a
plan may actually delay increases in the collections side of the program by reducing incentives to seek a child support award.

The figures in table 7.2 show that the income-tested assured benefit
(rows 1b, 2b, 3b, and 4b) costs much less than the nonincome-tested
benefit (rows 1a, 2a, 3a, and 4a), but still reduces the poverty gap and
AFDC recipiency by sizable amounts. This is to be expected, since an
income-tested benefit attempts to provide benefits only to those with
low incomes. An advantage of the nonincome-tested benefit is that it
is available to those who are near-poor; information about the distributional effects of the two assured benefits is presented in table 7.3.

As expected, the income-tested benefit assists the poor, with 90
percent of the $3,000 benefit under the medium improvement scenario
going to those with incomes less than poverty (table 7.3, row 3b). In
comparison, 75 percent of the nonincome-tested benefit goes to the
poor (table 7.3, row 3a). The nonincome-tested benefit provides substantial assistance to the near-poor, with 21 percent of the same benefit going to those with incomes between 101 percent and 200 percent
of poverty. The table also shows that as the private child support
system becomes more effective (moving down the panels), the percentage of benefits going to the poor increases, for two reasons: first,
as the system improves, more poor families receive child support
awards and thus more become eligible for the assured benefit; second,
as the system improves, the nonpoor receive more private child support benefits and thus do not need the assured benefit. Similarly,
larger assured benefits generally reach farther up into the income
distribution, since some of the near-poor would be attracted to a large
benefit but not a small one.

Table 7.3 furthermore shows the effect of the income-tested and
nonincome-tested assured benefits on average custodial family incomes. Because the nonincome-tested benefit is available to more
people, it results in higher mean incomes than the income-tested
benefit. For example, under the medium improvement scenario with
a $3,000 benefit, the nonincome-tested benefit raises mean annual
incomes by $300, compared to $100 for the income-tested benefit.

CONCLUSIONS

The simulation results presented in this chapter suggest that a child
support assurance system that included an assured benefit available

Table 7.3 DISTRIBUTION OF ASSURED BENEFITS TO CUSTODIAL FAMILIES AND ESTIMATES OF MEAN FAMILY INCOME UNDER FOUR SCENARIOS

Scenario	0%–100% Poverty	101%–200% Poverty	201%+ Poverty	Mean Custodial Family Income ($1,000s)
Number of Custodial Families	41.0%	22.6%	36.3%	19.3
	Percentage of Net Assured Benefits to Families with Incomes of			
	0%–100% Poverty	101%–200% Poverty	201%+ Poverty	
1. Child Support System in 1985				
a. Families with awards (nonincome-tested)				
$1,000	42.0	37.7	20.2	19.4
$2,000	35.9	33.2	30.9	19.5
$3,000	33.1	29.9	37.0	19.9
b. Low-income families with awards (income-tested)				
$1,000	82.4	14.2	3.4	19.3
$2,000	86.7	9.6	3.7	19.3
$3,000	83.4	12.9	3.7	19.4
2. Percentage Standard Implemented				19.7
a. Families with awards (nonincome-tested)				
$1,000	59.5	29.4	11.0	19.7
$2,000	47.7	30.4	21.8	19.8
$3,000	41.4	29.1	29.4	20.0
b. Low-income families with awards (income-tested)				
$1,000	82.5	12.6	4.9	19.7
$2,000	88.1	8.4	3.4	19.7
$3,000	87.3	9.9	2.7	19.8

continued

Table 7.3 DISTRIBUTION OF ASSURED BENEFITS TO CUSTODIAL FAMILIES AND ESTIMATES OF MEAN FAMILY INCOME UNDER FOUR SCENARIOS (continued)

Scenario	Percentage of Net Assured Benefits to Families with Incomes of			Mean Custodial Family Income ($1,000s)
	0%–100% Poverty	101%–200% Poverty	201%+ Poverty	
Number of Custodial Families	41.0%	22.6%	36.3%	20.3
3. Medium Improvements in Awards and Collections				
a. Families with awards (nonincome-tested)				
$1,000	75.3	16.8	7.8	20.3
$2,000	70.6	19.7	9.6	20.4
$3,000	67.9	21.2	10.9	20.6
b. Low-income families with awards (income-tested)				
$1,000	87.6	5.9	6.4	20.3
$2,000	89.6	6.1	4.4	20.3
$3,000	90.3	7.0	2.8	20.4
4. Perfect child support system				21.3
a. Families with awards (nonincome-tested)				
$1,000	84.2	10.7	5.1	21.3
$2,000	75.8	16.0	8.3	21.5
$3,000	72.8	17.6	9.6	21.7
b. Low-income families with awards (income-tested)				
$1,000	90.5	4.7	4.7	21.3
$2,000	90.3	4.9	4.7	21.3
$3,000	91.6	5.5	2.9	21.4

Source: Microsimulation results based on 1986 CPS—CSS.

Notes: For the nonincome-tested version, income taxes paid on the public portion of the assured benefits have been subtracted to give "net assured benefits." For the income-tested version, the custodial surtax has been subtracted. The first three columns may not add to 100 percent because of rounding.

to all custodial families with awards could increase the incomes of poor custodial families. The labor supply of custodial parents is not predicted to change much, and many of the families would leave AFDC. Achieving such a major reduction in poverty and welfare recipiency is not, however, estimated to cost a great deal. In fact, when combined with improvements on the collections side, the nonadministrative costs of a CSAS may actually be less than the nonadministrative costs of the child support system in 1985.

Four eligibility options were simulated, comparing the basic results (assured benefits available to all custodial families with awards) to assured benefits available to low-income families with awards, single-parent families with awards, and all custodial families (with and without awards). As expected, the benefits are less when eligibility restrictions are made, with the assured benefit available to all decreasing the poverty gap and AFDC recipiency by at least twice as much as the benefit available only to those with awards. Compared to a benefit available only to those with awards, limiting eligibility to single-parent families decreases the benefits only slightly, whereas limiting it to poor families shows a somewhat larger decrease. As expected, cost estimates also vary dramatically with different eligibility rules. In the medium improvement scenario, an assured benefit of $3,000 is estimated to cost $1.9 billion. An assured benefit of $3,000 available to all families costs three times as much, an assured benefit that is available only to single-parent families with awards costs about $0.3 billion less, and an income-tested assured benefit costs about $1.2 billion less. An income-tested benefit focuses its assistance on families below the poverty line. A nonincome-tested benefit provides more benefits to those near poverty, at a higher total cost.

This chapter has reviewed conceptual arguments about the advantages and disadvantages of limiting eligibility for an assured child support benefit and has provided dollar estimates of some of the costs and benefits of these limitations. As expected, trade-offs are involved: a benefit that is available to more people does more to decrease poverty and welfare recipiency, but at a higher cost. If an assured child support benefit is to become policy, decisions on eligibility will need to be made; the conceptual arguments presented here and the estimates of the costs and benefits involved can inform this policy decision.

Whatever eligibility rules are selected, we believe that an assured benefit would be a desirable income security policy, providing significant benefits for a very poor group without costing much in public dollars.

Notes

The research reported in this chapter was supported in part by a grant from the Office of the Assistant Secretary for Planning and Evaluation, U.S. Department of Health and Human Services, to the Institute for Research on Poverty. Any opinions expressed here are those of the authors alone and not of the sponsoring institutions.

1. This section borrows heavily from Garfinkel (forthcoming).

2. Some would argue that any type of assured benefit would change the incentives in custody determination, providing an additional benefit to those who gain custody. This issue is particularly relevant in this context, in that a nonincome-tested assured benefit may mean that high-income custodial fathers receive regular public benefits because the awards assessed on lower-income custodial mothers may be low.

3. Although this is true if a nonincome-tested plan is compared to an income-tested plan, if a nonincome-tested plan is compared to the current system, the labor supply effect for nonworking AFDC recipients is positive; for working AFDC recipients the effect could be either positive or negative; and for non-AFDC recipients the effect is negative. The aggregate effect is unknown.

4. The CSAS simulated in Wisconsin included a wage subsidy and taxed back the difference between the assured benefit and the amount of private child support. Garfinkel, Robins, Wong, and Meyer (1990: 24, table 5, row 4) provide the results for an assured benefit of $3,000 without a wage subsidy; these are the results described here.

5. For a more complete description of the CPS—CSS, see Robins (1987). The 1986 CPS—CSS has five major problems. First, not all those eligible for child support (and thus not all those eligible for the CSAS) are included. For example, custodial fathers and custodial parents younger than age 18 are not included. (The omission of younger custodial parents was corrected in the 1988 CPS—CSS, and the other omissions are scheduled to be corrected in the 1992 CPS—CSS). Women who have only been married once and are currently married, but who were single parents prior to the marriage, are also not included. Second, no information is gathered on the noncustodial parent. Third, self-reports of welfare recipiency are used, and AFDC recipiency is significantly underreported, making identification of recipients and estimation of welfare savings difficult. Fourth, only annual data are reported, creating problems in identifying those eligible for the CSAS for only part of the year and those who are part-year AFDC recipients. Finally, the CPS—CSS may have incorrectly identified older women as being child-support eligible (see Robins 1987). For this reason, only women younger than age 60 were used in the simulation.

6. To do this, we first divided every case into a portion that we assumed had a child support award and a portion that did not, based on a logit equation. An alternate approach would accept the information provided by each woman on whether or not there was an award, and then increase the percentage with awards by randomly selecting cases without awards. Our approach was consistent with the idea that each case, being part of a sample, "represents" many cases like it. What we have done is similar to dividing each case into 100 families and then giving, say, 67 of these families an award and 33 families no award. For more details on the estimation of the model we employed to adjust award rates, see Meyer et al. (1991).

7. These procedures have been used in other simulations, and are also summarized in Garfinkel and Oellerich (1989). There are two reasons to believe that these estimates were conservative: first, Garfinkel and Oellerich applied their estimating procedures to three samples in which we have information on both the custodial parent and the income of the noncustodial parent and found that the estimates consistently underestimated the actual incomes of nonwhites and were lower than (or slightly above) the

incomes of whites. Second, a different methodology reported in Michalopoulos and Garfinkel (1989) would have resulted in estimates of noncustodial income that are about 10 percent higher than our estimates.

8. We used the 1982 estimates without the deduction reported by Fraker et al. (1985) when available. When they were not, we adjusted their 1982 estimates with the deduction or their 1981 estimates. Unfortunately, estimates from some small states were not available for either of these years. Using the rates of other states in the same region, we imputed a rate to states that have neither a 1982 nor a 1981 estimate.

9. The total amount of AFDC reported in our sample is $7.33 billion. We know, however, that only 76 percent of AFDC is reported (U.S. Bureau of the Census 1990); thus, the $7.33 billion reported could be equivalent to $7.33/.76, or about the $10.0 billion that we simulate here. Our approach thus appears to rectify the problem of underreporting.

We have not, however, dealt with the problem of CSAS-eligible cases systematically missing from the CPS—CSS. The total amount of AFDC benefits reported in administrative records in 1985 is $15 billion. Subtracting the cases eligible for AFDC who are not eligible for the CSAS (those eligible through the unemployment, incapacitation, or death of a parent) results in a total amount of $12.7 billion. We assume that the difference between the $12.7 billion from administrative records and the $10 billion we estimated is for AFDC cases who are not in the CPS—CSS. We ignored this additional $2.7 billion of AFDC benefits, which is equivalent to assuming that none of these people leave AFDC and that we collect no additional child support from their partners.

10. Because no research has been done on the labor supply of *remarried* women, we are not sure if their labor supply responses are more like those of married women or like those of single women. We use the parameters for single heads of households for all women and, for remarried women, treat the spouse's income as exogenous.

11. As Moffitt (1986) and Hausman (1985) have noted, the error term can generally be thought of as representing a combination of measurement error, optimization error, and unmeasured heterogeneity. In our application, it may also represent differences between SIME-DIME, the sample used by Johnson-Pencavel (1984), and this sample. For purposes of this chapter, however, the error term is assumed to arise only because of unmeasured heterogeneity, since we assume that observed hours of work are equal to the optimal hours of work, and participation and labor supply decisions are based on utility maximization.

12. We used the 1985 schedule for federal income taxes, assuming that all income except AFDC and child support was taxable and that women used either the "unmarried head of household" or "married, filing jointly" status with only the standard deduction and exemptions for all members of the family. To simplify the model, we assumed that the current marginal tax rate applies to all levels of hours. For simplicity we ignored state income taxes.

13. Unfortunately, identifying custodial fathers of child-support-eligible children is difficult. If we add the male custodial fathers in Wisconsin, and adjust their sample weight so that they total an estimate of the number of custodial fathers nationally, costs increase but there is little effect on the estimates of the percentage reductions in the poverty gap or the AFDC caseload.

14. The other common guideline type, income shares, is used by 34 states. Income shares guidelines determine the percentage of income based on both parents' income. However, the two types of guidelines usually yield identical awards when the income categories are wide (Lewin/ICF 1990).

15. The assured benefit in the $1,000 plan does not exceed the AFDC maximum benefit for one child in any state; for two through five children, however, AFDC maximums are less than the assured benefit in two through nine states, depending on family size. The highest assured benefit is greater than AFDC benefits in 21 to 26 states, depending on

family size. In our base results, when AFDC is less than the assured benefit, a family is assumed to participate in AFDC only if there is not a child support award.

16. The particular income-tested version we implement is the one that was planned for the Wisconsin demonstration: the assured benefit is limited to those with incomes less than $2,000 less than the median income for each family size; the benefit is taxed back at the rate of 17 percent for every dollar of custodial parent income if there is one child, at the rate of 25 percent for two children, and so forth, following the Wisconsin percentages required from noncustodial parents.

References

Burtless, Gary, and Jerry A. Hausman. 1978. "The Effect of Taxation on Labor Supply: Evaluating the Gary Income Maintenance Experiment." *Journal of Political Economy* 86:1103–30.

Featherman, David, and Robert M. Hauser. 1978. *Opportunity and Change.* New York: Academic Press.

Fraker, Thomas, Robert Moffitt, and Douglas Wolf. 1985. "Effective Tax Rates in the AFDC Program." *Journal of Human Resources* 20:251–63.

Garfinkel, Irwin. Forthcoming. *Child Support, Poverty and Welfare* [working title]. New York: Russell Sage Foundation.

Garfinkel, Irwin, and Marygold Melli, eds. 1982. *Child Support: Weaknesses of the Old and Features of a Proposed New System, vol. 1.* Institute for Research on Poverty Special Report 32A. Madison: University of Wisconsin–Madison, Institute for Research on Poverty.

Garfinkel, Irwin, and Sara S. McLanahan. 1986. *Single Mothers and Their Children: A New American Dilemma.* Washington, D.C.: Urban Institute Press.

Garfinkel, Irwin, and Donald Oellerich. 1989. "Noncustodial Fathers' Ability to Pay Child Support." *Demography* 26:219–33.

Garfinkel, Irwin, and Marieka M. Klawitter. 1990. "The Effect of Routine Income Withholding of Child Support Collections." *Journal of Policy Analysis and Management* 9:155–77.

Garfinkel, Irwin, Donald Oellerich, and Philip K. Robins. 1991. "Child Support Guidelines: Will They Make a Difference?" *Journal of Family Issues* 12:404–29.

Garfinkel, Irwin, Charles Manski, and Charles Michalopoulos. 1992. "Micro Experiments and Macro Effects." In *Evaluating Welfare and Training Programs*, edited by Charles F. Manski and Irwin Garfinkel. Cambridge, Mass.: Harvard University Press.

Garfinkel, Irwin, Philip K. Robins, Pat Wong, and Daniel R. Meyer. 1990. "The Wisconsin Child Support Assurance System: Estimated Effects on

Poverty, Labor Supply, Caseloads, and Costs." *Journal of Human Resources* 25:1–31.

Hausman, Jerry. 1985. "The Econometrics of Nonlinear Budget Sets." *Econometrica* 53:1255–82.

Hill, Martha, Sue Augustiniak, and Michael Ponza. 1985. "The Impact of Parental Marital Disruption on the Socioeconomic Attainments of Children as Adults." University of Michigan, Institute for Social Research, Ann Arbor. Photocopy.

Johnson, Terry R., and John H. Pencavel. 1984. "Dynamic Hours of Work Functions for Husbands, Wives, and Single Females." *Econometrica* 52:363–89.

Lerman, Robert I. 1989. "Child Support Policies." In *Welfare Policy for the 1990s*, edited by Phoebe H. Cottingham and David T. Ellwood. Cambridge, Mass: Harvard University Press.

Lewin/ICF. 1990. *Estimates of Expenditures on Children and Child Support Guidelines*. Report prepared for the U.S. Department of Health and Human Services. Washington, D.C.: Lewin/ICF.

McLanahan, Sara S. 1988. "Family Structure and Dependency: Early Transitions to Female Household Headship." *Demography* 25:1–16.

Meyer, Daniel, Irwin Garfinkel, Philip K. Robins, and Donald Oellerich. 1991. "The Costs and Effects of a National Child Support Assurance System." Institute for Research on Poverty Discussion Paper 940-91. Madison: University of Wisconsin–Madison, Institute for Research on Poverty.

Michalopoulos, Charles, and Irwin Garfinkel. 1989. "Reducing the Welfare Dependence and Poverty of Single Mothers by Means of Earnings and Child Support: Wishful Thinking and Realistic Possibility." Institute for Research on Poverty Discussion Paper 882-89. Madison: University of Wisconsin-Madison, Institute for Research on Poverty.

Moffitt, Robert. 1986. "The Econometrics of Piecewise-Linear Budget Constraints." *Journal of Business and Economic Statistics* 4 (July):317–28.

National Commission on Children. 1991. *Beyond Rhetoric: A New American Agenda for Children and Families*. Washington, D.C.: National Commission on Children.

Oellerich, Donald T. 1984. "The Effects of Potential Child Support Transfers on Wisconsin AFDC Costs, Caseloads, and Recipient Well-being." Institute for Research on Poverty Special Report 35. Madison: University of Wisconsin–Madison, Institute for Research on Poverty.

Oellerich, Donald T., Irwin Garfinkel, and Philip K. Robins. 1991. "Private Child Support: Current and Potential Impacts." *Journal of Sociology and Social Welfare* 18:3–23.

Robins, Philip K. 1986. "Child Support, Welfare Dependency, and Poverty." *American Economic Review* 76:768–88.

————. 1987. "An Analysis of Trends in Child Support and AFDC from 1978 to 1983." Institute for Research on Poverty Discussion Paper 842-87. Madison: University of Wisconsin–Madison, Institute for Research on Poverty.

U.S. Bureau of the Census. 1990. *Money Income and Poverty Status in the United States: 1989 (Advanced Data from the March 1990 Current Population Survey). Current Population Reports,* ser. P-60, no. 168. Washington, D.C.: U.S. Government Printing Office.

Chapter Eight

THE ECONOMIC IMPACT OF CHILD SUPPORT REFORM ON THE POVERTY STATUS OF CUSTODIAL AND NONCUSTODIAL FAMILIES

Ann Nichols-Casebolt

One out of every five children in the United States today is eligible for child support (Garfinkel and Melli 1982). That is, 13.5 million American children have a living parent not residing with them who could be contributing to their financial support. Many of these children are poor; of all the children eligible to receive child support in 1981, 35 percent were living in poverty and almost 30 percent received some assistance from welfare (Oellerich 1984).

The lack of child support awards, inadequate awards, and nonpayment of awards all contribute to the poverty status of these children. As cited in previous chapters in this volume, census data indicate that in 1982 only 59 percent of all families eligible for child support even received a legally enforceable award. And of those with an award, the average award was less than $2,200 per year. In addition, only about half received the full amount of child support payment due them, and about one-quarter received nothing (U.S. Bureau of the Census 1983).

But can fathers who do not live with their children pay more in child support than they are currently paying?[1] Most studies have suggested that absent fathers can increase their child support payments (Cassetty 1978; Garfinkel and Melli 1982; Jones, Gordon, and Sawhill 1976; McDonald, Moran, and Garfinkel 1983; and Oellerich 1984). However, a critical question still remains—how much more should they pay? There is considerable disagreement over this issue because the answer depends not only on the income of the absent fathers but also on judgments concerning how much of that income should be shared with the child.

Although many issues must be considered before making decisions regarding child support reform (e.g., the effect on parent-child relationships, remarriage, etc.), a major concern in the controversy is the extent to which various reform regimes alleviate the poverty of solo-mother families. What is often ignored, however, is the impact of child support reform on the economic status of absent fathers and any new dependents they acquire. It is clear that female-headed families are at great risk for poverty, but it is unclear to what extent absent fathers can alleviate the poverty of their children without themselves slipping into poverty. To date, there have been no research findings on the economic consequences of an improved child support system on the absent parent.

This chapter begins to fill this gap by examining the impact of one current child support reform proposal on the economic status of both the custodial and noncustodial families. Specifically, it compares current levels of child support payment to potential levels under the reform, and then determines the effect of the current and reform systems on the poverty status of these families.

CURRENT SYSTEM OF CHILD SUPPORT AND A PROPOSAL FOR REFORM

The establishment of a child support order is a mechanism to enforce the financial responsibility of noncustodial parents for their children. Although most states have codified the right of a child to the support of both parents, the operation of the child support system within each state is handled chiefly by local judiciary. For a family to be eligible for child support, there must be a court order or a court-approved voluntary agreement. The amount to be paid, however, is determined on a case-by-case basis, and historically the guidelines given the courts have been very broad (Chambers 1979; Krause 1981; Melli 1984).

As welfare costs have mounted in the last several decades, congressional interest in private child support payments has grown. As described in previous chapters, between 1950 and 1984, the U.S. Congress enacted a series of bills to strengthen public enforcement of private child support, including, most significantly, in 1975, Part D to Title IV of the Social Security Act, thereby establishing the Child Support Enforcement (or IV-D) program; and, in the summer of 1984, the Child Support Enforcement Amendments, requiring all states to (a) initiate a process to withhold child support from the wages of noncustodial parents who are delinquent in their child support payments for one month and (b) appoint blue-ribbon commissions to devise statewide standards for child support.

Then, in 1988 under the Family Support Act, states were required to establish mandatory guidelines for child support awards and provide for immediate wage withholding for all new and revised orders for child support.

A Reform Proposal

In the summer of 1980 a research team from the Institute for Research on Poverty (IRP), University of Wisconsin–Madison, began to examine the child support system to find ways to improve it. The team concluded that the current system of child support fostered parental irresponsibility, was inequitable, and failed to alleviate poverty (Garfinkel and Melli 1982). Their report recommended a new child support assurance program aimed at rectifying these defects. Under a child support assurance system, all parents living apart from their children would be obligated to share income with their children. The sharing rate would be specified by law and would depend only upon the number of children owed support. The obligation would be collected through payroll withholding, in the manner of social security and income taxes. Children with a living noncustodial parent would be entitled to benefits equal to either the child support paid by the noncustodial parent or a socially assured minimum benefit, whichever was higher.[2]

The success of this reform depends in great measure on the potential for increased child support collections. It is based on the premise that noncustodial parents have an untapped ability to pay more in child support. That premise is examined here.

DATA AND METHODOLOGY

This study utilizes the Michigan Panel Study of Income Dynamics (PSID), a national longitudinal study that began in 1968. The 1968 interviews were conducted with 4,902 families: 1,872 from a low-income sample and 2,930 from a national cross-section of the population. Weighting was done to adjust for the oversampling of low-income families and differential response rates. In each year the PSID attempted to follow all individuals in the original 1968 sample, whether or not they remained in the same family. The overall sample size of the PSID decreased periodically because of nonresponse and increased periodically because of new family formation (Duncan and Morgan 1978).

For this analysis the 13-year individual tape of the PSID was utilized. The individual tape contains a record for each person living in
a panel family at the time of the interview. In addition to the information unique to each individual (age, education, etc.), each record
contains all the data for the family in which the person was living. In
1980, the 13th year of the study, there were 6,533 families with almost
23,000 individuals in the sample. (Sample size increased between
1968 and 1980 because more new families were formed than families
that were lost from the sample.)

Theoretically, with this dataset we could observe characteristics of
both the custodial and noncustodial families. However, to be able to
"match" custodial and noncustodial parents, only those couples who
resided in the same family at some point during the survey period
were selected. Thus, our sample consists of married couples who
experienced a divorce or separation at some point in the 13 years of
the study and who had children younger than age 18 at the time of
the marital split. This excludes all those who divorced or separated
prior to 1968 as well as those parents who never married (i.e., paternity cases).

Ideally, we wanted to observe both members of the couple prior to
and after the split. However, attrition and an "unfortunate" feature of
the survey meant that this was not always the case. The PSID attempted to follow only members of the original 1968 families. Thus,
nonsample members who married sample members were not followed
after a marital split. This meant that the only cases in which both
parents were followed after a marital split were those in which the
two individuals were original sample members. Although there are a
few cases in which two sample members married subsequent to 1968,
essentially only couples who were married in 1968 met this criterion.

Data were collected, however, on nonsample spouses during the
time they resided with the sample member. Therefore at the very least
we obtained "pre-split" information on both mother and father. With
this in mind, the selection criteria were designed to capture records
that had "post-split" information on both mother and father when
these were available, as well as records in which post-split information on one or the other was missing. Of the total cases selected, 343
were those in which the father became a nonrespondent after the
marital split and only the mother's record was retained; 216 were
those in which the mother became a nonrespondent and only the
father's record was retained; and in 141 cases both the mother and
father were retained in the sample.[3]

Because of the limited number of father custody cases, the sample was also restricted to those cases in which the mother was the custodial parent of at least one of the children.

Methodology

The first step in the analysis was to determine the income of the noncustodial father. Income was defined as all nonwelfare monies received by the father. This included earnings, dividends, pensions, interest, and social insurance (e.g., Social Security benefits, Unemployment Compensation, and Worker's Compensation) income. For fathers who remained in the sample, it was the total of such income received in the last sample year. For those who left the sample, the income from the year prior to the split was used as a proxy for current income.[4] The effects of inflation were corrected by adjusting all income to 1981 dollars.

When these income levels were determined, the next step was to compare current levels of payment with an estimate of the amount of child support that could potentially be collected under the Wisconsin reform proposal. As described in earlier chapters, the Wisconsin proposal outlines a percentage-of-income standard that would be applied to gross income, based on the number of children. The proposed rates are 17 percent for one child, 25 percent for two children, 29 percent for three children, 31 percent for four children, and 34 percent for five or more children. The final step was to determine the impact of these potential child support amounts on the economic status of both the custodial and noncustodial families.

RESULTS

Table 8.1 presents the relationship of child support payments to the income of the noncustodial father. The data for this analysis are based upon the Michigan survey weighted subsample of cases in which the mother was retained in the sample and current child support information was available.[5] The weighted subsample for this and subsequent analyses was used to retain the representativeness of the sample (see note 3).

It can be seen that the higher the income of the father, the more likely he is to pay child support, but even in the highest income category not quite half the fathers make payments (column 3, table 8.1). In addition, the average amount paid by those paying the most—

Table 8.1 CURRENT AND POTENTIAL CHILD SUPPORT PAYMENTS BY INCOME OF NONCUSTODIAL FATHER

Income of Father	Number of Fathers (1)	Number Paying Support (2)	Percentage Paying Support (3)	Mean Support Paid ($) (4)	Potential Mean Support, Using Standard ($) (5)
0–$1,500	240	1	.4	109	70
$1,501–$3,000	143	37	26	153	425
$3,001–$5,000	353	60	17	583	1,082
$5,001–$7,500	1,044	141	14	2,174	1,493
$7,501–$10,000	911	216	24	2,773	2,246
$10,001–$15,000	2,074	1,120	54	2,031	2,882
$15,001–$20,000	2,221	948	43	2,552	4,320
$20,001–$25,000	964	427	44	2,922	5,351
$25,000+	1,853	880	47	3,062	8,937
Totals	9,803	3,830	39	2,502	4,218

Notes: Data in table and in subsequent tables in this chapter are based on the Michigan survey weighted subsample. The unweighted sample size totals 484 absent fathers. The sample for this analysis includes all cases in which the mother was retained in the sample and current child support information was available.

$3,062—is substantially below the 1981 poverty level of $6,110 for a family of two. Comparing the current child support amounts to the potential under the reform proposal clearly indicates that there would be substantial improvement (column 5, table 8.1). Even assuming there is no increase in the numbers of those paying, the average payment would increase by almost 69 percent (from $2,502 to $4,218).

An integral part of this reform proposal, however, is that collections would also improve because of automatic income assignment. If we assume that such a procedure would be 100 percent effective (i.e., all noncustodial fathers pay a percentage of their income for child support), the improvement over the current system would be well over 300 percent. Even if we assume, as is likely, that the income assignment would only be 80 percent effective, the result remains nontrivial—an increase of almost 250 percent.

Although it seems evident from these data that the reform proposal would be a great improvement over the current system, its impact upon the economic status of the families still needs to be addressed. Table 8.2 presents the percentages of women at various poverty levels. The first and fourth columns (pre-split) show their distribution prior to the divorce, the second and fifth columns (post-split) show their distribution in the current year, and the third and sixth columns (with reform) predict their distribution under a 100 percent effective reform proposal. Poverty levels were determined on the basis of total nonwelfare family income and family size. Welfare income was not included in any of these income estimates because such benefits rise (or decline) dollar for dollar in response to the decrease (or increase) in child support. Excluding such income, of course, overestimates the actual number of poor persons, but I believe it gives a clearer picture of how effective child support is, and can be, in contributing to the economic self-sufficiency of such households. Because we expected that nonwhites will have significantly lower incomes than whites, and therefore receive less in child support payments, the sample was disaggregated by race.

Probably the most striking result in table 8.2 is the post-split increase in poverty for whites. Not only does the percentage of all those below the poverty line increase, but the largest proportion of these have nonwelfare incomes of less than one-half the poverty level. For nonwhites the increase is not as substantial, but again, those below the poverty line tend to be very poor.

A comparison of the current system (columns 2 and 5, table 8.2) and the application of the standard (columns 3 and 6) indicates that

Table 8.2 POVERTY LEVELS OF CUSTODIAL FAMILIES PRE-SPLIT, POST-SPLIT, AND WITH THE PERCENTAGE-OF-INCOME STANDARD AND 100 PERCENT EFFECTIVE COLLECTIONS

	Whites (%)			Nonwhites (%)		
Poverty Level[a]	Pre-split (1)	Post-split (2)	With Reform (3)	Pre-split (4)	Post-split (5)	With Reform (6)
.0–.5	2.3	15.7	9.7	10.0	30.7	24.6
.5–1.0	7.6	13.0	12.1	23.4	13.7	11.5
1.0–1.5	10.8	12.2	7.9	23.0	9.8	15.3
1.5–2.0	16.5	16.2	14.7	13.6	21.3	12.0
2+	62.7	42.9	55.7	30.1	24.5	36.5
Percentage below poverty line	9.9	28.7	21.8	33.4	44.3	36.1
Average income ($)	22,210	13,483[b]	18,486[c]	14,836	9,373[b]	11,179[c]
N (weighted sample size)		238 (7,901)			246 (1,902)	

Note: The weighted sample for this analysis includes all cases in which the mother was retained in the sample and current family income was available.

[a] Proportion of nonwelfare income to poverty line.

[b] Significantly different from pre-split ($p < .01$).

[c] Significantly different from pre-split and post-split ($p < .01$).

the number below the poverty line would be reduced under a 100 percent effective reform. There would be a 6.9 percentage point reduction in the poverty rate for whites and a comparable 8.2 percent reduction for nonwhites. Although a substantial number would remain poor, their relative poverty status would improve. The percentages below .5 of poverty would decrease from 15.7 percent to 9.7 percent for whites and from 30.7 percent to 24.6 percent for nonwhites. This trend is reflected in the average income of these families. Income drops significantly for post-split families, and although it would rise somewhat with a 100 percent effective reform, it would not reach the original pre-split level.

The next question is, What is the impact of a reformed child support system on the economic status of the noncustodial family? Would we in fact be impoverishing fathers (and possibly their new families) in an effort to improve the economic status of children from a previous marriage? The data in table 8.3 address that issue. These data were obtained from cases in which we had current information on the father (i.e., those in which the father had remained in the sample).

The most significant finding from this analysis is the difference between the poverty levels of custodial and noncustodial families after divorce. Whereas women experience a substantial increase in poverty, men experience a substantial decrease. Comparing columns 2 and 5 with columns 3 and 6 of table 8.3, one sees that poverty rates do increase for noncustodial families with the application of the standard. For whites, they increase 1.5 percentage points, but the overall rate is still less than one-third that of custodial families. For nonwhites, there is an 8.9 percent increase, with the resulting poverty rate only 1 percentage point lower than that of custodial mothers.

Changes in the average incomes of noncustodial families are also shown in table 8.3. One sees that, for white fathers, income increases after the split, and although it would decline with the reform, it is still higher than the income of white mothers. For nonwhites, income drops after the split and would be further reduced with the reform.[6] In fact, with the reform the average income of noncustodial nonwhite fathers would be lower than for noncustodial mothers.

In summary, the percentage-of-income standard under this reform proposal does have the potential for improving the economic status of custodial families, but it would at the same time impoverish some noncustodial families. The least improvement and greatest impoverishment under this system would be for nonwhites—not surprising, in view of the lower income of our nonwhite sample.

Table 8.3 POVERTY LEVELS OF NONCUSTODIAL FAMILIES PRE-SPLIT, POST-SPLIT, AND WITH THE PERCENTAGE-OF-INCOME STANDARD AND 100 PERCENT EFFECTIVE COLLECTIONS

	Whites (%)			Nonwhites (%)		
Poverty Level[a]	Pre-split (1)	Post-split (2)	With Reform (3)	Pre-split (4)	Post-split (5)	With Reform (6)
.0–.5	4.0	1.3	2.4	11.7	12.7	18.7
.5–1.0	5.2	3.5	3.9	24.0	13.4	16.3
1.0–1.5	6.7	6.2	12.7	14.9	14.3	13.2
1.5–2.0	15.1	8.7	7.5	9.0	7.9	11.6
2+	69.0	80.3	73.5	40.5	51.8	40.1
Percentage below poverty line	9.2	4.8	6.3	35.7	26.1	35.0
Average income ($)	23,728	24,984[b]	19,701[c]	14,682	13,579[b]	10,868[c]
N (weighted sample size)	187 (5,328)			170 (1,399)		

Note: The weighted sample for this analysis includes all cases in which the father was retained in the sample and current family income was available.

[a] Proportion of nonwelfare income to poverty line.

[b] Significantly different from pre-split ($p < .01$).

[c] Significantly different from pre-split and post-split ($p < .01$).

CONCLUSIONS

The issue of child support reform is of national importance. Demographers project that nearly one-half of all children born today will become potentially eligible for child support before they reach adulthood (Bumpass 1984). Although issues other than alleviating poverty must be considered in setting new directions (see for example, the issues raised by Kelly 1985: 174–79), a major goal of all proposed reforms of the current child support system is to improve the economic well-being of families eligible for child support (and concomitantly reduce welfare costs). An examination of one group of such families—those who have been married—does indicate that the current system leaves many custodial families well below the poverty level.

This analysis shows that the application of one proposed alternative to the current system could reduce poverty for these families. It also indicates, however, that this alternative, compared to the current system, would increase poverty for the noncustodial family. But we have noted that noncustodial families as a whole remain better off than before the split and are consistently better off than the custodial families after the split.

Such results certainly add to the complexity of policy decisions in this area, and given the shortcomings of this particular dataset (e.g., attrition, and the exclusion of never-married and father-custody families), it is clear that further research on the economic impact of alternative child support regimes is necessary before concrete conclusions can be drawn. Although empirical results can provide information on how both custodial and noncustodial parents would be affected, the normative questions remain: Should a noncustodial parent (typically the father) be required to share some of his income with his child regardless of the impact on his economic status? Do the needs of the child take precedence over the needs of the parent and the parent's subsequent children? What is an equitable child support obligation? Given the vulnerability of the populations at stake, it is hoped that answers to these questions will soon be forthcoming.

Notes

From *The Journal of Marriage and The Family* 48 (Nov. 1986): 875–880. Copyrighted 1986 by The National Council on Family Relations, 3989 Central Ave., N.E., Suite 550, Minneapolis MN 55421. Reprinted by permission.

1. Nationwide, only 8.7 percent of all families eligible for child support are headed by fathers (Kamerman 1985).

2. The argument for a socially assured benefit is two-fold. First, it would reduce the risk to children whose noncustodial parents became unemployed or unable to work. In such cases, the child support payments would fall only to the socially assured benefit level, not to zero. Second, the assured benefit, when combined with earnings, would lift many single-parent households out of poverty and remove them from welfare. Custodial parents going to work would not face a dollar-for-dollar reduction in their child support payments, as they do under AFDC.

3. Reweighting techniques have been employed throughout sampling years to correct for differential nonresponse of sample members. Michigan researchers argue that the weighted sample remains representative (Duncan and Morgan 1978). However, my comparison of several family characteristics prior to the marital split by record type (i.e., only father remained in sample, only mother remained in sample, and both remained in sample) indicated that the men and women who are no longer in the sample had lower education, lower earnings, and lower total family income. The largest differences were between those couples in which one member left the sample and those in which both were retained. Those in which both members of the couple remained in the sample were more likely to be white, older, have more children, and have significantly more income. On the basis of these characteristics, it appears that estimations of current economic status that exclude those who left the sample will be biased upward, and caution will have to be exercised in drawing firm conclusions from these data.

4. Using pre-split income as a proxy for current income assumes that the father's income does not change significantly from one time period to another. A comparison of pre- and post-split income for those who remained in the sample indicates that there was, in fact, no significant change in "head's nonwelfare income" between the two time periods.

5. Excluding records in which the mother left the sample means that there may be a potential overestimate in the average child support currently paid and the potential under the reform. This is because, on average, these fathers have lower income and fewer children than cases in which the mother was retained in the sample.

6. Although we would expect that a decrease in income after the split would increase the percentage of those below poverty, it should be kept in mind that poverty status is based on income *and* family size. Because family size decreased, on average, after the split, economic status was improved.

References

Bumpass, Larry. 1984. "Children and Marital Disruption: A Replication and An Update." *Demography* 21:71–82.

Cassetty, Judith. 1978. *Child Support and Public Policy*. Lexington, Mass.: Lexington Books.

Chambers, David. 1979. *Making Fathers Pay: The Enforcement of Child Support*. Chicago: University of Chicago Press.

Duncan, Greg, and J. N. Morgan. 1978. *Five Thousand American Families: Patterns of Economic Progress*, vol. 6. Ann Arbor, Mich.: University of Michigan, Institute for Social Research.

Garfinkel, Irwin, and Marygold Melli. 1982. *Child Support: Weaknesses of the Old and Features of a Proposed New System*. Madison: University of Wisconsin–Madison, Institute for Research on Poverty.

Jones, Carol, N. M. Gordon, and I. V. Sawhill. 1976. "Child Support Payments in the United States." Urban Institute Working Paper 992-03. Washington, D.C.: Urban Institute Press.

Kamerman, Sheila. 1985. "Young, Poor, and a Mother Alone: Problems and Possible Solutions." In *Services to Young Families*, edited by Harriette McAdoo and T. M. Jim Parham (1–38). Washington, D.C.: American Public Welfare Association.

Kelly, Robert F. 1985. "The Family and the Urban Underclass." *Journal of Family Issues* 6: 159–184.

Krause, Harry O. 1981. *Child Support in America: The Legal Perspective*. Charlottesville, Va.: Michie.

McDonald, Thomas, J. Moran, and I. Garfinkel. 1983. *Wisconsin Study of Absent Fathers' Ability to Pay More Child Support*. Madison: University of Wisconsin–Madison, Institute for Research on Poverty.

Melli, Marygold. 1984. *Child Support: A Survey of the Statutes*. Madison: University of Wisconsin–Madison, Institute for Research on Poverty.

Oellerich, Donald. 1984. *The Effects of Potential Child Support Transfers on Wisconsin AFDC Costs, Caseloads, and Recipient Well-Being*. Madison: University of Wisconsin–Madison, Institute for Research on Poverty.

U.S. Bureau of the Census. 1983. "Child Support and Alimony." *Current Population Reports*, ser. P-23, no. 124. Washington, D.C.: U.S. Government Printing Office.

THE USE OF NORMATIVE STANDARDS IN FAMILY LAW DECISIONS: DEVELOPING MATHEMATICAL STANDARDS FOR CHILD SUPPORT

Irwin Garfinkel and Marygold S. Melli

The 1980s marked an important institutional shift in American family law from the individualized judicial determination of certain issues to the use of normative standards. This change represents a major break with traditional decision making in family law, which has been highly individualized, with decisions made at the discretion of the trial judge and great deference accorded the trial court's decision by appellate courts.

Probably the most visible example of this change is in the establishment of child support awards. Traditionally, this amount has been set on a case-by-case basis by a judge in a judicial hearing at which both parents have the opportunity to present relevant evidence. This approach has been said to be necessary to allow the trial judge to tailor the order to the needs of a particular family. No two families were seen to be alike, and flexibility was needed in the system to enable the judge to weigh the equities of each situation and arrive at the best solution for the family involved.[1]

Federally mandated standards have now reduced that flexibility. The Child Support Enforcement Amendments of 1984 required the states to develop mathematically formulated guidelines for use by the courts in setting child support. The Family Support Act of 1988 has made those formulae presumptive (i.e., courts are required to use them or to give written reasons for not doing so).[2] This pioneering effort to change the structure of child-support decision making is in its initial stages. Theories on how a normative standard for child support ought to be developed are still evolving. This chapter attempts to add to the growing literature on how to structure a workable formula. It describes the policy analysis that led to the development of the flat percentage-of-income standard, pioneered by Wisconsin in 1983. That standard and the income-shares standard developed by the federal Office of Child Support Enforcement are the two most widely adopted standards. As of mid-1989, 24 states and territories had adopted the income-shares approach,[3] 13 had adopted the flat per-centage-of-income approach,[4] and another 10 had adopted a varying percentage-of-income standard.[5]

The development of the income-shares standard and the reasons for choosing it have been described at length elsewhere (Williams 1987). This chapter compares and contrasts the income-shares standard with the Wisconsin flat percentage-of-income standard. The objective is to provide sufficient information on the theoretical differences between these two competing formulae to enable the states to make informed assessments as they refine and reform their standards.

The first section of this chapter briefly reviews the reasons behind the trend toward normative child support standards. The second section discusses the two major alternative philosophical approaches to child support standards—cost sharing and income sharing—and then describes the percentage-of-income and the income-shares standards, both of which are based upon the income-sharing approach. Five succeeding sections focus on critical issues on which the two standards differ: how to choose the percentage of income that nonresident parents[6] should transfer to their children; whether the percentage should vary depending on the income of the nonresident parent; whether the percentage should depend on the income of the resident parent; whether the child support obligation should depend upon actual expenditures on children; and how simple or complex the standard should be. The final section is a summary and conclusion.

BACKGROUND

The impetus for abandoning the principle that child support amounts should be determined on a case-by-case basis came from the documented failure of the traditional approach to provide adequate support for children in single-parent households. Although recognition of problems with provision of support for children by absent parents can be traced back at least to 1907 (when the issue had become sufficiently serious to attract the attention of the National Conference of Commissioners on Uniform State Laws, which approved a Uniform Desertion and Nonsupport Act in 1910),[7] little effective action was taken until the 1950s, when Congress became concerned about the expenditures of funds under the Aid to Families with Dependent Children (AFDC) program. AFDC is the public assistance program established by the Social Security Act in 1935 as a joint state-federal effort to provide a minimal standard of living for children who had lost their primary supporting parent. Because the bulk of single mothers then were widows, the drafters of the Social Security Act had not envisioned the program as a measure to shore up a system of divorce and paternity establishment that failed to provide sufficiently for children. But by 1949 the Social Security Administration estimated that the total bill for aid to families where the father was living but absent and not supporting was about $205 million.

In 1950 Congress enacted the first federal child support legislation. Between 1950 and 1984, as divorce, separation, and out-of-wedlock births increased and costs of the AFDC program escalated, Congress enacted a series of bills to strengthen child support enforcement. In 1975 a congressional committee investigating the causes of the rapidly increasing costs of the AFDC program concluded: "The problem of welfare in the United States is, to a considerable extent, a problem of the nonsupport of children by their absent parents" (U.S. Congress 1975). As a result, in 1975 the Child Support Enforcement Program was added to the Social Security Act (Title IV-D) (Social Security Amendments of 1974: Sec. 651 et seq.). In 1984 amendments to Title IV-D (Child Support Enforcement Amendments of 1984: Sec. 654–66) mandated that the states provide enforcement services for all children—non-AFDC as well as AFDC recipients—and required that mathematical guidelines be developed by all the states by October 1, 1987. The guidelines could be used by the courts to determine child support obligations but were not binding. Following upon these amendments, the Family Support Act of 1988 (Sec. 466[b][3][A]) requires states to make their guidelines the presumptive child support obligation—that is, judges can depart from the guidelines only if they justify the departure in writing.

There are three reasons for this rather dramatic shift from judicial discretion to presumptive standards in the establishment of child support awards. The first is that the old system resulted in child support awards that were much too low,[8] For example, U.S. Bureau of the Census reported that existing child support awards to resident mothers totaled nearly $10 billion in 1983, but a more recent study estimated that if either the percentage-of-income standard adopted by Wisconsin or the income shares standard adopted by Colorado had been applied in all cases, the total would have been between $28 and $30 billion, or about two and one half times the amount of existing awards (Garfinkel and Oellerich 1989: 219). It is important to note, however, that the problem of low awards may be due as much to the failure to update awards over time as to the size of the initial awards.[9] Indeed, data from Wisconsin suggest that the state's problem of low awards resulted uniformly almost from a failure to increase awards over time as the incomes of nonresident parents increased.[10] However, preliminary analyses of national data suggest that initially low awards as well as the failure to update awards account for the low level of current awards. (Garfinkel, Oellerich, and Robins 1990).

The second reason for the marked shift in the establishment of child support awards is that judicial discretion led to inequity in child support awards. Research has shown that even within the same jurisdiction, supporting parents in similar circumstances were treated very differently.[11] When the number of broken marriages and out-of-wedlock births was small, greater equity was perhaps achieved by the old individualized system. In small communities, the judge knew the parents and the circumstances, so justice was perhaps better served by taking account of all particulars. But when the number of cases is large and the system impersonal, this method breaks down. In practice, judges now do very little to tailor child support to particular circumstances.

The third reason is that in view of the existence of public programs such as AFDC that assure a minimum income to children who are potentially eligible for child support, the public has a direct financial stake in the amount of private child support paid by nonresident parents whose children are potential recipients of public benefits. The lower the amount of support paid by nonresident parents, the greater must be the burden on taxpayers. How the support of poor children should be apportioned between the resident parent, the nonresident parent, and the public is a public policy issue more appropriate to the legislative branch than the judicial branch of government.

NORMATIVE STANDARDS

Any normative standard must be based on an attempt to recognize and balance the sometimes competing values that a child support award seeks to serve. Those values relate to the three different persons involved in a child support award: the child, the resident parent, and the nonresident parent.

The child needs an adequate standard of living and fair treatment by the nonresident parent. This means that the child is entitled to as high a standard of living as his or her parents can provide. Current statistics show that the standard of living of nonresident parents usually increases after divorce, while the living standard of children and the resident parent drops (see Duncan and Hoffman 1985: 485 and Weitzman 1988, chap. 10). As a matter of public policy, this discrepancy in treatment should be minimized in the interest of fairness to the child.

The resident parent, of necessity, provides support for the child because he or she shares resources with the child. The resident parent, therefore, is entitled to help from the child's other parent and to fair treatment in relation to the other parent. A resident parent, for example, should not be required to be the sole support for a child because the nonresident parent wishes to parent another family.

Finally, the needs of the nonresident parent must be considered. He or she has need of a decent standard of living and the right to pursue an independent life. Although a nonresident parent has a duty to provide the child as adequate a standard of living as possible, this responsibility ought not prevent the parent from living adequately apart from the family.[12] A public policy that recognizes and endorses liberal divorce must acknowledge this problem.

Choosing the Basic Approach

Child support awards are based on the theory that by parenting a child, a person takes on the responsibility to share income with that child as well as the cost of raising that child. There are two approaches to setting the amount of this share: cost sharing and income sharing (Cassetty 1983: 5).

Cost sharing was the traditional way of setting child support in the individualized, case-by-case system. The base for beginning calculations was the budget submitted by the resident parent. Courts reviewed the budget, sometimes adjusting it downward if particular expenditures were found to be inconsistent with the family's standard of living prior to divorce. Once the budget for the child was set, the court examined the nonresident parent's living costs and income to determine how much that parent was able to pay. Sometimes when the parent's expenditures were so great that nothing appeared to be left for the child, the court did not count certain types of expenditures. Basically, however, the courts operated on the premise that nonresident parents were entitled to spend their money as they saw fit, with the child receiving some of what was left over. The rationale for this gentle treatment of nonresident parents was fear that the parent would refuse to pay anything by absconding or quitting work and the child would be worse off.

When cost sharing is used as the basis for developing a normative standard, the problem becomes more complex because an individual budget is not the base point. A normative figure must now be established for the cost of raising a child. Yet this cost differs considerably, depending on the parents' incomes—parents with higher incomes spend proportionately more money on their children. Because of the dilemma in setting a standard, none of the states has adopted standards based on a pure cost-sharing approach.

The focus of income sharing, the other approach to setting the amount of child support, is the income of the nonresident parent. Both of the mathematical standards discussed in this paper are based on the income-sharing approach. This choice is predicated on the belief that the income-sharing approach reflects more accurately how parents treat children in intact families. If parents with more income spend more on their children, it makes good sense to develop a standard based on this sharing of income by the nonresident parent.

The Percentage-of-Income and Income-Shares Standards

The percentage-of-income standard is rooted in a system developed by the Michigan Friend of the Court, but it is now most closely associated with the state of Wisconsin. It is quite simple. Unlike the mathematical formulae used by some states, in which a variety of factors considered relevant to the child support award are evaluated, the percentage-of-income standard is based on the principle that the two most important features in the determination of a child support award are the nonresident parent's income and the number of children to be supported.[13] By taking a certain percentage of the nonresident parent's income, varied by the number of children supported, it is possible to tie child support amounts to income. Thirteen states, including Wisconsin, use this form of percentage standard. Nine other states use the percentage standard, but vary the percentage, based on the income of the nonresident parent.

The income-shares standard was first used by Washington State and then refined and developed in a study commissioned by the federal Office of Child Support Enforcement (Advisory Panel on Child Support Guidelines and Williams 1987; Sawhill 1983). It is considerably more complex than the percentage-of-income standard. The basic child support obligation is computed by multiplying the combined income of both parents by percentages that decline with income. For example, the percentage for one child ranges from 21.5 percent for incomes between $5,976 and $11,800 to 11.8 percent for incomes over $64,250. The total child support obligation is determined by adding actual work-related child-care expenses and extraordinary medical expenses to the basic obligation. The total obligation is then prorated between each parent, based on his or her proportionate share of income. The resident parent's obligation is assumed to be met in the course of everyday sharing with the child. The nonresident parent's obligation is payable as child support.

The two standards are similar in that they both begin with an income-sharing approach. The income-shares approach, however, has elements of cost sharing, in that it considers actual expenditures for child care and medical care. Under the income-shares approach, the child support obligation declines as a percentage of the nonresident parent's income as total income increases, and it varies depending on the resident parent's income. Each of these differences is discussed later in this chapter. But we begin with the more general issue of how the percentages to be shared were determined.

CHOOSING THE PERCENTAGES

There are two possible ways to address how much income a nonresident parent should share with his or her child. One approach with intuitive appeal is to set the nonresident parent's share at a rate that would equalize income for the resident and nonresident households. This type of income sharing is known as income equalization. The object is to ensure that the children maintain the same living standard as the nonresident parent. Although income equalization has been advocated by some academics, it has not been implemented anywhere (Dodson 1988: 4, 6). It is generally opposed because equalizing incomes in the nonresident and resident households would benefit the parent living with the children by raising that parent's standard of living along with that of the children and would entail substantially greater child support obligations for most upper-middle-income and upper-income nonresident parents than other standards. Of course, any child support award benefits the resident parent because that parent lives with the children; income equalization is simply the most obvious and most extreme case.

The second approach to determining how much a parent should pay in child support is to base the amount on the proportion of the parents' incomes that would be spent on the children if they all lived together. This also has intuitive philosophical appeal, and is the starting point for both the percentage-of-income standard and the income-shares standard. However, the manner in which the authors of the two standards arrived at the amount of the child's share differed in two respects: (1) how they viewed the difficulty of estimating the percentage of income that two-parent families devote to their children and (2) how they viewed the value judgments involved in translating the child's share in a two-parent family to the share in a single-parent family.

Determining the amount of their income that parents devote to their children is far more complex than is immediately apparent. Although there is a considerable body of economic literature on the amounts parents spend raising children, social science research has not been able to provide the exact proportions, primarily because so many expenses, such as food, housing, and transportation, are jointly consumed. Determining how to allocate these common expenditures among individual family members with differing ages and needs and decision-making capacities is the principal problem.

The architects of the income-shares approach resolved this difficulty by ultimately ignoring all but one study of expenditures on children.[14] In the 1987 report to the federal Office of Child Support Enforcement, Robert Williams, the principal designer of the income-shares standard, justified ignoring the bulk of the existing economics literature on the grounds that the 1960s data upon which these studies were based were outdated (Advisory Panel and Williams 1987). Instead, the report relied almost exclusively on the Espenshade study (1984), which was based on 1972 data. This made the task of deriving percentages for the child support standard very simple. One merely extrapolated from the estimated percentages in the two-parent family. Following this line of reasoning, however, one could now claim that the Espenshade study has been superseded by studies using data from the 1980s. But such an argument has little scientific merit, because there are no grounds for believing that the pattern of sharing between parents and their children has shifted radically during the past 30 years.

In contrast, the authors of the Wisconsin percentage-of-income standard saw the problem as far more intricate and value laden. As part of the child support research conducted by the Institute for Research on Poverty (University of Wisconsin–Madison) under a contract from the Wisconsin Department of Health and Social Services, Jacques Van der Gaag (1982: 1–44) conducted a comprehensive, 12-study review of the economics literature on expenditures on children. One of his major findings was that the range of estimates of the share of income that parents devote to their children is enormous. Even after limiting the studies to those he judged to be the most theoretically and methodologically sound, Van der Gaag found that the estimates of the proportion of income devoted to the first child ranged from 16 percent to 24 percent. Taking the midpoint of this range, he concluded that 20 percent was the best point estimate. But he cautioned, "other observers might easily reach a different point estimate."

Van der Gaag's (1982) other major conclusions were that expenditures on children were proportional up to very high income levels, and that the shares of income devoted to the second and third child were about half that devoted to the first. This research was used as a starting point, but *only* the starting point, for recommending the percentages used in the Wisconsin standard. The authors of that standard recognized that even if it were possible to determine the proportion of income spent on children in a two-parent household, it did not necessarily follow that the children should receive the same proportion of parental income when the parents live apart.

For at least three reasons, the proportion of income that nonresident parents devote to their children should be lower than the proportion they would have spent had they been living with the children. First, a parent who lives apart from, rather than together with, the child, has a much different, perhaps less satisfying relationship with that child. Second, the nonresident parent will incur some costs for the child in the course of normal visitation. Third, child support orders that are too high a percentage of the nonresident parent's income may preclude a decent standard of living for the nonresident parent and will encourage evasion.

On the other hand, there is one important reason why nonresident parents should share more than if they lived with the child. Because so many expenses, like housing, are jointly consumed when the parent and child live together, the cost to a parent of providing a given standard of living to the child is smaller if they live together. The child as well as the parent can derive the full benefits of living in a nice house, for example, at no extra cost to the parent—so long as they live together. To keep the child at the same standard of living, therefore—which is an explicit objective of nearly every child support statute in the country—requires that the nonresident share more when living apart.

None of these reasons for expecting nonresident parents to share more or less of their income with their children suggests an exact amount or percentage. Ultimately, the determination of how much the nonresident parent should pay also depends upon value judgments about how to balance the conflicting objectives of providing well for the children, minimizing public costs, and retaining incentives and a decent standard of living for the nonresident parent. Establishing a child support standard cannot be a purely scientific exercise. After considering the reasons for expecting nonresident parents to share more (or less) of their income with their children than if they lived with them and weighing the foregoing conflicting objectives, the final decision by the designers of the Wisconsin percentage-of-income standard was that the support rates for nonresident parents should equal 17 percent of gross income for one child and 25 percent, 29 percent, 31 percent, and 34 percent for two, three, four, and five or more children, respectively.

One final note: none of the studies reviewed by either Van der Gaag (1982) or the Advisory Panel on Child Support Guidelines and Williams (1987) took into account the foregone family income in a two-parent family that results from a parent—usually the mother—not working or taking a job that pays less than she can command in the market in order to have time to care for the children. As Van der Gaag showed, this implicit cost of a child may be larger than the explicit costs of a child that are included in the studies of expenditures on children. Ignoring this cost raises questions about even those standards that make the modest claim that the share of income that children would have received if the parents lived together is a reasonable starting point for determining how much child support should be paid. For standards that claim that the child should get the exact share that he or she would have enjoyed if the parents lived together, ignoring this cost makes the exercise a mockery.

To summarize, whereas both the percentage-of-income standard and the income-shares standard take as their starting point the proportion of family income that the child would receive if the parents lived together, the architects of the income-shares model proceed as though it is a simple scientific exercise to ascertain how much of two-parent families' income is spent on their children. In contrast, the architects of the Wisconsin percentage-of-income standard stress both the large range in estimates of how much of their income parents spend on their children as well as the inescapable need to make value judgments in determining child support obligations.

SHOULD THE PERCENTAGES VARY WITH THE INCOME OF THE NONRESIDENT PARENT?

As noted earlier, a critical difference between the percentage-of-income standard and the income-shares standard is that in the former, the percentage of income that the nonresident parent pays in child support is the same irrespective of income, whereas in the latter, the percentage declines substantially as income increases. This section explores the grounds for determining whether a proportional or regressive structure of sharing rates in child support standards is preferable.

Both the proportionality of the Wisconsin percentage-of-income standard and the regressivity of the income-shares standard were originally justified by their designers as reproducing the pattern of income sharing when both parents live with the children. As noted earlier, Van der Gaag's (1982) review concluded that the proportion of income devoted to children was relatively constant up to very high income levels.[15] In contrast, the federal report (Advisory Panel and Williams 1987) concluded that the proportion of income that parents spent on their children declined as income increased.

The evidence presented in the federal report (Advisory Panel and Williams 1987) is unconvincing. Of the five studies the report reviewed, only Espenshade's (1984) study supported its conclusion; three of the other four failed to examine how the costs of children varied with income, and the remaining study found the costs to be roughly proportional. One out of five is hardly solid evidence for rejecting the proportionality assumption. Moreover, the report's technical argument for preferring the Espenshade study was neither directly related to the proportionality issue nor supported by the weight of professional economics opinion.[16]

On the other hand, neither the evidence reviewed by Van der Gaag (1982) nor the work published since then has presented convincing evidence that the costs of children are proportional to income. Although all of the studies have shown that expenditures on children increase with income, most have indicated that expenditures as a proportion of income decline as income rises. Van der Gaag (1982: 21) noted, however, that one common approach to estimating the costs of children builds in this result. Moreover, of the studies he reviewed, the two that found rough proportionality—including one of his own— also appeared to be superior on methodological grounds to most other studies.[17] Furthermore, as already noted, none of the studies reviewed took account of the indirect costs of children that arise from a mother giving up or reducing market work and earnings in order to care for her child. Finally, none of the studies on the costs of children was concerned primarily with the issue of whether expenditures on children increase in proportion to income. In short, before either flat or declining percentages of income in a child support standard can be satisfactorily justified by appeal to the proportion of income that children would receive if both parents lived together, more research is warranted.

The absence of reliable scientific evidence on child expenditures by income class may be a blessing in disguise, in that it makes abundantly clear that value judgments are required to design a child support standard. We suspect that once the value judgments implicit in the two standards are made explicit, the flat percentage-of-income standard will have wider appeal than the declining percentages in the income-shares standard. It is hard to justify state legislation that requires a working-class nonresident parent to contribute a much larger proportion of his or her income to his or her children than that required by a middle-income nonresident parent and requires a middle-income nonresident parent to contribute a much larger share of his or her income than that required by the upper-middle-income nonresident parent. Regressive taxes are widely perceived to be unfair. A regressive child support standard is unlikely to command greater support. In contrast, a proportional child support standard like the Wisconsin percentage-of-income standard is likely to be perceived as equitable.

SHOULD CHILD SUPPORT DEPEND ON THE INCOME OF THE RESIDENT PARENT?

Probably the most controversial aspect of the percentage-of-income standard is that it does not take into account the income of the resident parent. In this respect, it represents a complete break with past practice. Traditionally in child support law, the financial resources of the resident parent played a critical role. That law, as stated earlier, was based on a cost-sharing approach and was framed around two issues: the needs of the child and the ability of the nonresident parent to pay. It was assumed that the more income the resident parent had, the more of the child's needs were already being met with this income and, therefore, the less child support was needed from the nonresident parent.

The income-sharing approach to establishing child support obligations assumes that both parents have an obligation to share their income with their children. The percentage-of-income standard does not consider the income of the resident parent at all in setting the amount the nonresident parent should pay. It excludes the resident parent's income for several reasons. First, income sharing is based on the principle that to parent a child is to incur an obligation to share income with the child. Conditioning the obligation on the income of the resident parent undermines this principle.

Second, the child is entitled to a share of both parents' incomes. When the parents live together, the child shares the benefits (and bears some of the costs as well) if both parents work. There is no evidence that the share of income the child receives from the father declines if the child's mother starts working. Indeed, as conventionally measured, the proportion of total family income devoted to the child will actually be higher when both parents work, because of child care expenses. A child in a single-parent household with two income-producing parents should enjoy the advantages of that situation, as though the family lived as one unit.

Finally, the percentage-of-income standard assumes that resident parents share their income with the children with whom they live. The resident parent bears the burden of a multitude of hidden expenses associated with being a single parent that are ignored in most considerations of the cost of caring for a child. Some of these costs include, for example, the need to provide child care because there is no parent available to babysit while the other parent goes shopping, to the dentist, or to a school conference for an older child; as well as the increased cost of a household where one parent must both support and care for the family alone so that time is limited, more expensive convenience items must be used, and advantage cannot be taken of sales (Bruch 1987). Furthermore, the resident parent's income will depend in large part upon how much he or she works. But the more the resident parent works, the greater the child care costs. If resident parent income is to be counted in the determination of the nonresident parent's child support obligation, the child care expenses the resident parent incurs to earn that income cannot be ignored. Not surprisingly, the income-shares standard does take into account child care expenditures. But as discussed later in this chapter, doing so both weakens the income-sharing principle by inserting an element of cost sharing and substantially complicates the determination and updating of child support awards.

Under the income-shares standard, the child support obligation of the nonresident parent declines as the income of the resident parent increases. But this is only an accidental byproduct of the fact that the percentages in the standard decline as income increases. If the percentages in the income-shares standard were constant rather than declining, the income of the resident parent would play no role in determining the obligation of the nonresident parent. Indeed, if it were the case that the percentage of family income spent on children increased with family income, the income-shares standard would lead to the absurd result that the higher the income of the resident parent, the greater would be the child support obligation of the nonresident parent. This is not generally perceived, and therefore is worth explaining.

Recall that under the income-shares standard, the child support obligation is computed by multiplying the combined income of both parents by percentages that are determined by how much of their income two-parent families spend on their children. The obligation is then prorated between the parents based on their proportionate shares of income. The resident parent's obligation is assumed to be met in the course of everyday sharing with the child. The nonresident parent's obligation is payable as child support.[18]

Now suppose that research showed that two-parent families spent 20 percent of their income on one child at all income levels. Consider a case in which the nonresident father has a $20,000 income and the resident mother has a $10,000 income. Their total income is $30,000. The total child support obligation is $6,000. His share is two-thirds of the total, or $4,000. Now suppose that the resident mother's income is $20,000. Total income is now $40,000. The total obligation is $8,000. But the father's share is only one-half the total, or once more, $4,000. Resident-parent income would be irrelevant in determining the child support obligation in the income-shares standard if the percentages were constant rather than declining. What if research showed that families with incomes below $40,000 spent 20 percent on their children, whereas those with $40,000 or more spent 25 percent of their income on their children? In this case, as the income of the resident mother increased from $10,000 to $20,000, the child support obligation of the nonresident father would increase from $4,000 to $5,000.

There may, of course, be arguments for taking resident-parent income into account when setting a child support award. For example, failure to consider it leads to what some consider to be inequitable results, especially in extreme cases. The argument is that whereas it is fair for a nonresident parent earning $20,000 to pay $3,400 in child support if the resident parent has no income, it is unfair to expect the nonresident parent to pay the same amount if the resident parent earns $60,000. It is up to public policymakers to decide whether these circumstances overcome the income-sharing principle of child support, which suggests that there is nothing inequitable about nonresident parents paying a constant share of their income irrespective of the income of the resident parent, thus enabling the child to benefit from two income-producing parents. But taking resident-parent income into account in the unsatisfactory manner used by the income-shares standard is certainly not the answer.

SHOULD CHILD SUPPORT DEPEND UPON EXTRAORDINARY EXPENDITURES?

Under the income-shares standard, child support obligations depend upon actual child care expenditures and extraordinary medical care expenditures. These expenditures are irrelevant in the Wisconsin percentage-of-income standard.

There are numerous objections to basing child support obligations on actual expenditures. To begin with, as mentioned earlier, the practice is inconsistent with the income-sharing principle underlying both the income-shares and percentage-of-income standard. Furthermore, simply adding a prorated share of these costs to the basic child support obligation violates the claim of the architects of the income-shares standard that the child support obligation secures for the child the same portion of the nonresident parent's income as the child would have enjoyed if the parents lived together. The expenditure data used to derive the proportion of income that two-parent families devote to their children include expenditures on child care and medical care. If the percentages reported in the Espanshade (1984) study were correct, adding a prorated share of these expenses to the percentages makes the total child support obligation too high. Child care and medical care expenditures are being counted twice.

How much the resident parent spends on child care depends upon both the kind and amount of care purchased. The amount needed will depend primarily upon how much the resident parent works. What is the justification for increasing the child support paid by the nonresident parent in response to increases in work by the resident parent? It is difficult to think of one. After all, the more the resident parent works, the more income he or she will have. More generally, it seems inappropriate to base the child support obligation of the nonresident parent on lifestyle choices of the resident parent.

The argument for adjusting the child support obligation in response to extraordinary medical care expenditures is more convincing, precisely because such expenditures are presumably involuntary. Furthermore, in the rare cases when medical catastrophes occur, the average medical care cost incorporated in a child support standard will obviously be totally inadequate. One can hardly make the case that the resident parent should bear the entire cost of a medical catastrophe. By the same token, one can hardly contend that any family should bear the entire cost. The real problem is our nation's failure to institute a national health insurance system. This creates pressures to twist the child support system out of shape to compensate for a broader social problem.

Finally, basing the child support obligation upon actual child care and medical care expenditures further complicates the determination of child support because such expenditures change substantially from year to year. Should this year's child support be based upon last year's expenditures? Or upon expenditures anticipated in the coming year? As is discussed in more detail in the next section, each complication deepens the cost and makes it more difficult to update child support awards.

THE COSTS AND BENEFITS OF SIMPLICITY

The Wisconsin percentage-of-income standard is designed to maximize simplicity. The child support obligation equals a percentage of the nonresident parent's income, which depends only upon the number of children owed support. The income-shares standard is more complex: the percentages of support owed vary with the income of the nonresident parent and also depend upon the income of the resident parent and expenditures on child care and medical care.

Simplicity itself may be a virtue because it enhances public understanding and eases the burden on the courts. Most people can readily understand that under the Wisconsin percentage-of-income standard, child support in most cases equals 17 percent of the nonresident parent's income. Parents who enter the court system in Wisconsin have no difficulty in assessing the dollar magnitude of their entitlements or obligations. The percentage standard is also easy for the courts to administer because (1) it requires that only limited information be provided the court (the income of the parent and the number of children); and (2) the process for determining the amount of the award is the simple one of multiplying the income by the percentage set for the number of children entitled to support.

In contrast, even though the income-shares standard is simpler than other standards and entails only a few more variables than the Wisconsin standard, it is far more difficult to understand.

Whether simplicity promotes or sacrifices equity is a more complicated issue. To the extent that equity depends upon tailoring child support awards to the unique circumstances of each case, obviously simplicity is the enemy of equity. No one seems to be arguing this position now, however. Indeed, the country has adopted the position that equity is better served by the rough average justice produced by numerical child support standards.

Yet, a general presumption is no substitute for examining the consequences for equity of the specific differences in simplicity between the two standards. The Wisconsin standard is simpler in that it uses a constant rather than a declining percentage, it ignores the resident parent's income, and it takes no account of expenditures for child care and medical care. Based on our analysis in previous sections, we conclude: (1) having one constant percentage is more equitable than having declining percentages; (2) ignoring the income of the resident parent may in some extreme cases entail some sacrifice in equity; and (3) ignoring child care costs entails no sacrifice in equity and probably promotes it, although ignoring catastrophic costs for medical care entails a sacrifice in equity. In terms of the specifics, therefore, the verdict on the relationship between the greater simplicity of the Wisconsin standard and equity appears mixed. To the extent that the simplicity of the Wisconsin standard facilitates updating of child support awards, however, the relationship between simplicity and equity is substantially strengthened.

Recall that one of the widely perceived problems with the old child support system was that child support awards were too low, and furthermore that a large part of the problem of low awards is attributable to the failure to update awards over time. Why are modifications of child support awards so rare? One reason is that most state laws in the past have adopted practices and legislation that discourage parents from seeking modifications of child support orders. The Uniform Marriage and Divorce Act (1979; Sec. 316, 9A) suggests a modification "only upon a showing of changed circumstances so substantial and continuing as to make the terms unconscionable." But to say that laws and regulations discourage modifications begs the question. What is the rationale for this discouragement? The answer is that under the old system of individualized determinations of child support awards, modifications were quite costly in terms of court time. In essence, updating a child support award is equivalent to reopening and rehearing the case. If the average child support case has a 10-year-obligation life, annual modification or updating under the old system would increase the burden on the courts tenfold.

Numerical child support standards reduce the burden on the court system of both establishing the initial child support award and modifying or updating the award over time. But the reduction in burden is directly related to the simplicity of the standard. The more complex the standard, the more information the court must obtain, verify, and process. Even in the age of computers, obtaining, verifying, and processing information is costly.

To appreciate the difference in the costs of updating a child support award derived from the Wisconsin percentage-of-income standard and one derived from the income-shares standard, it is useful to consider what actions a child support agency would have to take under the two standards. Consider the most common case in which both the nonresident and resident parents are employed wage earners with no unearned income. Under the Wisconsin standard, the child support agency notifies the nonresident parent's employer of the percentage of income to be withheld and forwarded to the agency.[19] As the income of the nonresident parent increases (or decreases) over time, the child support withheld and paid changes automatically as well. The only additional action the child support agency must take is to verify the income tax returns of the nonresident parent each year to ascertain if he or she has received additional earned or unearned income.

Even though the income-shares standard has only a few more variables than the Wisconsin percentage-of-income standard, updating awards entails a substantially greater administrative burden. Each year the child support agency must collect income tax returns from both the resident and nonresident parent as well as information from the resident parent on the costs of child care and medical care. Some method of securing and verifying these expenditures will have to be developed. The records of the two parents must be linked. Each year a new child support obligation must be calculated. Because only the child support agency has all the data upon which the revised child support obligation is based, each year the agency must notify the employer, the resident parent, and the nonresident parent of the new obligation.

Updating the income-shares standard is feasible but will be substantially more costly than updating the Wisconsin standard. Consequently, it will at the very least delay implementation of updating. It is even conceivable that the extra administrative burdens imposed by the income-shares standard will permanently discourage updating. That may seem difficult to imagine in view of the current strong political support for strengthening child support enforcement, but the political euphoria for child support enforcement may not last indefinitely. In view of the importance of updating to the adequacy of child support awards, this makes the simplicity of the Wisconsin percentage-of-income standard especially attractive.

SUMMARY AND CONCLUSIONS

This chapter has attempted to add to the information available to the states on how to develop a numerical child support standard as required by federal legislation. It has compared and contrasted the two most popular types, the percentage-of-income model and the income-shares model. Both standards begin with the philosophical premise of income sharing—that to parent a child is to incur a responsibility to share income with the child and that the child's share of the non-resident parent's income should be based upon the proportion the child would receive if the parent lived with the child.

The standards depart from one another in application, however, both because there is a wide range of estimates of the extent and nature of income sharing in two-parent families and because a host of other value judgments must be made to derive child support orders. Under the income-shares approach, the child support obligation declines as a percentage of the nonresident parent's income as income increases, and consequently the obligation decreases as the resident parent's income increases. Moreover, the obligation also depends upon expenses for child care and medical care. In contrast, under the percentage-of-income standard, the obligation is a flat percentage of the nonresident parent's income and depends neither upon the resident parent's income nor upon expenses for child care and medical care.

Economic research on expenditures on children in two-parent families provides mixed evidence on whether the percentage of income spent on children declines as income increases. Moreover, whereas the proportion of income that would have been spent on the child if the parents had remained together is a useful starting point for determining the proportion of income that a nonresident parent should provide for his child, value judgments are involved as well in determining the size of the child support award. Our own values are such that we think a proportional child support standard is more appealing than one that is regressive.

Similarly, whether the income of the resident parent should affect the child support obligation of the resident parent is principally a value judgment. Although counting the income of the resident parent is consistent with the old cost-sharing approach to determine child support obligations and has an intuitive appeal on the grounds of equity, ignoring the resident parent's income is consistent with the income- sharing philosophy that underlies both standards. Moreover, on closer inspection, the equity case is not clear. In a two-parent family, if both parents work, the child shares the monetary fruits along with the parents. Why should it be any different when the family is separated?

The income-shares model accepts this line of reasoning in principle, but because obligations as a percentage of income decline as income increases, in practice obligations decline as the resident parent's income increases. If the income-shares standard were proportional instead of regressive, the income of the resident parent would be irrelevant. Adjusting the child support obligation to take account of child care and medical care costs departs from the income-sharing philosophy underlying both standards and complicates the standard.

One of the most attractive features of the Wisconsin percentage-of-income standard is its simplicity. Simplicity promotes public comprehension, is at least consistent with equity, and facilitates updating of awards. The latter function may be the most important single consideration for the states in the future in constructing mathematical child support standards. Failure to update awards is a major source of inadequate child support awards. A scheme to provide quick and efficient updating is an essential tool for child support enforcement.

Notes

Reprinted by permission of the American Bar Association. This chapter originally appeared as "The Use of Normative Standards in Family Law Decisions: Developing Mathematical Standards for Child Support," by Irwin Garfinkel and Marygold Melli in *Family Law Quarterly*, vol. XXIV(2), 1990. Copyright 1990 American Bar Association.

A working draft of this paper was published in 1989 by the Institute for Research on Poverty, University of Wisconsin–Madison, as Discussion Paper 900-89.

This work was supported in part by the Wisconsin Department of Health and Social Services, the U.S. Department of Health and Human Services, the Ford Foundation, and the Institute for Research on Poverty, University of Wisconsin–Madison. Any opinions and conclusions expressed are solely those of the authors and should not be construed as representing the opinions or policy of the sponsoring institutions.

1. Historically, statutes authorized courts to set child support according to their discretion, with only very general guidelines such as an amount "deemed just and reasonable." In the 1970s, concern about the need for more determinative standards arose and legislative and administrative guidelines proliferated, outlining lists of factors to be considered by the court in establishing the amount of a support award. See, for example, Freed and Walker (1987: 550–51).

2. The Family Support Act of 1988, P.L. 100-485 §103, 102 Stat. 2343, 2346, codified as 42 U.S.C. §667 (b)(2), effective October 14, 1989, provides:

> (2) There shall be a rebuttable presumption, in any judicial or administrative proceeding for the award of child support, that the amount of the award which would result from the application of such guidelines is the correct amount of child support to be awarded. A written finding or specific finding on the record that the application of the guidelines would be unjust or inappropriate in a particular case, as determined under criteria established by the State, shall be sufficient to rebut the presumption in that case.

3. Alabama, Arizona, Colorado, Florida, Guam, Kansas, Kentucky, Maine, Maryland, Michigan, Missouri, Montana, Nebraska, New Jersey, New Mexico, Ohio, Oklahoma, Oregon, Rhode Island, South Carolina, Utah, Vermont, Virginia, Washington.

4. Alaska, Connecticut, Georgia, Idaho, Illinois, Louisiana, Mississippi, Nevada, New Hampshire, North Carolina, Tennessee, Texas, Wisconsin.

5. Arkansas, California, District of Columbia, Iowa, Massachusetts, Minnesota, New York, North Dakota, Puerto Rico, Wyoming.

6. The terms *residential* and *noncustodial* are used to clarify the parent who has physical custody of the child, as distinguished from legal custody.

7. This act authorized legal action against fathers who failed to support their children under 16 years of age. The act was adopted with various modifications by 24 states, but proved less than successful. Taking criminal action against the nonsupporters took them away from their jobs and furthermore labeled them as criminals, making future employment more difficult; in addition, the out-of-state parent had to be returned to the home state for trial at great expense.

In 1950, the National Conference of Commissioners on Uniform State Laws replaced the Uniform Desertion and Nonsupport Act with the Uniform Reciprocal Enforcement of Support Act, providing interstate enforcement in a civil action. But, although the conference had withdrawn the Desertion and Nonsupport Act, it remains the basis for the nonsupport statutes of many of the states (see Melli 1984).

8. It should be noted, however, that the problem is also caused in part by the failure to obtain child support awards. Awards are obtained in only 60 percent of the cases. More serious is the failure to obtain awards in more than 80 percent of out-of-wedlock births (U.S. Bureau of the Census 1987). In a large percentage of out-of-wedlock cases, the failure to establish paternity precludes the possibility of establishing a child support award.

9. For a discussion of how price inflation, the growth of a child, and wage increases restructure a support order, see Eden (1979: 2).

10. The data indicate that initial child support awards during the period 1980–83, prior to the publication of the Wisconsin percentage-of-income standard, were almost identical to the percentages of the noncustodial parents' income called for by the Wisconsin percentage-of-income standard (see Garfinkel 1986).

11. The two most frequently cited empirical studies on this point are those of White and Stone (1976: 83) and Yee (1979: 21). White and Stone studied 532 cases disposed of in Orange County, Florida, between July 1, 1971, and the end of 1974. Nine variables were identified that were considered to cover all essential factors in determining the

amount of a child support award. These were: estimated financial needs of wife, estimated financial needs of husband, total assets, total liabilities, number of children, age of children, net income of husband, net income of wife, and duration of the marriage. For all 532 cases, the rank ordering of seven of the variables was: (1) net income of the husband, (2) estimated financial needs of the wife, (3) number of children, (4) estimated financial needs of the husband, (5) net income of the wife, (6) total assets, and (7) total liabilities. However, when an analysis was made of the cases decided by each of the nine judges involved (the number of cases handled by the judges ranged from 28 for two judges to 72 for one judge), the ranking of the variables was quite different. For example, for three judges the most important variable was the income of the husband; for two, the estimated financial needs of the husband was the most important variable; the other four judges each had used another variable as the most significant (needs of the wife, duration of the marriage, the number of children, and the net income of the wife). The conclusion was that although each judge was consistent as to his own model, there was no uniformity among the judges. To obtain consistency, the researchers suggested that a model be developed to be followed by the courts in setting child support and alimony. The researchers asserted that in addition to ensuring more equitable treatment, considerable judicial time would be saved.

Yee (1979) examined a random sample of 135 cases handled in the Denver, Colorado, District Court between January 1, 1977, and September 30, 1978. Unlike the White and Stone study, which focused on divorces, this one was limited to support actions brought under the Uniform Reciprocal Enforcement of Support Act. Yee selected six items as possibly affecting the amount of the child support award: the income of the noncustodial parent, the judge who heard the case, the presence or absence of an attorney for the noncustodial parent, the pattern of conduct by the district attorney's office, the fixed living expenses of the noncustodial parent, and the time of year at which the case was heard.

Yee found great variation in the amount of child support awards. For example, one judge ordered child support payments of $120 in one case and $60 in another, although both cases involved two children and fathers who had net monthly incomes of $450. Furthermore, that same judge ordered another father of two children to pay only $50 a month child support, although his net monthly income of $900 was twice that of the other fathers. Yee concluded that none of the six factors she examined—some of which rationally ought to relate to the amount of the award, although others ought not affect it—adequately explained the wide variation in amounts of awards. She further concluded that there was no consistency between judges, and that individual judges were erratic as to the amount of the award.

12. Commentators have suggested that judges may give too much weight to this objective (see Bruch 1982: 49, 51; and Lieberman 1986: 37).

13. A study of 236 randomly selected cases in Wisconsin revealed that the number of children, the income of the supporting parent, and the couple's estimated net worth accounted for almost 50 percent of the variation in the amount of child support (Melli, Erlanger, and Chambliss 1988: 1133, 1164).

14. These are discussed in Advisory Panel and Williams (1987).

15. The architects of the Wisconsin standard recommended that the flat percentages apply only to the first $50,000 or $60,000 of income in 1980 dollars. In part, the recommendation was based on the Van der Gaag (1982) finding of proportionality only up to very high incomes. Another consideration was that the public interest in assuring children a share of their parents' income declined at very high income levels. The Wisconsin Department of Health and Social Services rejected the idea of an income cap to the standard, but the legislature was more flexible. As adopted, the statute allows the court to depart from the standard when it finds that use of the percentage standard is unfair to any of the parties. Presumably, this would cover cases in which the nonresident parent income is unusually high (see Wis. Stat. § 767.25 [1M] [1987–88]).

16. The federal Advisory Panel and Williams's (1987) argument in support of Espenshade (1984) was that, among the studies using the most recent data available, Espenshade used the share of expenditure spent on food rather than that spent on adult goods (such as tobacco, alcohol, and adult clothing) as the measure of the standard of living. The former is a larger, more stable, and more reliably reported share of total consumption. The Advisory Panel and Williams ignored the Van der Gaag and Smolensky (1981) study, which used the same dataset as Espenshade (1984), but followed a more general approach for measuring the standard of living, one preferred by many economists. Use of the food share as a measure of welfare is only appropriate when children's needs for food relative to all other goods and services are the same as adults' needs. Two of the most prominent economists in the field have recently argued that it is more plausible to assume children need more food relative to other goods than adults (Deaton and Muellbauer 1986: 720–44). If their contention is true, the food share method overestimates child costs. (Deaton and Muellbauer would prefer the adult goods method if expenditures of adult goods were accurately measured.)

17. Van der Gaag (1982: 40) recommended that future research expand upon the direct approach to measuring the cost of children (see also Gordon and Garfinkel 1989).

18. To simplify, we ignore child care expenses and extraordinary medical expenses.

19. This example assumes that the initial child support order is expressed in percentage terms rather than in dollar terms, which is as yet true in only a minority of cases in the state. Most of the courts have been reluctant to issue percentage orders because no mechanism is in place to verify the income of the noncustodial parent and thereby to ascertain that the amount being withheld and forwarded by employers is correct.

References

Advisory Panel on Child Support Guidelines and Robert Williams. 1987. *Development of Guidelines for Child Support Orders: Advisory Panel Recommendations and Final Report to U.S. Office of Child Support Enforcement*. Williamsburg, Va.: National Center for State Courts. September.

Bruch, Carol. 1982. "Developing Normative Standards for Child Support Payments. A Critique of Current Practice." *University of California, Davis, Law Review* 49: 51.

————. 1987. "Problems Inherent in Designing Child Support Guidelines." In *Essentials of Child Support Guidelines Development: Economic Issues and Policy Considerations* 41. Washington, D.C.: Department of Health and Human Services, Office of Child Support Enforcement.

Cassetty, Judith. 1983. "Emerging Issues in Child Support Policy and Practice. In *The Parental Child Support Obligation*, edited by Judith Cassetty. Lexington, Mass.: Lexington Books.

Child Support Enforcement Amendments of 1984, P.L. 98-378, codified as 42 U.S.C.

Deaton, A.S., and John Muellbauer. 1986. "On Measuring Child Costs: With Applications to Poor Countries." *Journal of Political Economy* 94: 720–744.

Dodson, Diane. 1988. "A Guide to the Guidelines." *Family Advocate* 10 (Spring): 4, 6.

Duncan, Greg, and Saul Hoffman. 1985. "A Reconsideration of the Economic Consequences of Marital Dissolution." *Demography* 22: 485.

Eden, Philip. 1979. "How Inflation Flaunts the Court's Orders." *Family Advocate* 1 (Spring): 2.

Espenshade, T. 1984. *Investing in Children: New Estimates of Parental Expenditures.* Washington, D.C.: Urban Institute Press.

Family Support Act of 1988. P.L. 100-485, codified as 42 U.S.C.

Freed, Doris, and Timothy Walker. 1987. "Family Law in the Fifty States: An Overview." *Family Law Quarterly* 20: 439, 550–51.

Garfinkel, Irwin. 1986. *Utilization and Effects of Immediate Income Withholding and the Percentage-of-Income Standard: An Interim Report on the Child Support Assurance Demonstration.* Institute for Research on Poverty, Special Report 42. Madison: University of Wisconsin–Madison, Institute for Research on Poverty.

Garfinkel, Irwin, and Donald Oellerich. 1989. "Noncustodial Fathers' Ability to Pay Child Support." *Demography* 26 (May): 219.

Garfinkel, Irwin, Donald Oellerich, and Philip Robins. 1990. "Child Support Guidelines: Will They Make a Difference?" Institute for Research on Poverty Discussion Paper 912-90. Madison: University of Wisconsin–Madison, Institute for Research on Poverty.

Gordon, Anne R., and Irwin Garfinkel. 1989. "Child Costs as a Percentage of Family Income: Constant or Decreasing as Income Rises?" Institute for Research on Poverty Discussion Paper 889-89. Madison: University of Wisconsin–Madison. August.

Lieberman, J. 1986. *Child Support in America.* Cambridge, Mass.: Yale University Press.

Melli, Marygold. 1984. *Child Support: A Survey of the Statutes.* Institute for Research on Poverty, Special Report 33. Madison: University of Wisconsin–Madison, Institute for Research on Poverty.

Melli, Marygold, Howard Erlanger, and Elizabeth Chambliss. 1988. "The Process of Negotiation: An Exploratory Investigation in the Context of No-Fault Divorce." *Rutgers Law Review* 40: 1133, 1164.

Sawhill, Isabel V. 1983. "Developing Normative Standards for Child Support Payment." In *The Parental Child Support Obligation,* edited by Judith Cassetty. Lexington, Mass.: Lexington Books.

Social Security Amendments of 1974. P.L. 93-647, codified as 42 U.S.C. Uniform Marriage and Divorce Act.

U.S. Bureau of the Census. 1987. *Child Support and Alimony: 1985.* Current Population Reports, ser. P-23, No. 152. Washington, D.C.: U.S. Government Printing Office.

U.S. Congress, Senate Committee on Finance. 1975. *Child Support Data and Materials.* 94th Cong., 1st Sess.

Van der Gaag, J. 1982. "On Measuring the Costs of Children." In *Child Support; Weaknesses of the Old and Features of a Proposed New System,* edited by Irwin Garfinkel et al. Institute for Research on Poverty Special Report 32C, vol. 3 (1–44). Madison: University of Wisconsin–Madison, Institute for Research on Poverty.

Van der Gaag, J., and E. Smolensky. 1981. "True Household Equivalence Scales and Characteristics of the Poor in the United States." *Review of Income and Wealth*, ser. 28 (1): 17–28.

Weitzman, Lenne J. *The Divorce Resolution: The Unexpected Social and Economic Consequences for Women and Children in America*, chap. 10. New York: Free Press 1985.

White, Kenneth R., and R. Thomas Stone. 1976. "Study of Alimony and Child Support Rulings with Some Recommendations." *Family Law Quarterly* 10(1): 75–91.

Williams, Robert. 1987. "Guidelines for Setting Levels of Child Support Orders." *Family Law Quarterly* 21: 281.

Yee, Lucy M. 1979. "What Really Happens in Child Support Cases: An Empirical Study of the Establishment and Enforcement of Child Support Awards in the Denver District Court." *Denver Law Journal* 57(1): 21–70.

Chapter Ten

THE EFFECT OF ROUTINE INCOME WITHHOLDING ON CHILD SUPPORT COLLECTIONS

Irwin Garfinkel and Marieka M. Klawitter

This chapter examines the effects on child support collections of one major reform of the American private child support enforcement system—routine income withholding. *Private child support* refers to payments from a nonresident parent to the parent who resides with his or her children. *Routine income withholding* refers to the requirement that employers routinely withhold child support obligations from the salaries of nonresident parents. The proceeds are mailed to the courts, thereby ensuring that the custodial parent receives regular support payments.

The Family Support Act of 1988 requires all states to adopt routine withholding for all child support cases by 1994. The state of Wisconsin, which has been at the forefront of the child support reform movement, was the first in the nation to pilot and adopt a routine income withholding system as part of its proposed new child support assurance system (CSAS). Between January and June 1984, 10 Wisconsin counties began to use routine income withholding. Legislation in 1985 made the percentage-of-income standard[1] the presumptive child support obligation as of July 1987, allowed additional counties to adopt routine income withholding, and required all counties to do so as of July 1987. Whereas the Child Support Enforcement Amendments of 1984 required withholding only in the event that payments were one month delinquent, the 1988 Family Support Act compels withholding of the child support obligation from the outset for all Title IV-D cases (those being handled by the federal Office of Child Support Enforcement) as of 1990 and for all child support cases as of 1994. To do so, states will be forced to develop the capacity to routinely monitor payments in all cases. Only seven states, including Wisconsin, had this capability as of 1988.

Previous research suggests that child support payments could be increased substantially, but that routine income withholding by itself is likely to result in only modest increases. Whereas nonresident fathers in the United States paid about $7 billion in child support in 1983, estimates of their income and family circumstances indicate that they could afford to pay between $24 billion and $28 billion annually (Garfinkel and Oellerich 1991).[2] Yet the gap between what was owed and paid was only about $3 billion. Obtaining more awards and raising the level of awards are more important than collecting a greater proportion of existing awards (McDonald, Moran, and Garfinkel 1983).[3]

This chapter uses data from Wisconsin's pilot counties and a set of control counties to evaluate the effects of routine income withholding on child support collections. The next section describes the data. The third section presents data on the extent to which withholding was implemented in the pilot and control counties on a routine basis. The fourth section presents estimates of the effects on child support collections of routine income withholding. The chapter ends with a brief summary and conclusion.

DESCRIPTION OF THE DATA

This study sampled family court records involving divorce, separation, and paternity cases in which there was at least one child under age 18 from 20 Wisconsin counties. Ten of the counties had agreed to utilize immediate income withholding on a routine basis in all cases in which it was possible. Ten control counties were chosen based on county population, geographic location, divorce rate, unemployment rate, and average per capita income. Table 10.1 shows that, in general, the pilot and control counties are fairly well matched. On average, the control counties have slightly higher populations, number of divorces, per capita incomes, and unemployment rates.

Predemonstration data were collected for three years. Cases for the baseline sample included only those that entered the court system for the first time during the period from July 1, 1980, through June 30, 1983.[4] Information on all these cases was collected through December 31, 1983.

The demonstration-period sample included cases that began one month after the implementation of routine withholding in each pilot county and at the same time in the "matching" control county. Case selection continued until May 31, 1986, and collection of all case activity continued until January 31, 1987. Table 10.1 shows the imple-

Table 10.1 CHARACTERISTICS OF PILOT AND CONTROL COUNTIES IN WISCONSIN STUDY

	1980 Population	1981, Number of Divorces	1980 per Capita Income ($)	1983 Unemployment Rate (%)
Pilot Counties (Implementation Date):				
Clark (1-15-84)	32,910	112	7,125	12.6
Dane (5-01-84)	323,545	1,741	10,364	6.8
Dunn (1-03-84)	34,314	118	6,875	7.7
Kewaunee (1-01-84)	19,539	67	8,067	14.3
Monroe (2-01-84)	35,074	191	7,995	10.1
Oneida (6-15-85)	31,216	188	8,023	10.4
Ozaukee (2-15-84)	66,981	303	12,245	9.4
Richland (1-03-84)	17,476	97	7,346	11.8
Sheboygan (3-15-84)	100,935	447	9,773	9.5
Winnebago (4-02-84)	131,703	658	9,772	9.2
Unweighted mean	79,369	392	8,775	10.2
Control Counties (Implementation Date):				
Calumet (5-19-87)	30,867	104	8,766	14.7
Dodge (4-01-86)	75,064	456	8,882	10.7
Green (3-17-87)	30,012	160	9,945	8.1
Jefferson (4-10-87)	66,152	336	9,017	11.4
Juneau (8-01-85)	21,039	93	7,395	11.4
Marathon (6-15-86)	111,270	341	8,240	11.4
Price (7-01-86)	15,788	79	7,225	11.7
Racine (8-01-87)	173,132	1,083	10,229	13.0
St. Croix (8-01-87)	43,262	213	8,087	8.7
Waukesha (8-01-87)	280,326	1,481	11,819	10.0
Unweighted mean	84,691	435	8,961	11.1

mentation dates for pilot counties as well as for the control counties, all of which later implemented routine income withholding.[5]

To facilitate early evaluation of the demonstration, the sampling method for the second and third years of the demonstration period was altered slightly. Cases were considered chronologically from the beginning of the case-selection period instead of being randomly selected over the entire selection period. Sampling continued until a predetermined sample size was reached or until the end of the case-selection period. The selection criteria were otherwise unchanged.

The entire sample is further divided into six cohorts by the year during which the case began. Table 10.2 shows the dates of case selection, the ending date of data collection, the resulting average number of months of data for each cohort, and the number of cases in each

Table 10.2 CASE SELECTION, DATA COLLECTION PERIODS, AND AVERAGE
NUMBER OF MONTHS OF DATA: WISCONSIN STUDY

Cohort	Case-Selection Period	Data Collection Ends	Average Number of Months of Data	Number of Cases
		Predemonstration Period		
Cohort 1	July 1, 1980–June 30, 1981	Dec. 31, 1983	36.6	1,093
Cohort 2	July 1, 1981–June 30, 1982	Dec. 31, 1983	24.5	1,099
Cohort 3	July 1, 1982–June 30, 1983	Dec. 31, 1983	12.5	1,083
		Demonstration Period		
Cohort 4	Feb. 1, 1984–Sept. 30, 1984[a]	Jan. 31, 1987	32.4	877
Cohort 5	Oct. 1, 1984–May 31, 1985	Jan. 31, 1987	26.5	1,116
Cohort 6	Oct. 1, 1985–May 31, 1986	Jan. 31, 1987	14.8	1,167

[a]The case-selection period for cohort 4 varied by county. Cases were collected beginning one month after the county implementation date for immediate withholding.

cohort. Within each county, from about 30 to 150 cases were chosen in each cohort. In some small counties, all eligible cases were used. In larger counties, a larger number of cases, but a smaller proportion of the caseload, was used. Weights were constructed to adjust for differences in the proportion of cases selected in each county and cohort by case type.

For each case, information was collected about every court action during the data-collection period. This included the dates and purposes of the actions, custody and visitation agreements, child support orders, and other types of monetary obligations. Payment data were also collected, including the amount and dates of all payments sent to the county clerk of courts. Wisconsin law requires nonresident parents to make child support payments through the county clerk of court, but payments are occasionally sent directly to the resident parent. Such payments are not included in these data. Although the court data indicated that about 3 percent of cases had legal direct payment agreements, a separate survey estimated that some direct payment occurs in about 7 percent of child support cases.[6] To the extent that routine income withholding results in a substitution of payments through the court for direct private payments, our data overestimate the true effect of routine income withholding on total child support payments.[7]

In addition to information on child support payments, the court record includes some demographic information such as the number and ages of children, and income and employment information for both parents. Unfortunately, much of the income and employment data are missing in the court record.

DEGREE OF IMPLEMENTATION OF ROUTINE INCOME WITHHOLDING IN PILOT AND CONTROL COUNTIES

The effects of any policy depend in large part on the extent to which the policy is implemented. Similarly, an evaluation of a policy that is based on comparing outcomes in pilot and control counties is reliable to the extent that the policy was implemented in the former but not the latter. Thus, the extent to which routine income withholding was implemented in both pilot and control counties is of great interest.

Full implementation of routine income withholding would entail issuance of an income withholding order to the employer or other source of income of the obligor at the outset of the child support obligation in every case where it was possible to withhold income. Unfortunately, because some obligors are self-employed and others are unemployed, it is not possible to withhold income in all cases at the outset of the child support obligation.

Table 10.3 presents data on the potential for using withholding by county and by predemonstration and demonstration periods. In this and all subsequent tables in this chapter, only sole (legal) custody divorce and paternity cases with support orders are included, and cases with private pay agreements are excluded, leaving a total of 3,620 cases.[8] These and all other descriptive statistics in this chapter are weighted to account for the sampling scheme.[9]

The assignable income sources identified in the court record were wages or salary paid by others and unemployment compensation. Any other source was assumed to be unassignable. Since the court record included information on income source in only about three-quarters of the sample, table 10.3 gives the proportion of cases with missing information and two projections of the potential proportion of cases with assignable income.[10]

The first column for both time periods in table 10.3 gives the proportion of all cases with missing data on income source for the nonresident parent. The proportion of such cases decreased dramatically in pilot counties during the demonstration period. Prior to the demonstration, pilot and control counties had about equal proportions of missing information—25 percent and 24 percent, respectively. How-

Table 10.3 PERCENTAGE OF PATERNITY AND DIVORCE CASES WITH MISSING
INCOME SOURCE AND ASSIGNABLE INCOME SOURCE BY COUNTY,
BEFORE AND DURING DEMONSTRATION PERIOD: WISCONSIN STUDY

| | Predemonstration Period | | | Demonstration Period | | |
| | | Assignable Income (%) | | | Assignable Income (%) | |
	Missing Data	Lower Bound	Upper Bound	Missing Data	Lower Bound	Upper Bound
Pilot Counties						
Clark	18	55	67	5	67	71
Dane	21	67	86	13	73	84
Dunn	33	58	86	36	53	83
Kewaunee	18	65	80	0	90	90
Monroe	31	56	81	18	69	84
Oneida	35	50	77	29	55	77
Ozaukee	21	71	89	11	81	91
Richland	35	53	82	19	64	79
Sheboygan	36	61	95	15	83	97
Winnebago	15	66	78	11	71	80
All pilots	25	63	84	14	73	85
Control Counties						
Calumet	25	67	89	24	65	85
Dodge	29	60	84	19	71	88
Green	13	70	81	28	65	90
Jefferson	25	60	81	16	73	88
Juneau	35	56	86	46	40	73
Marathon	27	62	85	18	67	82
Price	18	69	84	35	49	76
Racine	23	68	87	12	72	81
St. Croix	29	65	92	23	60	77
Waukesha	23	72	93	20	71	89
All controls	24	67	88	18	69	85

Note: See text for explanation of data.

ever, the proportion of missing data in pilot counties during the demonstration decreased to 14 percent, whereas the proportion in control counties decreased to 18 percent. This program effect is to be expected: when information is needed to run a program, it is more likely to be recorded.

The second column in table 10.3 gives a conservative estimate of the proportion of cases with assignable income sources: the number of cases with a known assignable income source divided by the total number of cases (including cases without income information). This lower-bound estimate assumes that no cases with missing information on income source have an assignable income source.

The third column in table 10.3 gives a more generous estimate of assignable income: the number of cases with a known assignable income source divided by the number of cases with information on income source. This higher estimate assumes that the proportion of cases with assignable incomes among the cases with missing income information equals the proportion for the cases with known income sources.

The estimates of assignable income for pilot counties during the demonstration are probably the most accurate assessment of the potential for using routine withholding. Those figures suggest that in about 73 percent to 85 percent (the lower and higher estimates) of divorce and paternity cases, the nonresident parent has income that can be assigned.

Given the experience of pilot counties, the higher estimate of assignable income may be a fairly accurate estimate of the level of assignable income. For the pilot counties, the proportion of cases with missing income source decreased by 11 percentage points from the predemonstration to demonstration periods, increasing the pool of cases with income source information. At the same time, the percentage of cases with assignable income (based on the conservative estimate) increased by 10 percentage points. This implies that the "new" cases with income information had about the same proportion of assignable income as the "original" cases.

The actual use of withholding is shown in table 10.4, by county and cohort. A case was defined as having a routine assignment if an income assignment was issued within 60 days of the first court action with a child support order. Cases with an income assignment dated more than 60 days after the court action, or with no effective date in the court record, were not labeled as immediate assignments.[11]

Table 10.4 shows that the use of routine income assignments has increased in both pilot and control counties over the court-record period. In pilot counties, the proportion of cases with assignments rose from levels of 4–6 percent in the first three cohorts to levels of 57 percent, 56 percent, and 65 percent, respectively, in the demonstration-period cohorts. Although the increase in assignments in pilot counties during the demonstration period was dramatic, levels remained substantially below the potential levels reported in table 10.3. Even by the third year, routine income withholding was not fully implemented in the pilot counties.

Less-than-complete implementation may not be a serious problem for analysis, since no policy is ever fully implemented. Is there reason to expect that national implementation of routine withholding will be

Table 10.4 USE OF IMMEDIATE INCOME ASSIGNMENT, BY COUNTY AND
COHORT: WISCONSIN STUDY

	Predemonstration Period (%)			Demonstration Period (%)		
	1	2	3	4	5	6
Pilot Counties						
Clark	9	17	0	50	71	56
Dane	3	4	8	57	47	52
Dunn	0	0	0	76	48	88
Kewaunee	9	13	19	67	—[b]	83
Monroe	15	13	22	31	42	61
Oneida	0	5	0	44	26	64
Ozaukee	4	2	7	70	75	82
Richland	7	3	0	54	62	69
Sheboygan	4	2	2	73	63	80
Winnebago	0	6	6	50	67	75
All pilots	4	5	6	57	56	65
Control Counties						
Calumet	10	7	6	19	25	32
Dodge[a]	7	0	0	22	22	70
Green	2	6	5	36	32	51
Jefferson	3	7	13	18	30	41
Juneau[a]	8	4	0	19	5	93
Marathon	0	0	0	5	5	52
Price	0	0	0	0	7	60
Racine	40	19	22	33	27	57
St. Croix	0	0	0	4	5	31
Waukesha	2	7	3	14	35	48
All controls	15	9	10	20	25	53

[a]Became a pilot county in cohort 6.
[b]No sole custody cases with awards for cohort 5.

any better than the Wisconsin experience? The Wisconsin data do suggest that implementation improved over time. At the least, therefore, a comparison of increases in child support payments in pilot and control counties in the first two years of the demonstration will underestimate the long-run effects of national implementation of routine income withholding.

A more serious problem is that use of routine withholding also increased in the control counties. Although control counties used routine withholding much less frequently than pilot counties in cohorts four and five (see table 10.4), the proportions (20 percent and 25 percent, respectively) were far in excess of zero, and by the sixth cohort, control counties were using assignments in over half the cases.

This widespread use of routine assignments in the control counties means that a simple comparison of collections in pilot and control counties would likely underestimate the effects of national implementation of routine income withholding.

ESTIMATING THE EFFECTS OF ROUTINE WITHHOLDING

Child support payments, the key outcome variable in the analysis, were measured in this study by (1) the ratio of dollars of child support paid to dollars of child support due, and (2) the ratio of months in which a child support payment was made to months in which there was a child support obligation.[12] The former measures the collection rate of child support dollars, and the latter reflects the regularity and timeliness of payments. Both of these were calculated for the time between the first month of child support owed and the last month of court record data collected. These measures, averaged over the data period, were used to study the effects of withholding over the first few years after a support order. Monthly measures, described later in this section, were subsequently used to study differences in the impact of withholding over time.

The impact of routine income withholding on child support payments was measured by us in three different ways. The first was simply the difference in increases in child support payments between cases in pilot and control counties. The second was derived from the relationship between the extent of utilization of immediate income assignments in counties and child support payments in those counties. The third measure was the difference in child support payments between cases with and without immediate income assignments.

As discussed earlier, the difference in child support payments between pilot and control counties is expected to be an underestimate of the long-run effect of national implementation of routine income withholding. There are two reasons for believing that extrapolating from the relationship between county use of routine withholding and county payment rates may overestimate the effects of routine income withholding. First, differences in the utilization of routine withholding across counties may be attributable to county differences in the proportion of cases in which assignments are possible. Second, the differences may reflect administrative discretion on the part of the courts, which is correlated with other efforts the courts make to enforce payments. For both reasons, counties with higher levels of routine withholding might have had higher payment rates even without the withholding.

The third measure may furthermore result in an overestimate of the impact of withholding on child support payments because cases with routine income assignments may be better prospective payers. Courts cannot issue assignments to those with no income. On the other hand, courts may be reluctant to issue assignments to well-known, influential members of their community. In about 80 percent of the cases, we had data on whether or not the nonresident parent had income that could be withheld. But that still left about 20 percent of the cases in which we could not control for the absence of assignable income. On balance, therefore, it is likely that the difference between payments in cases with and without immediate assignments will be an overestimate of the effects of implementing routine withholding.

In short, the first measure of the impact of routine income withholding is likely to be an underestimate, whereas the second and third measures are likely to be overestimates.

Table 10.5 presents the ratios of child support dollars paid to dollars owed and months paid to months owed by pilot county status and period, by county withholding level, and by case withholding status. All of the measures suggest that routine withholding probably has positive effects. The smallest differences are between the pilot and control counties. The ratio of dollars paid to dollars owed increased by 7 percentage points in the pilot counties, compared to only 4 percentage points in the control counties. The payment rates in counties that used routine assignments in less than 10 percent of their cases were nearly 9 percentage points less than the rates in counties that used assignments in over 60 percent of their cases. Also, payment rates for cases with routine withholding were 17 percentage points higher than for cases without withholding. Note, however, that even those subject to routine withholding paid only 70 percent of what they owed. This suggests that routine withholding by itself is not a cure-all.

Because the policy variables may be correlated with other variables, we used multivariate regression analyses to further explore the relationship between the policy variables and child support payments. The values of the dependent variables in these regressions are constrained to be between 0 and 100, so we estimated tobit regressions.[13]

The first policy variable is a dummy variable equaling one for cases opened in a county after the county became a pilot county and equal-

Table 10.5 PERCENTAGE OF CHILD SUPPORT DOLLARS PAID-TO-OWED AND
MONTHS PAID-TO-OWED BY PILOT COUNTY STATUS AND PERIOD,
COUNTY WITHHOLDING LEVEL, AND INDIVIDUAL CASE
WITHHOLDING: WISCONSIN STUDY

Experimental County Status	Dollars Paid-to-Owed (%)	Months Paid-to-Owed (%)
Pilot Counties:		
Predemonstration period	55.16	54.00
Demonstration period	62.03	61.10
Control Counties:		
Predemonstration period	55.12	56.94
Demonstration period	59.10	58.80
County Withholding Level:		
0% to 10%	56.12	55.36
11% to 30%	56.57	58.11
31% to 45%	56.94	57.43
46% to 60%	61.15	60.70
61% and over	64.76	65.21
All	57.27	57.28
Individual Case Withholding:		
Immediate withholding cases	70.34	70.78
Nonwithholding cases	53.17	53.04

ing zero for all other cases. The second policy variable equals the percentage of cases in a county using immediate withholding during the period in which a case got an award. The third variable is a dummy variable equal to one if the case had immediate withholding and zero otherwise. Each of the policy variables is used alone in separate regressions.

In addition to the policy variable, each regression also contains the following independent variables: a dummy variable equaling one if the case was a paternity case, a dummy variable equaling one if the case was one in which the mother rather than the father was the payer, a dummy variable equaling one if the payer had a reported income of zero, a dummy variable equaling one if the payer had reported assignable income, a dummy variable equaling one if the payer had missing income amount (the omitted variable being a dummy equaling one if the payer had income that was neither missing nor assignable), the dollar amount of the payer's income (set to the mean if missing), and a set of dummy variables for the cohort and county of the case. The coefficients of the other independent variables are not very sensitive to the policy variables included in the regression. Thus, only the policy variable coefficients are reported in the chapter tables, with the full set of regression coefficients presented in Appendix 10.A.

Table 10.6 presents the coefficients of the three alternative specifications of the policy variable from separate tobit analyses. In addition to the coefficients of the policy variables, the table also presents the percentage increases in child support payments that are implied by the coefficients. These impacts were calculated as the differences in the predicted means for the control and experimental statuses as a percentage of the control county mean in the demonstration period. For the second policy variable, the level of withholding, the experimental impact was evaluated as a change of 50 percentage points in the level of withholding.

All of the policy coefficients in table 10.6 are positive, and, as indicated by the *t*-ratios in parentheses, all but one are statistically significant at the 5 percent level or better. Not surprisingly, the percentage increases in payments implied by the coefficients are much larger for the second and third measures of the impact of withholding than for the first. Based on the previous argument that the first measure is an underestimate and the second and third are overestimates of the impact of implementing routine income withholding, the estimates in table 10.6 suggest that routine income withholding will increase child support payments by more than 11 percent and less than 30 percent.[14]

Note also that the effects on the ratios of months paid to months owed are larger than those on the ratios of dollars paid to dollars owed. This makes sense insofar as payment irregularity is a problem distinct from nonpayment. Routine income withholding should have an effect on the regularity of payments as well as on total payments.

So far, we have examined the average effects of routine income withholding. Reports from state civil servants who monitored the implementation of routine income withholding, however, have indicated that the process was relatively chaotic for the first five or six months of implementation. This suggests that the implementation of routine income withholding may actually have had a negative effect in the early months of implementation and an increasingly positive effect thereafter. Furthermore, as table 10.4 indicates, the proportion of cases in pilot counties in which an income assignment was implemented increased notably in the third year, which suggests that the estimated effects of withholding should be larger in the sixth cohort.

To test for the possibility that the effects of income withholding may have varied over time, monthly child support payment data were

Table 10.6 EFFECTS OF EXPERIMENTAL VARIABLES ON SUMMARY RATIOS OF
DOLLARS AND MONTHS PAID-TO-OWED FROM TOBITS: WISCONSIN
STUDY

	Dollars Paid-to-Owed		Months Paid-to-Owed	
	Coefficient (t-ratio)	Impact (%)	Coefficient (t-ratio)	Impact (%)
Experimental county dummy	5.86 (1.74)	11.0	7.38 (2.29)	14.4
County withholding level	.23 (2.73)	22.0	.25 (3.06)	24.5
Individual case withholding	14.83 (5.92)	28.4	14.94 (6.24)	29.6

Notes: Impacts are calculated as the difference in the predicted pay-to-owe ratio due
to experimental status as a percentage of demonstration period control county mean.
The impact for the county withholding level is evaluated for a 50 percentage point
increase in withholding.

used to construct a variable equal to the number of months between
the first month in which support was owed and the first month with
no payment. This variable was used to estimate a hazard rate—the
probability of having no payment in a month—given that there has
been no previous month without payment. The model used for the
hazard rate estimated here is a type of proportional hazard based on
a Weibull distribution for the number of months until a nonpayment.
This model allows the estimated hazard rate to either increase or
decrease monotonically over time, but not to change directions. The
independent variables are assumed to shift the hazard rate up or down
proportionately over the entire spell length. The percentage change in
the hazard for a unit change in the independent variable is $e^B - 1$,
where b is the coefficient.

An additional policy variable was constructed to assess changes in
the effectiveness of withholding as the county gained administrative
experience. This variable, the county withholding experience, equals
the number of months between the first month the county began routine withholding and the first month support was owed for the case.
It equals zero both for cases in the predemonstration period and for
control county cases in the demonstration period.

Table 10.7 shows the coefficients for the experimental and county
experience variables from the hazard functions (complete results are
in Appendix 10.B). Also shown are the estimated changes in the

Table 10.7 EFFECTS OF EXPERIMENTAL VARIABLES ON WEIBULL HAZARD
RATE OF HAVING A MONTH WITH NO CHILD SUPPORT PAID:
WISCONSIN STUDY

	Policy Variable Coefficient (t-ratio)	Coefficient on Months of County Withholding Experience (t-ratio)	Impact with 12 Months of County Experience (%)
Experimental county	.11 (0.92)	−.02 (2.83)	−12.2
County withholding level	−.004 (1.89)	−.01 (1.97)	−27.4
Individual case withholding	−.34 (5.09)	−.01 (2.45)	−36.9

Notes: Proportional change in hazard is calculated as e^B for experimental county and individual case withholding. Change for county withholding level is $e^{B \times 50}$ (the impact of increasing withholding by 50 percentage points).

hazard rate of a nonpayment, calculated for a county with 12 months of withholding experience. The coefficient estimated for the experimental county variable is positive but statistically insignificant. On the other hand, in the same regressions, the coefficient on the variable measuring county withholding experience is negative and statistically significant. Taken together, these coefficients suggest that nonresident parents who entered the court system in the pilot counties soon after the pilots commenced were somewhat more likely to miss a payment than nonresident parents in control counties, but that as the pilot counties gained more experience with routine income withholding, income withholding became more effective.

The county withholding level and the individual case withholding coefficients are both negative, as are the accompanying pilot county experience coefficients. Note that the county experience coefficients in these regressions are half the size of the coefficient in the regression with the experimental county dummy. This makes sense in that presumably part of the effect of more experience is attributable to more widespread use of income withholding, which would be picked up by the county withholding level and individual case coefficients.

Survival rates, the proportions of cases expected to not yet have had a month with no payment, can be calculated from the estimated hazard rates. Figure 10.1 shows the survival rates over the months in

Figure 10.1 EXPECTED PROPORTION OF CASES WITHOUT A NONPAYMENT
MONTH BY MONTHS SINCE SUPPORT ORDER

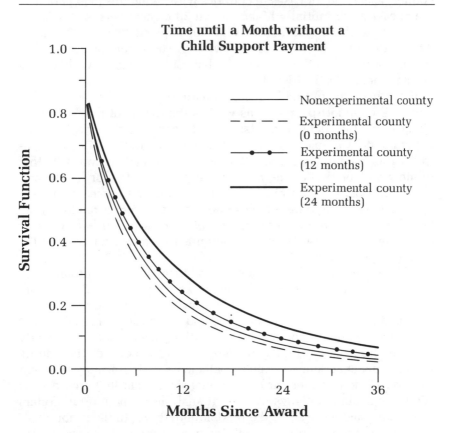

a case for the hazard function associated with the experimental
county dummy variable. The survival rates are calculated at the mean
value for all control variables. Separate lines are graphed for cases in
nonexperimental counties and for cases in experimental counties at
three levels of county withholding experience: 0 months, 12 months,
and 24 months. For the nonexperimental counties, only about 20 percent of the cases would be expected to go 12 months without a nonpayment month, and only about 10 percent would last 24 months.
Experimental county cases starting in the first month of county implementation (0 months of county experience) had slightly lower survival rates than the nonexperimental counties because of the negative
coefficient on the experimental county dummy. However, for cases
starting after 12 months of county withholding experience, the sur-

vival rates were slightly higher than those for the nonexperimental county cases. And for cases in counties with 24 months of experience, the rates are substantially higher: about 30 percent versus 20 percent 12 months after the first month owed and 15 percent versus 10 percent 24 months after the first month owed. In short, the hazard models provide support for the hypothesis that routine income withholding became more effective over time.

To further explore this hypothesis with respect to the regularity of later child support payments as well as the timing of the first delinquency, monthly data were also used to estimate the effects of the experimental variables on payment in a given month while also controlling for the number of months the case had had an award. Both a dummy variable indicating any payment in a particular month and the ratio of dollars paid-to-owed in that month were used as dependent variables. The data for these analyses are from a randomly selected month out of the case history for each case. This was done to eliminate the possibility of correlation across errors for the months belonging to the same case.

Table 10.8 presents the coefficients and t-statistics from probit equations estimating the chance of having any payment in the random month. Whereas the county withholding level and individual case withholding coefficients are positive and statistically significant, the experimental county coefficient is negative, though not significantly different from zero. Unlike the hazard model, none of the county withholding experience variable coefficients is significantly different from zero, and two even have the wrong sign. Table 10.9 presents the coefficients and t-statistics from tobit analyses of the ratio of dollars of support paid-to-owed in the random month. As in the probit analyses, none of the county withholding experience variables is significantly different from zero.

On the other hand, in a probit and a tobit analysis (not reported in tables 10.8 and 10.9) that included all three experimental variables, as well as the county experience variables, the county withholding experience variable coefficient was positive, though only in the probit was it statistically significant.

Unlike the hazard analysis, therefore, the probit and tobit analyses provide, at best, mixed evidence that routine withholding became more effective over time. It should be noted that the three analyses, though related, do not capture the same phenomenon. The hazard measures the length of time until the first month when there is no payment, whereas the probit measures the probability of a payment in any month and the tobit measures the proportion of the obligation

Table 10.8 PROBIT ANALYSIS OF EFFECTS OF EXPERIMENTAL VARIABLES ON HAVING A PAYMENT IN A RANDOM MONTH: WISCONSIN STUDY

Experimental county	-.13 (1.09)	—	—
County withholding level	—	.006 (2.42)	—
Individual case withholding	—	—	.35 (5.25)
County withholding experience	.007 (1.05)	-.003 (0.59)	-.0005 (0.11)
Case time	-.004 (1.32)	-.005 (1.44)	-.005 (1.60)
Paternity case	.09 (1.62)	-.09 (1.60)	-.10 (1.77)
Mother-payer case	-.10 (0.48)	-.12 (0.54)	-.08 (0.40)
Nonresident parent's income variables			
Zero income dummy	-.32 (2.31)	-.33 (2.35)	-.29 (2.08)
Assignable income dummy	.70 (12.93)	.69 (12.83)	.64 (11.72)
Income amount	.0001 (6.83)	.0002 (6.87)	.0002 (7.00)
Missing income dummy	-.28 (4.68)	-.29 (4.72)	-.28 (4.66)
Cohort variables			
Cohort 2	.32 (4.32)	.32 (4.39)	.32 (4.36)
Cohort 3	.40 (4.89)	.40 (4.91)	.40 (4.87)
Cohort 4	.32 (3.48)	.13 (1.34)	.19 (2.27)
Cohort 5	.46 (3.34)	.30 (3.14)	.34 (4.07)
Cohort 6	.41 (4.00)	.18 (1.37)	.23 (2.17)
Intercept	-1.13 (13.77)	-1.12 (13.73)	-1.10 (13.50)
Log likelihood	-2088.9	-2086.6	-2075.6

Notes: Absolute values of t-statistics are in parentheses.

Dashes (—) denote omitted variables.

County dummies were also included in regressions, though not reported here.

Table 10.9 TOBIT ANALYSIS OF EFFECTS OF EXPERIMENTAL VARIABLES ON MONTHLY RATIOS OF DOLLARS PAID-TO-OWED: WISCONSIN STUDY

	Model 1	Model 2	Model 3
Experimental county	−.46 (1.55)	— —	— —
County withholding level	— —	.00002 (0.004)	— —
Individual case withholding	— —	— —	.49 (2.96)
County withholding experience	.007 (0.43)	−.009 (0.70)	−.01 (1.07)
Case time	−.001 (0.17)	−.002 (0.19)	−.002 (0.30)
Paternity case	−.02 (0.18)	−.02 (0.13)	−.03 (0.24)
Mother-payer case	−.06 (0.13)	−.07 (0.15)	−.06 (0.13)
Nonresident parent's income variables			
Zero income dummy	−.46 (1.58)	−.46 (1.58)	−.41 (1.42)
Assignable income dummy	1.16 (8.60)	1.16 (8.62)	1.08 (7.94)
Income amount	.0001 (6.13)	.0001 (6.23)	.0001 (6.28)
Missing income dummy	−.38 (2.57)	−.38 (2.57)	−.37 (2.53)
Cohort variables			
Cohort 2	.43 (2.29)	.43 (2.31)	.43 (2.32)
Cohort 3	.73 (3.86)	.73 (3.87)	.73 (3.87)
Cohort 4	.63 (2.88)	.46 (2.00)	.33 (1.70)
Cohort 5	.88 (4.16)	.77 (3.24)	.63 (3.10)
Cohort 6	.80 (3.22)	.74 (2.29)	.51 (2.03)
Intercept	−2.42 (10.78)	−2.38 (10.78)	−2.35 (10.63)
Log likelihood	−5101.7	−5103.8	−5095.5

Notes: Absolute values of t-statistics are in parentheses.
Dashes (—) denote omitted variables.
County dummies were also included in regressions though not reported here.

that is paid in any month. Still, there is no obvious explanation for the seemingly inconsistent results. At this point, therefore, we concluded that there is no consistent support for the hypothesis that routine withholding increases in effectiveness as counties gain implementation experience.

Moreover, note that in table 10.9 neither the experimental county dummy nor the county withholding level coefficients are significantly different from zero, and the former has the wrong sign. Only the individual case withholding dummy is positive and significantly different from zero. It is unclear why the withholding coefficients in the random month pay-to-owe tobit regressions are weaker than those in the average pay-to-owe tobit regressions. One possibility is that routine withholding may have a smaller effect on one-month ratios because of variation in pay periods or work availability for a payer, but may lead to a higher collection of delinquent payments when the payer is working. In any case, in view of the fact that the random-month regressions are based on much less information, more confidence should be placed in the average results reported here.

SUMMARY AND CONCLUSION

This chapter has focused on but one of numerous recent changes in the U.S. system of enforcing private child support—that of routine income withholding.

Ten Wisconsin counties began piloting routine income withholding in 1984. As originally conceived, the evaluation design consisted of a cross-county, before-after study. Data on child support obligations and payments and the use of income withholding were collected from the court records of child support cases entering the court system between 1980 and 1986 in 10 pilot and 10 matched control counties. Because the control counties began to use routine income withholding in a large number of cases, the cross-county, before-after comparison understates the true effect of income withholding. On the other hand, because income withholding cannot be implemented in some cases in which payment is unlikely, and because we can control for such selectivity only imperfectly, a comparison of child support payments of those with and without income withholding orders is likely to overstate the true effect of routine withholding. The former comparison suggests that routine income withholding increases child support payments by 11 percent, whereas the latter suggests an increase of 30 percent.

Whether an increase of 11–30 percent in child support payments is large or small depends upon the basis of comparison. Relative to gains achieved by most program interventions, this one is quite substantial. However, in terms of the difference between current child support payments and estimated ability to pay child support—which implies potential gains of close to 400 percent—this gain is quite small. What this suggests is that although routine income withholding will increase child support payments by a modest amount, it is no panacea. Attention should now be turned toward evaluating the independent and interactive effects of other reforms such as increased paternity establishment, numeric child support standards, and regular updating of awards on child support payments.

Notes

From the *Journal of Policy Analysis and Management*, Vol. 9, No. 2 (Spring 1990), pp. 155–177. Copyright 1990 by The Association of Public Policy Analysis and Management. Reprinted by permission of John Wiley & Sons, Inc.

A working draft of this chapter was published in 1989 by the Institute for Research on Poverty, University of Wisconsin–Madison, as Discussion Paper 891-89.

This research was supported in part by the Wisconsin Department of Health and Social Services, the U.S. Department of Health and Human Services, the Ford Foundation, and the Institute for Research on Poverty, University of Wisconsin–Madison. Any opinions and conclusions expressed here are those of the authors and do not represent the opinions or policy of the sponsoring institutions.

1. The percentage-of-income standard, established by the Wisconsin Department of Health and Social Services, stipulated child support awards of 17 percent of the non-resident parent's income for one child, and 25 percent, 29 percent, 31 percent, and 34 percent for two, three, four, and five or more children, respectively.

2. The upper and lower figures in the range are derived by applying, respectively, the Wisconsin percentage-of-income standard and the Colorado child support guidelines, two of the most widely used standards in the country (see chapter 3, this volume).

3. McDonald, Moran, and Garfinkel (1983) estimated that if Wisconsin were to collect 100 percent of the amount of child support owed by fathers of children on Aid to Families with Dependent Children (AFDC), collections would increase by $19 million; if the amount of the child support awards of those with awards were increased to the level specified by the percentage-of-income standard, collections would increase by $20 million; finally, if child support awards were secured in 100 percent of the cases, with no increase in the amounts of awards and no improvement in the proportion of the award collected, collections would increase by $26 million.

4. Cases just entering the court system were collected to evaluate the effects of routine withholding from the start of the payment history. Routine withholding could also be used in cases returning to court, but the effects in this type of case are not evaluated here.

5. Two control counties, Dodge and Juneau, implemented routine withholding before the end of case selection for cohort 6. They are treated as pilot counties for cohort 6 cases.

6. This information is from the Survey of Children, Income, and Program Participation, conducted by the Institute for Research on Poverty, University of Wisconsin–Madison, in 1985.

7. The extent of substitution in the pilot counties is not likely to have been large because, as described in the text following, withholding was not implemented in a large proportion of cases. It is likely that private direct payment cases were excepted.

8. About 3 percent of the cases had legal direct payment agreements, and about 20 percent had no child support order in the entire case history. In 30 percent of the cases, there was a change in legal custody, joint custody, or custody granted to someone other than the parents. These cases were excluded because of possible changes in the payer.

9. The sampling scheme and weights are available from the authors.

10. The income source information (and later income level information) is taken from the data for the final judgment in cases in which one had been issued. (A final judgment is issued in divorce cases at the time of property division. Although there is often a temporary child support order prior to the final judgment, income information is often available only at the time of the final judgment.) For cases with no final judgment, the income information from the first court action was used.

11. There are also cases in which assignments are made at a later action in response to delinquency. These were excluded by looking only at assignments made at the time of the first order. Also, it appears that in some cases assignments are issued at the time of the first order, but are not immediately sent to the employers and therefore have no effective date. These may be activated later in the event of a delinquency in payment, or if an unemployed nonresident parent later secures a job. These are not included in our definition of routine withholding. (Some of the cases are from pilot counties after the demonstration commenced.)

12. For awards expressed as percentages, the exact dollar amount owed is unknown to us. For these cases, the amount owed was estimated as the percentage ordered in the last court action multiplied by the income amount stated in that action. If no income information was available, the case was dropped from this analysis. Not all support orders mandate monthly payments (e.g., some use weekly or biweekly payments). Monthly equivalents were calculated for these cases.

13. The ratio of dollars paid to dollars owed could be greater than 1 if the nonresident parent pays more than the ordered amount. However, taken as an average over the entire case life, it seems rare for the payments to exceed the amount owed. Therefore, the cases with high pay-to-owe ratios are likely to be data errors and were treated as censored at 100 percent by using tobit models with an upper point of truncation at 100. The monthly data used later have many cases with payments of more than the monthly amount owed, so there a single (lower) point of truncation was used.

14. The three experimental variables were also included simultaneously in a single regression on the ratio of dollars paid-to-owed, and one on months paid-to-owed. In those regressions, only the individual case withholding dummy coefficients were significant. The impact of withholding calculated from those regressions was slightly larger than in the regressions reported in the text.

Appendix 10.A TOBIT ANALYSIS OF EFFECTS OF EXPERIMENTAL VARIABLES ON CHILD SUPPORT PAID-TO-OWED: WISCONSIN STUDY

	Dollars Paid-to-Owed					
Experimental county	5.86	(1.74)	—	—	—	—
County withholding level	—	—	.23	(2.73)	—	—
Individual case withholding	—	—	—	—	14.83	(5.92)
Paternity case	−6.31	(3.09)	−6.29	(3.09)	−6.71	(3.30)
Mother-payer case	−13.28	(1.83)	−14.33	(1.97)	−12.91	(1.75)
Nonresident parent's income variables						
Zero income dummy	−26.16	(5.28)	−26.09	(5.29)	−25.05	(5.11)
Assignable income dummy	19.67	(9.43)	19.50	(9.36)	16.96	(8.07)
Income amount	.003	(8.89)	.003	(8.95)	.003	(8.86)
Missing income dummy	−21.73	(9.70)	−21.90	(9.81)	−21.80	(9.83)
Cohort variables						
Cohort 2	.55	(0.19)	.71	(0.25)	.66	(0.23)
Cohort 3	1.27	(0.44)	1.60	(0.56)	1.42	(0.50)
Cohort 4	2.12	(0.59)	−1.47	(0.37)	.64	(0.19)
Cohort 5	9.43	(2.70)	5.88	(1.52)	7.68	(2.44)
Cohort 6	3.12	(0.89)	−3.99	(0.82)	−1.13	(0.36)
Intercept	42.20	(11.30)	41.14	(3.64)	42.64	(11.73)
Sigma	49.32	(61.47)	49.21	(61.60)	49.02	(61.47)
Log likelihood	−14062		−14060		−14045	

	(1)	(2)	(3)
Experimental county	7.38 (2.29)	—	—
County withholding level	—	.25 (3.06)	—
Individual case withholding	—	—	14.94 (6.24)
Paternity case	−12.16 (6.00)	−12.26 (6.04)	−12.60 (6.26)
Mother-payer case	−15.28 (2.26)	−17.35 (2.55)	−15.68 (2.29)
Nonresident parent's income variables			
Zero income dummy	−25.36 (5.08)	−25.27 (5.06)	−23.95 (4.86)
Assignable income dummy	21.72 (10.70)	21.53 (10.59)	19.09 (9.33)
Income amount	.003 (9.54)	.003 (9.52)	.003 (9.45)
Missing income dummy	−19.96 (9.17)	−20.08 (9.23)	−19.94 (9.26)
Cohort variables			
Cohort 2	4.43 (1.60)	4.55 (1.63)	4.49 (1.63)
Cohort 3	6.19 (2.24)	6.30 (2.28)	6.25 (2.28)
Cohort 4	2.60 (0.74)	−.76 (0.20)	1.56 (0.48)
Cohort 5	9.94 (2.97)	6.74 (1.81)	8.96 (2.92)
Cohort 6	6.36 (1.91)	−.88 (0.19)	2.79 (0.93)
Intercept	40.06 (11.19)	38.51 (10.97)	39.87 (11.41)
Sigma	47.35 (63.89)	47.36 (63.89)	47.07 (63.64)
Log likelihood	−13814	−13812	−13796

Notes: Absolute values of *t*-statistics are in parentheses.
Dashes (—) denote omitted variables.
County dummies were also included in regressions though not reported here.

Appendix 10.B RESULTS OF WEIBULL HAZARD ANALYSIS OF TIME UNTIL FIRST MONTH WITH NO CHILD SUPPORT PAYMENT: WISCONSIN STUDY

	Model 1	Model 2	Model 3
Experimental county	.11 (0.92)	—	—
County withholding level	—	-.004 (1.89)	—
Individual case withholding	—	—	-.34 (5.09)
County withholding experience	-.02 (2.83)	-.01 (1.97)	-.01 (2.45)
Paternity case	.38 (6.71)	.38 (6.70)	.39 (6.87)
Mother-payer case	.18 (0.77)	.19 (0.78)	.16 (0.66)
Nonresident parent's income variables			
Zero income dummy	.53 (3.28)	.53 (3.32)	.52 (3.25)
Assignable income dummy	-.52 (9.07)	-.52 (9.04)	-.48 (7.99)
Income amount	-.03 (11.74)	-.03 (11.80)	-.03 (11.47)
Missing income dummy	.51 (8.35)	.51 (8.30)	.51 (8.36)
Cohort variables			
Cohort 2	.12 (1.78)	.12 (1.74)	.11 (1.59)
Cohort 3	.26 (3.16)	.26 (3.12)	.25 (3.03)
Cohort 4	-.44 (0.50)	.10 (1.07)	.08 (1.10)
Cohort 5	.72 (0.84)	.18 (2.00)	.18 (2.23)
Cohort 6	.41 (4.04)	.57 (4.49)	.56 (5.42)
Intercept	1.47 (13.67)	1.45 (0.00)	1.51 (14.36)
Sigma	1.38 (37.59)	1.40 (37.67)	1.38 (37.77)
Log likelihood	-6236.7	-6235.7	-6227.1

Notes: Absolute values of t-statistics are in parentheses.
Dashes (—) denote omitted variables.
County dummies were also included in regressions though not reported here.

References

Garfinkel, Irwin, and Donald Oellerich. 1991. "Non-Custodial Fathers' Ability to Pay Child Support." *Demography* 25(4): 641–645.

McDonald, Thomas, James Moran, and Irwin Garfinkel. 1983. *Wisconsin Study of Absent Fathers' Ability to Pay More Child Support.* Institute for Research on Poverty Special Report 34. Madison: University of Wisconsin–Madison, Institute for Research on Poverty.

Chapter Eleven

THE EFFECT OF ROUTINE INCOME WITHHOLDING OF CHILD SUPPORT ON AFDC PARTICIPATION AND COST

Marieka M. Klawitter and Irwin Garfinkel

In the last 10 years, the number of families eligible for child support has risen dramatically, while the amount of support paid has remained low (U.S. Bureau of the Census 1989). Concern about the inadequacy of private child support and the cost to the taxpayer of providing public support to fill the gap has spurred efforts to reform federal and state child support legislation. Indeed, recent federal reforms mandate that states improve paternity establishment, enact numeric standards for child support awards, institute periodic updating of awards, and improve enforcement mechanisms. Many of these reforms have initially targeted families participating in the Aid to Families with Dependent Children (AFDC) program.

This chapter analyzes the effects of one support enforcement mechanism, routine income withholding, on participation in and costs of AFDC. As discussed in chapter 10, in routine income withholding, child support payments are deducted from the paychecks of nonresident parents and transferred to resident parents by a state agency. Unlike wage garnishment in response to payment delinquency, routine withholding begins at the time of the initial support obligation and avoids the stigma and potential delays of delinquency withholding. The Family Support Act of 1988 requires states to begin using routine income withholding in all child support cases by 1994.[1] This chapter uses data from a pilot demonstration of routine withholding in Wisconsin (described in detail in chapter 10) to discuss the mechanism's potential for reducing AFDC costs and participation.

EXPECTED EFFECTS OF ROUTINE WITHHOLDING ON AFDC

It is commonly assumed that higher rates of child support collection associated with routine withholding could lead to reductions in AFDC caseloads and the public cost of AFDC. Theoretically, by increasing the income available to resident parents, higher child support collections could decrease the number of families ever on AFDC or decrease the length of time a family stays on AFDC. Higher child support payments could, in addition, make some families ineligible for AFDC and would allow some to choose not to participate. The more likely reality, however, is that the increase in child support resulting from routine withholding alone would not be large enough to greatly affect participation rates, since award levels for AFDC families are usually low. At the same time, as a condition for receiving AFDC, parents must transfer to the state their right to receive child support payments. Therefore, if routine withholding increased the amount of child support collected for families on AFDC, state AFDC costs would decrease.

It is also possible, though, that an increase in collections in conjunction with the $50 child support disregard could be a source of increased AFDC participation. Under the disregard, a family considering applying for AFDC would not only receive a welfare check but also the first $50 a month the absent parent pays in child support. This is tantamount to increasing that family's monthly AFDC check by up to $50, thus increasing the incentive not only to apply for and receive AFDC but to stay on it as well. However, so long as child support collections exceed $50 per month, further increases in collections will reduce public expenditures for families on AFDC. Also as noted, if the support collected is high enough, families will no longer be eligible for AFDC or will choose to leave the program, and both participation and public expenditures will drop.

Families applying for AFDC are required to pursue a child support award through the state child support enforcement agency (the "IV-D" office). Since families in this group are already on AFDC when they enter the court system, they are more likely to be on AFDC after a child support order than are families not entering the court system through this office. The IV-D cases may also be treated differently by court administrators, who may be concerned with the level of public expenditures.[2] Nationwide, only about 60 percent of eligible IV-D families have child support awards, and less than 40 percent of those receive any payment (U.S. Congress 1989: 662, table 2). Routine withholding may have a larger effect on IV-D cases, since most of the families involved in those cases are on AFDC in the absence of withholding. It is also possible, though, that even with routine withholding, child support payments to this group will be very low because of low award amounts and unstable incomes of the nonresident parents.

Previous research suggests that the effects of routine withholding alone on AFDC costs and caseloads may not be large. Using 1980 data, McDonald, Moran, and Garfinkel (1983), for example, found that if the state of Wisconsin were to collect 100 percent of current child support obligations of the fathers of children on AFDC, the state's caseload would decrease by only 1,200 (2 percent), and AFDC savings would amount to only $26 million (about 7 percent). Similarly, Robins (1986), using 1981 Current Population Survey (CPS) data, estimated that full enforcement of child support orders nationally would lead to no change in AFDC participation rates and about an 8 percent decrease in AFDC costs. Bergmann and Roberts (1987) used 1979 CPS data to estimate a 6.1 percent decrease in AFDC participation and a 9.7 percent decrease in welfare expenditures with complete collection of child support. These and other studies (e.g., Oellerich, Garfinkel, and Robins [1989]) suggest that even perfect enforcement of child support at current levels would not lead to large changes in AFDC participation or costs.

The actual effects of routine withholding are likely to be smaller than these estimates. Withholding will not lead to 100 percent collections, since it cannot be used when the payer has no job or is self-employed. Garfinkel and Klawitter (1990) have estimated that only between 70 percent and 85 percent of the nonresident parents in the Wisconsin sample had assignable incomes. Also, as documented by Graham and Beller (1989), unobservable family differences may affect AFDC participation, child support, and a mother's earnings. These connections imply that routine withholding may not be effective for the women most at risk for AFDC, since potential market earnings may also be low for this group. The aggregate effect of enforcement reforms also depends on the ability to establish child support awards. Penkrot (1989) suggested that only about 25 percent of children on AFDC in 1985 were covered by child support orders. Further, of cases in which a social security number was available, only 20 percent of the remaining noncustodial parents earned over $10,000 a year and thus were likely to be able to pay support.

In combination with other types of child support reform, however, increased enforcement could have large effects. McDonald et al. (1983) estimated that if child support orders were obtained in all cases, the award amounts were based on the Wisconsin percentage-of-income standard, and 100 percent of the amount owed was collected, the number of families on AFDC would decrease by 12 percent to 15 percent and costs would decrease by about 36 percent. Even a 75 percent collection rate, in combination with the other reforms, was estimated to result in a 6 percent decrease in cases and a 28 percent decrease in costs.

Estimates from other national studies are similar to these. Oellerich et al. (1989) calculated reductions of about 16 percent in caseload and 30 percent in AFDC costs if orders were set in all cases using the Wisconsin standard and collections were 100 percent. Robins (1986) estimated that if awards were ordered in all cases (at 1982 levels) and were perfectly enforced, participation in AFDC would decrease by 3 percent to 6 percent and costs would decrease by 26 percent. Bergmann and Roberts (1987) estimated a much larger impact of fully collected awards in all cases at then-existing levels—a decrease in AFDC participation of one-third and in expenditures of one-half.[3]

The results of these simulations suggest that the effects of routine withholding by itself on AFDC costs will not be large, and that there may be no effect at all on participation rates. The Wisconsin demonstration data used in this study provide a better estimate of the effects of increasing child support enforcement by incorporating family labor supply adjustments and realistic implementation levels of the policy.

THE WISCONSIN DEMONSTRATION AND DATA

Background

As described in chapter 10, during January to June 1984, 10 Wisconsin counties contracted with the state for the pilot demonstration of routine withholding[4] as one component of the state's new child support assurance system (CSAS). These pilot counties were to use routine income withholding of child support whenever possible. Ten control counties provided a comparison group during the demonstration period, and a predemonstration sample from pilot and control counties allowed baseline comparison.[5] By using pilot counties rather than random cases within a county, the demonstration could capture the possible spillover effects of changing a county's system of support collection.

Family court records from the 20 counties thus provided information on a sample of new divorce, separation, and paternity cases involving at least one child under the age of 18.[6] The cases first entered the court system in the three-year period prior to the demonstration (1980–83) or in the three years after the demonstration's start (1984–87).[7] Data for each family are available for one to three years, depending on when they entered the court system. The data include the dates and purposes of each court action, custody and visitation agreements, and the amounts of child support and other monetary obligations. Records of the amounts and dates of all child support payments sent through the county clerk of court office were also available. Because Wisconsin requires child support payments to be made through the clerk of court, these records document the great majority of child support payments.[8] Social security numbers from the court record were checked against Wisconsin AFDC records for the period between July 1980 and January 1987 to obtain the amounts of AFDC payments for each family.

For the analysis presented here, the sample includes only cases in which the mother had legal custody of all children for the entire sample period and a social security number was available for her. Also, only cases with a child support order were used, since routine withholding can only be used in cases with awards.[9] The sample size is 3,309 cases.

Pilot counties used routine withholding in about 60 percent of the cases during the demonstration period. Control counties also began using routine withholding during the demonstration and used it overall in about 30 percent of the demonstration-period cases. Use of withholding increased over time in pilot and control counties. Even in the last year of the demonstration, however, pilot county levels of withholding (65 percent) were below the estimated potential of 70–85 percent of cases (Garfinkel and Klawitter 1990). The incomplete implementation of routine withholding in pilot counties and the use of withholding in control counties make the evaluation of withholding more complex.

The Demonstration Cases:
Can Routine Withholding Have an Effect?

As already mentioned, even perfect collection of child support may not result in large changes in AFDC participation or expenditures. The potential effects of routine withholding on AFDC depend in part on how many families would participate in the program in the absence of greater amounts of child support. If most families entering the family court system were not at risk of participating, then the overall effects on this population would be small.

Table 11.1 shows the proportion of cases in our sample that were on AFDC at the petition date (just prior to the first court appearance) as well as at any time in the court record period.[10] These are shown for the predemonstration and demonstration period and for pilot and control counties. Prior to the withholding demonstration, both pilot and control counties had about 35 percent of cases on AFDC at the petition date and more than half on AFDC at some time during the court record period. With this large proportion of cases on AFDC, a change in the level of child support collected could have a significant impact on AFDC costs.

Table 11.1 also shows that AFDC participation rates changed between the predemonstration and demonstration periods. During the demonstration, about 45 percent of all cases started out on AFDC—an increase of about 10 percentage points over the predemonstration rate. The proportion of cases ever on AFDC also increased, but not so dramatically. The increase in the proportion of cases on AFDC prior to entering the court system would be a problem in a simple before/after analysis of the effects of routine withholding, but can be handled by comparing pilot and control counties.

Cases on AFDC at the petition date are likely to spend a much greater proportion of their time on AFDC than are other cases (table 11.2). Before the demonstration, cases not starting on AFDC spent an average of 16 percent and 22 percent of months on AFDC in pilot and control counties, respectively. In the same period, cases on AFDC at petition spent about 80 percent of the time on AFDC in pilot and control counties. Clearly, there is much room for reduction in the amount of time spent on AFDC for cases entering the court system through the AFDC program.

The effects of changes in child support collection rates also depend on the levels of awards. If award levels are very low for families at risk of needing AFDC, then payment enforcement will have little impact on AFDC. Table 11.2 shows that cases on AFDC at the petition date had monthly child support awards that were much lower than those of cases not on AFDC, especially in the demonstration period. Awards in cases not on AFDC at petition averaged $300 in pilot and $323 in control counties prior to the demonstration, but cases on AFDC had awards of only $132 in pilot counties and $164 in control during that time. Thus, prior to the demonstration, awards for the cases most at risk for AFDC were about half the amount of those for other cases.[11]

During the demonstration period these differences were exacerbated. Awards in cases not on AFDC at petition increased to $342 and $392 in pilot and control counties, respectively, while awards decreased for cases on AFDC at petition in control counties to $137 (there was no significant change in pilot-county cases) (see table 11.2). These changes in the award levels may reflect early use of the Wisconsin percentage-of-income standard for award amounts.[12] The ef-

Table 11.1 THE PROPORTION OF CASES ON AFDC AT PETITION DATE AND AT ANY TIME, BY PERIOD AND PILOT COUNTY STATUS: WISCONSIN STUDY

	Predemonstration (%)		Demonstration (%)	
	Pilot	Control	Pilot	Control
Proportion of cases on AFDC at petition	36	35	44	45
Proportion of cases with any AFDC in court period	52	56	58	59

Source: Data from demonstration of routine income withholding in 10 Wisconsin counties.

Table 11.2 AVERAGE PROPORTION OF MONTHS ON AFDC, AMOUNT OF FIRST CHILD SUPPORT AWARD, AND PROPORTION OF CHILD SUPPORT COLLECTED, BY AFDC STATUS, PERIOD, AND PILOT COUNTY STATUS: WISCONSIN STUDY

	Predemonstration		Demonstration	
	Pilot	Control	Pilot	Control
Cases Not on AFDC at Petition:				
Average percentage of months on AFDC in court period	16	22	18	14
Amount of first award ($)	300	323	342	392
Category of first award (%):				
$1–$50	5	7	8	4
$51–$100	14	9	12	9
Over $100	81	84	81	87
Percentage of child support collected	61	63	70	67
Cases on AFDC at Petition:				
Average percentage of months on AFDC in court period	81	80	86	85
Amount of first award ($)	132	164	131	137
Category of first award (%)				
$1–$50	25	17	23	15
$51–$100	31	23	26	23
Over $100	44	60	52	62
Proportion of child support collected	46	41	49	49

Source: Data from demonstration of routine income withholding in 10 Wisconsin counties.

fects of routine withholding on AFDC could be mitigated by any decrease in award levels for the cases most likely to participate in the AFDC program.

Awards of less than $50 per month are particularly significant because of the child support AFDC disregard. Net AFDC costs will not be offset by even perfect collection of child support in cases with awards less than $50, though income to the families would be increased. For cases with awards from $51 to $100, increased child support could make a marginal difference in AFDC. However, without significant earnings by the custodial parent, it seems unlikely that increased child support could affect AFDC participation for these cases. Increases in child support collection rates may make the most difference in AFDC participation and costs for the group of cases with awards over $100 per month.

Table 11.2 shows that cases on AFDC at petition are more likely to have awards not exceeding $50 (25 percent and 17 percent of pilot- and control-county cases, respectively) than are cases not starting on AFDC (5 percent and 7 percent of pilot and control cases, respectively) prior to the demonstration. Also, pilot counties have greater proportions of low-award cases than do control counties for cases on AFDC at petition. Among the cases not starting on AFDC, the proportions of low awards in pilot and control counties were very similar. There was not much change in these patterns in the demonstration period.

More than 80 percent of cases not on AFDC at petition had awards greater than $100 per month in the predemonstration period, but the corresponding proportion for cases on AFDC was only 44 percent in pilot and 60 percent in control counties (see table 11.2). The proportion for AFDC cases grew slightly in the demonstration period (to 52 percent in pilots and 62 percent in controls) but remained well below the proportions for cases not on AFDC.[13] Cases most at risk for AFDC participation are more likely to have low awards, but over half of these cases have awards over $100 per month—not enough to support a family, but potentially a significant addition to income.

Award levels are an upper limit on the potential impact of routine withholding, but withholding will have only a marginal impact on payments, so the current payment levels are also of interest. Table 11.2 furthermore shows the average proportion of child support collected over the court record period. Prior to the demonstration, the collection rate was much lower in cases starting on AFDC (about 46 percent in pilots and 41 percent in controls) than in non-AFDC cases (61 percent in pilots and 63 percent in controls). On the brighter side, there is much room for improvement in support collections for AFDC families and so withholding could have an impact. On the darker side, the rates are so low to begin with that one questions the potential for improvement. Consistent with the pessimistic view, collection rates increased in pilot counties for non-AFDC cases during the withholding demonstration, but increased only slightly for families starting out on AFDC. On the other hand, collections increased in AFDC cases in control counties during the demonstration to the same level as those in pilot counties.

Overall, it seems that a significant proportion of custodial families participate in the AFDC program, but those who do are likely to have low child support awards and payments. These results point to only a small potential for AFDC savings from routine withholding alone, especially in the presence of the $50 child support disregard. On the other hand, if award levels are adjusted over the life of a court case, potential collections may be higher than indicated by these initial levels. This could be especially important in families with young noncustodial parents who may have greater earnings as they age. Routine withholding may then be a tool for maintaining contact and improving opportunities for later collection of support.

ROUTINE WITHHOLDING AND AFDC

This section estimates the effects of routine withholding on AFDC participation and public expenditures. Again, AFDC participation is the proportion of months a family spent on AFDC between the first month of the child support obligation and the end of the sample period. Net AFDC expenditures are the sum of AFDC payments to the resident parent in the same period, minus the child support sent to the state to offset the family's AFDC costs, averaged over the time since the child support order.[14] The child support disregard is reflected in the expenditure measure by excluding up to $50 of the child support paid in each month that the family was on AFDC.[15] The measure reflects the cost of AFDC to the state and federal governments (excluding administrative costs) net of the child support recovered.

Policy Variables Used in Analysis

The effects of routine withholding on the AFDC outcomes were measured by three alternative policy variables providing a range of estimates. The first variable is an indicator equaling one for cases in pilot counties during the demonstration period (experimental-county cases) and zero for all other cases. This specification (Model 1 in the subsequent tables in this chapter) allowed us to compare AFDC participation and costs in experimental-county cases with levels in predemonstration and control-county cases. This comparison could underestimate the effects of routine withholding, since pilot counties did not fully implement withholding and control counties began to use withholding in the demonstration period. It does, however, capture any spillover effects of the policy on all cases in the pilot counties.

The second measure (Model 2) uses the level of implementation of withholding to estimate the effects on AFDC. For each case this variable equals the proportion of cases in which withholding was used in the county and cohort (the year the case entered the court system). This measure can account for the use of withholding in control counties and the incomplete implementation in pilot counties. However, if differences in the level of implementation were related to the ability of counties to use withholding or the level of other county efforts in child support collection, this measure may overestimate the potential impact of withholding in an average county. On the other hand, counties perceiving AFDC caseloads as problematically high might use routine withholding more often, resulting in a possible underestimate of the impact.

The third measure (Model 3) compares cases in which routine withholding was used with all other cases. A dummy variable indicates cases in which the county issued a withholding order to the nonresident parent's employer within 60 days of the first court date.[16] This measure could also result in an overestimate of the effects of withholding, if routine withholding were used more often in cases with better prospective payers. Again, if routine withholding is used more often in AFDC cases, this measure could alternatively underestimate the AFDC effects on an average case.

Table 11.3 presents the mean values of the proportion of months on AFDC and the net AFDC expenditures by each of the policy variables. Cases in pilot counties spent slightly less time on AFDC than did control-county cases before the demonstration, but during the demonstration the proportions were nearly equal. AFDC costs were slightly lower in pilot counties than in control counties prior to the demonstration, but pilot-control costs were about the same during the demonstration period. None of these differences, however, is statistically significant. No clear patterns are apparent in AFDC participation

Table 11.3 AVERAGE PROPORTION OF MONTHS ON AFDC AND NET AFDC
EXPENDITURES, BY PILOT COUNTY STATUS AND PERIOD, COUNTY
WITHHOLDING LEVEL, AND CASE WITHHOLDING STATUS:
WISCONSIN STUDY

Policy Variables	Average Proportion of Months on AFDC (%)	Average Net AFDC Expenditures per Month ($)	Proportion of Cases in Policy Category (%)
Pilot-county cases			
Predemonstration period	39	171	27
Demonstration period	48	208	22
Control-county cases			
Predemonstration period	42	178	27
Demonstration period	47	209	24
County withholding level			
0% to 10%	36	156	51
11% to 30%	51	221	19
31% to 45%	47	200	13
46% to 60%	56	260	10
61% and over	48	196	8
Case withholding status			
Immediate withholding cases	47	192	24
Nonwithholding cases	42	188	76

Source: Data from demonstration of routine income withholding in 10 Wisconsin counties.

or expenditures based on comparisons of county withholding level.
Unexpectedly, cases with routine withholding had higher costs and
participation levels than did cases not receiving withholding orders.
This could indicate selective use of the policy by courts determined
to enforce child support payments in AFDC cases. The following multivariate analysis controls for some case characteristics and may thus
mitigate the selection bias in the estimation of effects of routine withholding on AFDC costs and participation. Indeed, routine withholding cases are associated with *lower* AFDC expenditures after controlling for case and county characteristics, though not significantly so.

Tobit Analyses of AFDC Participation and Costs

The multivariate analysis measures the effects of routine withholding
while controlling for other county and case differences. The amount

of child support paid (CS) is assumed to be a function of the routine withholding policy variable (RW) and of other variables (X_1):

$$CS = f(RW, X_1). \tag{11.1}$$

The AFDC outcomes are assumed to be affected by the amount of child support paid and by other factors (X_2):

$$AFDC = g(CS, X_2). \tag{11.2}$$

We estimate a reduced-form model:

$$AFDC = b_0 + b_1RW + b_2X + E, \tag{11.3}$$

where X includes all variables affecting child support and AFDC outcomes. The coefficients in this model will reflect both the effects of the explanatory factors on child support and the effects on AFDC.

Since the dependent variables—AFDC participation and net AFDC expenditures—are limited in their ranges, tobit analyses were used to estimate the models. Two-limit tobits account for the limits on the proportion of months on AFDC to between zero and 100. Net expenditures are limited to be at or above zero, and so tobits with a single limit at zero were used for those analyses. The three measures of routine withholding are used in separate tobits (Models 1, 2, and 3) to estimate the range of its effects. In addition to the policy variables, variables control for county and family differences. The explanatory variable sample means and standard deviations are listed in Appendix 11.A.

The monthly award amount from the first child support order (in hundreds of dollars) measures the potential child support payments. Since child support payments may decrease with time since the court action, the number of months the case was in the sample were included. A dummy variable captures the differences between paternity and divorce cases. The regressions contain several controls for the nonresident parent's income. The amount of monthly income (in hundreds of dollars) is included and equals the mean value for cases with missing values.[17] Dummy variables indicate a missing income amount, a reported income amount of zero, and a reported income source that was assignable (a source with which routine withholding could be used). The number of children and the age of the mother are controlled for with dummy variables (with dummies for one child and mother's age under 25 omitted).[18] The age of the youngest child is included, since it may affect the resident parent's cost of entering the labor market. Finally, a set of cohort dummies (the first cohort is the omitted category) indicates the year that the case entered the court system, and county dummy variables (Waukesha County omitted) control for baseline county differences. The cohort and county dummy coefficients are not reported here.[19]

The results of the tobit regressions on the proportion of months on AFDC are in table 11.4, and the regressions on net AFDC costs are in table 11.5. In neither set of regressions are any of the policy variables statistically significant—implying no robust negative association of routine withholding with the AFDC outcomes.

Table 11.4 TOBIT ANALYSIS OF PROPORTION OF MONTHS ON AFDC: WISCONSIN STUDY

	Model 1		Model 2		Model 3	
Constant	114	(7.94)	114	(7.96)	115	(7.98)
Policy variables:						
Experimental-county dummy	2	(0.30)	—	—	—	—
Level of county withholding	—	—	.09	(0.57)	—	—
Case withholding dummy	—	—	—	—	4	(0.73)
Award amount ($100s)	−12	(9.00)	−12	(9.01)	−12	(9.01)
Months of data	−1	(4.07)	−1	(4.07)	−1	(4.09)
Paternity-case dummy	40	(7.63)	40	(7.63)	40	(7.63)
Nonresident parent income:						
Amount ($100s)	−3	(7.50)	−3	(7.51)	−3	(7.52)
Missing income dummy	14	(2.85)	14	(2.84)	14	(2.84)
Zero income dummy	−2	(0.21)	−2	(0.22)	−2	(0.19)
Assignable income dummy	1	(0.22)	1	(4.07)	0	(0.09)
Number of children:						
Two children	17	(3.65)	17	(3.66)	17	(3.66)
Three children	39	(5.81)	39	(5.82)	39	(5.81)
Four or more children	49	(5.73)	49	(5.73)	49	(5.71)
Age of mother:						
Age missing dummy	−17	(1.28)	−17	(1.28)	−17	(1.29)
25 to 34 years	−18	(4.02)	−18	(4.02)	−18	(4.02)
Over 34 years	−29	(3.65)	−29	(3.65)	−29	(3.64)
Age of youngest child (years)	−7	(9.67)	−7	(9.67)	−7	(9.66)
Sigma	85	(39.83)	85	(39.83)	85	(39.83)
Log likelihood	-8032		−8031		−8031	
Dependent mean			46			
N			3,309			

Source: Authors' estimates from data from demonstration of routine income withholding in 10 Wisconsin counties.

Notes: Absolute values of T-statistics are in parentheses. Dummy variables for counties and for year of petition date were also included.

Table 11.5 TOBIT ANALYSIS OF NET AFDC EXPENDITURES: WISCONSIN STUDY

	Model 1		Model 2		Model 3	
Constant	357	(8.82)	357	(8.86)	355	(8.80)
Policy variables:						
Experimental-county dummy	5	(0.24)	—	—	—	—
Level of county withholding	—	—	.22	(0.48)	—	—
Case withholding dummy	—	—	—	—	−5	(0.38)
Award amount ($100s)	−43	(11.21)	−43	(11.22)	−43	(11.19)
Months of data	−3	(3.45)	−3	(3.45)	−3	(3.44)
Paternity-case dummy	136	(9.25)	136	(9.25)	136	(9.26)
Nonresident parent income:						
Amount ($100s)	−6	(6.36)	−6	(6.36)	−6	(6.37)
Missing income dummy	44	(3.20)	44	(3.19)	44	(3.20)
Zero income dummy	10	(0.36)	10	(0.35)	10	(0.37)
Assignable income dummy	−16	(1.31)	−17	(1.33)	−15	(1.19)
Number of children:						
Two children	79	(5.75)	79	(5.76)	79	(5.74)
Three children	162	(8.54)	162	(8.55)	162	(8.54)
Four or more children	228	(9.28)	228	(9.28)	228	(9.28)
Age of mother:						
Age missing dummy	−45	(1.19)	−44	(1.18)	−45	(1.19)
25 to 34 years	−35	(2.86)	−35	(2.85)	−35	(2.85)
Over 34 years	−70	(3.04)	−70	(3.04)	−70	(3.04)
Age of youngest child (years)	−23	(11.79)	−23	(11.78)	−23	(11.80)
Sigma	255	(59.21)	255	(59.21)	255	(59.20)
Log likelihood	−14687		−14687		−14687	
Dependent mean			$196			
N			3,309			

Source: Authors' estimates from data from demonstration of routine withholding in 10 Wisconsin counties.
Notes: *T*-statistics are in parentheses. Dummy variables for counties and for year of petition date were also included.

Earlier work has shown that implementation of withholding was gradual and that withholding may have been more effective over time (Garfinkel and Klawitter 1990). Here, we explore the possibility of greater AFDC impacts over time by adding a measure of county withholding experience similar to the one used in that study. This measure is the number of months between the initial county implementation of routine withholding and the month the case entered the court system. For cases entering the system prior to the demonstration, the variable is zero. If counties used withholding more effectively with practice, then there could be larger AFDC impacts associated with greater withholding experience. The tobit results with this additional variable are included in table 11.6 for the participation outcome and table 11.7 for net AFDC expenditures.

Again, the static policy measures of routine withholding have insignificant coefficients in the analyses of proportion of months on AFDC (table 11.6). In each model in table 11.6, county withholding experience is estimated to be negatively (though insignificantly) associated with AFDC participation time. The county withholding experience measure is also negatively associated with net AFDC expenditures (table 11.7), and the Model 1 coefficient is significant. In that specification, the experimental-county indicator has a positive coefficient, implying that pilot counties initially had higher AFDC expenditures, but that the expenditures decreased with withholding experience.

Several interesting patterns appeared in the control variable coefficients from the tobits and are almost identical across models. The amount of the child support award is significantly related to both the proportion of months on AFDC and the net AFDC expenditures. An award higher by $100 implies a lower proportion of time on AFDC by 4 percentage points and lower net monthly AFDC expenditures of $26. (The impacts reported in this section are calculated from the tobit coefficients.[20]) Although these relationships may result from higher awards contributing to greater amounts of child support paid, it is also possible that the award level is an additional proxy for the family socioeconomic status.

The number of months in the case was negatively related to both the proportion of months on AFDC and net AFDC expenditures. With each additional month since the first court support award, the proportion of months on AFDC decreased by one-half a percentage point and the average monthly AFDC expenditures fell by $2. This may result from families being able to leave the AFDC program if income sources become greater or more stable over time.

Not surprisingly, families from paternity cases (compared to families involved in divorce cases) spend a significantly greater proportion of months on AFDC and cost the program more.

Nonresident parents' income is negatively related to the levels of AFDC participation and expenditures. Cases in which the nonresident parent's income is higher by $100 have, on average, proportions of months on AFDC lower by 1 percentage point and AFDC expenditures lower by $4. This is consistent with previous work on child support, which found that higher nonresident income had a significant impact on the collection rates of child support (Garfinkel and Klawitter 1990).

Table 11.6 TOBIT ANALYSIS OF PROPORTION OF MONTHS ON AFDC WITH
COUNTY EXPERIENCE VARIABLE: WISCONSIN STUDY

	Model 1		Model 2		Model 3	
Constant	118	(8.05)	115	(8.00)	115	(8.01)
Policy variables:						
Experimental-county dummy	13	(1.19)	—	—	—	—
Level of county withholding	—	—	.16	(0.09)	—	—
Case withholding dummy	—	—	—	—	4	(0.80)
County withholding experience	−1	(1.32)	−.4	(0.95)	−.3	(0.73)
Award amount ($100s)	−12	(8.99)	−12	(9.00)	−12	(9.00)
Months of data	−2	(4.27)	−1	(4.17)	−1	(4.16)
Paternity-case dummy	40	(7.65)	40	(7.64)	40	(7.64)
Nonresident parent income:						
Amount ($100s)	−3	(7.54)	−3	(7.53)	−3	(7.54)
Missing income dummy	14	(2.86)	14	(2.84)	14	(2.85)
Zero income dummy	−2	(0.19)	−2	(0.20)	0	(0.16)
Assignable income dummy	1	(0.25)	1	(0.23)	0	(0.11)
Number of children:						
Two children	18	(3.67)	18	(3.68)	17	(3.67)
Three children	39	(5.82)	39	(5.84)	39	(5.82)
Four or more children	49	(5.72)	49	(5.71)	49	(5.70)
Age of mother:						
Age missing dummy	−17	(1.26)	−17	(1.26)	−17	(1.28)
25 to 34 years	−18	(4.04)	−18	(4.01)	−18	(4.01)
Over 34 years	−29	(3.65)	−29	(3.64)	−29	(3.63)
Age of youngest child (years)	−6	(9.64)	−7	(9.66)	−7	(9.65)
Sigma	85	(39.83)	85	(39.83)	85	(39.83)
Log likelihood	−8031		−8031		−8031	
Dependent mean			46			
N			3,309			

Source: Authors' estimates from data from demonstration of routine income withholding in 10 Wisconsin counties.
Notes: T-statistics are in parentheses. Dummy variables for counties and for year of
petition date were also included.

Time on AFDC and AFDC expenditures increase with the number of
children and decrease as the age of the mother and the age of the
youngest child increase.

As noted earlier, the effects of routine withholding could be different in families participating in the AFDC program prior to entering
the court system or those entering the court system through the IV-D
office. However, tobit results for the sample of cases on AFDC at the

Table 11.7 TOBIT ANALYSIS OF NET AFDC EXPENDITURES WITH COUNTY
EXPERIENCE VARIABLE: WISCONSIN STUDY

	Model 1		Model 2		Model 3	
Constant	373	(9.08)	359	(8.92)	357	(8.85)
Policy variables:						
Experimental-county dummy	54	(1.80)	—	—	—	—
Level of county withholding	—	—	54	(1.07)	—	—
Case withholding dummy	—	—	—	—	−4	(0.25)
County withholding experience	−3	(2.17)	−2	(1.57)	−1	(1.21)
Award amount ($100s)	−43	(11.21)	−43	(11.21)	−43	(11.17)
Months of data	−4	(3.89)	−4	(3.67)	−4	(3.59)
Paternity-case dummy	136	(9.27)	136	(9.26)	136	(9.27)
Nonresident parent income:						
Amount ($100s)	−6	(6.40)	−6	(6.40)	−6	(6.40)
Missing income dummy	44	(3.21)	44	(3.18)	44	(3.20)
Zero income dummy	11	(0.39)	11	(0.38)	11	(0.40)
Assignable income dummy	−16	(1.29)	−16	(1.29)	−15	(1.17)
Number of children:						
Two children	80	(5.78)	80	(5.78)	79	(5.75)
Three children	163	(8.56)	163	(8.58)	163	(8.56)
Four or more children	228	(9.28)	228	(9.27)	228	(9.27)
Age of mother:						
Age missing dummy	−43	(1.16)	−44	(1.16)	−44	(1.18)
25 to 34 years	−36	(2.89)	−35	(2.85)	−35	(2.84)
Over 34 years	−70	(3.03)	−69	(3.02)	−70	(3.03)
Age of youngest child (years)	−23	(11.76)	−23	(11.77)	−23	(11.79)
Sigma	254	(59.21)	254	(59.21)	255	(59.20)
Log likelihood	−14685		−14686		−14687	
Dependent mean			$196			
N			3,309			

Source: Authors' estimates by authors from data from demonstration of routine income withholding in 10 Wisconsin counties.
Notes: T-statistics are in parentheses. Dummy variables for counties and for year of
petition date were also included.

petition date (not reported here) resulted in impacts only slightly
larger than those for the entire sample.

Effects of Routine Withholding on AFDC Participation and Costs

Table 11.8 contains the estimated impact of routine withholding on
AFDC participation (top panel) and net expenditures (bottom panel)

Table 11.8 ALTERNATIVE MEASURES OF THE IMPACT OF ROUTINE
WITHHOLDING ON THE PROPORTION OF MONTHS ON AFDC AND
NET AFDC EXPENDITURES: WISCONSIN STUDY

Specification	Model 1	Model 2	Model 3
	Proportion of Months on AFDC (percentage points)		
Policy variables only (table 11.4)	1	2	1
Policy variables and county experience (table 11.6)			
0 months	4	3	1
12 months	1	1	0
24 months	−2	0	−1
36 months	−5	−2	−2

Dependent variable mean: 46 percentage points

	Model 1	Model 2	Model 3
	Net AFDC Monthly Expenditures ($)		
Policy variables only (table 11.5)	3	7	−3
Policy variables and county experience (table 11.7)			
0 months	35	17	−2
12 months	9	4	−11
24 months	−16	9	−20
36 months	−39	−21	−29

Dependent variable mean: $196

Source: Authors' estimates from data from demonstration of routine income withholding in 10 Wisconsin counties. Calculated from tobit coefficients in tables 11.4
through 11.7.

implied by the coefficients in tables 11.4 to 11.7. For the specifications
that included the county withholding experience measure, the impact
is evaluated at 0, 12, 24, and 36 months of experience. It should be
noted that in tables 11.4 to 11.7 the policy variable coefficients are not
significant, although county withholding experience in table 11.7,
Model 1, is significant. However, the point estimates of the coefficients
are generally consistent in sign, and the calculated impacts can provide a sense of the magnitude of the effects.

As the size of the coefficients in the tobit analyses suggests, the
impacts in table 11.8 estimated in the specifications without the withholding experience variable are small and almost all positive. How-

ever, after adding the county experience measure, it looks as though AFDC participation and costs may initially be higher, but will decrease over time. For cases entering the court system in the first month of implementation (zero months of county experience), AFDC participation is expected to be between 1 and 4 percentage points higher (between 2 percent and 9 percent of the mean) under routine withholding. Net AFDC expenditures at 0 months of experience are estimated to be between $35 higher and $2 lower per month. Routine withholding appears to start to "pay off" sometime after 12 months of implementation experience. After 36 months of experience, routine withholding is associated with lower participation by between 2 and 5 percentage points (4 percent to 11 percent of the mean) and expenditures lower by $21 to $39 (11 percent to 20 percent of the mean). These estimates are within the range suggested by the simulation studies discussed earlier and, as expected, are quite low.

CONCLUSION

Federal legislation requires states to begin to use routine withholding of child support payments in all cases as of 1994 and earlier for IV-D cases. In 1984, 10 Wisconsin counties began using routine withholding as part of a three-year demonstration. That experience suggests that routine withholding increases the collection of child support obligations by between 11 and 30 percent. This effect alone may justify implementing routine withholding.

The effects of routine withholding on AFDC participation and expenditures were not expected to be large. Other studies have suggested that, by itself, routine withholding would only marginally affect AFDC caseloads and would only decrease AFDC costs by about 7 percent, but in combination with increases in both the number of families with child support awards and the amounts of those awards, withholding could result in large decreases in AFDC participation and costs.

In this study, we have shown that child support awards and payments were very low for the group most at risk of receiving AFDC, leaving little potential for a large impact from withholding alone. Consistent with that, we found that on average routine withholding did not decrease AFDC participation or net AFDC expenditures. On the other hand, we found that the implementation of routine withholding initially increases AFDC participation and costs, but results in decreases as counties gain implementation experience. For cases entering the family court system three years after initial implementation, our estimates suggest that AFDC participation is lower by 4 percent to 11 percent and that net AFDC expenditures are lower by 11 percent to 20 percent.

Routine withholding alone will not dramatically lower the level of public expenditures on AFDC. However, it is just one of several reforms being implemented in Wisconsin and nationwide. As more child-support-eligible families receive awards, and as award amounts increase, routine withholding may help to ensure higher levels of private child support payments and lower levels of public AFDC costs.

Notes

A working draft of this chapter was published in 1991 by the Institute for Research on Poverty, University of Wisconsin–Madison, as Discussion Paper 961-91.

This research was supported in part by the Wisconsin Department of Health and Social Services, the U.S. Department of Health and Human Services, the Ford Foundation, and the Institute for Research on Poverty, University of Wisconsin–Madison. Any opinions and conclusions expressed here are those of the authors and do not represent the opinions or policy of the sponsoring institutions. Patricia Brown and Elizabeth Uhr were immensely helpful in the creation of this paper.

1. Federal legislation in 1984 required states to use withholding in response to delinquency in child support payments, and it was used even earlier in Wisconsin (starting in 1980). The Family Support Act of 1988 required the use of routine withholding in cases handled by the Office of Child Support Enforcement as of 1990.

2. It does appear that in cases in which the resident parent was on AFDC at the petition date, routine withholding was more likely to be used. In a probit regression (not reported here), a dummy variable indicating the use of routine withholding was used as the dependent variable. Resident parents on AFDC at the petition date were estimated to be 14 percent more likely to get a routine withholding assignment after controlling for income and other characteristics.

3. Unlike most of the other studies, the Bergmann and Roberts (1987) model included a labor supply effect. They may, however, overestimate the effects of child support on work and AFDC participation because of possible endogeneity of child support payments. See Graham and Beller (1989) for a discussion of these issues.

4. See also Garfinkel and Klawitter (1990) for a detailed description of the withholding.

5. Two of the control counties, Dodge and Juneau, officially became pilot counties during the demonstration period. Cases in these counties that entered the system after they became pilots (cohort-six cases) were treated as experimental-county cases.

6. The sample was further limited to cases with the first court action within a year of the court petition date and in which there was a living nonresident parent for at least a year following the first court action. These selections limited the sample to cases in which child support could be ordered.

7. Weights based on the proportion of the total caseload sampled for each case type (divorce, paternity, separation) in each county and cohort are used for the descriptive statistics reported here.

8. In this dataset, about 3 percent of cases had legal agreements to make payments directly to the resident parent; these cases were dropped since there was no information on child support paid. In a separate survey, the Survey of Children, Income, and Program Participation (conducted by the Institute for Research on Poverty, University of Wisconsin–Madison, in 1985), it was estimated that some direct payment occurs in about 7 percent of Wisconsin cases.

9. This selection could cause problems if there was a change in the demonstration period in the pool of cases receiving child support orders. The pool of cases with awards may have changed with alterations in the child support standard for all cases, or with changes in paternity adjudication for paternity cases. Although the Wisconsin percentage-of-income child support standard was not yet the presumptive standard, it had been published and could have been used in the demonstration period.

Routine withholding itself could have effects on the number of parents going to court to seek child support awards. If parents perceive greater gains from having awards (higher payment levels), they may choose to go to court to pursue an award. This seems unlikely to have happened in the short period of the demonstration, however.

10. The petition date is the date that a request for court action is filed. The petition date was, on average, three months before the court date and at most one year prior to the first court action (because of the sample selection procedures).

11. Differences in award levels may be due in part to differences in the number of children in the family.

12. The percentage-of-income standard was published shortly before the beginning of the demonstration period, but use of the standard was not mandatory until July 1987.

13. To account for these differences, we controlled for award levels in our estimations of the effects of withholding.

14. In some cases the amount of child support recorded as having been sent to the state was greater than the amount of AFDC paid out. This could happen if child support was being allocated for AFDC costs occurring prior to the support order. However, many of these cases had no AFDC record and are probably one of three types of errors. They could be errors in the AFDC record-matching process, the parent could have been on AFDC in another state (since we have only Wisconsin AFDC data), or the payments may have gone to the resident parent but were incorrectly recorded as going to the state. Because it was not possible to ascertain which cases had legitimate negative values for net expenditures, all of these cases were deleted from the sample used here.

To test the importance of payment-type error, we constructed an alternative measure that does not depend on the record of payment type. For that measure, all child support paid (regardless of recorded type) in months when the resident parent's family was on AFDC was subtracted from the sum of AFDC checks (adjusted for the $50 disregard). This measure ignores child support paid to the state in non-AFDC months for prior AFDC, but includes all child support paid (even that recorded as going to the resident parent) in AFDC months. The results of analyses using this dependent variable are not reported here, but were very similar to the results reported.

15. The $50 disregard, part of the 1984 federal Deficit Reduction Act, did not take effect until October 1984, and the first checks were not paid in Wisconsin until July 1985. To avoid a "built-in" difference in AFDC expenditures in the two periods, the measure is calculated as though the disregard were in effect during both the predemonstration and demonstration periods.

16. In some cases, income assignments were made at the first court date but were not immediately sent to the employer. These could be used later in the event of delinquency in payment, or if an unemployed nonresident parent later secured employment. These

are not labeled as routine withholding here. There were, in addition, cases in which assignments were made in a later court action in response to a payment delinquency. These are also not included in our definition of routine withholding.

17. Income information was taken from the court action of the final judgment (property division) for divorce cases in which there had been a final judgment. For all other cases the information is from the first court action. The final judgment action was used because income is most likely to be recorded at that time. Income was missing in the court record in about 35 percent of the cases.

18. The number of children used here is the number involved in the court case studied. This may differ from the number in the household, for a number of reasons. In divorce cases this may be due to children born prior to or after the marriage ended by the court action. Paternity cases, by law, involve only one child. Separate cases are filed for each child, even if the parents are the same. In a few cases we were able to consolidate multiple paternity cases from the same parents. Otherwise, resident parents with more than one child involved in paternity cases will have more children than indicated here.

19. These coefficients are available from the authors.

20. The coefficients reported in the tables give the change in the (latent) continuous dependent variable. To calculate the expected change in the observed outcome for a marginal change in the explanatory variable, the coefficient is multiplied by the estimated probability of observing a value (not the limits of zero or 100). In the one-limit tobit, the coefficients are multiplied by the cumulative normal density evaluated at -xb/s (where x is the vector of means of the independent variables, b is the vector of coefficient estimates, and s is the estimated standard deviation). For the two-limit tobit, the coefficients are multiplied by the cumulative normal density evaluated at $(100 - xb)/s$ less the cumulative normal evaluated at -xb/s (see Maddala 1983: 160–61). The withholding impacts are calculated for each case as the difference between the outcome with and without routine withholding, then are averaged over the sample of cases.

Appendix 11.A VARIABLE MEANS BY AFDC STATUS AT PETITION DATE:
WISCONSIN STUDY

	Not on AFDC		On AFDC	
N	1,902		1,407	
Experimental-county dummy	.20	(.40)	.23	(.42)
Level of county withholding	20.8	(40.6)	23.2	(40.6)
Case withholding dummy	.24	(0.43)	.26	(.82)
County withholding experience	2.57	(7.12)	3.55	(7.55)
Award amount ($100s)	3.16	(3.04)	1.37	(1.06)
Months of data	21.2	(9.99)	19.04	(9.76)
Paternity-case dummy	.14	(.35)	.56	(.50)
Nonresident parent income:				
Amount ($100s)	16.24	(15.24)	11.54	(6.18)
Missing income dummy	.25	(.43)	.49	(.50)
Zero income dummy	.02	(.15)	.06	(.24)
Assignable income dummy	.72	(.45)	.53	(.50)
Number of children:				
Two children	.36	(.48)	.18	(.38)
Three children	.13	(.37)	.08	(.27)
Four or more children	.08	(.26)	.04	(.21)
Age of mother:				
Age missing	.01	(.11)	.02	(.15)
25 to 34 years	.45	(.50)	.33	(.25)
Over 34 years	.29	(.45)	.07	(.25)
Age of youngest child (years)	5.7	(4.8)	3.1	(2.85)

Source: Data from demonstration of routine income withholding in 10 Wisconsin
counties.
Note: Standard deviations are in parentheses.

References

Bergmann, B., and M. Roberts. 1987. "Child Support, Work, and Welfare." In
Gender in the Work Place, edited by Clair Brown and Joseph A.
Pechman. Washington, D.C.: Brookings Institution.

Garfinkel, I., and M. Melli. 1982. Child Support: Weaknesses of the Old and
Features of a Proposed New System, vol. 1. Institute for Research on

Poverty Special Report 32A. Madison: University of Wisconsin–
Madison, Institute for Research on Poverty.

Garfinkel, I., and M. Klawitter. 1990. "The Effect of Routine Income Withholding on Child Support Collections." *Journal of Policy Analysis
and Management* 9(2): 155–77.

Graham, John W., and Andrea H. Beller. 1989. "The Effect of Child Support
Payments on the Labor Supply of Female Family Heads: An Econometric Analysis." *Journal of Human Resources* 24(4): 664–89.

Maddala, G. S. 1983. *Limited-Dependent and Qualitative Variables in Econometrics.* New York: Cambridge University Press.

McDonald., T., J. Moran, and I. Garfinkel. 1983. "Wisconsin Study of Absent
Fathers' Ability to Pay More Child Support." Institute for Research
on Poverty Special Report 34. Madison: University of Wisconsin–
Madison, Institute for Research on Poverty.

Oellerich, D., I. Garfinkel, and P. Robins. 1989. "Private Child Support: Current and Potential Impacts." Institute for Research on Poverty Discussion Paper 888-89. Madison: University of Wisconsin–Madison,
Institute for Research on Poverty.

Penkrot, J. 1989. "Can AFDC Parents Pay Child Support?" *Journal of Policy
Analysis and Management* 8(1): 104–10.

Robins, P. 1986. "Child Support, Welfare Dependency, and Poverty." *American
Economic Review* 76(4): 768–88.

U.S. Bureau of the Census. 1989. *Child Support and Alimony: 1985.* Current
Population Reports, ser. P-23, no. 154. Washington, D.C.: U.S. Government Printing Office.

U.S. Congress. House. Committee on Ways and Means. 1989. *Background
Material and Data on Programs within the Jurisdiction of the Com-
mittee on Ways and Means.* Washington, D.C.: U.S. Government
Printing Office.

Chapter Twelve

THE EFFECT OF ROUTINE INCOME WITHHOLDING ON THE LABOR SUPPLY OF CUSTODIAL PARENTS

Nancy Maritato and Philip K. Robins

This chapter presents the results of a preliminary empirical analysis of the effects of immediate wage withholding—one of three primary features of the Wisconsin child support assurance system (CSAS)—on the labor supply of custodial parents. As discussed in more detail in the next section, economic theory suggests that an increase in child support income (resulting from immediate wage withholding) will have different labor supply effects for AFDC and non-AFDC families. For AFDC families, labor supply is expected to increase, whereas for non-AFDC families, labor supply is expected to decrease. When averaged over all families, labor supply may either increase, decrease, or not change at all in response to immediate withholding. The aggregate response will depend on the distribution of families with respect to welfare status and the size of the response within each welfare status.

Despite economic theory's relatively unambiguous predictions, this chapter's analysis indicates no discernible effects of immediate withholding on the labor supply of either AFDC or non-AFDC families. In certain cases, weak positive effects occur for AFDC families, consistent with the theory, but these effects are rarely statistically significant. The weak effects may be due in part to a lack of response, but they may also be due to a contaminated control environment (e.g., the fact that immediate withholding was implemented to some degree in control counties as well as in pilot counties). Although we attempted to account for the contaminated control environment through use of a statistical correction procedure, this exercise was generally uninformative. Throughout, small sample sizes plague the analysis, leading to estimates that are statistically imprecise. Overall, although suggestive of small positive effects for the population as a whole, our analysis of the Wisconsin data does not lead to definitive conclusions about the effects of immediate wage withholding on the labor supply of custodial parents.

The remainder of this chapter is organized in four sections: section two describes the theoretical effects of immediate withholding on labor supply; section three discusses the data and empirical methodology; section four presents the results of the analysis; and section five summarizes the findings and provides suggestions for further research.

THEORETICAL EFFECTS OF IMMEDIATE WAGE WITHHOLDING

The primary purpose of immediate wage withholding is to increase the level of child support income received by the custodial parent.[1] In addition, if the custodial parent is currently not employed and is receiving AFDC benefits, then immediate withholding is also intended to encourage work effort and discourage welfare dependence.

The labor supply effects of withholding can be analyzed using the economic theory of labor supply. Under this approach, immediate withholding affects labor supply by altering the budget constraints facing families. Figure 12.1 shows how an increase in child support income affects the budget constraint of AFDC and non-AFDC families. In this figure, the solid lines represent budget constraints for AFDC and non-AFDC families not receiving child support, and the dashed lines represent the budget constraints for AFDC and non-AFDC families receiving child support. The solid line *BDG* is the composite budget constraint for families without child support, and the dashed line *CEF* is the composite budget constraint for families with child support. In the figure, it is assumed that the effective tax rate on child support for AFDC families is zero for the first $50 per month of child support received and 100 percent for child support received in excess of $50 per month. In other words, current law allows the family to keep the first $50 of child support, with the rest to be used to offset the AFDC benefit on a dollar-for-dollar basis. Figure 12.1 also assumes that the effective tax rate on earnings under the AFDC program is less than 100 percent.[2]

If the child support withholding amount exceeds $50 per month, then *AT* will exceed *BC*, with *BC* being equal to $50. The effect of increased child support is to reduce the AFDC break-even level from point *D* to point *E*. This change in the break-even level causes a differential response for AFDC and non-AFDC families. For AFDC families, labor supply will either rise or fall, depending on whether the families choose to remain on AFDC. If they choose to remain on

Figure 12.1 THE EFFECTS OF INCREASED CHILD SUPPORT INCOME ON THE
LABOR SUPPLY OF CUSTODIAL PARENTS

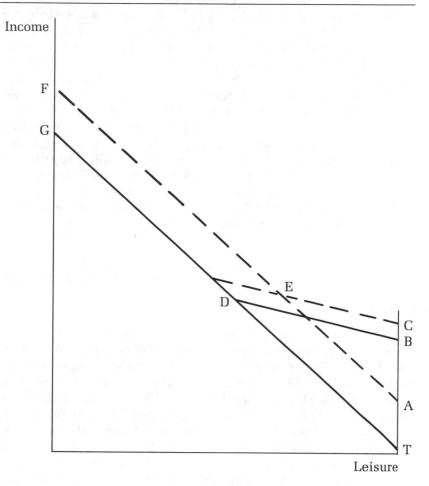

AFDC, labor supply will fall because of an income effect (the families will end up locating somewhere on the segment *CE*). If they choose to leave AFDC, labor supply will rise because of a substitution effect that dominates the income effect (the families will end up locating somewhere on the segment *EF*). Because the child support disregard of $50 is generally small relative to the average withholding amount, the number of families increasing labor supply is expected to exceed the number decreasing labor supply. Hence, on average, labor supply of AFDC families is expected to increase.

For non-AFDC families, labor supply will unambiguously decrease because of an income effect. The decrease should be larger than the decrease for families remaining on AFDC because the rise in income is larger (*TA* versus *BC*). Thus, for the entire population of custodial parents, the net effect of increased child support income on labor supply is uncertain and will depend on the size of the increase in child support income, the size of the income and substitution effects on labor supply, and the distribution of families along the budget constraint *BDG* prior to the increased child support.

The differential response for AFDC and non-AFDC families suggests that in attempting to empirically estimate the effects of immediate withholding on labor supply, it is useful to allow separate responses according to the family's initial welfare status. This way, even if there is a zero aggregate response, the consistency of the results with respect to economic theory can be assessed. This strategy is adopted in the following empirical analysis.

DATA AND METHODOLOGY

Data and Samples

The empirical analysis is based on data collected as part of the demonstration of the effects of immediate wage withholding in Wisconsin (see chapter 10 for a detailed description). The base dataset was taken from official court records for cases entering the courts between July 1980 and June 1986. The sample frame for the court records includes child-support-eligible family court cases: divorce, legal separation, and paternity actions, in which a payer potentially could have made child support payments.[3]

Data were collected from 20 Wisconsin counties. Ten of the counties agreed to pilot immediate withholding as a way to collect child support payments, while the other 10 counties continued to ask noncustodial parents to pay child support directly to the clerk of courts. The 10 control counties were matched with the 10 pilot counties, based on aggregate characteristics such as population size, geographic location, divorce rate, unemployment rate, average per capita income, and AFDC expenditures (Manning, Seltzer, and Schaeffer 1987). As discussed later in the chapter, the demonstration was not "pure"; this is because many child support cases in the control counties also had immediate withholding. This "contamination" in control counties has implications for the specification of the response models.

Parents in paternity and divorce cases could not choose whether or not their case would be heard in a pilot or control county. This means that the allocation of cases to pilot counties was not a matter of choice; consequently, estimates of program effects can be made without worrying about the possibility of bias introduced by individuals' own decision to be "selected" into the program.

The Wisconsin Parent Survey (PS) complements the Court Record Database (CRD) by obtaining detailed information not available in the court record for a sample of cases in the CRD. The Parent Survey was conducted by telephone and included cases with originating petition dates at least one month after the date a county agreed to begin implementing immediate withholding. Implementation dates varied from January 1984 to June 1986. Data were collected in nonimplementing counties for the same variable time frame. The Parent Survey identifies custodial and noncustodial parents on the basis of where the children actually lived during 1986 rather than on who had legal custody of the children (Manning et al. 1987). A total of 4,377 individuals were reached, and interviews were successfully completed for 2,891 individuals. Of the 2,891 individuals, 1,536 were custodial parents.

Information on AFDC status of individuals was obtained from files on benefit history held by the Wisconsin Department of Health and Social Services (DHSS). An AFDC check-history file provides monthly data on AFDC benefits from 1980 to the present.

For the empirical analysis in this chapter, cases were excluded for several reasons. First, individuals who were self-employed anytime during the sample period (1986) were excluded. Second, those without a child support award were excluded because they are not eligible for CSAS. The one widow of the sample was also excluded. And those for whom a social security number was unavailable were excluded because welfare status was determined by matching social security numbers of parents to the AFDC check-history file.

The final analysis sample consisted of 1,118 custodial parents, of which 27 individuals were missing certain information such as age or household income. In these cases, the sample mean among non-missing cases was substituted for the missing information.

The reference year for the Parent Survey is 1986. Therefore, all labor supply outcome measures analyzed in this study refer to the year 1986. In addition, some of the outcome measures (described later here) cover a period extending through the first half of 1987.

Approximately 26 percent (270) of the cases had an initial court date sometime after January 1, 1986. For these cases, the policy variables used to estimate response are not fully exogenous to the individuals' labor supply decisions. To account for this potential problem of endogeneity, all analyses were performed excluding cases having initial court dates subsequent to January 1, 1986. For comparative purposes, results are also presented for the samples including these cases.

Empirical Models

As indicated in the previous section, because of expected differential response according to initial welfare status, this analysis is performed for AFDC and non-AFDC families separately as well as for all families jointly. The basic equations estimated in this paper are as follows:

$$Y = b_1 PA + b_2 P(1 - A) + cI, \text{ and} \tag{12.1}$$

$$Y = b'P + c'I, \tag{12.2}$$

where Y is the labor supply outcome measure, P is a vector of CSAS policy variables, A is a dummy variable denoting initial AFDC status ($1 =$ AFDC), and I is a vector of control variables. The coefficient b_1 is an estimate of the policy effect for AFDC families, the coefficient b_2 is an estimate of the policy effect for non-AFDC families, and the coefficient b' is an estimate of the policy effect for all families. Based on the discussion in the previous theoretical section, it is expected that $b_1 > 0$, $b_2 < 0$, and $b' \gtrless 0$.

Dependent Variables

Seven labor supply outcomes are analyzed here and were created from responses to questions in the Parent Survey. The first three outcomes are static measures of labor supply and the remaining four are dynamic. The first outcome is a dichotomous variable equaling one if the individual was employed at anytime during 1986, and zero otherwise. The second outcome is the total number of hours that the individual worked in 1986. The third outcome is the total number of weeks the individual worked in 1986. (An individual was counted as working an entire week if he or she worked anytime during the week in question.)

The four dynamic labor supply outcomes are measures of duration in a particular employment state. Samples were created from the primary sample in terms of spells rather than individuals. For example, an individual working two jobs within the observation period, January

1986 through June 1987, appears in the job sample twice. An individual not holding any jobs within the observation period does not appear in the job spell sample. Samples were created for employment spells, job spells, unemployment spells, and out-of-the-labor-force (OLF) spells. All duration outcomes are measured in weeks. Many of the spells are "right-censored," meaning that the spell had not ended as of June 1987, the date of the Parent Survey. Some of the unemployment spells and out-of-the-labor-force spells are also "left-censored," meaning that the spell began prior to January 1986, but the actual start date was not available from the PS dataset. Start dates for job and employment spells are available and, therefore, left-censoring is not a problem for these labor supply outcomes. The implications of censoring are discussed later in the chapter.

Policy Variables

The percentage-of-income standard and immediate wage withholding are two of the key features of Wisconsin's Child Support Assurance System that existed during the time covered by this study. The percentage-of-income standard was made available to court commissioners in 1983, and legislation in 1985 (the 1985 Wisconsin Act 29) made the standard presumptive.[4] A principal advantage of the standard is the automatic indexing of awards. This advantage is lost when awards are expressed as a fixed amount. Although the standard is not the focus of this chapter, it must be considered in the empirical specification. Therefore, a dichotomous variable was created equaling one if the child support award was expressed as a percentage of income rather than a fixed dollar amount, and zero otherwise.

The second policy variable is a dichotomous variable equaling one if the case was tried in a pilot county demonstrating immediate wage withholding. In pilot counties, the level of use of immediate withholding ranged from 40 percent to 68 percent of the cases in the county. Unfortunately, for purposes of analysis, immediate wage withholding was also used in control counties during the time period covered by the analysis. The range of utilization in control counties was from zero to 50 percent. Because the pilot counties were not using immediate withholding assignments in all possible cases and because some of the control counties were making extensive use of immediate assignments, the true effects of immediate withholding using this policy variable will be underestimated.[5] In light of this, a third policy variable was created equaling one if immediate withholding was used in a particular case, and zero otherwise.

The use of a variable measuring whether withholding is used in a particular case is somewhat problematical, in that it may be endogenous (correlated with the error term in the labor supply response equation). For example, it may be that immediate withholding is more likely in cases where the custodial parent is not working. If this is true and if labor supply is highly correlated over time, then a negative correlation exists between the withholding dummy and labor supply that is unrelated to the response to immediate withholding. Hence, the coefficient of the withholding dummy would be a biased estimate of the true withholding effect. In the case of AFDC families, the coefficient would be an underestimate of the true (positive) effect, whereas in the case of non-AFDC families, the coefficient would be an overestimate (in absolute value) of the true (negative) effect. On the other hand, it is possible that withholding is more likely in cases where the custodial parent is working (because of complementarity between the labor supply of the mother and father). In this case, the biases in the coefficient of the wage withholding dummy would be opposite to those just described. We have no theoretical basis for judging which bias, if any, is most likely.

There are several ways to correct for the potential endogeneity of the withholding dummy.[6] One is to develop an instrumental variable for withholding (based on an estimated probability equation using a set of exogenous variables) and including this instrument in place of the actual withholding dummy in the estimated labor supply response equation. Another is to create a selectivity correction term based on the probability equation and to include this term in addition to the withholding dummy. The selectivity correction term essentially "purges" the correlation between the withholding dummy and the error term in the labor supply response equation.

Both of these approaches are difficult to implement in practice because of a possible identification problem. In models with selectivity bias, identification is generally achieved in two ways: through nonlinearities of the selectivity correction term and through omission of variables in the response equation that are included in the selectivity equation. Each of these is potentially problematical and could result in large standard errors of the estimated coefficients measuring the response to the CSAS. Given the relatively small size of the samples used in this study, we did not pursue such approaches for all outcomes analyzed in this study. Instead, we investigated the instrumental variables procedure for the static measures of labor supply analyzed. Generally, this exercise did not yield definitive conclusions about the existence of selectivity bias. Although there is no a priori reason to suspect any biases, the results obtained using the immediate withholding dummy should be interpreted with some caution.

Table 12.1 shows the extent of the utilization of immediate withholding among cases in pilot and control counties. As the table indicates, immediate withholding was used in about two-thirds of the cases in pilot counties and about one-third of the cases in control counties. Slightly higher percentages were used for non-AFDC families, but the relative utilization between pilot and control counties was about the same for both AFDC and non-AFDC families (approximately a two-to-one ratio). Thus, it is clear from the table that because of the utilization of immediate withholding in control counties, the coefficient of the pilot county dummy will be an underestimate of the true effect of immediate withholding on labor supply.

Table 12.1   USE OF IMMEDIATE WITHHOLDING IN PILOT AND CONTROL
COUNTIES: WISCONSIN STUDY

	Pilot County	Control County
All court cases		
Total		
Fraction with withholding	0.647	0.333
N	521	597
AFDC		
Fraction with withholding	0.605	0.323
N	195	235
Non-AFDC		
Fraction with withholding	0.672	0.340
N	326	362
Cases before January 1986		
Total		
Fraction with withholding	0.624	0.286
N	380	468
AFDC		
Fraction with withholding	0.551	0.258
N	136	178
Non-AFDC		
Fraction with withholding	0.664	0.303
N	244	290

Tables 12.2 through 12.6 present means and standard deviations of the various labor supply outcomes and policy variables for the samples analyzed in this study. During 1986, close to 80 percent of all custodial parents were employed. Average hours of work were 1,387 (1,765 among workers), and average weeks worked were close to 36. Those employed had been working on average about four years, with their current job having lasted about three years. Among those not working, the average duration of unemployment was about five months, and the average duration of time out of the labor force was about one year.

As one would expect, custodial parents on AFDC had lower labor supply than custodial parents not on AFDC. Just over one-half of the AFDC recipients were employed, compared to an employment rate of over 90 percent among non-AFDC recipients. A similar AFDC/non-AFDC relationship exists for the other labor supply outcomes. Overall, this sample of custodial parents in Wisconsin exhibits a somewhat higher employment rate than exists nationwide for custodial parents, particularly among AFDC recipients. In the April 1986 Child Support Supplement to the Current Population Survey, for example, 35 percent of custodial parents receiving AFDC were employed in 1985, whereas 84 percent of custodial parents not on AFDC were employed.[7]

Control Variables

To control for economic and demographic differences among custodial parents in pilot and control counties and among custodial parents with and without immediate withholding, several control variables were included in equations 12.1 and 12.2.[8] These control variables are fairly standard in models of labor supply (see Killingsworth 1983, for example).

The first control variable is the custodial parent's wage rate. Because the survey only provides a wage for individuals who worked during the survey period, an imputed wage—obtained from a wage equation estimated using the Heckman (1979) technique—was assigned to each sample member. Wages were imputed on the basis of age, education, race, and other control variables. The exact specification used, as well as the results, are presented in table 12.A-1 of the Appendix.

The second control variable is household nonwage income. This variable includes income of all household members, excluding the custodial parent's wage and salary income and any income-dependent transfers received by the household.[9] In addition, the amount of child support income received by the custodial parent is excluded.[10]

Table 12.2 MEANS AND STANDARD DEVIATIONS OF DEPENDENT AND POLICY VARIABLES: WISCONSIN STUDY

| | Dependent Variable | | | | Policy Variable | |
	1 = Employment	Hours of Work	Weeks Worked	1 = Percentage Award	1 = Pilot County	1 = Immediate Withholding
All court cases						
Total (N = 1,118)						
Mean	0.786	1,387.23	35.92	0.046	0.467	0.497
Standard deviation	0.410	1,035.98	22.19	0.209	0.499	0.500
AFDC (N = 430)						
Mean	0.563	686.75	20.74	0.037	0.456	0.451
Standard deviation	0.497	877.46	22.62	0.189	0.499	0.498
Non-AFDC (N = 688)						
Mean	0.926	1,825.04	45.40	0.051	0.474	0.497
Standard deviation	0.262	874.73	15.70	0.220	0.500	0.500
Cases before January 1986						
Total (N = 848)						
Mean	0.789	1,413.62	36.44	0.032	0.449	0.438
Standard deviation	0.408	1,033.74	22.02	0.176	0.498	0.496
AFDC (N = 314)						
Mean	0.561	722.07	21.61	0.032	0.436	0.385
Standard deviation	0.497	891.54	23.08	0.176	0.497	0.487
Non-AFDC (N = 534)						
Mean	0.923	1,820.26	45.17	0.032	0.457	0.468
Standard deviation	0.266	885.43	15.87	0.176	0.499	0.499

Table 12.3 SAMPLE STATISTICS FOR EMPLOYMENT SPELL ANALYSIS: WISCONSIN STUDY

	Employment Duration (Weeks)	1 = Right Censor	1 = Left Censor	1 = Percentage Award	Policy Variables	
					1 = Pilot County	1 = Immediate Withholding
All court cases						
Total (N = 1,005)						
Mean	213.79	0.787	0.000	0.047	0.476	0.502
Standard deviation	245.43	0.410	0.000	0.211	0.500	0.500
AFDC (N = 308)						
Mean	71.02	0.646	0.000	0.039	0.481	0.484
Standard deviation	79.02	0.479	0.000	0.194	0.500	0.501
Non-AFDC (N = 697)						
Mean	276.84	0.849	0.000	0.050	0.473	0.511
Standard deviation	266.63	0.358	0.000	0.219	0.500	0.500
Cases before January 1986						
Total (N = 756)						
Mean	225.82	0.794	0.000	0.033	0.460	0.462
Standard deviation	255.79	0.405	0.000	0.179	0.499	0.499
AFDC (N = 217)						
Mean	74.81	0.673	0.000	0.037	0.470	0.419
Standard deviation	75.14	0.470	0.000	0.189	0.500	0.495
Non-AFDC (N = 539)						
Mean	286.61	0.842	0.000	0.032	0.456	0.479
Standard deviation	276.86	0.365	0.000	0.175	0.499	0.500

Table 12.4 SAMPLE STATISTICS FOR JOB SPELL ANALYSIS: WISCONSIN STUDY

	Job Duration (Weeks)	1 = Right Censor	1 = Left Censor	1 = Percentage Award	Policy Variables	
					1 = Pilot County	1 = Immediate Withholding
All court cases						
Total (N = 1,465)						
Mean	168.24	0.599	0.000	0.047	0.472	0.507
Standard deviation	231.69	0.490	0.000	0.212	0.499	0.500
AFDC (N = 462)						
Mean	57.40	0.463	0.000	0.043	0.463	0.468
Standard deviation	74.32	0.499	0.000	0.204	0.499	0.499
Non-AFDC (N = 1,003)						
Mean	218.83	0.661	0.000	0.049	0.477	0.525
Standard deviation	260.32	0.474	0.000	0.216	0.500	0.500
Cases before January 1986						
Total (N = 1,089)						
Mean	179.76	0.609	0.000	0.032	0.448	0.459
Standard deviation	243.30	0.488	0.000	0.176	0.498	0.499
AFDC (N = 329)						
Mean	60.57	0.468	0.000	0.033	0.432	0.383
Standard deviation	71.85	0.500	0.000	0.180	0.496	0.487
Non-AFDC (N = 760)						
Mean	231.36	0.670	0.000	0.032	0.455	0.492
Standard deviation	271.61	0.470	0.000	0.174	0.499	0.501

Table 12.5 SAMPLE STATISTICS FOR UNEMPLOYMENT SPELL ANALYSIS: WISCONSIN STUDY

	Unemployment Duration (Weeks)	1 = Right Censor	1 = Left Censor	1 = Percentage Award	Policy Variables	
					1 = Pilot County	1 = Immediate Withholding
All court cases						
Total (N = 230)						
Mean	20.43	0.322	0.243	0.065	0.513	0.504
Standard deviation	29.07	0.468	0.430	0.247	0.501	0.501
AFDC (N = 141)						
Mean	22.78	0.305	0.270	0.071	0.525	0.475
Standard deviation	32.84	0.462	0.445	0.258	0.501	0.501
Non-AFDC (N = 89)						
Mean	16.70	0.348	0.202	0.056	0.494	0.551
Standard deviation	21.47	0.479	0.434	0.232	0.503	0.500
Cases before January 1986						
Total (N = 161)						
Mean	20.29	0.367	0.273	0.062	0.516	0.472
Standard deviation	23.90	0.483	0.447	0.242	0.501	0.501
AFDC (N = 93)						
Mean	22.86	0.333	0.312	0.065	0.548	0.419
Standard deviation	24.89	0.474	0.466	0.247	0.500	0.496
Non-AFDC (N = 68)						
Mean	16.77	0.412	0.221	0.059	0.471	0.544
Standard deviation	12.19	0.496	0.418	0.237	0.503	0.502

Table 12.6 SAMPLE STATISTICS FOR OUT-OF-THE-LABOR-FORCE ANALYSIS: WISCONSIN STUDY

| | OLF[a] Duration (Weeks) | 1 = Right Censor | 1 = Left Censor | 1 = Percentage Award | Policy Variables | |
					1 = Pilot County	1 = Immediate Withholding
All court cases						
Total (N = 380)						
Mean	59.40	0.626	0.568	0.037	0.442	0.439
Standard deviation	47.33	0.484	0.496	0.189	0.497	0.497
AFDC (N = 265)						
Mean	63.94	0.657	0.608	0.038	0.445	0.434
Standard deviation	51.00	0.476	0.489	0.191	0.498	0.497
Non-AFDC (N = 115)						
Mean	48.94	0.557	0.478	0.035	0.435	0.452
Standard deviation	35.58	0.499	0.502	0.184	0.498	0.500
Cases before January 1986						
Total (N = 285)						
Mean	59.88	0.625	0.579	0.305	0.421	0.396
Standard deviation	50.66	0.485	0.495	0.184	0.495	0.490
AFDC (N = 193)						
Mean	65.17	0.653	0.622	0.036	0.415	0.378
Standard deviation	56.14	0.477	0.486	0.187	0.494	0.486
Non-AFDC (N = 92)						
Mean	48.77	0.565	0.489	0.033	0.435	0.435
Standard deviation	34.27	0.498	0.503	0.179	0.498	0.498

[a]OLF, out of the labor force.

In addition to an imputed wage rate and household nonwage income, several other control variables are included in the equation. These are dichotomous variables indicating the custodial parent's marital status and race; the number of adults in the household; the number of children in the household; a dichotomous variable indicating whether any preschool children are present in the household; a dichotomous variable indicating gender of the respondent, age, and age-squared of the respondent; a dichotomous variable indicating whether the respondent had ill health that limited his or her work ability or capacity; a dichotomous variable denoting a paternity (as opposed to a divorce) case; and a set of dichotomous variables for each county. We note that the results of the analysis are generally insensitive to the inclusion of the county dummy variables; therefore, for simplicity and because the standard errors of the coefficients were somewhat higher when these variables were included, they were omitted from the final impact equations reported in this chapter.

Both the full sample (including all court cases) and the partial sample (including only court cases before January 1, 1986) were divided into two groups: AFDC recipients and non-AFDC recipients. Individuals were classified as an AFDC recipient if they were recorded as having received a welfare check during the month of their court date or any of the three months following that date. Equations were estimated for AFDC and non-AFDC families together (including and excluding those cases with court dates after January 1, 1986) and for AFDC and non-AFDC families separately.

RESULTS

Static Labor Supply Outcomes

UNADJUSTED EFFECTS

The estimation results for the effects of withholding that do not control for differences in economic and demographic characteristics of the sample members are presented in table 12.7. These estimates represent raw differences in labor supply between withholding and non-withholding counties (first three columns) and between withholding and nonwithholding cases (last three columns). As Table 12.7 indicates, none of the pilot-control differences is statistically significant at the 10 percent level or lower. This is probably a reflection of the

Table 12.7 UNADJUSTED EFFECTS OF IMMEDIATE WITHHOLDING ON LABOR SUPPLY: WISCONSIN STUDY

	Pilot County			Immediate Withholding		
	Employment Dummy	Hours	Weeks	Employment Dummy	Hours	Weeks
All court cases						
Total (N = 1,118)	0.020	−8.29	0.41	0.056[a]	71.23	2.66[a]
	(0.025)	(62.13)	(1.33)	(0.025)	(62.01)	(1.33)
AFDC (N = 362)	0.086	62.81	1.42	0.067	20.67	0.04
	(0.053)	(84.18)	(2.32)	(0.053)	(84.74)	(2.33)
Non-AFDC (N = 756)	−0.007	−29.76	0.19	0.021	3.01	1.89
	(0.021)	(65.89)	(1.21)	(0.021)	(65.74)	(1.21)
Cases before January 1986						
Total (N = 848)	0.035	18.80	0.91	0.064[a]	68.64	2.68
	(0.028)	(71.40)	(1.52)	(0.028)	(71.56)	(1.52)
AFDC (N = 280)	0.082	67.29	1.21	0.059	−35.63	−1.08
	(0.060)	(98.27)	(2.70)	(0.061)	(100.40)	(2.76)
Non-AFDC (N = 568)	0.016	5.10	0.99	0.027	3.26	1.98
	(0.022)	(75.01)	(1.33)	(0.022)	(74.82)	(1.33)

Notes: Standard errors are in parentheses. Data are not adjusted for effects of control variables.
[a]Statistically different from zero at .10 level or lower.

small samples and the contamination of the control sample with numerous families having immediate withholding.

A few significant differences occur for the withholding and non-withholding cases, however. In the sample of court cases before 1986, custodial parents with a withholding order are estimated to have a 6.4 percentage point higher probability of being employed than individuals without immediate withholding. In percentage terms, the difference is 7.8 percent, which is not large.

The theoretical discussion suggests that the expected effects of immediate withholding should be different for AFDC and non-AFDC families. In particular, a positive effect is expected for AFDC families and a negative effect is expected for non-AFDC families. The results are broadly consistent with this expected pattern for AFDC families, but not for non-AFDC families. However, none of the effects broken down by AFDC status are statistically significant at the 10 percent level or lower.

ADJUSTED EFFECTS OF WITHHOLDING

The estimation results for the effects of withholding that control for differences in economic and demographic characteristics of the sample members are presented in table 12.8 (ordinary least squares [OLS]) and table 12.9 (maximum likelihood).[11] Each model was run twice, once including the pilot county policy variable and once including the immediate withholding policy variable. The percentage standard policy variable and all control variables were included in both specifications.

The results in table 12.8 are very similar to the unadjusted results in table 12.7, with a slight improvement (of about 10 percent) in statistical precision. Nevertheless, despite the improvement in statistical precision, none of the pilot-control differences in table 12.8 is statistically significant at the 10 percent level or lower. Again, this is probably a reflection of the small sample sizes and the contamination of the control sample with numerous families having immediate withholding.

As with the unadjusted differences in table 12.7, a few significant effects occur in table 12.8 for the withholding dummy specification. In the sample of court cases before 1986, custodial parents with a withholding order are estimated to have a 4.8 percentage point higher probability of being employed than similar individuals without immediate withholding, slightly lower than the unadjusted differences in table 12.7. The estimated percentage effect of 5.9 percent is again not large.

Table 12.8 ADJUSTED EFFECTS OF IMMEDIATE WITHHOLDING ON LABOR SUPPLY USING ORDINARY LEAST SQUARES: WISCONSIN STUDY

	Pilot County			Immediate Withholding		
	Employment Dummy	Hours	Weeks	Employment Dummy	Hours	Weeks
All court cases						
Total	0.017	−22.72	0.40	0.043[a]	42.68	1.95[a]
	(0.023)	(55.28)	(1.19)	(0.023)	(55.13)	(1.18)
AFDC	0.040	−25.01	0.33	0.070	75.89	1.42
	(0.048)	(83.39)	(2.17)	(0.049)	(84.23)	(2.19)
Non-AFDC	−0.004	−18.52	−0.24	0.019	6.33	1.76
	(0.019)	(63.76)	(1.15)	(0.019)	(63.04)	(1.13)
Cases before January 1986						
Total	0.036	12.12	0.73	0.048[a]	43.33	2.02
	(0.026)	(62.92)	(1.35)	(0.026)	(63.14)	(1.35)
AFDC	0.064	10.01	1.30	0.081	22.25	1.11
	(0.057)	(99.25)	(2.62)	(0.058)	(100.80)	(2.66)
Non-AFDC	0.015	11.96	0.19	0.013	−0.83	1.21
	(0.022)	(72.42)	(1.27)	(0.022)	(72.61)	(1.27)

Note: Standard errors are in parentheses. Results in this and all subsequent tables in chapter are adjusted for effects of control variables.
[a]Statistically different from zero at .10 level.

Table 12.9 MAXIMUM-LIKELIHOOD ESTIMATES OF EFFECTS OF IMMEDIATE WITHHOLDING ON LABOR SUPPLY: WISCONSIN STUDY

	Pilot County			Immediate Withholding		
	Employment Dummy	Hours	Weeks	Employment Dummy	Hours	Weeks
All court cases						
Total	0.075	−22.38	2.83	0.163[a]	71.18	9.52[a]
	(0.093)	(71.68)	(6.02)	(0.093)	(70.95)	(5.93)
	[0.023]	[−19.24]	[0.61]	[0.039]	[61.71]	[2.10]
AFDC	0.119	−23.10	3.15	0.190	87.15	8.04
	(0.129)	(150.20)	(7.43)	(0.129)	(147.60)	(7.35)
	[0.029]	[−13.10]	[0.97]	[0.076]	[49.41]	[2.47]
Non-AFDC	−0.051	−18.44	−0.50	0.098	8.29	7.79
	(0.160)	(69.95)	(7.84)	(0.160)	(72.59)	(8.21)
	[−0.001]	[−18.01]	[−0.06]	[0.004]	[8.10]	[1.01]
Cases before January 1986						
Total	0.179	20.26	5.77	0.207[a]	77.48	10.32
	(0.111)	(82.21)	(7.24)	(0.111)	(83.13)	(6.98)
	[0.020]	[17.77]	[1.25]	[0.064]	[67.95]	[2.24]
AFDC	0.183	14.05	6.64	0.227	30.55	8.45
	(0.154)	(181.50)	(10.06)	(0.155)	(180.80)	(10.13)
	[0.068]	[8.08]	[1.84]	[0.090]	[17.57]	[2.37]
Non-AFDC	0.121	12.88	3.48	0.060	0.96	5.04
	(0.192)	(80.30)	(8.63)	(0.191)	(86.45)	(8.74)
	[0.006]	[12.59]	[0.83]	[0.002]	[0.94]	[0.60]

Notes: Standard errors are in parentheses; effects evaluated at the mean in brackets. Estimation techniques are probit for the employment dummy, tobit for hours of work, and two-limit tobit for weeks worked.
[a]Statistically different from zero at .10 level.

As in table 12.7, the results in table 12.8 are broadly consistent with the expected pattern for AFDC families, but not for non-AFDC families. Also, as in table 12.7, none of the effects broken down by AFDC status is statistically significant at the 10 percent level or lower. It should be noted, however, that all of the estimated effects in table 12.8 for the sample of AFDC cases before 1986 are positive, consistent with the theory. However, all but one of the estimated effects for non-AFDC families are also positive, which deviates from the predictions of the theory.

Maximum-likelihood estimates for the three static labor supply outcomes (adjusted for the effects of the control variables) are presented in table 12.9.[12] In addition to the estimated coefficients and standard errors of the policy variables, the estimated effects at the mean for each subsample are presented in brackets. The maximum-likelihood estimates, evaluated at the mean, are very similar to the ordinary least squares estimates in table 12.8. Once again, pilot/control county differences appear to be very small for the full sample and all subsamples, and none of the estimates is statistically significant. For the immediate withholding policy variable, all the coefficients are positive, but only a few are statistically significant. For employment status, only a few (following the pattern of the OLS estimates) are statistically significant at the 10 percent level or lower.

ACCOUNTING FOR POSSIBLE ENDOGENEITY OF THE IMMEDIATE WITHHOLDING VARIABLE

As indicated earlier, the variable measuring whether withholding is used in a particular case may be endogenous, and therefore the estimated effects of withholding when this variable is used may be biased. To examine this issue, the ordinary least squares models were reestimated using an instrumental variables technique. More specifically, the specification in table 12.8 was reestimated using two-stage least squares.[13]

With any instrumental variable procedure, identification is an important issue. For this analysis, identification is achieved in two ways—creation of a nonlinear instrument using a first-stage probit equation, and including certain variables in the probit equation that do not appear in the impact equation. Specifically, the additional variables in the probit equation that are not in the impact equation are the county dummies and the education level of the custodial parent.[14]

The instrumental variable estimates for the static measures of labor supply are presented in table 12.10. Of major note in these estimates

Table 12.10 TWO-STAGE LEAST SQUARES ESTIMATES OF EFFECTS OF
IMMEDIATE WITHHOLDING ON LABOR SUPPLY: WISCONSIN STUDY

	Immediate Withholding		
	Employment dummy	Hours	Weeks
All court cases			
Total	−0.016	−156.99	−0.51
	(0.068)	(164.02)	(3.52)
AFDC	−0.035	−52.33	−5.31
	(0.166)	(262.31)	(7.32)
Non-AFDC	−0.054	−251.56	−2.39
	(0.056)	(177.32)	(3.25)
Cases before January 1986			
Total	0.017	1.68	2.74
	(0.068)	(164.16)	(3.52)
AFDC	0.007	116.80	−0.86
	(0.151)	(242.79)	(6.77)
Non-AFDC	−0.010	−111.15	−0.19
	(0.055)	(185.68)	(3.24)

Note: Standard errors are in parentheses.

is that the standard errors are about triple the already sizable standard errors in table 12.8. Thus, the statistical precision of these instrumental variables estimates is quite low. In fact, none of the estimates in table 12.10 is statistically significant at the 10 percent level or lower.

Despite the lack of statistical precision, however, the instrumental variables estimates for cases before 1986 are broadly consistent with the theory outlined earlier. Two out of the three effects for AFDC families are positive in sign, and all three of the effects for non-AFDC families are negative in sign. The net effect for all three outcomes is positive in sign.[15] Nevertheless, because of the low level of statistical precision, these results must be interpreted with caution.

Dynamic Labor Supply Outcomes

The estimated effects of immediate withholding on the four dynamic labor supply outcomes are presented in tables 12.11 through 12.14.[16] These estimates are based on hazard models explaining the duration of employment, jobs, unemployment, and time out of the labor force. The hazard models are estimated using maximum likelihood.[17] Two different assumptions are made about the form of the hazard function: first, an exponential distribution is assumed, and second, a Weibull distribution is assumed.[18] The distributions produced very similar results for all samples.

For the hazard analysis, the coefficients are presented in terms of survival probabilities, rather than exit or hazard probabilities. Thus, the coefficients can be interpreted as the effect of a change in the independent variable on the log of the survival probability.

Table 12.11 presents the results of the survival analysis for employment spells. All coefficients on both the pilot-control county policy variable and the immediate withholding policy variable are negative, indicating that a pilot county or an immediate withholding case has a lower employment survival probability. In other words, those living in a pilot county or those with an immediate withholding order are less likely to remain employed than similar persons in a control

Table 12.11 MAXIMUM-LIKELIHOOD ESTIMATES OF EFFECTS OF IMMEDIATE WITHHOLDING ON EMPLOYMENT DURATION: WISCONSIN STUDY

| | Pilot County | | Immediate Withholding | |
	Exponential Distribution	Weibull Distribution	Exponential Distribution	Weibull Distribution
All court cases				
Total	−0.166	−0.209	−0.084	−0.178
	(0.129)	(0.217)	(0.127)	(0.213)
Exp(coefficient) − 1	−0.153	−0.189	−0.081	−0.163
AFDC	−0.241	−0.252	−0.007	−0.015
	(0.191)	(0.253)	(0.182)	(0.244)
Exp(coefficient) − 1	−0.214	−0.223	−0.007	−0.015
Non-AFDC	−0.072	−0.090	−0.258	−0.417
	(0.194)	(0.318)	(0.199)	(0.324)
Exp(coefficient) − 1	−0.069	−0.086	−0.228	−0.341
Cases before January 1986				
Total	−0.192	−0.237	−0.167	−0.294
	(0.155)	(0.243)	(0.150)	(0.238)
Exp(coefficient) − 1	−0.175	−0.211	−0.154	−0.255
AFDC	−0.241	−0.246	−0.267	−0.323
	(0.256)	(0.303)	(0.234)	(0.285)
Exp(coefficient) − 1	−0.214	−0.218	−0.234	−0.276
Non-AFDC	−0.034	−0.036	−0.192	−0.315
	(0.224)	(0.358)	(0.222)	(0.348)
Exp(coefficient) − 1	−0.033	−0.035	−0.175	−0.270

county or without a withholding order. The percentage effect is indicated by the term Exp{coefficient} − 1. Although negative coefficients were not expected for AFDC recipients, the negative coefficients for non-AFDC families are consistent with the theory. However, as with the static measures of labor supply, none of the coefficients in this table is statistically significant at the 10 percent level or lower.

The results for job duration are presented in table 12.12. When all court cases are included, it is estimated that individuals living in a pilot county are less likely to remain on a job than individuals living in a control county. Although the effects for AFDC families are again unexpectedly negative, the effects for non-AFDC families are uniformly more negative, consistent with the pattern suggested by the theory. The sample including only cases with initial court dates prior to January 1, 1986 indicates that individuals on AFDC and living in a pilot county are more likely to continue working on a job than indi-

Table 12.12 MAXIMUM-LIKELIHOOD ESTIMATES OF EFFECTS OF IMMEDIATE WITHHOLDING ON JOB DURATION: WISCONSIN STUDY

	Pilot County		Immediate Withholding	
	Exponential Distribution	Weibull Distribution	Exponential Distribution	Weibull Distribution
All court cases				
Total	− 0.068	− 0.099	− 0.026	− 0.081
	(0.069)	(0.125)	(0.069)	(0.124)
Exp(coefficient) − 1	− 0.066	− 0.094	− 0.026	− 0.078
AFDC	− 0.053	− 0.041	0.131	0.127
	(0.119)	(0.151)	(0.117)	(0.147)
Exp(coefficient) − 1	− 0.052	− 0.040	0.140	0.135
Non-AFDC	− 0.082	− 0.144	− 0.160[a]	− 0.291[a]
	(0.095)	(0.176)	(0.096)	(0.178)
Exp(coefficient) − 1	− 0.079	− 0.134	− 0.148	− 0.252
Cases before January 1986				
Total	− 0.026	− 0.044	0.064	0.032
	(0.085)	(0.145)	(0.083)	(0.143)
Exp(coefficient) − 1	− 0.026	− 0.043	− 0.062	0.033
AFDC	0.045	0.055	0.088	0.079
	(0.158)	(0.183)	(0.146)	(0.169)
Exp(coefficient) − 1	0.046	0.057	0.092	0.082
Non-AFDC	− 0.071	− 0.131	− 0.082	− 0.153
	(0.113)	(0.204)	(0.115)	(0.205)
Exp(coefficient) − 1	− 0.069	− 0.123	− 0.079	− 0.142

[a]Statistically different from zero at .10 level.

viduals living in a control county and that individuals not on AFDC are *less* likely to remain on the job. Both of these effects are consistent with the theory. However, again, none of the estimated pilot-control county differences are statistically significant.

Immediate withholding does seem to affect the probability of remaining on a job differently for AFDC recipients, compared to non-AFDC recipients. Custodial parents on AFDC with an immediate withholding order appear more likely to remain on a job than those with similar characteristics but without an immediate withholding order. The opposite is true for individuals not on AFDC. This pattern of coefficients is generally consistent with the theory; however, only in the case of non-AFDC recipients (for the full court case sample) are the effects statistically significant (table 12.12).

The results for unemployment spells are presented in table 12.13.

Table 12.13 MAXIMUM-LIKELIHOOD ESTIMATES OF EFFECTS OF IMMEDIATE WITHHOLDING ON UNEMPLOYMENT DURATION: WISCONSIN STUDY

	Pilot County		Immediate Withholding	
	Exponential Distribution	Weibull Distribution	Exponential Distribution	Weibull Distribution
All court cases				
Total	0.074	0.073	0.192	0.211
	(0.151)	(0.241)	(0.149)	(0.237)
Exp(coefficient) − 1	0.077	0.076	0.212	0.235
AFDC	0.035	0.072	.203	0.273
	(0.210)	(0.350)	(0.194)	(0.323)
Exp(coefficient) − 1	0.036	0.075	0.225	0.314
Non-AFDC	0.108	0.112	0.004	−0.097
	(0.313)	(0.415)	(0.345)	(0.432)
Exp(coefficient) − 1	0.114	0.119	0.004	−0.092
Cases before January 1986				
Total	0.116	0.074	0.343[a]	0.385
	(0.194)	(0.304)	(0.184)	(0.290)
Exp(coefficient) − 1	0.123	0.077	0.409	0.470
AFDC	−0.014	0.018	0.274	0.335
	(0.306)	(0.446)	(0.306)	(0.451)
Exp(coefficient) − 1	−0.014	0.018	0.315	0.398
Non-AFDC	[b]	−0.327	[b]	−0.091
	[b]	(0.468)	[b]	(0.428)
Exp(coefficient) − 1	[b]	−0.278	[b]	−0.087

[a]Statistically different from zero at .10 level.
[b]Function did not converge.

These estimates are extremely imprecise, owing to the small sample sizes. Coefficients on both policy variables are positive for AFDC recipients when all court cases are included. Pilot-control differences are smaller than immediate withholding/nonimmediate withholding differences; however, none of the effects is statistically signfiicant. The samples excluding later court cases produce similar estimates for AFDC recipients.

Individuals not on AFDC, using the smaller sample, are estimated to be less likely to remain unemployed if they have an immediate withholding child support order than are those in the control group. These estimates are obtained when the Weibull distribution is assumed. Because some of the unemployment spells are left-censored, the Weibull results may be biased.

The results for out-of-the-labor-force (OLF) spells are presented in table 12.14. All coefficients obtained on the immediate withholding variable (except for those in the models that did not converge) are negative, indicating that immediate withholding stimulates labor force participation for both AFDC and non-AFDC recipients. The result for AFDC recipients is consistent with the theory, but the result for non-AFDC recipients is not. The coefficients for the sample including all court cases are statistically significant at the 10 percent level for non-AFDC recipients and for the total sample, whereas the coefficients for the sample including only cases with an initial court date prior to January 1, 1986, are statistically significant for AFDC recipients (assuming the exponential distribution). Results for non-AFDC recipients using the smaller sample are not available because the likelihood function did not converge.

SUMMARY AND CONCLUSIONS

This chapter has presented a preliminary analysis of the labor supply effects of the immediate withholding provision of the Wisconsin child support assurance system. A theoretical analysis suggests that immediate withholding would be expected to increase the labor supply of custodial parents on AFDC and decrease the labor supply of custodial parents not on AFDC.

An empirical analysis was performed using data from the 1986 Parent Survey and court records. Seven different labor supply outcomes were analyzed: employment status, weeks worked, hours of work, duration of employment, duration of jobs, duration of unem-

Table 12.14 MAXIMUM-LIKELIHOOD ESTIMATES OF EFFECTS OF IMMEDIATE
WITHHOLDING ON OUT-OF-THE-LABOR-FORCE DURATION:
WISCONSIN STUDY

	Pilot County		Immediate Withholding	
	Exponential Distribution	Weibull Distribution	Exponential Distribution	Weibull Distribution
All court cases				
Total	−0.262	−0.269	−0.342[a]	−0.352[b]
	(0.164)	(0.178)	(0.171)	(0.180)
Exp(coefficient) − 1	−0.230	−0.236	−0.290	−0.297
AFDC	−0.368	−0.370[b]	−0.203	−0.204
	(0.210)	(0.220)	(0.213)	(0.216)
Exp(coefficient) − 1	−0.308	−0.309	−0.184	−0.185
Non-AFDC	0.044	0.046	−0.805[a]	−0.800[a]
	(0.344)	(0.353)	(0.331)	(0.327)
Exp(coefficient) − 1	0.045	0.047	−0.553	−0.551
Cases before January 1986				
Total	−0.286	−0.292	−0.371[b]	−0.383[b]
	(0.196)	(0.210)	(0.199)	(0.210)
Exp(coefficient) − 1	−0.249	−0.253	−0.310	−0.249
AFDC	−0.405	−0.407	−0.428[b]	−0.429
	(0.252)	(0.263)	(0.259)	(0.264)
Exp(coefficient) − 1	−0.333	−0.334	−0.348	−0.349
Non-AFDC	c	c	c	c
	c	c	c	c
Exp(coefficient) − 1	c	c	c	c

[a]Statistically different from zero at .05 level.
[b]Statistically different from zero at .10 level.
[c]Function did not converge.

ployment, and duration of time out of the labor force. The analysis
yields results broadly consistent with the theoretical expectations,
particularly for custodial parents on AFDC. However, low precision
levels (due to small sample sizes) make the findings extremely tenta-
tive.

The empirical analysis utilized two specifications to estimate the
effects of immediate withholding. First, labor supply of families in
pilot counties was compared to labor supply of families in control
counties, controlling for differences in observed personal characteristics. The interpretation of the adjusted pilot-control differences is
clouded somewhat by the fact that immediate withholding was uti-

lized in control counties during the period studied (although the frequency of utilization was less than in pilot counties). This led to a second specification in which families with immediate withholding were compared directly to families without immediate withholding. However, this specification is also potentially problematical because the use of immediate withholding may have been influenced by the custodial parent's labor supply. An attempt was made to account for this potential endogeneity of the withholding variable by using the technique of instrumental variables, but the level of statistical imprecision became even greater. Nevertheless, the signs of the effects were broadly consistent with the theory. However, the results should be viewed with extreme caution because of the low levels of statistical precision.

Thus, we must tentatively conclude that the Wisconsin data used in this study are unable to reveal any clear effect of a system of immediate withholding on the labor supply of custodial parents. The lack of an effect may be due in part to the absence of a response, but it may also be due to the contaminated control environment—for example, the fact that immediate withholding was implemented to some degree in control counties as well as in pilot counties—and to our limited ability to account for the contaminated control environment using a statistical correction procedure.

Notes

The research reported in this paper was supported in part by the Wisconsin Department of Health and Social Services and by the Ford Foundation.

1. As discussed in Garfinkel, Corbett, MacDonald, McLanahan, Robins, Schaeffer, and Seltzer (1988), the regularity of income flows is also expected to increase as a result of withholding. In general, reducing the uncertainty of child support income should have similar effects on labor supply as increasing the level of child support income (see Graham and Beller 1987).

2. See Garfinkel et al. (1988) for a more thorough discussion of the assumptions underlying these budget constraints.

3. Child-support-eligible cases meet all these criteria: (1) the potential for child support payments exists for at least two months; (2) there is at least one minor child; (3) there is a temporary order or a final judgment (i.e., the court decided the case rather than leaving it pending); and (4) the date of the originating petition of the action and the date of a support order decision are between 1980 and 1986 (Manning, Seltzer, and Schaeffer 1987).

4. The percentage-of-income standard is specified in administrative code. The rate prescribed by the code depends exclusively on the number of children owed support. Seventeen percent of the noncustodial parent's gross income is ordered for one child and 25 percent, 29 percent, 31 percent, and 34 percent, respectively, are ordered for two, three, four, and five or more children. The percentage-of-income standard can be expressed in two ways, first as a fixed dollar amount equaling a percentage of the noncustodial parent's income at the time of the order, and second as a percentage of the noncustodial parent's income that adjusts to changes in that income.

5. For example, suppose that the same portion of cases in both pilot and control counties used immediate withholding. Assuming no other differences between pilot and control counties, the estimated response (the coefficient of the pilot county dummy variable) would be zero regardless of what the true effect is. The coefficient of the pilot dummy approaches the true effect of immediate withholding as the number of cases with immediate withholding in the control counties approaches zero.

6. See Barnow, Cain, and Goldberger (1980) for a discussion of the available statistical techniques.

7. The Current Population Survey includes only female custodial parents, whereas the Wisconsin sample contains both male and female custodial parents.

8. Including control variables in the equations may also increase the precision of the estimated responses if they are not highly correlated with the policy variables. For comparative purposes later in the text, we also present "unadjusted" estimates that do not include the control variables.

9. Respondents were asked to report all sources of income for themselves and all other members of their household. The household nonwage income variable includes: spouse's and other members' wage, salary and self-employment income, rental income, social security income, strike pay, unemployment compensation, pension income, interest income, and child support or alimony received by the respondent's spouse or other household members. Missing information for any of these sources of income was substituted with the sample median for that type of income. Sources excluded from the variable include: the respondent's wage, salary and self-employment income, Supplemental Security Income (SSI), AFDC income, general relief income, food stamp income, and energy assistance.

10. Child support income received by the custodial parent was excluded because it is an outcome variable affected by immediate withholding.

11. The full results for the entire sample, including all court cases, are presented in Appendix 12.A, table 12.A-2.

12. All estimates were generated using the LIMDEP program (see Green 1986).

13. Two-stage least squares was also applied to the maximum-likelihood probit and tobit specifications of table 12.9 and yielded conclusions similar to the two-stage least squares estimates of the specification in table 12.8.

14. The other variables in the probit model are whether the award is in percentage terms, household nonwage income, the custodial parent's marital status and race, whether it is a paternity case, and whether the custodial parent is a male.

15. Note that for the weeks variable, the net effect is positive, whereas the individual effects for AFDC and non-AFDC families are negative. This perverse result is possible when two-stage least squares is used.

16. The full results (for the combined AFDC/non-AFDC sample that includes all court cases) are presented in Appendix 12.A, table 12.A-3.

17. See Kiefer (1988) for a general discussion of econometric techniques used to estimate hazard models.

18. The exponential distribution assumes that the hazard rate does not vary over time, whereas the Weibull distribution allows the hazard rate to increase or decrease with the duration of the spell. For the exponential distribution, neither right censoring nor left censoring creates a problem in estimation, because of the assumption that the process generating the spells is "memoryless." For the Weibull distribution, right censoring is not a problem; however, left censoring is because the start date of the spell is used to estimate the duration dependence parameter. In estimating the Weibull model for unemployment and out-of-the-labor-force spells, we include spells with missing start dates (left-censored spells). Thus, these results could be biased and should be interpreted with caution. Note that for employment and job spells, start dates are available for all observations. Also note that we made no attempt to allow the policy effects to vary with the duration of the spell, although this may be worth pursuing in future research.

Appendix 12.A WAGE EQUATION ESTIMATES AND RESULTS FOR LABOR SUPPLY AND DURATION MEASURES

Table 12.A-1 WAGE EQUATION ESTIMATES: WISCONSIN STUDY

	Dummy for Observed Wage (Probit)	Wages in Natural Logs (Ordinary Least Squares)
Female	−0.433[a]	−0.473[a]
	(0.184)	(0.055)
White	0.315	0.189[b]
	(0.257)	(0.118)
Age	−0.005	0.070[a]
	(0.049)	(0.017)
Age^2	0.000	−0.001[a]
	(0.001)	(0.000)
Limiting ill health	−0.707[a]	—
	(0.154)	—
High school education	0.424[a]	0.227[a]
	(0.135)	(0.068)
Some college education	0.409[a]	0.315[a]
	(0.140)	(0.068)
College degree	0.307	0.518[a]
	(0.226)	(0.087)
Some graduate education	0.395	0.597[a]
	(0.291)	(0.106)
Never married	0.163	−0.224
	(0.420)	(0.197)
Separated	0.422	−0.147
	(0.448)	(0.207)

Table 12.A-1 WAGE EQUATION ESTIMATES: WISCONSIN STUDY *(continued)*

	Dummy for Observed Wage (Probit)	Wages in Natural Logs (Ordinary Least Squares)
Divorced	0.611	−0.109
	(0.414)	(0.201)
Family size	−0.008	—
	(0.038)	—
Preschool children present	−0.338[a]	—
	(0.114)	—
Nonwage household income (in $ thousands)	−0.002	—
	(0.003)	—
Unemployment rate of residing county	−0.023	—
	(0.038)	—
Wisconsin SMSA	—	0.136[a]
	—	(0.030)
Lambda	—	0.000
	—	(0.157)
Intercept	0.475	0.486
	(1.004)	(0.410)
N	1118	840
R^2	—	.28
Log likelihood	−570.01	—

Note: Dashes (—) denote not included or not applicable.
[a]Statistically different from zero at .01 level.
[b]Statistically different from zero at .10 level.

Table 12.A-2 FULL RESULTS FOR LABOR SUPPLY MEASURES: WISCONSIN STUDY (ALL COURT CASES)

	Ordinary Least Squares			Maximum Likelihood		
	Dummy for Employment	Hours of Work	Weeks Worked	Dummy for Employment (Probit)	Hours of Work (Tobit)	Weeks Worked (Two-Limit Tobit)
Immediate withholding	0.043[c] (0.023)	42.68 (55.13)	1.95[c] (1.18)	0.163[c] (0.093)	71.18 (70.95)	9.52[c] (5.93)
Percentage award	0.015 (0.055)	9.27 (131.80)	1.44 (2.84)	0.066 (0.219)	14.38 (174.00)	6.20 (14.00)
Predicted wage[d]	0.276[a] (0.084)	697.56[a] (201.90)	16.80[a] (4.35)	1.130[a] (0.337)	735.39[a] (246.50)	74.54[a] (21.65)
Adults in household	0.014 (0.018)	56.29 (43.29)	1.12 (0.95)	0.049 (0.072)	28.06 (53.28)	4.57 (4.64)
Children in household	-0.043[a] (0.013)	-132.65[a] (31.60)	-3.12[a] (0.68)	-0.172[a] (0.053)	-174.56[a] (38.04)	-16.54[a] (3.43)
Preschool children present	-0.070[b] (0.031)	-92.95 (73.48)	-2.64[c] (1.58)	-0.321[a] (0.126)	-156.78[c] (94.50)	-12.40 (7.77)
Nonwage household income (in $ thousands)	-0.000 (0.001)	-3.55 (2.44)	-0.01 (0.05)	-0.000 (0.004)	-2.93 (2.95)	0.01 (0.26)
Paternity case	-0.133[b] (0.062)	-501.42[a] (149.4)	-8.28[a] (3.22)	-0.394 (0.221)	-596.63[a] (203.00)	-37.23[b] (15.42)
Never married	0.075 (0.126)	148.29 (302.70)	8.26 (6.53)	0.225 (0.429)	70.67 (338.70)	4.13 (29.22)
Separated	0.091 (0.143)	-75.27 (343.70)	5.21 (7.41)	0.192 (0.501)	-72.86 (404.60)	-13.51 (34.17)

Divorced	0.086	-12.30	6.20	0.188	54.12	-8.10
	(0.135)	(325.50)	(7.02)	(0.463)	(379.50)	(31.61)
Not white	-0.158	-402.08[b]	-10.45[a]	-0.430	-424.53	-40.91[c]
	(0.076)	(182.30)	(3.93)	(0.273)	(284.30)	(21.69)
Male	0.021	417.68[b]	3.60	0.616[c]	439.06[a]	59.68[a]
	(0.056)	(135.1)	(2.91)	(0.344)	(165.30)	(18.23)
Age	0.00	66.89[c]	1.82[c]	-0.004	60.73	7.69[c]
	(0.02)	(37.74)	(0.81)	(0.065)	(50.47)	(4.11)
Age^2	-0.000	-0.75	-0.02[b]	0.000	-0.63	-0.09
	(0.000)	(0.51)	(0.01)	(0.001)	(0.71)	(0.06)
Limiting ill health	-0.188[a]	-492.94[a]	-9.79[a]	-0.679[a]	-537.48[a]	-47.82[a]
	(0.044)	(105.70)	(2.28)	(0.163)	(135.90)	(10.96)
Intercept	0.243	-820.23	-26.89[c]	-0.834	-833.88	-163.33
	(0.269)	(646.50)	(13.94)	(1.061)	(846.70)	(70.70)
Sigma	—	—	—	—	1120.20	77.29
	—	—	—	—	(29.47)	(4.79)
N	1118	1118	1118	1118	1118	1118
R^2	.163	.239	.229	—	—	—
Log likelihood	—	—	—	-485.15	-7448.10	-1772.20

Note: Dashes (—) denote not available or not applicable.
[a]Statistically different from zero at .01 level.
[b]Statistically different from zero at .05 level.
[c]Statistically different from zero at .10 level.
[d]Predicted wage is expressed in terms of natural logs.

Table 12.A-3 FULL RESULTS FOR DURATION MEASURES: WISCONSIN STUDY (ALL COURT CASES, EXPONENTIAL DISTRIBUTION)

	Job Duration	Employment Duration	Out-of-the-Labor-Force Duration	Unemployment Duration
Immediate withholding	-0.026 (0.069)	-0.084 (0.127)	-0.342[b] (0.171)	0.192 (0.149)
Percentage award	-0.116 (0.148)	0.242 (0.301)	0.396 (0.491)	-0.480[c] (0.283)
Predicted wage[d]	1.021[a] (0.276)	1.236[b] (0.527)	0.158 (0.538)	-3.444[a] (0.605)
Adults in household	-0.035 (0.055)	-0.051 (0.103)	0.017 (0.140)	0.243[b] (0.117)
Children in household	-0.100[a] (0.040)	-0.240 (0.069)	0.009[a] (0.094)	0.040 (0.087)
Preschool children present	0.267[a] (0.088)	0.246 (0.163)	0.801[a] (0.217)	-0.002 (0.191)
Nonwage household income (in $ thousands)	-0.006[b] (0.003)	0.004 (0.005)	0.001 (0.007)	-0.002 (0.005)
Paternity case	-0.053 (0.193)	-0.466 (0.310)	0.239 (0.370)	-0.155 (0.451)
Never married	-1.384[a] (0.459)	-1.311[b] (0.664)	0.544 (0.702)	-0.084 (0.649)

Separated	−1.294[a] (0.515)	−1.992[a] (0.771)	0.498 (0.849)	−1.263 (0.795)
Divorced	−1.177[b] (0.498)	−1.570[b] (0.742)	0.381 (0.769)	−0.389 (0.747)
Not white	−0.721[a] (0.230)	−0.897[b] (0.445)	−0.109 (0.468)	0.076 (0.409)
Male	0.656[a] (0.206)	1.950[a] (0.628)	−0.928 (0.738)	1.164 (0.773)
Age	0.269[a] (0.039)	0.320[a] (0.066)	0.206[a] (0.073)	0.530[a] (0.080)
$Age^2/100$	−0.287[a] (0.052)	−0.331[a] (0.091)	0.244[b] (0.108)	0.738[a] (0.108)
Limiting ill health	−0.355[b] (0.147)	−0.566[b] (0.263)	0.663[b] (0.295)	0.187 (0.248)
N	1465	1005	380	230
Log likelihood	−1859.00	−806.80	−394.45	−377.11

[a]Statistically different from zero at .01 level.
[b]Statistically different from zero at .05 level.
[c]Statistically different from zero at .10 level.
[d]Predicted wage is expressed in terms of natural logs.

References

Barnow, B., G. Cain, and A. Goldberger. 1980. "Issues in the Analysis of Selectivity Bias." *Evaluation Studies Review Annual* 5: 43–59.

Garfinkel, I., T. J. Corbett, M. MacDonald, S. McLanahan, P. K. Robins, N. C. Schaeffer, and J. A. Seltzer. 1988. "Evaluation Design for the Wisconsin Child Support Assurance Demonstration." Institute for Research on Poverty, University of Wisconsin, Madison. Photocopy.

Graham, J. W., and A. H. Beller. 1987. "The Impact of Income Uncertainty on Labor Supply: The Case of Child Support." University of Illinois, Champaign. Photocopy. February.

Green, W. H. 1986. *LIMDEP User's Manual*, Econometric Software, Inc., Bellport, NY.

Heckman, J. J. 1979. "Sample Selection Bias as a Specification Error." *Econometrica* 47(1, Jan.): 153–161.

Kiefer, N. M. 1988. "Economic Duration Data and Hazard Functions." *Journal of Economic Literature* 26(2, June): 646–679.

Killingsworth, M. R. 1983. *Labor Supply.* Cambridge, England: Cambridge University Press.

Manning, W., J. Seltzer, and N. C. Schaeffer. 1987. "Wisconsin Child Support Project Data Sets: Court Record Database, Parent Survey, and Children Incomes and Program Participation Survey." Institute for Research on Poverty, University of Wisconsin, Madison. Photocopy.

Chapter Thirteen

EFFECTS OF CHILD SUPPORT ON REMARRIAGE OF SINGLE MOTHERS

Kwi-Ryung Yun

As the number of female-headed families in the United States has almost tripled over the past three decades, controversy has surrounded the effects of governmental programs on family structures. Critics argue, in particular, that the Aid to Families with Dependent Children (AFDC) program encourages female headship by rewarding behaviors such as out-of-wedlock births and marriage breakups (Murray 1984). Although this argument is not strongly supported by empirical studies (Corcoran et al. 1985; Ellwood and Bane 1984; Hoffman and Duncan 1988), uneasiness about AFDC grows as female headship and welfare costs increase. At the same time, concern for child support has recently risen, accompanied by a growing sense that parents should take responsibility for providing care for their children regardless of the parents' living arrangement. The primary purpose of child support is for noncustodial fathers to share their income with their children. The federal child support program, however, may have indirect effects on the behavior of custodial parents, such as remarriage or employment.

This study focuses on the relationship between child support and remarriage of custodial mothers. It comprises five sections. Section one describes the theoretical framework; section two briefly reviews empirical results of previous studies; section three describes the data and methodology used in this analysis; section four presents the study's empirical findings; and section five provides a summary and conclusion.

THEORETICAL FRAMEWORK

The remarriage behavior of women can be analyzed by applying marital search theory. Becker and his colleagues were the first to apply the job search theory to the marriage market (Becker 1981: chap 10;

Becker, Landes, and Michael 1977). They used the search theory
mainly to explain marital dissolution, rather than to study the marriage formation process (Oppenheimer 1988). Later, others (Beller and
Graham 1985; Hutchens 1979; Oppenheimer 1988) applied the search
theory to analyze the marriage behavior of women.

According to Becker (1974), the behavior of a woman in the marriage
market is determined by her own benefit and cost analysis, given an
expected distribution of marriage offers. The distribution of marriage
offers varies across women according to the differences in the value
that potential marriage partners assign to these women's characteristics. Assuming risk neutrality, the woman compares the expected level
of well-being in marriage with that of remaining single, and chooses
a lifestyle that seems to provide the highest level of well-being.[1] There
are, of course, constraints on her behavior, a major one being the cost
of searching for a marriage partner. The search involves both direct
and indirect costs. Direct costs refer to the financial costs of obtaining
information on potential marriage partners, as well as the emotional
costs. Indirect costs refer to opportunity costs, such as earnings foregone when a person spends time searching or when a potential partner
is already married.

Owing to search costs, the woman typically does not continue to
search until the perfect match is achieved. Rather, she searches until
the value to her of any expected improvement in the mate she can find
is no greater than the cost of her time and other inputs into additional
search. Therefore, the greater the benefits expected from additional
searching, the longer will be the search. The participation in a search
and the duration of the search will thus determine the probability of
marriage over a certain time period.

Income Effect, Independence Effect, and Child Support

An increase in child support has two opposing effects: On the one
hand, it increases the probability of remarriage of a single mother by
encouraging her to participate in a search for a new marriage partner.
On the other hand, it decreases the probability of remarriage by allowing her to extend the duration of her marital search.

An increase in child support provides a woman, first of all, with
search costs, such as for clothing or babysitting. The added income
may facilitate her marital search for a potential partner.

Moreover, her improved economic attractiveness (resulting from the
likelihood that her future mate would benefit from the increased child
support) may induce a higher quantity and quality of marriage offers

from the demand side of the marriage market. This can be called a dowry effect.

An increase in child support may furthermore increase her expected gain from remarriage because of her altruistic attitude toward her family and a potential marriage partner (Becker 1974: s14; Becker 1981: chap. 8). For a woman who cares about her family, her well-being depends positively on the well-being of family members. If a single mother remains single, her well-being depends on the well-being of herself and her children. However, if she remarries a man whom she cares for, and shares the increased child support income with him, her well-being can be even more enhanced as his well-being increases.

Taken together, the gains from provision of search costs, the dowry effect, and an altruistic attitude are called, in this study, the income effect.[2] In sum, the income effect amplifies the probability of remarriage by facilitating a woman's participation in a marital search.

However, an increase in child support also reduces the probability of remarriage by increasing a woman's economic independence. With the added income, a woman may not have to remarry in a hurry just to survive economically. Becoming more selective in choosing a husband, she is more likely to extend the duration of her marital search, in turn reducing the probability of remarriage over the short term. In this study, this effect is called the independence effect.

The net probability of remarriage is therefore determined by the magnitude of the income effect and the independence effect. Owing to the problems of measuring the size of each effect, it is difficult to predict the net effect of child support on the probability of remarriage of female heads. This question must be addressed empirically.

PREVIOUS STUDIES

Just as theory does not predict the direction of the effect of child support on the probability of remarriage, previous studies do not provide a conclusive answer either. Of the limited amount of work that has been done on the relationship between child support and remarriage of women, only three studies are relevant to this chapter's analysis: those of Beller and Graham (1985), Hutchens (1979), and Hoffman and Duncan (1988). Beller and Graham (1985) examined the relationship between child support and remarriage of divorced/separated mothers using the March/April 1979 match file of the Current

Population Survey (CPS). Child support was operationalized on the basis of whether a woman was awarded child support, whether child support was due in 1978, and the amount of child support due per child. Results from Beller and Graham's logistic analysis indicated that although having a child support award increases the probability of remarriage, being due support in 1978 decreased the probability of remarriage by a larger amount than the award increased it. Also, according to the authors, an increase in the amount of child support due per child reduces the probability of remarriage. Therefore, the authors concluded that child support has a negative impact on the probability of remarriage. Their results, however, were based on child support awards ordered by the court, rather than actual payments; neither the women's income nor AFDC variables were included.[3]

Hutchens' (1979) study, which focused on the effects of AFDC on remarriage of female heads, contained variables on nonwage income including child support and alimony. Utilizing data from the Panel Study of Income Dynamics (PSID [Institute for Social Research, University of Michigan, Ann Arbor]), Hutchens followed the remarriage behavior of female heads for two years. Results from his logistic regression model indicate that nonwage income has a negative, but statistically insignificant, impact on the probability of remarriage. The problem with this result is that the variable does not distinguish between child support and alimony. This is a critical disadvantage in terms of studying a relationship between child support and remarriage, since the level of alimony payments unambiguously falls if a woman remarries, whereas the level of child support income does not change upon remarriage.

Hutchens (1979) argued that the negative effect of the variable stems mainly from alimony, which, he claimed, took into account most of the variation in the variable. However, in general, alimony is very small relative to child support, as evidenced in Beller and Graham's (1985) study, which showed that whereas the average amount of child support receipt in 1978 was $915, that of alimony was only $199. If a similar ratio holds for Hutchens's data, the estimate of nonwage income may be weighted more by child support than by alimony. In short, it is difficult to draw any conclusion on the relationship between child support and remarriage from Hutchens's data, despite the suspicion that the negative impact of nonwage income may stem from child support as well as from alimony.

Hoffman and Duncan's (1988) study also included nonwage income and focused on the relationship between welfare and remarriage of separated and divorced women, using PSID data. The variable, nonlabor income, also included both child support and alimony. This study differed from the Hutchens (1979) study, however, in that it used the nested logit model in addition to the multinomial logit model, and estimated the model as a discrete-time hazard model of time until remarriage. Hoffman and Duncan claimed that the nested logit model offers an important advantage over a multinomial logit, the latter of which has a critical assumption that the elements of the choice set are statistically independent of one another. The nested logit model was considered by Hoffman and Duncan to selectively relax the independence supposition by assuming a hierarchical decision process. In the authors' study, for instance, a single mother is assumed to face a set of "nested" choice sets—that is, first, a choice between remarriage and remaining single, and, second, a choice between entering or not entering welfare. The women who remain single, they argue, share some common unmeasured characteristics regardless of their decision on welfare recipiency, such as the absence of husbands. Therefore, the choices of receiving or not receiving welfare may be more closely related to one another than either one is to the remarriage alternative. Changes in the value of either being on welfare or off welfare are expected to have stronger effects on each other than on remarriage choice.

The estimated results from Hoffman and Duncan's (1988) two models are different, and are in contrast to Hutchens's finding. An estimate from the multinomial logit indicates a positive effect of non-wage income on the probability of remarriage, statistically significant at .05 level. From the nested logit model, the nonwage income shows a still positive but not statistically significant effect on the remarriage decision of female heads. The results suggest that, at the least, the nonlabor income does not have a negative impact on the probability of remarriage.

In sum, the previous studies do not provide conclusive answers to the issue of the direction and magnitude of the net effect of child support on remarriage of women.

METHODOLOGY AND DATA

Event History Analysis

There are two methods of event history analysis: continuous time methods, which assume time is measured continuously; and discrete-time methods, which measure time in discrete time units. This study employs the discrete-time model, mainly because it is easier to incorporate time-varying covariates within discrete-time methods.

Event history analysis permits effective use of data by utilizing information on the timing of events and on those who are censored. The analysis accomplishes this by focusing on the rate of the event—the number of events per unit of time—and by virtue of the fact that a rate at a particular time is allowed to depend on the values of the independent variables at a particular time. This rate is called the hazard rate, the fundamental dependent variable in an event history model. The independent variables can be either time-varying covariates, which have different values at each time, or fixed variates, which are constant over time.

The hazard rate is expected to change autonomously with time. With remarriages, one may expect a decline in the hazard rate, simply because as a woman ages, the pool of marriage partners will be reduced. On the other hand, a woman may not remarry right after the marital dissolution, thus showing a low hazard rate in the initial period. With the discrete-time model, one can allow for any variation in the hazard rate by letting the intercept be different at each point in discrete time.

Let P_{it} be the probability of individual i remarrying in time period t. $X1_i$ denotes a vector of fixed variates, and $X2_{it}$ indicates a vector of time-varying covariates. α, $\beta1$, and $\beta2$ are the parameters to be estimated. The time unit is measured as a three-month period, assuming the hazard rate is constant within these periods. If the effects of independent variables are constant over time, and if the effects of the variables are linear in the logistic, then

$$\log(P_{it}/(1-P_{it}) = a_t + \alpha_t + \beta1X1; + \beta2X2_{it} \qquad (13.1)$$

This model can be *estimated* through maximum-likelihood procedures.

Data

The data used in this analysis consist of four datasets; the Court Record Database (CRDB), tax records, welfare records, and the Parent Survey. The first three datasets are administrative records collected by counties or the state of Wisconsin.[4] The fourth dataset, the Parent Survey, is conducted by the Institute for Research on Poverty, University of Wisconsin–Madison.[5] In combining the datasets for this study, first, the sample was drawn from the CRDB, then the other three datasets were merged with the CRDB, extracting a sample of 2,803 cases. From this larger sample, a subset of 1,025 women, consisting of white divorced mothers who have physical custody of children, was selected for this analysis. Separated mothers were excluded from the sample because, in the absence of information on their separation date, it was difficult to determine the time when they started to search for remarriage partners. Never-married mothers were also omitted, both because only a few of them go through the court system and because their partner-seeking behavior might differ from that of divorced mothers. The remarriage behaviors of the women in the sample were followed from the date of divorce until the date of their remarriage or interview.

VARIABLES

The dependent variable is whether a single mother remarried in a given period. *Remarriage* is defined as a legal remarriage to a man other than the father of the woman's children. Neither cohabitating with a man nor reconciliation with the noncustodial father was considered remarriage in this study—because of the lack of information on cohabitation and because of the different effects of child support on reconciliation when the father is the payer of child support. This study assumes that risk of remarriage starts from date of divorce.

In this analysis, child support and other economic variables (AFDC, income of divorced mothers) are critical factors. The analysis controls for the mother's socioeconomic status at the time of divorce (income of noncustodial fathers and education), and includes demographic variables (age at divorce, age at first marriage, number of children, age of the youngest child, whether the mother lived in an urban county). The study also contains variables related to the parents' divorce process (whether father wanted to end the marriage, duration of divorce process). The economic variables are time-varying covariates, whereas other independent variables are fixed variables measured at the time of divorce, unless indicated otherwise. Measuring the economic variables was problematic because of the time and multiple steps involved in the remarriage process. It is not known which value of the economic variables affects each step of the remarriage process.[6] Hence, the history of the economic situation of women since divorce is used, rather than their economic status at a certain time. More information on the time-varying covariates follows.

Child Support   In this study, child support is categorized according to the mother's welfare status: child support received while the mother was not on welfare (child support—off welfare) and child support received while the mother was on welfare (child support—on welfare). Child support—on welfare should have a different effect from child support—off welfare, since welfare mothers receive only up to $50 of child support, regardless of actual payments from the noncustodial fathers. Moreover, these mothers may not be aware of the portable characteristic of their child support benefits. Child support is operationalized as: (1) a dummy variable indicating availability of child support; (2) the amount of child support; (3) the standard deviation of the payments that measures irregularity of child support payments.

The amount of child support (X_{ip}) is measured from the divorce date to the previous period, and is averaged for the monthly figure. That is, the amounts of child support are calculated by

$$X_{ip} = \frac{\sum_{p=1}^{p-1} X'_{ip}}{P-1} \tag{13.2}$$

where X'_{ip} refers to the monthly average amounts of child support received by an individual i in period p.

AFDC Status   AFDC is operationalized as a binary variable rather than a continuous variable, because the entire sample is from Wisconsin, and thus each receives the same benefit level, holding family size and economic status constant. AFDC status reflects whether a divorced mother experienced AFDC up to the previous period.

Income   Unlike the variables of child support and AFDC, which measure receipt of income from divorce to the previous period, the mother's income variable reflects an average monthly income for the previous year, because it is obtained from the tax records, which report income annually. Since earned income accounts for most of the variation in this income variable, this is used as a proxy for earned income. Missing cases (37 percent) are denoted with a dummy variable.

Characteristics of the Sample

Characteristics of the sample, based on the variables used, are given in table 13.1. Most of the women had received child support at least once since divorce. The average amount of child support received at all times is about $230. About two-thirds of the women received child support while not on welfare. One-third of the women received child support while they were experiencing welfare. Not surprisingly, the

Table 13.1 CHARACTERISTICS OF SAMPLE: EFFECTS OF CHILD SUPPORT ON REMARRIAGE OF SINGLE MOTHERS

Variables	Original Data	Discrete-Time Data
CHILD SUPPORT—ALL TIMES[a]		
Dummy	0.829	0.799
Amount[b]	233.596	233.046
Standard deviation	126.017	109.492
CHILD SUPPORT—OFF WELFARE[a]		
Dummy	0.676	0.595
Amount[b]	199.427	186.440
Standard deviation	109.942	94.596
CHILD SUPPORT—ON WELFARE[a]		
Dummy	0.321	0.301
Amount[b]	34.168	36.605
AFDC[a]		
Dummy	0.387	0.389
Amount[b]	142.363	243.293
INCOME[a]	1,025.042	1,071.274
FATHERS' INCOME	1,773.587	1,752.399
EDUCATION[c]		
Less than high school	0.082	0.083
High school[d]	0.453	0.448
Some college	0.361	0.363
College or more	0.104	0.106
AGE AT DIVORCE		
< 20 years old	0.018	0.018
20–25 years old[d]	0.128	0.129
26–30 years old	0.259	0.251
31–40 years old	0.448	0.451
> 40 years old	0.148	0.150
Mean	32.094	32.137
NUMBER OF CHILDREN		
1[d]	0.481	0.485
≥ 2	0.519	0.515
Mean	1.655	1.627
AGE OF YOUNGEST CHILD		
≤ 5 years old	0.514	0.596
≥ 5 years old[d]	0.486	0.404
Mean	5.691	5.657
AGE AT FIRST MARRIAGE		
< 17 years old	0.048	0.047
17–19 years old	0.274	0.282
20–22 years old[d]	0.377	0.367
> 23 years old	0.248	0.244
Missing	0.054	0.059
Mean	21.404	21.256
FATHER ENDED 1ST MARRIAGE		
Dummy	0.187	0.197

(continued)

Table 13.1 CHARACTERISTICS OF SAMPLE: EFFECTS OF CHILD SUPPORT ON REMARRIAGE OF SINGLE MOTHERS *(continued)*

Variables	Original Data	Discrete-Time Data
DIVORCE PROCESS[e]	284.216	289.980
URBAN COUNTY	0.608	0.618
DIVORCE YEAR		
1984[d]	0.160	0.228
1985	0.453	0.521
1986	0.415	0.285
DURATION	21.707	25.505
REMARRIED	0.193	0.028
CASES	1,025	
PERSON-PERIOD		7,040

[a]Amount and standard deviation of CHILD SUPPORT, AFDC, and INCOME are time-varying covariates. Time-varying covariates reported for the orignal dataset are measured as monthly average values from divorce.
[b]Monthly averages are measured in $100s.
[c]Education is measured at time of survey, owing to lack of information on education at time of divorce.
[d]Omitted categories.
[e]Divorce process is calculated by subtracting petition dates from divorce dates.

amount of child support—off welfare is much higher than child support—on welfare, $199 versus $34, respectively.

The average age of women at divorce was 32. About 40 percent of the divorces occurred before age 30, and a little less than half of the women were in their thirties; about a quarter were in their late twenties. Only 15 percent of the divorces occurred in women over age 40. This age distribution is comparable to that of data used by Bumpass et al. (1989).[7] Most of the women in the current sample married at a young age. About a third of the divorces were to teenage marriages, and the average age at first marriage was about 21.[8]

EMPIRICAL RESULTS

Remarriage behavior of mothers who divorced during the period from January 1984 to June 1986 was observed for an average of 22 months, ranging from 3 months to 44 months. Among 1,025 women, about a fifth of them legally remarried to men other than the fathers of their children. Of those who remarried, all but 2 remarried within three years after divorce, and about 40 percent within a year.

Table 13.2 presents results regarding the effect of child support and other variables on remarriage rates of divorced mothers. For brevity, the discussion focuses on the effects of child support. Note that the estimates shown here are not remarriage rates over these women's lifetimes. Since the observation periods are relatively short, increases in child support may result in delays in remarriage after the observation periods, rather than actually reducing the chance of remarriage over a lifetime. The first two columns of table 13.2 indicate the parameter estimates from the event history analysis and their *t*-ratios. The last column refers to the remarriage rate change with a one-unit increase in each variable. A predicted rate of remarriage for a woman with average characteristics is about 2 percent.[9]

In model 1 (table 13.2), child support variables are related to child support that the divorced mothers have received at all times—regardless of their welfare recipiency. In model 2, child support—off welfare is separated from child support—on welfare to separate the effect of child support from the influence of AFDC. Since child support—off welfare is a general type of child support, child support and child support—off welfare will be used interchangeably hereafter.

When child support—off welfare was separated from child support—on welfare in model 2 (table 13.2), the explanatory power of the model increases (the log likelihood is changed from −845.79 to −840.92). The dummy variable, the availability of child support—off welfare, has a positive and statistically significant effect on remarriage. According to the last column of table 13.2, women with child support—off welfare have a 9 percent higher rate of remarriage than those without child support—off welfare. Note that the dummy variable is not statistically significant when child support—off welfare is not distinguished from child support—on welfare, in model 1. Child support recipients who are able to stay off welfare are more likely to remarry than are other mothers. Also, those with child support—off welfare have unmeasured characteristics different from those without the support, which may imply the existence of selection effects.

The amount of child support has a negative effect on the rate of remarriage, but is not statistically significant. These results are consistent with Beller and Graham's (1985) findings, though their study used the child support award rather than actual payments.

Variation of child support payments appears to be a critical factor affecting the remarriage behavior of divorced mothers. Variation of child support payments increases the likelihood of remarriage, and the effect is statistically significant at the 0.01 level. Moreover, if the regularity measure is excluded from model 2 (table 13.2), the coeffi-

Table 13.2 EFFECTS OF CHILD SUPPORT ON RATE OF REMARRIAGE

Variables	Model 1	Model 2	Percentage Change of Rate[d]
CHILD SUPPORT—ALL TIMES[a]			
Dummy	0.137 (0.66)		
Amount	−0.046 (−1.34)		
Standard deviation	0.001 (3.13)		
CHILD SUPPORT—OFF WELFARE[a]			
Dummy		0.360 (1.96)	8.91
Amount		−0.047 (−1.37)	−1.18
Standard deviation		0.001 (3.02)	0.02
CHILD SUPPORT—ON WELFARE[a]			
Amount		−0.303 (−2.28)	−7.52
AFDC STATUS		0.041 (0.20)	1.03
INCOME[a]		−0.032 (−2.00)	−0.80
FATHER'S INCOME[a,b]		0.015 (1.72)	0.37
AGE AT DIVORCE			
<20 years old	−0.774 (−1.02)	−0.743 (−0.97)	−17.76
25–29 years old	0.240 (0.98)	0.224 (0.92)	5.58
30–39 years old	−0.177 (−0.61)	−0.183 (−0.63)	−4.56
>40 years old	−0.697 (−1.74)	−0.704 (−1.76)	−16.90
NUMBER OF CHILDREN (≥ 2)	−0.045 (−0.28)	−0.001 (−0.01)	−0.03
YOUNG CHILD[c]	−0.047 (−0.24)	0.001 (0.01)	0.02
AGE AT MARRIAGE			
>17 years old	0.412 (1.24)	0.368 (1.10)	9.09
17–19 years old	−0.132 (−0.72)	−0.158 (−0.86)	−3.94
>23 years old	−0.470 (−2.09)	−0.482 (−2.14)	−11.83

EDUCATION			
<High school	-0.410 (-1.29)	-0.414 (-1.29)	-10.20
Some college	0.052 (0.32)	0.050 (0.31)	1.26
College/more	-0.236 (-0.79)	-0.189 (-0.63)	-4.71
FATHER ENDED 1ST MARRIAGE	-0.529 (-2.46)	-0.561 (-2.60)	-13.66
DIVORCE PROCESS	-0.001 (-3.00)	-0.002 (-3.10)	-0.04
URBAN COUNTY	0.110 (0.70)	0.143 (0.90)	3.58
PERIOD 3	2.602 (4.87)	2.589 (4.86)	43.01
PERIOD 4	1.955 (3.53)	1.936 (3.51)	37.39
PERIOD 5	2.275 (4.15)	2.256 (4.12)	40.51
PERIOD 6	2.134 (3.82)	2.108 (3.78)	39.17
PERIOD 7	2.174 (3.84)	2.141 (3.79)	39.48
PERIOD 8	1.736 (2.86)	1.700 (2.81)	34.56
PERIOD 9	2.686 (4.75)	2.662 (4.72)	43.47
PERIOD 10	2.158 (3.49)	2.126 (3.44)	39.34
PERIOD 11	2.010 (2.92)	1.968 (2.86)	37.74
PERIOD 12	2.755 (4.13)	2.719 (4.08)	43.81
PERIOD 13	2.371 (2.67)	2.347 (2.64)	41.27
CONSTANT	-4.916 (-7.45)	-5.047 (-7.76)	-49.36
Log likelihood	-845.79	-840.92	-3.68

Notes: T-ratios are in parentheses. Dummy variable for CHILD SUPPORT—ON WELFARE is not included because of high correlation with its amount. Property settlement after divorce is excluded because it was not significant and did not improve the fit of the model.
[a] Amount and standard deviation of CHILD SUPPORT, INCOME, and FATHER'S INCOME are measured in $100.
[b] Monthly average of father's income a year prior to divorce.
[c] Binary variable equaling 1 if age of youngest child is less than six years old.
[d] Changes in probability are calculated using the formula: $\exp(B)/(1 + \exp(B)) \times 100 - 50$.

cient of the amount of child support changes from −0.047 to 0.002, and the *t*-ratio changes from −1.37 to 0.083—indicating almost no impact. This result implies the importance of the regularity of child support in affecting the rate of remarriage; that is, regular payments provide economic security, which reduces remarriage in the short run.

In short, variation of child support is an important determinant of the rate of remarriage. The more varied the child support, the more likely that the women will remarry. Availability of child support has a positive impact; as payments increase, however, the positive effect is reduced. Therefore, child support appears to have a positive impact until payments reach a certain level. The next section tries to identify the level at which child support decreases remarriage.

Child Support Level and Decreasing Remarriage

Suppose there are five divorced mothers without child support payments and with mean values for other independent variables. Their estimated rate of remarriage is the same, 0.017. If they are provided different amounts of child support, how would the remarriage rate change? Table 13.3 explains the changes in the rate for the women according to the different increases in child support, using the coefficients of model 2, table 13.2. The first six columns describe amounts of child support that the five hypothetical women received over the six-month period. The last column reports the estimated rates of their remarriage.

The first woman, A, does not have any child support during the six-month period. Because A's child support income does not change, her rate of remarriage remains the same, 0.017. B receives payments of $250 each month, which increases her remarriage rate to 0.021. However, C, who has the highest remarriage rate of the five, has the same average amounts of child support as B but is paid irregularly. The remarriage rate of C, 0.033, is almost twice that of A. The child support payment for D is nearly doubled, compared to that of C, but with the same variation. The doubled amounts of child support lead D to be slightly less likely to remarry than C. The most interesting result is shown in the case of E. E receives the highest amount of child support among the five women over the 6 months ($750 per month), and it is paid regularly. Her remarriage rate, 0.017, is the same as that of A, who does not have any child support. If child support beyond $750 were paid regularly to a woman, the rate would be less than 0.017. That is, she would be less likely to remarry than the woman without any child support. In other words, child support tends to have a positive effect on the remarriage rate until the amount reaches

Table 13.3 CHILD SUPPORT LEVEL AND ESTIMATED RATES OF REMARRIAGE: HYPOTHETICAL CASES

Cases	Child Support in Each Month ($)						Estimated Rates
	1	2	3	4	5	6	
A	0	0	0	0	0	0	0.017
B	250	250	250	250	250	250	0.021
C	0	0	1,500	0	0	0	0.033
D	0	680	0	1,500	800	0	0.030
E	750	750	750	750	750	750	0.017

Note: Rates estimated based on coefficients of model 2, table 13.2.

$750; beyond that amount and paid regularly, child support decreases the remarriage rate.

THEORETICAL EXPLANATION

This phenomenon can be explained, in part, by offsetting income and independence effects.[10] Child support increases both the income and independence of the mother. Up to a certain level, however, the income effect is stronger, because, say, a first few hundred extra dollars may not be enough for the mother to feel secure about the future. If she has a marriage offer, and her expected level of future offers is not much higher than the current one, her opportunity costs of rejecting the offer would be greater than the situation in which she senses financial security. Therefore, her pessimistic expectation for future marriage offers may lead her to accept the offer. Because of this, child support below a certain level may increase her incentive to remarry, but not the duration of marital search. The woman with some child support tends to increase her rate of remarriage when observed over a relatively short period of time.

However, child support above a certain level may make a woman feel financially secure for the future, and, therefore, the independence effect will dominate. The opportunity costs of rejecting the current offer are not so great as in the previous case. The woman's selectiveness in choosing a marriage partner and her duration of search would be increased. Therefore, the initial positive effect of having child support would be reduced as the extra income increased.

Substantial amounts of child support, however, are not enough to ensure a secure future. Economic security dictates that child support be paid regularly, as proven by the diminishing effects of the amount of child support when variation of child support is omitted from the model, as mentioned earlier.

In sum, child support tends to have a strong income effect at first, but as income increases and is paid regularly, the independence effect increases as well.

This explanation can be further illustrated by regressing child support on the quality of husbands. If the availability of child support has a negative effect on the quality of men, whereas a substantial amount of child support has a positive influence, then one may assert that the results regarding the effect of child support on the remarriage rate and the quality of husbands are consistent. The following subsection addresses this topic in more depth.

Child Support and the Quality of Husbands

The quality of husbands is measured in this study by annual income and years of education of the new spouses, with a separate analysis conducted for each quality, and employing ordinary least square (OLS) estimation.[11] The results are presented in table 13.4.[12] The first two columns describe estimates on income of new husbands and the next two columns report estimates on education. For each quality, model 1 enters the availability and amount of child support along with other control variables, and model 2 adds variation of child support amount.

When the annual income of new husbands is used as a measure for the quality of husbands, the result supports the theoretical explanation: the availability of child support reduces income of new husbands, but an increase in the amount of child support enhances their income. According to model 1 (table 13.4), the coefficients and t-ratios are -51.248 and -1.714, respectively, for the availability, and 10.757 and 2.77 for the amount, respectively. If variation of child support amount is added in model 2, the coefficient and statistical significance of the amount are reduced substantially, owing to the high correlation between the two variables (Pearson correlation coefficient is 0.86).

The negative effect of the availability needs more explanation. As mentioned previously, child support under a certain level may facilitate the remarriage process, because the income effect is stronger than the independence effect. The lower level of child support, however, seemed to cause women to hurriedly remarry men who often had less income than if the women had had a higher level of child support. As defined earlier, the income effect includes raises in the dowry effect along with increases in search costs and expected gain from remarriage. The dowry effect may induce more remarriage offers, but not necessarily a higher quality of offers if the amount of child support is not high enough. As amount of child support increases, however, the quality of offers may increase as well.

Table 13.4 EFFECTS OF CHILD SUPPORT ON QUALITY OF NEW HUSBANDS

Variables	Effects on New Husband's Income		Effects on New Husband's Education	
	Model 1	Model 2	Model 1	Model 2
INTERCEPT	90.369 (0.805)	92.486 (0.820)	13.924 (12.015)	13.922 (11.970)
CHILD SUPPORT—OFF WELFARE[a]				
Dummy	−51.248 (−1.714)	−43.029 (−1.289)	0.146 (0.455)	0.153 (0.436)
Amount	10.757 (2.770)	5.958 (0.633)	−0.068 (−1.440)	−0.072 (−0.717)
Standard deviation		2.354 (0.560)		0.002 (0.047)
CHILD SUPPORT—ON WELFARE[a]				
Amount	12.575 (0.523)	10.628 (0.436)	0.023 (0.091)	0.022 (0.084)
AFDC Dummy	8.943 (0.208)	5.224 (0.120)	−0.546 (−1.216)	−0.549 (1.207)
INCOME[a]	8.132 (2.954)	7.861 (2.804)	−0.009 (−0.297)	−0.009 (−0.300)
FATHER'S INCOME[a]	1.733 (0.831)	2.139 (0.966)	0.016 (1.153)	0.017 (0.997)
AGE AT DIVORCE				
<20 years old	−199.816 (−1.384)	−196.712 (−1.357)	−0.855 (−0.465)	−0.853 (−0.462)
25–29 years old	23.560 (0.489)	21.435 (0.442)	0.525 (1.121)	0.525 (1.116)
30–39 years old	153.932 (2.633)	151.938 (2.586)	0.354 (0.629)	0.354 (0.625)
>40 years old	132.707 (1.660)	135.296 (1.684)	0.717 (0.935)	0.719 (0.933)
AGE AT MARRIAGE	−5.028 (−1.047)	−5.282 (−1.091)	−0.060 (−1.171)	−0.060 (−1.168)
EDUCATION				
<High school	−69.409 (−1.100)	−71.015 (−1.121)	−0.075 (−0.126)	−0.077 (−0.129)
Some college	−13.230 (−0.501)	−15.514 (−0.579)	0.772 (2.736)	0.770 (2.691)
College/more	−44.217 (−0.791)	−38.078 (−0.666)	3.062 (5.740)	3.065 (5.667)
NUMBER OF CHILDREN (≥2)	−36.134 (−1.286)	−31.864 (−1.091)	0.155 (0.517)	0.158 (0.514)
YOUNG CHILD[b]	143.410 (3.989)	143.357 (3.975)	−0.150 (−0.409)	−0.149 (−0.405)
DIVORCE TIME	−1.208 (−0.664)	−1.152 (−0.630)	−0.009 (−0.523)	−0.009 (−0.517)
F-VALUE	2.186	2.083	3.275	3.100
ADJUSTED R-Square	0.158	0.153	0.196	0.191
N	127	127	188	188

Notes: T-ratios are in parentheses. Dummy variable for CHILD SUPPORT—ON WELFARE is not included because of high correlation with its amount. Property settlement after divorce is excluded because it was not significant and did not improve the fit of the model.
[a]INCOME OF NEW HUSBANDS, amount and standard deviation of CHILD SUPPORT, INCOME, and FATHER'S INCOME are measured in $100.
[b]Binary variable equaling 1 if age of youngest is less then six years old.

One may argue that the annual income may not measure lifetime earning power of young men accurately, and that their education may be the better measure. When child support was regressed on the education of new husbands, however, neither the availability nor the amount of child support was statistically significant. This result differs from the expectation that an increase in child support will enhance the education of new husbands. Also, if only child-support-related variables are entered in the regression, the amount of child support indicates a positive, though not statistically significant, influence on the education of new husbands. The Pearson correlation coefficient between income and education of new spouses is positive (0.24). Therefore, disregarding other factors, one may conclude that child support that increases the income of new husbands would also increase their educational level; however, the regression analysis indicates otherwise.

This result on the education of new husbands does not provide a conclusive answer to the question of whether child support increases the quality of husbands. However, the finding on the income of new husbands suggests that the availability of child support, which facilitates the remarriage decision of divorced mothers, has a negative impact on income of new husbands. Also, since an increase in the amount of child support delays women's remarriage decision, the increase would allow them to meet new husbands with higher incomes.

Child Support—On Welfare

Compared to the effect of child support—off welfare, child support—on welfare shows a stronger negative impact on remarriage.[13] The last column of table 13.2 shows that $100 per month of child support while on welfare decreases remarriage by 7.5 percent. There are three possible explanations for the stronger effect of child support on welfare mothers. First, child support—on welfare may have an indirect impact on remarriage through its effect on the labor supply of welfare recipients. Since child support—on welfare is not reduced as earnings increase, it may encourage welfare mothers to work more hours than allowed by AFDC.[14] Thus, child support—on welfare would enhance their wage income, thus inducing the independence effect. However, average child support—on welfare is about $120 per month for those who ever receive it, and 36 percent of this group have child support of less than $50 per month. Given this relatively small amount, I doubt that the effect on the work incentive of child support—on welfare is powerful enough to account for the negative effect on remarriage.

The second explanation involves the relationship between child support and AFDC payments. Among AFDC-experienced mothers, 76 percent received child support—on welfare. (Child support to AFDC mothers is extra money in addition to the AFDC payments.) An average AFDC income for those who were ever on welfare is about $400 per month. Since the average amount of AFDC income is not only already a little higher than the average ($300 per month) of child support received while not on welfare and paid regularly, the extra money up to $50 is likely to create the independence effect. Moreover, because women are supposed to receive AFDC regularly on a monthly basis, the extra income may increase their selectiveness and extend their duration of search. In addition, even though welfare mothers may recognize the portable characteristic of child support, its relatively small amount may not help them to remarry out of fear that the cost of losing AFDC benefits would be greater than the expected gain from remarriage, including receipt of the full (but still a small) amount of child support after remarriage. This hypothesis can be tested by substituting values for child support on welfare. Instead of entering the total child support—on welfare payments from noncustodial fathers, using just the amounts of child support received by the custodial mothers—that is, amounts of up to $50—would give the effects of actual money rather than the effects of the total payments with portable characteristics. If the amount up to the $50 disregard shows significant effects, one may conclude that it is the actual amounts of child support—on welfare, rather than the total amounts, that create the strong negative effect on the remarriage rate by increasing the independence effect. The empirical result tends to support the hypothesis, but not conclusively. Actual amounts that substitute the total amount for the child support—on welfare of model 2 of table 13.2 produce a higher coefficient but with a bigger standard error, resulting in a lower statistical significance. The coefficient is changed from -0.303 to -0.804, and the t-ratio changes from -2.28 to -1.56.

The final possibility is related to the demand side of the remarriage market. For the economically better-off mothers, quality of remarriage offers would be higher than for the other mothers. Although child support increases the independence effect while it decreases remarriage, the attractiveness of a relatively high quality of remarriage offers may weaken the independence effect. However, for those with economic difficulties, remarriage offers from potential partners would not be appealing enough to offset the negative effect of the independence effect. Since we do not know the actual distribution of remarriage offers to those who experienced economic difficulty after divorce and to those who did not, this hypothesis cannot be tested in this analysis. The most probable possibility would be that the three explanations are together responsible for the phenomenon. In short, the amount of child support—on welfare has a strong negative impact on the rate of remarriage of divorced mothers who have experienced welfare.

SUMMARY AND CONCLUSION

This study explores the relationship between child support and remarriage of divorced mothers. Because effects of child support and AFDC are intertwined with each other, child support received while mothers are not on welfare is distinguished from child support received while mothers are on welfare.

Results from the discrete-time event history analysis indicate that child support has a significant impact on remarriage of divorced mothers. However, rather than a simple linear relationship, its effect differs depending on its availability, amount, and variation of its payments. The availability of child support increases the rate of remarriage of divorced mothers significantly, but as the amount increases, the magnitude of the positive impact decreases. However, in determining remarriage, variation of child support payments is more important than the amount itself. That is, the more varied the child support payment is, the more likely is remarriage. It is estimated that child support becomes a negative force against the propensity to remarry when it exceeds $750 and is paid regularly. This phenomenon is explained with the income effect and the independence effect of child support: the first few hundred dollars may increase remarriage by providing search costs and attracting potential marriage partners (income effect). At the same time, the extra income may decrease remarriage by increasing the independence of women (the independence effect). The independence effect dominates the positive income effect when the amount of child support exceeds a certain level.

This explanation is further developed by regressing child support on the quality of new husbands measured according to their annual income and education. If the availability of child support facilitates the remarriage decisions of divorced mothers within short periods, then the availability is expected to have a negative impact on the quality of remarriage. On the other hand, an increase in the amount of child support that delays the remarriage decisions of women would enhance the quality of their husbands. This hypothesis is supported when new husbands' income is used to evaluate the quality of husbands, but not when their education is used. It is unclear why the results on income and education are different. Further investigation is necessary.

This study's results have the following implications: First, the finding that the availability of child support has a positive impact on remarriage suggests that government should help divorced mothers, especially those with economic motivation to remarry, by granting them higher child support awards and enforcing child support collection. Second, the finding that an increase in the amount of child support delays women's remarriage decision but allows them to remarry better husbands implies that the increase could reduce the chance of another marriage disruption in the future. Third, the finding that regularity of child support is the negative factor in decisions to remarry implies that enforcing the immediate withholding component of child support would decrease the remarriage of divorced mothers by strengthening their economic security for the future.

Child support does not impose remarriage over remaining single, for example. However, it certainly helps divorced mothers to avoid a potentially undesirable lifestyle, whether involving remarrying or staying single, in which they must depend on someone else substantially. The direction of public policy should be toward helping to ensure the adequacy of child support payments to these women, thereby protecting and enlarging their options for living.

Notes

1. Well-being within marriage is assumed to be approximated by the sum of an expected stream of real income or commodities produced by households such as "the quality of meals, the quality and quantity of children, prestige, recreation, companionship, love, and health status" (Becker 1973: 816). According to Becker, gains from marriage depend on each person's having something different to trade. For example, a woman's comparative advantage in home production typically leads her to specialize in that domain, whereas the man specializes in employment in the market.

2. The terms *income effect* and, in the text upcoming, *independence effect* were first applied to the marriage market by Hannan, Tuma, and Groeneveld (1978).

3. Beller and Graham (1985) did include a variable of women's wealth at divorce, which was shown to be insignificant.

4. See chapter 1, for further description of these datasets.

5. Parent Survey was sampled from the Court Records selecting a sample of people who had their first child support award orders during the period from January 1984 to June 1986. The survey collected basic individual characteristics and retrospective marital histories using telephone interview conducted in 1987 and early 1988. In addition to information on marital history, characteristics of current husbands (for those who remarried) are also available in this dataset.

6. If the amount of child support received each month, for example, were used to determine its effects on remarriage that same month, then the assumption is that the extra income affects remarriage of the same month. It is known that this is not true, however. If information were available on the behavior of remarriage—such as the number of marriage offers the mother received and the times that she rejected or accepted the offers, then determining a child support value would be less difficult.

7. The Bumpass et al. (1989) study was based on marital histories from the June 1980 and June 1985 Current Population Surveys. Their sample included separated cases as well as divorced cases. Since the age of their sample was at the time of separation rather than of divorce, their sample was slightly younger than mine. They reported that more than half of marital disruptions occurred before age 30, about a third before age 25, and about 15 percent to women over the age of 40.

8. Bumpass et al. (1989) indicated an even higher marital disruption rate of young marriages. Almost half of the marriage disruptions were to teenage marriages, and one-sixth were to women under age 18 in a first marriage.

9. The 2 percent figure is estimated based on the pooled dataset, which has 7,040 person periods. The actual remarriage percentage using the dataset is 2.8 percent (198/7,040 × 100).

10. Another explanation for the contrasting result relates to unobserved heterogeneity in this remarriage propensity. Important sources of variation in the propensity to remarry are already controlled for in the model by variables such as income and other personal and family variables. Nevertheless, a cautious interpretation of this phenomenon is that it is partly attributable to some unobserved heterogeneity among single mothers, such as physical attractiveness or personality differences.

11. Hectman's selection model was tried, but data in this study were not suited to the model.

12. Control variables in table 13.4 are the same as those in table 13.2, except that FATHER ENDED 1ST MARRIAGE, DIVORCE PROCESS, and URBAN COUNTY are excluded because they are not only statistically insignificant but also reduce the fit of the model. Instead, DIVORCE TIME measured by total months between the divorce month and January 1984 is entered in the equations.

13. I tested child support—on welfare, including a dummy variable, and its regularity as well. Adding these two variables, which were not statistically significant, however, neither changed overall estimates, nor did they help to increase the explanatory power of the model.

14. Bergmann and Roberts (1987) argued that replacing welfare with child support will act as an incentive for the single mother to work, and that improving child support awards and strict administration would cut poverty incidence by one-fourth. However, Burtless (1987) contends that Bergmann and Roberts made critical errors by excluding a large proportion of working single mothers from their sample and by estimating

earnings function rather than a wage rate equation. Graham and Beller (1989) estimated that, holding AFDC participation constant, a $1,000 increase in child support income per year reduces work by just two hours per year, whereas other nonwage income reduces work by 48 hours per year.

References

Becker, Gary S. 1973. "A Theory of Marriage: Part I." *Journal of Political Economy* 81(4):813–46.

————. 1974. "A Theory of Marriage: Part II." *Journal of Political Economy* 82(2):s11–s33.

————. 1981. *A Treatise on the Family.* Cambridge: Harvard University Press.

Becker, Gary S., Elizabeth M. Landes, and Robert T. Michael. 1977. "An Economic Analysis of Marital Instability." *Journal of Political Economy* 85(6):1141–87.

Beller, Andrea H., and John W. Graham. 1985. "Variations in the Economic Well-Being of Divorced Women and Their Children: The Role of Child Support Income." In *Horizontal Equity, Uncertainty, and Economic Well-Being.* Martin David and Timothy Smeeding, eds., National Bureau of Economic Research, The Univeristy of Chicago Press: 471–509.

Bergmann, Barbara R., and Mark D. Roberts. 1987. "Income for the Single Parent: Child Support, Work, and Welfare." In *Gender in the Work Place.* Clair Brown and Joseph A., eds. The Brookings Institution: 247–63.

Bumpass, Larry, James Sweet, and Teresa Castro-Martin. 1989. *"Changing Patterns of Remarriage."* Working Paper 89-02, Center for Demography and Ecology, University of Wisconsin, Madison.

Burtless, Gary. 1987. "Comments by Gary Burtless." In *Gender in the Work Place.* Clair Brown and Joseph A., eds. The Brookings Institution: 263–7.

Corcoran, M., G. Duncan, G. Gurin, and P. Gurin. 1985. "Myth and Reality: The Causes and Persistence of Poverty." *Journal of Policy Analysis and Management* 4(4):516–536.

Ellwood, David, and Mary J. Bane. 1984. "The Impact of AFDC on Family Structure and Living Arrangements." *Research in Labor Economics* 7:137–207.

Graham, John W., and Andrea H. Beller. 1989. "The Effect of Child Support Payments on the Labor Supply of Female Family Heads; An Econometric Analysis." *The Journal of Human Resources* 24(4):664–687.

Hannan, Michael T., Nancy B. Tuman, and Lyle P. Groeneveld. 1978. "Income and Independence Effects on Marital Dissolution: Results from the Seattle and Denver Income Maintenance Experiments." *American Journal of Sociology* 84(3):611–633.

Hoffman, Saul D., and Greg J. Duncan. 1988. "A Comparison of Choice-Based Multinomial and Nested Logit Models—The Family Structure and Welfare Use Decisions of Divorced or Separated Women." *Journal of Human Resources* 23(4):550–562.

Hutchens, Robert M. 1979. "Welfare, Remarriage, and Marital Search." *The American Economic Review* 69(3):369–379.

Murray, Charles. 1984. *Losing Ground: American Social Policy 1950–1980*. New York: Basic Books.

Lam, David. 1988. "Marriage Markets and Assortative Mating with Household Public Goods: Theoretical Results and Empirical Implications." *The Journal of Human Resources* 23(4):462–497.

Oppenheimer, Valerie Kincade. 1988. "A Theory of Marriage Timing." *American Journal of Sociology* 94(3):563–591.

Chapter Fourteen

PUBLIC OPINION ABOUT A CHILD SUPPORT ASSURANCE SYSTEM

Thomas Corbett, Irwin Garfinkel, and Nora Cate Schaeffer

Since the 1980s, the U.S. child support system has come under increasing attack, on the grounds that it condones (and therefore fosters) parental irresponsibility, that it is inequitable and therefore exacerbates tensions among former spouses, and that it impoverishes children.

In 1983, some 8.7 million women were living with children whose legally liable fathers were absent from the household, while only about 4 million had child support awards during that calendar year.[1] Of those, half received the entire award, another quarter received partial payments, and one out of four received no support at all. Consequently, only one-third of eligible households obtained any child support, while less than one out of four received the full amount awarded. It is estimated that in recent years about $4 billion has gone unpaid annually.

When awards are made, they are likely to be insufficient. In 1983, the average monthly child support obligation amounted to slightly more than $200 per month. Real child support transfers (1983 dollars) actually declined by almost 15 percent between 1978 and 1983. Support payments accounted for an estimated 13 percent of the absent parents' income, a proportion substantially below what the sharing rate would be in intact households.

Failures in the child support system have serious economic consequences for female-headed households.[2] The proportion of female-headed families classified as poor ranges from 25 to 40 percent, depending on how in-kind government transfers are counted; individuals in such families account for more than half the poor (Danziger, Haveman, and Plotnick 1986: 56). Their vulnerability to poverty is not surprising. In 1984, the mean income for two-parent families was $34,379, whereas the comparable figure for female-headed households was $13,257. Two-parent families with children experienced real income growth of some 14 percent between 1967 and 1984, as opposed to a 6.5 percent decline for their single-parent counterparts (Danziger and Gottschalk 1986: 6). Between 1970 and 1984, the real value of the Aid to Families with Dependent Children (AFDC) program benefits to female-headed households with children declined by 33 percent (U.S. Congress 1984: 305–8).

Public support is a significant part of the child support system. Public transfers to poor families with children eligible for child support substantially exceed private child support transfers to all children. Whereas about $7 billion in private child support was paid in 1983, federal AFDC expenditures on families eligible for child support equaled about $8 billion in 1985. If the costs for Medicaid and food stamps are included, public transfers equaled nearly $21 billion, or three times private child support transfers.

The AFDC program was established in 1935 for purposes quite different from those it now serves. It was intended to provide support for the families of deceased fathers in a society that considered it undesirable for mothers with children to work. Today, the program is primarily for children who have a living, absent parent legally liable for their support and a custodial parent who increasingly is expected to work.

The structure of this system encourages dependency. Because AFDC, like any welfare program, is designed to aid only the poor, benefits are reduced when earnings increase. After four months on a job, a woman on AFDC faces a benefit reduction of one dollar for every dollar of net earnings. This is equivalent to a 100 percent tax on earnings. It is not surprising, therefore, that the majority of mothers on welfare do not work during the months they receive benefits. And yet, even if they were fully employed, one-half of welfare recipients could earn no more than the amount of their welfare grant, whereas the earnings of another quarter of recipients would exceed their grant by $1,000 or less (Sawhill 1976: 201–11). If they received child support from the children's noncustodial father, some, but not all, of these families would attain an income above the poverty level. Clearly, the only way to alleviate this kind of poverty without creating total dependency is to supplement rather than replace the earnings of these custodial mothers.

Finally, the number of female-headed families with children is growing. In 1983 about one out of five households was headed by a woman with children under age 18,[3] more than twice the 1987 rate.[4] According to Senator Daniel Patrick Moynihan, more than half of all children born in the 1980s will spend some portion of their minority years in single-parent households.[5]

WISCONSIN CHILD SUPPORT ASSURANCE SYSTEM

Previous chapters in this volume have described in detail the state of Wisconsin's effort to develop an alternative child support system and the outgrowth of this endeavor, the child support assurance system (CSAS). The three main provisions of the CSAS—the Percentage of Income and Asset Standard (PIAS) for establishing child support obligations, routine income withholding of child payments, and a socially assured child support level—have also been examined in depth.

Although justifiable on programmatic grounds, each of the provisions of the CSAS has controversial aspects. The percentage of income and asset standard has been criticized for not taking into account the following: (1) unusual debts encumbering the obligor; (2) remarriage and start of a new family by the noncustodial parent; and (3) the income or remarriage of the custodial parent. It has also been criticized for being inflexible, eroding judicial discretion, and diminishing the ability of parents to negotiate a child support arrangement that is uniquely tailored to their circumstances. Furthermore, this provision calls for administrative rather than legal procedures to be used to modify support obligations. If the obligation is expressed as a percentage of income, it changes automatically as the obligor's income changes. Some argue that all changes in support orders should be based on a judicial review of relevant factors.

The immediate income-withholding provision has evoked both positive and negative reactions. Many believe that it is the most efficient mechanism for collecting support obligations: it avoids the necessity of making sensitive decisions regarding when to impose such an order—an action traditionally represented as a penalty for noncompliance—and minimizes the accumulation of unpaid support with all the legal and economic complexities that result. Others construe withholding as an unnecessary intrusion of government into a private transaction, a variant of the "big government" argument. Opponents also believe that withholding penalizes obligors who intend to meet their obligations, and that it eliminates the personal touch associated with paying child support. Finally, it has been argued that employment-related problems will ensue, either because employers will object to the costs associated with administering the wage assignment or because employees will experience embarrassment vis-à-vis their employer.

Since the assured child support level has had the least public exposure, little is known about possible public reaction to this provision. Several possible objections can be identified. First, publicly guaranteed child support may be seen as an unwarranted extension of government responsibility by those who view child support—unless welfare is involved—as essentially a private transaction. Second, there may be concerns about potential costs, particularly with respect to how large an increase (if any) the public would accept. And third, some may view the assured benefit as an extension of welfare under a different name.

The Wisconsin child support assurance system is of national interest. Federal child support legislation passed unanimously by Congress in 1984, the Child Support Enforcement Amendments, moved the nation substantially in the direction of a child support assurance system by requiring all states to adopt nonbinding child support guidelines and income-withholding laws in response to a 30-day delinquency. In addition, the 1984 law allows Wisconsin to use federal funds, which would otherwise have gone to AFDC, to help fund an assured benefit. Subsequently, the Family Support Act of 1988 required states to make their guidelines binding and to adopt immediate income-withholding laws.

This chapter focuses on pubic opinion with regard to the three main provisions of a CSAS: (1) the factors that should determine the size of child support payments and the appropriateness of the percentages used in the PIAS; (2) the use of immediate income-withholding to collect obligations; and (3) the introduction of the assured child support guarantee.

DATA AND METHODS

In the spring of 1985, researchers at the Institute for Research on Poverty, University of Wisconsin, Madison, conducted a telephone survey of Wisconsin households. Known as the Children's Income and Program Participation Survey (CHIPPS), the interview incorporated a number of questions about the state's child support program, including questions designed to tap public perceptions regarding key provisions of the reform. The survey used a random digit dialing design to sample 1,073 households.[6] When there was a custodial or noncustodial parent in the household, that parent was selected as the respondent; otherwise, one of the principal earners in the household was selected. The average household income of those answering the vignettes was $27,970, their average age was 44 years, 67 percent were female, and 45 percent had more than a high school education.

For each of the three child support issues examined, a vignette was written and a set of factorial objects was generated. The factorial survey approach used in CHIPPS provides a technique for exploring the structure of complex judgments such as those concerning child support.[7] The method works as follows:

Step 1. Identify the dimensions thought most important in influencing the judgment process being studied. Specify the range of values that each of these variables can take. This step draws on knowledge of the substantive area and on awareness of the information that might cause respondents to change their judgment.

Step 2. Write a short story, or vignette, that can be used to present values of these dimensions and to elicit judgments. The vignette is built around the set of dimensions identified in step 1, and is completed by assigning a value to each dimension. Several completed vignettes can be presented to each respondent.

Step 3. Each case in the analysis is a completed vignette and the judgment elicited by the vignette. The way the dimensions affect judgments is examined by estimating a regression equation in which the judgment is the dependent variable and the dimensions in the vignette are independent variables.

Because values for dimensions are generated randomly with equal probabilities, the dimensions are uncorrelated except for random error. Furthermore, because objects are generated in random order, they are randomly assigned to respondents, and the dimensions are thus uncorrelated with respondent characteristics except for random error.

CHIPPS used the factorial survey technique for three issues related to the child support assurance system, making it possible to describe the way in which judgments about child support obligations, approval of universal withholding, and the approval of the assured benefit are affected by dimensions that operationalize situational variables. Two or three completed vignettes for each issue were randomly assigned to each respondent. In addition to the vignette questions, CHIPPS included force-choice questions about the conditions under which child support obligations should be modified.

Vignettes and Questions on Child Support Obligations

The vignettes used to obtain judgments about child support obligations included the following five dimensions or variables: income and remarriage of the noncustodial father, number of children owed support, and income and remarriage of the custodial mother.[8] In the text of the following vignette, a phrase in italics indicates that the phrase is the value of a dimension (values for the dimensions used in the vignettes are listed in table 14.1).

> Frequently when a father does not live with his children and their mother, he makes regular payments to their mother for support of the children. I am going to describe some situations to you in which children live with their mother and the father lives apart from them. For each situation, I will ask you how much money, if any, you think the father "should" contribute each month for the support of his children. Here is the first [next] situation: A father *who has not remarried* has *two young children who live with their mother*. The mother *has remarried* and *makes $500 a month after taxes*. The father makes *$2,000 a month after taxes*. How much, if anything, should the father contribute each month for the support of his children in this situation?

Each respondent was presented with three vignettes. The items are time-consuming to administer over the telephone and may be confusing or fatiguing for respondents. For these reasons, the language of the vignette and the selection of variables entailed simplifying assumptions, which may restrict the generalizability of the results. For example, the vignettes describe only the most common situation, in which the mother is the custodial parent and the father is the noncustodial parent. Judgments for the reverse situation may differ considerably from judgments given in this study.

Forced-choice questions were asked about conditions under which the respondent would favor automatic adjustments for child support obligations (values for the dimensions used in the vignette are listed in table 14.2).

> I am going to mention some ways in which the situation of the family might change. I will then ask whether or not you think the amount of the father's child support payment should be adjusted automatically for that kind of change. First, when the cost of living changes, do you think the amount a father contributes to support his children should be automatically adjusted for this or not? When the father's income changes, do you think the amount a father contributes to support his children should be automatically adjusted for this or not? If the father remarries and starts a new family, do you think the amount a father contributes to support his children should be automatically adjusted for this or not?

Finally, respondents were also asked the following forced-choice question:

Table 14.1 APPROPRIATE PATERNAL CHILD SUPPORT OBLIGATIONS: CHIPPS
SURVEY

| Dimensions and Values[a] | Percentage of Father's Income That Should Be Paid in Child Support (Original Response) | | | |
| | Given in Dollars[b] | | Given in Percentages | |
	Coefficient	SE[c]	Coefficient	SE[c]
Constant (%)	21.43	—	24.65	—
Father remarried:				
No	—	—	—	—
Yes	−1.75[d]	.63	−3.10	1.67
Mother remarried:				
No	—	—	—	—
Yes	−4.47[d]	.63	−6.72[d]	1.68
Number of children:				
One	—	—	—	—
Two	4.78[d]	.76	1.93	2.12
Three	6.81[d]	.77	5.71[d]	2.02
Mother's monthly income:				
$0	—	—	—	—
$500	−1.25	.77	1.60	2.05
$1,500	−6.22[d]	.78	−1.71	2.05
Father's monthly income:				
$500	—	—	—	—
$1,000	1.79	1.02	6.40[d]	2.62
$2,000	.47	.99	10.21[d]	2.63
$3,000	−1.15	.98	9.67[d]	2.66
$5,000	−3.21[d]	1.00	12.32[d]	2.59
R^2	.10		.12	
Number of vignettes	2,199		457	

[a]Reference category for each set of dummy variables is shown first.
[b]Transformed into percentages for the analysis. This permits a direct comparison with the Wisconsin Percentage of Income and Asset Standard.
[c]SE, standard error.
[d]Coefficient is at least twice its standard error.

Do you think that the amount that the father contributes in child support should depend on how much money the mother makes or should not depend on how much money the mother makes?

Vignettes on Immediate Income Withholding

The vignettes used to obtain judgments about universal withholding included three dimensions: the proportion of obligors who fail to pay support, percentage improvements in support collections, and per-

Table 14.2 PERCENTAGE FAVORING AUTOMATIC ADJUSTMENT OF PATERNAL
CHILD SUPPORT OBLIGATIONS IN RESPONSE TO CHANGES IN COST
OF LIVING, INCOME, AND MARITAL STATUS: CHIPPS SURVEY

Situational Characteristics	Percentage	N
Change in:		
Cost of living	74.3	947
Noncustodial father's income	73.6	949
Father remarries and starts a new family	36.5	941
Custodial mother's income	74.5	962

Notes: The first three items asked whether or not paternal child support obligations should be changed when each of the three types of changes occurred. The fourth item asked whether or not paternal child support obligations should depend on the mother's income.

centage reductions in welfare costs. Each respondent was presented with two completed vignettes to judge. The exact wording of an illustrative vignette is given below. The percentages are in italics to indicate that they are the values assigned to a dimension (values for the dimensions included in the vignette are listed in table 14.3).

> Now we want your opinion about how the government should collect child support payments. A 1984 federal law requires all states to withhold child support payments from the paycheck of any parent who owes child support and misses payments for one month. The court then gives these payments to the parent who takes care of the children. Some people have proposed that the state withhold child support payments for all parents who owe child support, not just for parents who miss making payments. Please tell me how strongly you would favor or oppose withholding from all parents who owe support if the following were true. First, with the new federal law *20 percent* of all parents who owe child support miss their payments and therefore would be subject to withholding under either system. Second, withholding from all parents who owed child support would collect an additional *30 percent* of child support payments that are owed. Third, withholding from all parents who owed child support reduced welfare costs by *20 percent*. In this case, would you favor or oppose withholding from all parents who owe support? On a scale of 1 to 5, where 5 means strongly (favor/oppose) and 1 means weakly (favor/oppose), how strongly do you (favor/oppose) withholding from all parents who owe support?

Vignettes on the Assured Benefit

The vignettes used to obtain judgments about the assured benefit included two dimensions: changes in program costs and reductions in welfare use. The exact wording of the question is as follows, except that percentages in italics were varied. Each respondent was presented

Table 14.3 JUDGMENTS ABOUT IMMEDIATE INCOME WITHHOLDING AS
FUNCTION OF MISSED PAYMENTS, ADDITIONAL SUPPORT
COLLECTED, AND REDUCTION IN WELFARE COSTS: CHIPPS SURVEY

Dimensions and Values	Coefficient	SE[a]
Constant	6.33	.23
Percentage who miss payments:		
20	—	—
50	.05	.19
80	.54[b]	.19
Amount of additional child support collected:		
None	—	—
15 percent	.12	.26
30 percent	.18	.26
Reduction in welfare costs:		
None	—	—
10 percent	.70[b]	.20
20 percent	1.03[b]	.20
R^2	.03	
Number of vignettes	1,801	

[a]SE, standard error.
[b]Coefficient is at least twice its standard error.

with two vignettes, each with alternative percentages, to judge (values
for these dimensions are listed in table 14.4).

> Last, we need to know whether you favor or oppose a new program.
> Some people have proposed a new child support program to pay at
> least some support to all children legally entitled to child support. Un-
> der this new program each child would receive either the amount that
> the parent actually pays in child support or a benefit set by the state,
> whichever amount is larger. With this new program, all legally entitled
> children would receive a minimum level of financial support. I am
> going to describe some effects this new program might have and ask
> your opinion. First, if the new program plus welfare costs *20 percent
> less* than welfare does now, and if the program reduces the number of
> people who are dependent on welfare by *10 percent*, would you favor or
> oppose using state funds for this program? On a scale of 1 to 5, where
> 5 means strongly (favor/oppose) and 1 means weakly (favor/oppose),
> how strongly do you (favor/oppose) such a program?

RESULTS

The results indicated public perceptions relevant to each of the three
major components of the Wisconsin child support assurance system.
First, in examining judgments about awards, a central issue is whether

Table 14.4 JUDGMENTS ABOUT ASSURED CHILD SUPPORT BENEFIT AS
FUNCTION OF COSTS AND WELFARE CASELOADS: CHIPPS SURVEY

Dimensions and Values	Coefficient		SE[a]
Constant	6.78		.16
Cost of benefit plus welfare:			
20 percent above welfare alone	—		—
Same as welfare alone	1.03[b]		.18
20 percent below welfare alone	1.36[b]		.18
Reduction in number on welfare:			
10 percent	—		—
30 percent	.46[b]		.17
50 percent	.68[b]		.18
R^2		.04	
Number of vignettes		1,787	

[a]SE, standard error.
[b]Coefficient is at least twice its standard error.

the obligations suggested by the public as being fair approximate the awards that would be set under the percentage of income and asset standard. Judgments regarding the conditions under which support obligations should automatically be adjusted are also examined. The income-sharing concept underlying the reform is compatible with automatic adjustments, in that automatic adjustments assure that children share in both the increases and decreases in their noncustodial father's fortunes. Second, public opinion about the use of immediate income withholding as a means for collecting support obligations is analyzed. Of primary interest is whether public support is affected by various alternative effects on program outcomes and welfare caseloads. Third, public perceptions regarding implementing a publicly financed assured child support benefit are investigated. Since this provision contains possible cost implications, opinions were obtained under varying assumptions about the costs and effects of this provision.[9]

Perceptions Regarding Appropriate Child Support Obligations

The first analysis addresses how well awards suggested by citizens conformed to the levels established under the percentage of income and asset standard. If public opinion and the standard specified similar awards, we would find the following: First, the proportion of the absent parent's income allocated for child support for one child would be roughly 17 percent of gross income. Second, the proportion allocated for additional children would increase at a decreasing rate. Third, the percentage of the father's income awarded would be approximately constant over the different levels of his income. Finally, the proportion allocated for child support would not vary with factors considered irrelevant under the "standard" approach, such as the marital status of either party or income of the custodial parent.

Table 14.1 displays the results of the regression of judgments regarding the father's appropriate child support obligation on five situational dimensions: (1) marital status of the noncustodial father; (2) marital status of the custodial mother; (3) the number of children to be supported; (4) the mother's income; and (5) the father's income. An award suggested by a respondent is expressed as a percentage of the father's income in the vignette that elicited the suggested award. The constant is the predicted judgment of the appropriate child support obligation when neither parent is remarried, one child is involved, the custodial parent has no income, and the absent parent's gross income is $500 per month. Each effect—or dummy variable coefficient—expresses the difference in the predicted child support obligation between the reference category and the category for which the effect is presented. The results are presented in two columns. The first, which represents 83 percent of all responses, includes those who answered the questions about awards in terms of dollar amounts—for example, "I think the award should be $150 per month." For analysis, these answers were transformed into a percentage of the father's income. The second column presents responses originally given in percentage terms—for example, "I think the award should be 17 percent of the noncustodial father's income." Because most people responded in dollars, we give more emphasis to the first column. Because respondents suggested what they thought the father *should* pay, we refer to the suggested award as a "fair" award.[10]

For most cases, the suggested child support obligation was close to what is called for by the Wisconsin Percentage of Income and Asset Standard. The constant term gives what is perceived to be a "fair" obligation for the case in which there is one child, neither parent is remarried, the custodial parent does not work, and the noncustodial parent earns $500 per month. That it equals 21 percent suggests that Wisconsin adults believe that in this case the Percentage of Income and Asset Standard is somewhat low. For this situation, if the father is remarried, the obligation remains over 19 percent; if the mother is remarried, the obligation is almost 17 percent; if the mother earns $1,500 per month, the fair obligation drops to 15 percent. Only if the custodial mother both earns a great deal and is remarried would the child support award established under the Wisconsin standard substantially exceed what Wisconsin citizens deem to be a fair amount.

Public suggestions for child support obligations were fairly consistent with the standard on two other dimensions. First, the predicted obligations increased with each additional child, and at a decreasing rate. The predicted increments for the second and third child, however, were smaller than those in the standard—5 percent and 2 percent compared with 8 percent and 4 percent increases in the standard. Second, the predicted obligations remained constant as a proportion of income across most income levels for the noncustodial parent. Only at $5,000 per month income level did respondents suggest that a statistically significant lower proportion of the father's income be awarded as child support.

The respondents deviated from the premises underlying the standard in two important respects. If the father remarries, respondents suggested a small (less than 2 percent), though statistically significant, reduction in predicted support obligations. Substantively, the reduction is minor and does not appear to violate the assumption that child support is a debt that takes precedence over more recently established obligations. More important, the evidence suggests that respondents would allocate less to support obligations if the mother (custodial parent) were remarried or had at least a moderate level of income ($1,500 per month). Both findings may reflect a public belief that support obligations should be based, in part at least, on the child's financial needs. The better those needs are met by the custodial parent, the smaller would be the obligation imposed upon the absent parent. This would represent a departure from the strict income-sharing concept upon which the standard is based.

The second column of table 14.1 displays the results for the relatively small number of respondents who replied to the vignettes in terms of percentages. In most cases, the direction of the coefficients was the same. The most significant departures were that, compared to those who answer in dollars, those who responded in a percentage metric established higher support obligations and generally allocated a higher proportion of the absent parent's income the more that parent makes.[11]

Table 14.2 presents results from the forced-choice question format that examines factors respondents might feel should be taken into account when modifying support orders. There was considerable support for automatically modifying support obligations in response both to changes in the cost of living and to changes in a noncustodial father's income. Approximately three out of four respondents indicated support for automatic modifications of orders under these circumstances. On the other hand, there was much less support—only slightly more than one out of three—for automatically modifying orders (presumably downward) when the noncustodial parent remarries and starts a new family. The relatively small portion that favored automatic adjustment if the noncustodial father remarries is consistent with the vignette finding of only a very small—albeit statistically significant—adjustment regarding the appropriate support obligation in the event of remarriage.

These results conform, for the most part, to the premises underlying the proposed reform. The strong support for modifications when the noncustodial father's income changes and the much weaker support when that parent starts a new family are consistent with the reform. The former is clearly consistent with the income-sharing concept and the latter may be consistent with the concept, suggesting that respondents accept the notion that financial obligations to children from prior relationships take priority over new responsibilities.

Whether support for automatically modifying obligations in light of changes in the cost of living is consistent with the standard is open to interpretation. Unfortunately, the survey did not ask whether respondents would prefer that awards be indexed to cost-of-living changes or to changes in noncustodial income. What is clear is the high level of support for automatic adjustment based on one index or the other.

Finally, the strong support for basing support obligations upon the custodial mother's income is consistent with the vignette findings and suggests a serious difference between what most respondents believe is fair and the Wisconsin standard. This latter finding suggests that a sense of absolute need is operating here. Respondents may feel that meeting the financial needs of the child(ren) is the paramount concern, irrespective of which parent makes that contribution.

Perceptions of Immediate Income Withholding

Judgments about universal withholding involve balancing beliefs about the economic costs and benefits to be derived from enforced support collections against beliefs about individual privacy and the role of government. Therefore, support for this provision was expected to be conditional. It would depend, in part, on how many noncustodial parents missed payments in the absence of immediate income withholding; upon how effective withholding would be in collecting support obligations; and upon the effect of such increased collections on reducing welfare expenditures. In general, support for this provision of the reform was expected to be higher as the estimated proportion of parents who missed support payments increased. Similarly, more support was anticipated when the estimated effectiveness of this provision in both collecting support and reducing welfare increased.

Table 14.3 displays the regression of support ratings on (1) the percentage of parents missing payments; (2) the amount of additional child support collected; and (3) the consequent reduction in welfare expenditures. The responses were recoded on a 10-point scale in which 1 = strongly oppose, 5 = weakly oppose, 6 = weakly favor, and 10 = strongly favor. The constant is 6.33 when no additional support is collected, there is no reduction in welfare costs, and only 20 percent of absent parents miss their support payments. This suggests modest support for universal withholding even under the most conservative set of hypothetical circumstances. Apparently, concerns about individual privacy and government intrusion do not offset the perception of income withholding as a desirable public policy.

Not surprisingly, the degree of support increased as the relative costs and benefits of withholding were modified to make the provision more attractive. Support for immediate withholding increased marginally, though significantly, when 80 percent of absent parents missed payments. (Based on a sample of court records in 20 Wisconsin counties, nearly 70 percent of obligors were at least two months delinquent in paying support within three years of the support order.) Reductions in welfare expenditures had a stronger effect. Reducing welfare expenditures by 10 percent significantly increased the magnitude of support; a reduction of 20 percent increased the degree of support by 16 percent. The one surprising finding was that there was no significant change in the degree of support for withholding when the amount of support collected was varied, though the coefficients were in the expected direction. Respondents appeared to be most sensitive to the effect that withholding might have on them personally as taxpayers.

Perceptions of the Assured Benefit

Whether or not respondents favored a publicly financed assured benefit is likely to depend upon the benefit's cost relative to current welfare expenditures and upon its success in reducing welfare dependency. These expectations were incorporated into two vignette dimensions: (1) program costs relative to current welfare expenditures and (2) program effects on welfare utilization. It was expected that support for this provision of the reform would increase as the cost relative to current welfare expenditures decreased and as the number of people on welfare declined.

Table 14.4 displays the regression of support ratings on the dimensions. Again, the dependent variable is scaled from 1 (strongly oppose) to 10 (strongly favor). If welfare plus a publicly guaranteed child support payment would cost 20 percent more than the current welfare system and would reduce welfare dependency only 10 percent, the constant of nearly 7 indicates surprisingly strong support for this provision of the reform. Support significantly increased if total costs do not increase or if they decrease. Reductions in welfare dependency also increased support, but the effects were smaller than the effects of reductions in costs. If welfare dependency were halved and costs reduced by 20 percent, the estimated level of support for the guaranteed benefit would be 8.82 out of a possible 10.

Finally, the very low R^2 in both the immediate withholding and the assured benefit regressions—.035 and .04, respectively—indicates that the proportion of variance explained by the independent variables is quite low. This could be because support for or opposition to immediate withholding and the assured benefit is determined primarily by political beliefs or attitudes not measured in the survey. On the other hand, it is possible that many respondents found the vignettes too confusing to respond meaningfully. If the low R^2 is attributable to missing variables, it is not problematic. That is, it does not provide grounds for placing less confidence in our results. If the low R^2 reflects a confusing stimulus, however, it would be grounds for placing less confidence in our results. Unfortunately, with these data we cannot distinguish between these two possibilities. Future research should: (1) seek to improve on the vignettes, (2) include some attitudinal variables, and (3) include direct forced-choice questions about support or opposition to immediate withholding and the assured benefit.

SUMMARY

To enhance the role of child support in reducing welfare dependency and to improve the economic well-being of children not living with both liable parents, the state of Wisconsin has begun implementing a new child support assurance system. Central to the reform are three provisions: (1) to establish support obligations equal to a proportion of the obligor's gross income; (2) to withhold automatically support obligations from earnings and other forms of income in all applicable cases; and (3) to guarantee that all participating children receive no less than a socially assured child support benefit.

Public support for these provisions was examined using responses of a sample of Wisconsin citizens to a series of vignettes. Answers to these vignettes suggest that the public would generally agree to support obligations set in conformance with the PIAS approach. On average, respondents suggested awards somewhat higher than directed by the formula currently used in Wisconsin, except when the custodial mother both has substantial earnings and has remarried. Respondents also supported the provision allowing awards to automatically vary with changes in the obligor's income, and most rejected the notion of reducing awards when the obligor assumes new family obligations. In contrast to the Wisconsin standard, however, respondents considered the economic situation of the custodial parent. Finally, we found moderate public support for immediate income withholding and substantial public support for the guaranteed child support payment provisions of the reform. Although such support for these provisions was forthcoming under the most conservative set of contextual circumstances, it increased significantly when considered in terms of either reduced public assistance expenditures or caseloads.

Notes

This paper first appeared in *Social Service Review* (December 1988: 632–48). Copyright 1988 by the University of Chicago. Reprinted by permission.

1. Data presented in this and the paragraph following are found in U.S. Bureau of the Census (1986).

2. Approximately 90 percent of custodial parents are female.

3. For a detailed discussion of female-headed families, see Garfinkel and McLanahan (1986).

4. Also see Moynihan (1985).

5. Ibid., 47.

6. An oversample of custodial and noncustodial parents is excluded from the analyses presented here. Details of the sample are given in MacDonald (1986).

7. For a fuller discussion of this technique, see Rossi and Noch (1982).

8. A sixth dimension varied whether the incomes listed in the vignette were specified as "before tax" or "after tax" income. Preliminary analysis indicated that there is no significant difference between gross and net income. Therefore, that dimension was dropped for this analysis.

9. The number of respondents is almost exactly one-third (for vignettes about suggested awards), or one-half (for immediate income withholding and the assured benefit), the number of vignettes. Inflating the standard error (SE) or the t-value required to reject the null hypothesis is an equivalent way of adjusting for this clustering of vignettes within respondents, but the latter is simpler. Multiplying 1.96 by .5 gives 3.39, and by

2.5 gives 2.79, but using these inflated *t*-values overcorrects for clustering. The tables indicate coefficients that are more than twice their SEs; using even these conservative inflated *t*-values would have had little impact on the discussion. Four of the coefficients in table 14.1 have *t*-values less than 3.39, but those *t*-values are all 2.4 or greater. In tables 14.2 and 14.3, only one coefficient has a *t*-value below 2.79; its *t*-value is 2.71.

10. This does not suggest that the suggested award is the *only* award that a respondent would consider fair.

11. A pooled model was estimated that tested whether the coefficients were significantly different for those answering in dollars and those answering in percentages. All coefficients for father's income and the coefficient for mother's income of $1,500 per month were significantly different ($p < .01$).

References

Danziger, Sheldon H., and Peter Gottschalk. 1986. "How Have Families with Children Been Faring?" Institute for Research on Poverty Discussion Paper 801-86. Madison: University of Wisconsin–Madison, Institute for Research on Poverty.

Danziger, Sheldon H., Robert Haveman, and Robert Plotnick. 1986. "Antipoverty Policy: Effects on the Poor and the Nonpoor." In *Fighting Poverty: What Works and What Doesn't*, edited by Sheldon H. Danziger and Daniel H. Weinberg. Cambridge, Mass.: Harvard University Press.

Garfinkel, Irwin, and Sara S. McLanahan. 1986. *Single Mothers and Their Children: A New American Dilemma.* Washington, D.C.: Urban Institute.

MacDonald, Maurice. 1986. "Objectives, Procedures, and Sampling Results for CHIPPS: The 1985 Wisconsin Survey of Children, Incomes, and Program Participation." University of Wisconsin–Madison, Institute for Research on Poverty. Photocopy.

Moynihan, Daniel Patrick. 1985. *Family and Nation.* San Diego: Harcourt Brace Jovanovich.

Rossi, Peter H., and Steven L. Noch, eds. 1982. *Measuring Social Judgments: The Factorial Survey Approach.* Beverly Hills, Calif.: Sage Publications.

Sawhill, Isabel V. 1976. "Discrimination and Poverty among Women Who Head Families." *Signs* 2: 201–11.

U.S. Bureau of the Census. 1986. *Child Support and Alimony, 1983. Supplementary Report. Current Population Reports,* ser. P-23, no. 148. Washington, D.C.: U.S. Government Printing Office. October.

U.S. Congress. House. Committee on Ways and Means. 1984. *Background Material and Data on Programs within the Jurisdiction of the Committee on Ways and Means* (305–8). Washington, D.C.: U.S. Government Printing Office.

Bartfeld, Judith. 1991. "Parent Survey 2: Field Report," Institute for Research on Poverty. March.

Bartfeld, Judith, and Marygold Melli. 1991. "Use the Percentage Standard to Set Child Support in Wisconsin: Analysis of the Reasons Given by Courts in 20 Counties for Not Using It." Project Working Paper. January.

Betson, D. M. 1991. *Alternative Estimates of the Cost of Children from the 1980–86 Consumer Expenditure Survey.* Institute for Research on Poverty Special Report 51.

Brown, Pat. 1991. "Health Insurance Coverage for Children in Divorce and Paternity Cases in the State of Wisconsin." Project Working Paper. September.

Brown, Pat, and R. A. Monson. 1991. "Paternity Establishment in AFDC Cases: Three Wisconsin Counties." Project Working Paper. January.

Cassetty, Judith. 1978. *Child Support and Public Policy: Securing Support from Absent Fathers.* Lexington, Mass.: D.C. Heath and Company.

Cassetty, Judith. 1983. *The Parental Child Support Obligation.* Lexington, Mass.: Lexington Books.

Child Support Evaluation Team. 1988. "Cross Tabulations from the Child Support Parent Survey." Project Working Paper. October.

Corbett, Thomas. 1986a. "An Introduction to CHIPPS: The 1985 Wisconsin Survey of Children, Income, and Program Participation." Project Working Paper. February.

———. 1986b. "Child Support Assurance: Wisconsin Demonstration." *Focus* (Spring).

———. 1988. "Social Policy: Essays on the Difference between Expectation and Actuality." Unpublished dissertation, University of Wisconsin-Madison.

Corbett, Thomas, and Pat Brown. 1990. "A Preliminary Assessment of the Order Revision Pilot Project." Project Working Paper. October.

Corbett, Thomas, and Sandra Danziger. 1985. *The Child Support Assurance Program in Milwaukee County: Prospects for Implementation.* Report to Wisconsin Department of Health and Social Services. Institute for Research on Poverty. Summer.

Corbett, Thomas, and Ann Lewis. 1987. *An Evaluation of the Use of Immediate Income Witholding to Collect Child Support Obligations in Milwaukee County*. Report to the Wisconsin Department of Health and Social Services. Spring.

Corbett, Thomas, Pat Brown, and Kate Kost. 1991. "An Evaluation of the Order Revision Pilot Project." Project Working Paper. October.

Corbett, Thomas, Irwin Garfinkel, and Nora Cate Schaeffer. 1988. "Public Opinion about a Child Support Assurance System." *Social Service Review* 62(4):632–48.

Corbett, Thomas, Irwin Garfinkel, A. Skyles, and E. Uhr. 1986. "Assuring Child Support in Wisconsin." *Public Welfare* 44 (1, Winter):33–39.

Danziger, Sandra, and Ann Nichols-Casebolt. 1987/1988. "Teen Parents and Child Support: Eligibility, Participation, and Payment." *Journal of Social Service Research*.

————. Forthcoming. "Child Support for Children Born Outside of Marriage: An Analysis of Paternity Cases." Project Working Paper.

del Boca, D. 1986. "Children as Public Goods: An Economic Approach to Child Support Payments in Relation to Custody Decisions." Institute for Research on Poverty Discussion Paper 820-86.

Douthitt, Robin. 1988. "An Evaluation of Vertical Equity in Wisconsin's Percentage-of-Income Standard for Child Support." Institute for Research on Poverty Special Report 47. May.

————. 1990. "An Evaluation of the Relationship between the Percentage-of-Income Standard and Family Expenditures for Children." Institute for Research on Poverty Discussion Paper 921-90.

Garfinkel, Irwin. 1983. "The Role of Universal Demogrants and Child Support in Social Security Reform: An Essay in Honor of George F. Rohrlich." Festschrift in Honour of Dr. Rohrlich. *International Journal of Social Economics* 10 (6/7).

————. 1984. "Child Support: An Addition to the Social Security Menu." Working Paper 133, Mikroanalytische Grundlagen der Gesellschaftspolitik. Frankfurt and Mannheim: J. W. Goethe-Universität Frankfurt and Universität Mannheim. January.

————. 1986a. "Child Support." In *Encyclopedia of Social Work*, 18th ed. National Association of Social Work.

————. 1986b. "Utilization and Effects of Immediate Income Withholding and the Percentage-of-Income Standard: An Interim Report on the Child Support Assurance Demonstration." Institute for Research on Poverty Special Report 42.

————. 1988. "Child Support Assurance: A New Tool for Achieving Social Security." In *Child Support: From Debt Collection to Social Policy*, edited by Alfred Kahn and Sheila Kammerman. Beverly Hills, Calif.: Sage Publications.

————. 1990. "A New Child Support Assurance System." Institute for Research on Poverty Discussion Paper 916-90.

Garfinkel, Irwin, and Judi Bartfeld. 1990. "Utilization of the Percentage-of-Income Standard: A Preliminary Report." Project Working Paper. October.

————. 1991. "Utilization and Effects on Payments of Percentage-Expressed Child Support Orders: A Preliminary Report to the Wisconsin Department of Health and Social Services." Institute for Research on Poverty. June.

Garfinkel, Irwin, and Thomas Corbett. 1985. "A Design for an Economic Analysis: The Wisconsin Child Support Demonstration." In *Economic Evaluation of Public Programs: New Direction for Program Evaluation*, edited by James C. Catterall. San Francisco: Jossey Bass. June.

Garfinkel, Irwin, and Marieka Klawitter. 1990. "The Effect of Routine Income Withholding on Child Support Collections." *Journal of Policy Analysis & Management* (April).

Garfinkel, Irwin, and Sara McLanahan. 1986. *Single Mothers and Their Children: A New American Dilemma?* Washington, D.C.: Urban Institute Press.

————. 1987. "The Feminization of Poverty: Nature, Causes, and a Partial Cure." In *Poverty and Social Welfare in the United States*, edited by Donald Tomaskovic-Devey. Boulder, Colo.: Westview Press.

————. 1990. "The Effects of the Child Support Provisions of the Family Support Act of 1988 on Child Well-being." *Population Research and Policy Review* 9(3):205–234, September.

Garfinkel, Irwin, and Marygold Melli, eds. 1982. *Child Support: Weakness of the Old and Features of a Proposed New System*, Vols. I, II, and III. Institute for Research on Poverty Special Report 32A, B, and C.

————. 1987a. "Maintenance through the Tax System: The Proposed Wisconsin Child Support Assurance Program." *Australian Journal of Family Law* (January): 152–68.

————. 1990. "The Use of Normative Standards in Family Law Decisions: Developing Mathematical Standards for Child Support." *Family Law Quarterly* 24(2):157–178, Summer.

Garfinkel, Irwin, and Donald T. Oellerich. 1989. "Noncustodial Father's Ability to Pay Child Support." *Demography* 26(2):219–33, May.

Garfinkel, Irwin, and Q. Sullivan. 1986. "Immediate Income Withholding: A Preliminary Analysis of its Effects on Child Support Collections for AFDC Cases." Project Working Paper.

Garfinkel, Irwin, and E. Uhr. 1984. "Child Support and the Public Interest." *The Public Interest* (Spring).

Garfinkel, Irwin, and Patrick Wong. 1987. "Child Support and Public Policy." Institute for Research on Poverty Discussion Paper 854-87. Prepared for OECD Conference on Lone Parents: The Economic Challenge of Changing Family Structures, Paris, December 15–17.

Garfinkel, Irwin, Sara McLanahan, and Dorothy Watson. 1988. "Divorce and

Child Support Payment." In *Women's Life Cycle and Income Maintenance: Problems, Policy Issues, and Proposals*, edited by Hideo Ibe and Martha Ozawa. Japan Foundation for the Research and Development of Pension Schemes.

Garfinkel, Irwin, Sara McLanahan, and Patrick Wong. 1988. "Child Support and Dependency." In *Beyond Welfare: New Approaches to the Problem of Poverty in America*, edited by Harrell R. Rogers, Jr., Armonk, N.Y.: M.E. Sharpe.

Garfinkel, Irwin, D. R. Meyer, and G. D. Sandefur. 1991. "The Effects of Alternative Child Support Systems on Blacks, Hispanics, and Non-Hispanic Whites." Institute for Research on Poverty Discussion Paper 946-91.

Garfinkel, Irwin, Philip K. Robins, Patrick Wong, and D. R. Meyer. 1990. "The Wisconsin Child Support Assurance System: Estimated Effects on Participants." *Journal of Human Resources* (Winter).

Garfinkel, Irwin, Thomas Corbett, Maurice MacDonald, Sara McLanahan, Philip K. Robins, Nora Cate Schaeffer, and Judith A. Seltzer. 1988. "Evaluation Design for the Wisconsin Child Support Assurance Demonstration." Report prepared for the Wisconsin Department of Health and Social Services.

Gordon, Anne R. and Irwin Garfinkel. 1989. "Child Costs as a Percentage of Family Income: Constant or Decreasing as Income Rises?" Institute for Research on Poverty Discussion Paper 889-89. September.

Klawitter, Marieka, and Irwin Garfinkel. 1989. "The Effects of Routine Income Withholding of Child Support on AFDC Participation and Costs." Project Working Paper. October.

———. 1992. "Child Support, Routine Income Withholding, and Postdivorce Income for Divorced Mothers and their Children." *Contemporary Policy Issues* 10(1): 52–64, January.

Kost, Kate, and Pat Brown. 1991. "Ideal Practices Manual: Order Revision Pilot Project." Project Working Paper. November.

Levenson, L. 1991. "Report on States that Use a Percentage Standard to Determine Child Support Awards." Project Working Paper. May.

Lin, I. 1990. "Using Respondents as Proxies to Estimate the Characteristics of Nonrespondents." Master's thesis, Department of Sociology, University of Wisconsin-Madison. September.

MacDonald, Maurice. 1986a. "Economic and Demographic Characteristics of Custodial and Absent Parents in Wisconsin: Results from the 1985 Wisconsin Survey of Children, Income, and Program Participation (CHIPPS)." Institute for Research on Poverty Discussion Paper 809-86.

———. 1986b. "Objectives, Procedures, and Sampling Results for CHIPPS: The 1985 Wisconsin Survey of Children, Income, and Program Participation." Project Working Paper. February.

_____. 1988. "Child Support Reform Strategies to Reduce Children's Poverty." In *Proceedings of the American Council of Consumer Interests*, edited by Vickie L. Hampton, Columbia, Mo.: ACCI.

MacDonald, Maurice, and Margaret McMahon. 1989. "The Impact of Immediate Withholding of Child Support Payments on the Labor Supply of Wisconsin Noncustodial Parents: Early Results." Project Working Paper. September.

Manning, Wendy, Judith A. Seltzer, and Nora Cate Schaeffer. 1987. "Wisconsin Child Support Project Data Sets: Court Record Database, Parent Survey, and Children, Income, and Program Participation Survey." Project Working Paper. October.

Maritato, Nancy, and Philip K. Robins. 1989. "The Effects of Immediate Wage Withholding on the Labor Supply of Custodial Parents: Early Results from the Wisconsin Child Support Assurance System Demonstration." Project Working Paper. September.

McDonald, Thomas P., James R. Moran, and Irwin Garfinkel. 1990. "Absent Father's Ability to Pay More Child Support." *Journal of Social Service Research*, (Winter).

McLanahan, Sara, and K. Booth. Forthcoming. "Single Mothers and Their Children: Problems, Reproduction, and Politics." *Journal of Marriage and the Family*.

McLanahan, Sara, and Irwin Garfinkel. 1989. "Single Mothers, the Underclass, and Social Policy." *Annals of the American Academy of Political and Social Science* 501 (January): 92–104.

MaMahon, Margaret. 1989. "The Impact of Immediate Withholding of Child Support Payments on the Labor Supply of Wisconsin Noncustodial Parents." Master's thesis, Department of Consumer Science, University of Wisconsin–Madison.

Melli, Marygold. 1984. "Child Support: A Survey of the Statutes." Project Working Paper.

Meyer, D. R. 1989. "The Effects of Wisconsin's Child Support Reforms on Custodial Parents' Dependence on Government Transfers." Project Working Paper. January.

Mayer, D. R. 1990. "Child Support and Welfare Dependency in Wisconsin." Unpublished dissertation, University of Wisconsin-Madison.

_____. 1991. "Child Support and Welfare Dynamics: Evidence from Wisconsin." Institute for Research on Poverty Discussion Paper 939-91.

Meyer, D. R., Irwin Garfinkel, Philip K. Robins, and Donald T. Oellerich. 1991. "The Costs and Effects of a National Child Support Assurance System." Institute for Research on Poverty Discussion Paper 940-91.

Michalopoulos, C., and Irwin Garfinkel. 1989. "Reducing the Welfare Dependence and Poverty of Single Mothers by Means of Earnings and Child Support: Wishful Thinking and Realistic Possibility." Institute for Research on Poverty Discussion Paper 882-89. August.

Monson, R. A., and Sara McLanahan. 1990. "A Father for Every Child: Dilemmas of Creating Gender Equality in a Stratified Society." Project Working Paper.

Moran, James R. 1985. "Child Support and AFDC: Potential Impacts on Welfare Costs and Poverty." Unpublished dissertation, University of Wisconsin-Madison.

Nichols-Casebolt, Ann. 1986a. "The Economic Impact of Child Support Reform on the Poverty Status of Custodial and Noncustodial Families." *Journal of Marriage and the Family* (November).

_____. 1986b. "Teen Parents and the Child Support System." In *Proceedings: Research and Evaluation Track, 35th Annual Conference*, National Child Support Enforcement Association. Washington, D.C.: Office of Child Support Enforcement.

Nichols-Casebolt, Ann, and Sandra Danziger. 1989. "The Effect of Childbearing Age on Child Support Awards and Economic Well-being among Divorcing Mothers." *Journal of Divorce* 12.

Nichols-Casebolt, Ann, and Irwin Garfinkel. 1987. "A New Child Support Assurance Program: The Wisconsin Demonstration." *Social Work* (Sept.-Oct).

_____. 1991. "Trends in Paternity Adjudications and Child Support Awards." *Social Science Quarterly* 72(1):83–97, March.

Nichols-Casebolt, Ann, and Marieka Klawitter. 1989. "Child Support Enforcement Reform: Can It Reduce the Welfare Dependency of Families of Never-Married Mothers?" Institute for Research on Poverty Discussion Paper 895-89.

Nichols-Casebolt, Ann, Irwin Garfinkel, and Patrick Wong. 1988. "Reforming Wisconsin's Child Support System." In *State Policy Choices: The Wisconsin Experience*, edited by Sheldon Danziger and John F. Witte. Madison: University of Wisconsin Press.

Oellerich, Donald T. 1984. "The Effects of Potential Child Support Transfers on Wisconsin AFDC Costs, Caseloads and Recipient Well-being." Dissertation, University of Wisconsin-Madison, 1984 and Institute for Research on Poverty Special Report #35, Madison, Wis.: University of Wisconsin-Madison.

Oellerich, Donald T., and Irwin Garfinkel. 1983. "Distributional Impacts of Existing and Alternative Child Support Systems." *Policy Studies Journal* (September).

Oellerich, Donald, and Philip K. Robins. 1991. "Child Support Guidelines: Will They Make a Difference?" *Journal of Family Issues* 12(4):404–29, December.

Oellerich, Donald T., and Q. Sullivan. 1990. "Measuring National and State Performance in Pursuing Private Child Support." Project Working Paper.

Oellerich, Donald T., Irwin Garfinkel, and Philip K. Robins. 1991. "Private Child Support: Current and Potential Impacts." *Journal of Sociology and Social Welfare* 18(1):3–24, March.

Roan, Carol L. 1989. "The Relationship between Child Support Awards and Payments." Master's thesis, Department of Sociology, University of Wisconsin-Madison.

————. 1990. "A Comparison of Intrastate and Interstate Child Support Collections." Unpublished Manuscript. Department of Sociology, University of Wisconsin-Madison. April.

Robins, Philip K. 1987. "An Analysis of Trends in Child Support and AFDC from 1978 to 1983." Institute for Research on Poverty Discussion Paper 842-87.

————. 1988. "Federal Support for Child Care: Current Policies and a Proposed New System." *Focus* 11 (2, Summer).

————. 1989. "Why Are Child Support Award Amounts Declining?" Institute for Research on Poverty Discussion Paper 885-89.

————. 1990. "Federal Financing of Child Care: Alternative Approaches and Economic Implications." Institute for Research on Poverty Reprint 628.

Schaeffer, Nora Cate. 1987. "Principles of Justice in Judgments about Child Support." Institute for Research on Poverty Discussion Paper 852-87.

————. 1989. "The Frequency and Intensity of Parental Conflict: Choosing Response Dimensions." *Journal of Marriage and the Family* 51(3):759–66.

————. 1990. "Errors of Experience: Implications of Response Errors in Reports about Child Support for Questionnaire Design." Paper presented at conference on Autobiographical Data, University of Illinois at Champaign-Urbana, November 1990. Revised in 1991 in *Autobiographical Memory and the Validity of Retrospective Reports*, edited by Norbert Schwarz and Seymour Sudman. New York: Springer-Verlag.

Schaeffer, Nora Cate, and Hong-wen Charng. 1989. "Your Three Minutes Are Up: Experiments in Simplifying Response Categories for Telephone Interviews." Project Working Paper.

Schaeffer, Nora Cate, and I-F. Lin. 1990. "Using Respondents to Estimate Nonresponse Bias." Paper presented at annual meeting of the American Association for Public Opinion Research, Lancaster, Pa. May.

Schaeffer, Nora Cate, Judith A. Seltzer, and Marieka Klawitter. 1991. "Estimating Nonresponse and Response Bias: Resident and Nonresident Parents' Reports about Child Support." *Sociological Methods and Research* (August). Vol. 20, No. 1, pp. 30–59.

Seltzer, Judith A. 1989a. "Legal Custody Arrangements and the Intergenerational Transmission of Economic Welfare." Institute for Research on Poverty Discussion Paper 892-89.

————. 1989b. "Relationships between Fathers and Children Who Live Apart." NSFH Working Paper #4, Center for Demography and Ecology. Madison: University of Wisconsin.

————. 1990a. "Child Support Reform and the Welfare of U.S. Children." Paper presented at annual meeting of the American Sociological

Association, Washington, D.C. August.

————. 1990b. "Legal and Physical Custody Arrangements in Recent Divorces." *Social Science Quarterly* 71:250–66.

————. 1991a."Legal Custody Arrangements and Children's Economic Welfare." *American Journal of Sociology* 96 (January):895–929.

————. 1991b. "Relationships between Fathers and Children Who Live Apart: The Father's Role after Separation." *Journal of Marriage and the Family* 53:79–101.

Seltzer, Judith A., and Irwin Garfinkel. 1988. "Effects of Immediate Income Withholding on the Relationship between Property Settlements and Child Support Awards." Report prepared for the State of Wisconsin. January.

————. 1990. "Inequality in Divorce Settlements: An Investigation of Property Settlements and Child Support Awards." *Social Science Research* 19(March):82–111.

Seltzer, Judith A., and Nora Cate Schaeffer. 1989. "Another Day, Another Dollar: Effects of Legal Custody on Paying Child Support and Visiting Children." Paper presented at annual meeting of the American Sociological Association, San Francisco. August.

————. 1991. "Child Support and Family Dynamics." Project Working Paper. January.

Seltzer, Judith A., Nora Cate Schaeffer, and Hong-wen Charng. 1989. "Family Ties after Divorce: The Relationship between Visiting and Paying Child Support." *Journal of Marriage and the Family* 51(November):1013–31.

Takas, M. 1991. "The Treatment of Multiple Family Cases under State Child Support Guidelines." Washington, D.C.: U.S. Department of Health and Human Services.

Teachman, J. D., and K. Polonko. 1989a. "Negotiating Divorce Outcomes: Can We Identify Patterns in Divorce Settlements?" Institute for Research on Poverty Discussion Paper 886-89.

————. 1989b. "Providing for the Children: Socioeconomic Resources of Parents and Child Support in the United States." Institute for Research on Poverty Discussion Paper 887-89.

Wong, Patrick. 1988. "The Economic Effects of the Wisconsin Child Support Assurance System: A Simulation Study with a Labor Supply Model." Unpublished dissertation, University of Wisconsin-Madison.

ABOUT THE EDITORS

Irwin Garfinkel is currently professor of social work at the Columbia University School of Social Work. From 1970 to 1990 he was a faculty member at the University of Wisconsin School of Social Work and a research associate at the Institute for Research on Poverty (IRP). From 1975 to 1980, he was the IRP director. Between 1980 and 1990, he was the principal investigator of the IRP child support study. He is coauthor, with Sara McLanahan, of *Single Mothers and Their Children: A New American Dilemma*, published in 1986 by the Urban Institute, and author of *Assuring Child Support: An Extension of Social Security*, which will be published this fall by the Russell Sage Foundation.

Sara S. McLanahan is professor of sociology and public policy at Princeton University. She has published numerous articles on the growth and consequences of female-headed families and is coauthor of *Single Mothers and Their Children: A New American Dilemma* (with Irwin Garfinkel). She is currently writing a book on the consequences of single motherhood for children's long-term economic well-being.

Philip K. Robins is a professor of economics at the University of Miami and a research affiliate with the Institute for Research on Poverty at the University of Wisconsin-Madison. He is a widely published specialist in labor economics and the economic evaluation of social programs. His current research includes analyzing the economic effects of experimental social program interventions, the interrelationships among fertility, employment and child care, and child support enforcement policies.

ABOUT THE CONTRIBUTORS

Patricia R. Brown is a graduate student in sociology at the University of Wisconsin-Madison. She received an M.A. in public affairs from the Humphrey Institute at the University of Minnesota. She is currently working on a dissertation about the politics of gender, race, and class in paternity legislation in the American welfare state.

Thomas Corbett is assistant professor in the Department of Governmental Affairs of the University of Wisconsin-Madison. He is also a research affiliate with the Institute for Research on Poverty and teaches social policy in the School of Social Work. Acting as liaison between the Institute for Research on Poverty and the state of Wisconsin since the 1970s, he has been involved in a variety of collaborative university-state initiatives designed to enhance the prospects of the economically disadvantaged.

Marieka M. Klawitter is an assistant professor at the Graduate School of Public Affairs at the University of Washington. In addition to her work on child support, she studies women's marriage and employment choices, and teaches economics, statistics, and women's studies.

Nancy Maritato is a Ph.D. candidate in economics at the University of Wisconsin-Madison. From 1991 through 1992, she served as a junior staff economist on the President's Council of Economic Advisers. Her research has focused on the economic effect of public policy on families with children. Her most recent work uses a microsimulation model to evaluate the effect on poverty, welfare participation, and the income distribution of replacing federal income tax exemptions for children with a uniform child allowance.

Marygold S. Melli is Voss-Bascom Professor of Law at the University of Wisconsin-Madison, where she specializes in family law. She is the present director of the Child Support Reform Project at the Institute for Research on Poverty at the university. Her research interests relate primarily to problems of family dissolution and she has written about the divorce process, the negotiation of divorce settlements, mediation of custody disputes, and child support.

Daniel R. Meyer is an assistant professor at the School of Social Work at the University of Wisconsin-Madison and an affiliate of the Institute for Research on Poverty. His recent research has focused on the effect of child support reforms on the economic well-being of single-parent families.

Renee A. Monson received her Ph.D. in human geography from the University of Kentucky. She was a staff member of the survey management team at the Behavioral Sciences Laboratory, Institute for Policy Research, University of Cincinnati. She is currently associate researcher and project manager of the Wisconsin Child Support Demonstration Project at the Institute for Research on Poverty, University of Wisconsin.

Ann Nichols-Casebolt is associate professor and the director of the Ph.D. program in the School of Social Work at Arizona State University. She was previously a research associate at the Institute for Research on Poverty. Her interests are in the area of income support policy and poverty among single-mother families. She has published numerous articles on child support reform.

Donald T. Oellerich is an assistant professor of social work at Boston University and has recently served as a economist and policy analyst for the U.S. Department of Health and Human Services, Office of the Assistant Secretary for Planning and Evaluation. His research interests include income support policies, particularly as they relate to children; private child support; child welfare; and the use of microsimulations to address policy questions. He has authored and co-authored a dozen articles and papers on child support.

Nora Cate Schaeffer is associate professor of sociology at the University of Wisconsin-Madison and former assistant study director for the National Opinion Research Center in Chicago. Her next research project will examine the effects of nonparticipation on survey estimates of the factors predicting child support payments, and how the characteristics of child support awards affect perceptions of the fairness of awards, compliance with awards, and family conflict.

Judith A. Seltzer is associate professor of sociology and associate director for training at the Center for Demography and Ecology at the University of Wisconsin-Madison. Her research focuses on inequality within and between families and on the social definition of kinship. Her recent work examines the relationships among legal custody, paying child support, and parents' contact with children after divorce. She is also investigating the effects of child support payments, contact with parents, and conflict between parents on the welfare of children in the United States.

Kwi-Ryung Yun is a Ph.D. student in the department of social work at the University of Wisconsin-Madison where she was also a research assistant for the Institute for Research on Poverty. Her interest is in the relationship between the government and the family in the provision of care for the dependent population.